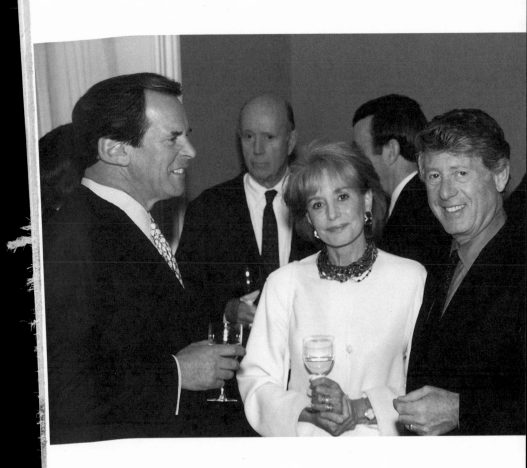

Roone

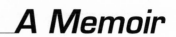

A Memoir

Roone

Roone Arledge

HarperCollins*Publishers*

HarperCollins books may be purchased for educational, business, or sales promotional use. For information, please write: Special Markets Department, Harper-Collins Publishers Inc., 10 East 53rd Street, New York, NY 10022.

Grateful acknowledgment is made for permission to reprint the following endpaper photographs: Roone Arledge, Richard Nixon, and Frank Gifford, photograph courtesy of the White House. Roone Arledge and Howard Cosell in 1974: photograph © ABC Photography Archive. Roone Arledge and Jim McKay at 1979 Olympics, Lake Placid: photograph © ABC Photography Archive. Peter Jennings, Barbara Walters, and Ted Koppel: photograph © ABC Photography Archive.

FIRST EDITION

Designed by Joseph Rutt

Library of Congress Cataloging-in-Publication Data
Arledge, Roone.
p. cm.
Includes index.
ISBN 0-06-019733-1 (hard : acid-free paper)
1. Arledge, Roone. 2. Television producers and directors—United States—
Biography.   I. Title.

PN1992.4.A72A3 2003
384.55'4'092—dc21   2003040712
[B]

03 04 05 06 07 ❖/RRD 10 9 8 7 6 5 4 3 2 1

Contents

Editor's Note

Roone Arledge was the perfect person to write a book about television as we've known it over its first half-century, for his amazing career mirrored the rise—and fall—of the great networks during those turbulent decades. He worked on the final manuscript of his memoir daily, right up to his death in December 2002, but, unfortunately, he didn't live to see the finished book. We have made every effort to avoid error in its publication. At the same time, we would like to thank the people who helped bring it to fruition: Peter Israel, without whom Roone would never have gotten to the meat of the story; Joni Evans and Ron Konecky, whose oversight was invaluable; Nancy Dobi, Roone's longtime assistant; and, most important, Gigi Shaw Arledge.

We are proud to be publishing Roone Arledge's memoir, which is about as inside as any reader will get to the workings of television. It stands as a lasting tribute to a major figure in the history of this great medium.

Lawrence P. Ashmead
February 11, 2003

Growing Up

I wonder what he'd have made of me.

I'm talking about the little boy with the thatch of red hair and the funny-sounding first name who grew up on suburban Long Island in the middle of the twentieth century: Roone Pinckney Arledge. What would he have thought of this full-grown graybeard in the next century, walking with a cane? What would he have made of my thirty-six Emmys and my directorships ranging from ESPN to the Council on Foreign Relations and Columbia University (*ESP—what?* he might ask), and my three wives and four children and five grandchildren? And the Lifetime Achievement Emmy I'm to receive for News, the first of its kind to be given by the Academy of Television Arts and Sciences? And, last but far from least, my late-life disease that now afflicts so many human beings?

A "legend in television," did you say?

I've been called that, much to my chagrin. Legends are the dead, people like Babe Ruth and Lou Gehrig whose images are carved in relief in deepest center field at Yankee Stadium. And I'm very much alive despite the cane, still chairman of ABC News and working on these memoirs in my spare time.

But which would be stranger to the little boy? The idea that he might grow up to win a lifetime achievement award in television?

Or television itself?

(Until I was eight, I don't think I had ever even heard of television.)

I have an equally hard time relating to the little boy I once was, the one his schoolmates nicknamed "Genius." (Whether he was or wasn't one he once lost a spelling bee because he muffed the word! That's right: "g-e-n-i-o-u-s"!). "Roone" was safer. The good thing about being called Roone, my father told me, was that people always remembered who you were. There are a lot of Johnnys, he said, a lot of Jims, Bobs, and Bills, but I've never run across another Roone.

He knew wherefrom he spoke: His name was Roone, too.

Dad was right, as he was about nearly everything. In all the years since, I only encountered one more Roone, and that's my son, who soon became known in the family as Boss and who christened his own first son . . . Benjamin!

Of course, there's always an exception, somewhere. In what was once East Berlin, an ABC crew once came across the statue of a Prussian field marshal who'd served as Bismarck's chief of staff. His inscribed name? "Roon." My ABC colleagues took a picture of the statue, simply added an *e* to the end, superimposed a photo of my face on the general's, and proudly presented it to me.

My father, in fact, had been christened without the *e*, too. My grandfather chose "Roon" for him, a minister's last name that he'd discovered written in an old family Bible. The Pinckney—my grandfather's middle name, as it was my own—was borrowed from an illustrious South Carolina family that went back to Revolutionary days, whereas we Arledges, at least through my grandfather's generation, were farmers from Scotland. As for "Roon," Dad added the *e*, went to Wake Forest, and after serving as a sergeant in France during World War I, came north to work as a real estate lawyer for Equitable Life Assurance.

My father's choice of the law was doubtless influenced by having grown up in a family famous for arguing and debating around the dinner table but even more so by his brother, Yates. Yates Arledge was locally celebrated for having defended the Carolina Power & Light Company in court against a farmer whose mule had been electrocuted by a fatal encounter with an electrified fence that had been erected by the company. The farmer wanted restitution for his mule. Yates filed a countersuit on behalf of the company, charging the mule with negligence. As everyone knew, he contended, mules were endowed with special intelligence. A horse might have run into such a fence, not knowing any better, but a mule? Never. The mule should have known!

The judge in question laughed both cases out of his courtroom.

My mother, Gertrude, was a Scot, too. I learned good manners from her, personal reserve, and most of all the love of excellence and attention to detail (a characteristic that, over the years, annoyed some of my ABC colleagues no end). But it was from my father, I think, that I got a passionate, an almost insatiable, curiosity about the world around me, and a devouring appetite for news and media. My earliest broadcasting memory is being huddled around the living room radio, a kind of mini-cathedral in dark wood with a lit doorway at the bottom where the dial was, listening to FDR's fireside chats. President Roosevelt was one of my father's heros. Another was Douglas MacArthur. I can summon to memory the announcement on our radio of the Japanese attack on Pearl Harbor. December seventh fell on a Sunday that year, and the special news bulletin broke into a football game. When not long afterward, we heard that the Japanese had invaded the Philippines, my father opined, "We've got MacArthur out there. He'll be terrific." The next day, in school, I remember being called upon to explain what had happened—probably my first experience in journalism.

World War II, needless to say, was *the* news story of my youth, and it ran every day for four astonishing years, on radio and in the newspapers. My father had tried to enlist but, much to his chagrin, was deemed too old to serve. Instead, he transformed our backyard into a victory garden and patrolled the streets of our Long Island community at night, wearing a Civil Defense helmet and watching for homes that failed to obey the blackout laws. I, in turn, committed the silhouettes of Japanese and German warplanes to memory—I think I could still, to this day, differentiate between a Japanese Zero and a German Stuka—and, as a Boy Scout, collected newspapers, household fats, and tinfoil for the war effort.

To all my readers who've grown up in the age of television, it is hard even to imagine the impact of radio on the generations before. We were *listeners*. Unlike today, when people who're listening to the radio tend to be doing something else at the same time, radio in those days was the center, the focal point, and, apart from going to the movies on Saturdays, *the* source of entertainment. Its stars and personalities were as significant in our lives as the Milton Berles, the Dinah Shores, and the Jackie Gleasons of the years to come. There were soap operas during the day, kiddie shows in the late afternoons, sitcoms, dramas, and variety shows at night—including the famous creaking door that introduced *The Inner Sanctum,* a kind of pre–Rod Serling radio horror show I loved—and the evening news from six to seven. All in all, it made for programming surprisingly similar to the typical television lineup of today. In wartime, then as now, a new brand of hero came into our living rooms—the foreign correspondent, broadcasting from the midst of danger. The stars of my youth were that intrepid CBS group—Edward R. Murrow speaking from the rooftops of London, Eric Sevareid, Howard K. Smith, Charles Collingwood, and so many others who brought the progress of the war vividly into our imaginations. I saw them as glamorous, their work as important, and when, in later years, they made the transition to the new medium of television— Murrow with the cigarette dangling out of his mouth doing his interviews on *Person to Person*—they aroused a fascination in me that never went away.

Like many of my generation, at least those of us in and around New York City, I first encountered television at the 1939 World's Fair in Flushing Meadows. Looking back, the fair was like a last oasis of peace and innocence before the war, with its famous Trylon and Perisphere and its fountains and its orchestra playing Sibelius's *Finlandia,* pavilions for all the nations of the globe, and a series of exhibits on the theme of "The World of Tomorrow." But more than anything, I remember standing wide-eyed before the demonstration of the technology, it was claimed, that would change the world.

Television.

It would be some years before I would be able to sneak off in the evenings to a friend's basement and spend secret hours watching its images on the large box with the tiny flickering screen, years more before, by a stroke of serendipitous luck, I got my first job in it. Meanwhile, back in the prosaic world of a Long Island high school, I served a journalistic apprenticeship as sports editor of our newspaper, rooted for the New York Giants in the National League and the Yankees in the American (the words "Brooklyn Dodgers" were never breathed in our household), learned the discipline and self-reliance of hunting on weekend trips with my father, and experimented in sweaty liaisons with demoiselles of my age and neighborhood.

Columbia University was where I wanted to go to college, and off I went at sixteen, only to discover—*after* my enrollment—that its famous school of journalism was for graduate students only! No matter. There was New York, and the more carefree pursuits of undergraduates. And there was the great and illustrious Columbia English faculty. Mark Van Doren was but one of their stars, but he taught literature as a dramatic weave spun from threads of sociology, psychology, history, and personal experience. My later sense of story bears his imprint, and so did the realization that poetry and the classics can come alive with the encouragement of a great professor, even in his seemingly offhand insights. Half a century later, I can still recall a discussion in his class of Cervantes's *Don Quixote*.

"Whom does Quixote represent?" Van Doren asked.

"God," some wiseass answered (*not* yours truly).

Whether the remark was meant fliply or seriously, I couldn't say, but Van Doren, after thinking about it for a moment, replied, "There are people who believe that. I wonder whether there has ever been a great story written in which God has *not* been one of the characters."

Van Doren would drop speculations like that into virtually every class, like pebbles tossed into still water, which would leave us arguing into the night about great stories that might—or might not—have had God in them.

Without any of us realizing it at the time, the air at 116th Street and Broadway was thick with future media mavens. Dick Wald, future editor of the *New York Herald-Tribune* and, later, president of NBC News, was one of my classmates. (Later still, Dick would become my senior vice president at ABC News.) So were Bob Gottlieb, president-to-be of Knopf and, subsequently, editor of *The New Yorker;* Max Frankel, executive editor of the *New York Times;* and Larry Grossman, another president-in-the-making, of NBC News and PBS. But I wonder how many among us knew where we were headed at the time. I know I didn't. Sometimes I thought of becoming an oilman, wildcatting for a thousand and one nights through the Arabian sands; at other times, I mused about sitting front-row center as a drama critic for *Newsweek* or *Time*. But the newsweeklies, as I found out, weren't hiring fresh-faced college grads, and a geologist I was not. Instead I drifted into Columbia's school of international relations, with the idea of specializing in the Middle East. What I didn't count on, though, was having to master the Arabic language. I was hopeless at it, I quickly discovered. After a few weeks, I dropped out and applied for a sportswriting job at a Long Island daily.

Not interested, the editor told me. You have no experience.

My next stop was the *Journal of Commerce,* in New York. They weren't looking for sportswriters but did ask me for a sample of my writing. The term paper I turned in made their interest exceedingly brief.

With no brighter prospects on the horizon that summer, and eager, like any feckless youth, to put career worries aside, I hopped a bus for Cape Cod, to take up the position my Ivy League liberal arts education seemed most suited for: headwaiter at the Wayside Inn in Chatham, Massachusetts. I'd worked at the inn between terms at Columbia. It was an establishment of local renown, as well known for the homey ministerings of its proprietress, a jolly, broad-of-beam woman named Marjorie Haven, as for its New England cuisine, including the oatmeal bread and blueberry muffins baked by Mrs. Haven's cousin Jesse.

There's a wry expression that's gained a certain currency in our contemporary world: "No good deed goes unpunished." It's a kind of irony, I guess, that reflects the skeptical spirit of this day and age. But fifty years ago, in a vastly more optimistic era, good deeds were something you still did because 1) they were the right thing to do; 2) they made you feel better about yourself; and 3) because sometimes, on occasion, they were even rewarded. And so it turned out for me, late that Cape Cod summer, in an unforeseen and incredibly serendipitous way.

Here's what happened.

It was late in the season, one Sunday night, when just after closing time a distinguished-looking gentleman arrived at the inn with his wife and several children. They'd just spent hours stuck in traffic, he told the hostess, and the kids were starving. Was it possible to reopen the now deserted dining room? Overhearing her turn him down, I stepped up and said, "It's okay. I'll wait on them myself."

I cajoled the chef into staying a little while longer to cook the family dinner, and then, once I served, they started rushing through it. I urged them to relax and enjoy themselves, and this they did. The grateful father asked my name.

Fast-forward to New York City, several months later.

I was no closer to finding permanent employment, but my dad came up with a lead for me. While working on a real estate transaction for Equitable with the DuMont television network, he learned that DuMont had an administrative position open and arranged for me to get an interview. Television had always intrigued me, although I didn't see any immediate fit there for my disparate interests—the Middle East, drama, music?—but now that the door was just a little bit ajar, and knowing how fierce the competition was for jobs with the major networks, I got excited about the prospect.

The interview turned into interviews. I was brought back at three successively higher levels, until at length, I was ushered into the office of DuMont's programming chief, James Cadigan. As I crossed a suite whose dimensions would have accommodated Mussolini, Mr. Cadigan was bent over his desk, examining my application. He looked vaguely familiar in the glow of the overhead light, but I couldn't see enough of his face to place him. Finally, he looked up and smiled.

A most gentlemanly smile. Even distinguished.

"How's everything at the Wayside Inn these days?" he said.

My jaw fell open, and I had to fight it shut. Incredibly, Mr. James Cadigan and his family had been my late arrivals, that Sunday evening on the Cape, many months before.

I started work the following Monday. And that was how I began an extraordinary life.

Forgotten today, DuMont was then at television's cutting edge. The demonstration I'd seen at the world's fair a dozen or so years before had been mounted by DuMont, and you could argue that without the long-life picture tube Allen B. DuMont had invented in his New Jersey garage, commercial broadcasting would never have happened. The high-quality, twenty-inch sets DuMont manufactured—when the likes of RCA and GE were turning out tinny, postcard-size models—were a wonder too and helped finance the network that bore his name. In reach, DuMont's sixteen stations in the Midwest and on the East Coast were too few to compete with the rest of the industry, but the company had made programming history, too: the first live network hookup between New York and Washington; the first regularly-scheduled children's show; the first daytime schedule; the first network newscast originating from Washington; the first network soap opera; the first prime-time telecasts of the National Football League. Ted Mack and *The Original Amateur Hour,* Ralph Kramden threatening to send Alice to the moon, Bishop Sheen bidding "'Bye now, and God loves you," Joe McCarthy having no comeback to Joseph Welch's "Have you no decency, sir?" during the Army-McCarthy hearings—all these were televised by DuMont, along with plays, symphonies, and *Howdy Doody*.

As with any of us starting at the bottom of the workaday ladder, the duties of an assistant-to-the-assistant-program-director were far from glamorous. I spent much of my day filling out forms. But, whenever a moment allowed, I sneaked away to the studios—and the more I saw, the more I became hooked. There was something magical about television: the immediacy; the drama of the countdown to air; the beaming live to an audience that, by then, counted in the millions; the technology; the bright lights; the studio hush. Little by little, I discovered what a television producer did, and I yearned for the chance to do it myself.

The striking, lively blonde I'd begun seriously dating thought it was a fine career choice as well. Her name was Joan Heise, and we'd known each other since high school where we'd acted in a number of plays together, invariably cast as a married couple. Next to her picture in my yearbook, Joan had written, "To my favorite husband." In high school, however, we hadn't so much as shared a soda together. The young lady in question was going steady with the class president. We lost touch during college, but after graduation, I learned that Joan was working at Republic Aviation, and, better for me, unattached. I called, and courtship began. Personally and professionally, everything seemed to be coming together—until, that is, a few months after I'd started work at DuMont, a letter arrived from the Selective Service Administration ordering one Roone Pinckney Arledge Jr. to report for induction into the United States Army.

Being drafted, particularly with the Korean War on, was decidedly not in my plans. In the early months of that so-called conflict, basic-training graduates were being chewed up at an alarming rate, and the only visible alternative to death in uniform, it seemed to me and my peers, was an endless tour of boredom. As it turned out, there were aspects of soldiering I enjoyed and was good at. Spit and polish was something I'd learned literally at my mother's knee, and my father had inculcated a love of the outdoors—plenty of which I saw during basic. The army also made me recognize that I'd grown up in a cocoon. Suddenly I was twenty-four hours a day, seven days a week with young men from hollers and ghettos, some whip smart, others barely able to read and write. You got along because you had to get along, and, in the process, I picked up an education that wasn't offered on Morningside Heights. Some other college boys were enrolled with me, and a few would become lifelong friends, like Larry Collins, who became Paris bureau chief for *Newsweek* and coauthor of the best-seller *Is Paris Burning?*; and Bernie Brillstein, who went on to become a Hollywood agent, owner of the *National Lampoon* franchise, and one of the most successful producers in television. But the U.S. Army made us all a part of the same American stew.

I'd hoped that wearing glasses would disqualify me as potential cannon fodder, but no such luck. Worse, tramping through the north woods with my dad after rabbits and deer had made me a dead shot, and with that now unwanted skill, I feared I'd end up hiding in a foxhole in a snowy no-man's-land on the other side of the planet. But the ways of the U.S. Army were indeed mysterious. The orders that came down after basic training commanded Private Arledge to stay put, assigned to public information as, among other things, a news announcer on the base radio station. Daily broadcasting of the latest promotions and personnel assignments was as mind-numbing as are most stateside army occupations, but I could hardly complain. For one thing, there were no incoming mortars to duck. For another, the duty was soft, and every weekend I was able to travel home, especially welcome, as Joan and I had succumbed to youthful impulse and gotten married. "War is hell," I'd say to her as I walked through the door.

The months dragged, but they passed. When, at last, I was mustered out, I fairly bolted to the phone to tell DuMont I was on my way back to work. My boss wasn't around, however, so I left a message for him. After a few days of hearing nothing, I called again and kept calling until I realized that they were ducking me. Finally, I informed a hapless assistant that the GI Bill of Rights entitled me to my old job, and that if employment weren't soon forthcoming, I'd see the network in court. That finally elicited a response. I could return, I was told, but someone would have to be fired to make room.

DuMont had hit on hard times. Allen DuMont was an engineer, not a corporate visionary of the Sarnoff or Paley stamp, and at a time when new television stations were opening all over the country and affiliating themselves with CBS and NBC, the much smaller DuMont network was obliged to lay people off.

The final blow had been an FCC decision freezing applications for further broadcast licenses, which left DuMont at a permanent disadvantage. The company, as a result, was hemorrhaging cash and in the midst of massive layoffs. Not long afterward, its assets would be sold off to investor John Kluge, whose holdings included independent channels in New York and Los Angeles. The network reruns on Kluge's stations had none of DuMont's innovation or élan, but they appealed to the right demographics in the right locations, and the empire he built on the remains of DuMont, renamed Metromedia, would bring him billions.

Meanwhile, much as I needed my job back, I wasn't about to cost someone else his. Consequently, I found myself looking for work all over again. But once again, chance came to the rescue. While I'd been safe-guarding my nation from behind the base broadcast microphone, Joan had switched employers and become a number two secretary to General David Sarnoff, founder and chairman of RCA, parent of NBC. Joan man-aged to get my name added to a list, which resulted in an interview for me, and before I had time to panic, I was on my way again.

NBC Years

I didn't exactly start at the top—or even at the network.

Well, neither did the General!

Joan invariably referred to David Sarnoff as "General," not even "the General," to the point that I at first thought "General" might be his first name! (He had, in fact, served briefly in uniform in World War II and was appointed a brigadier general by an act of Congress in 1944.) When I went to work at Rockefeller Center, NBC's owned-and-operated New York station, first known as WEAF in its radio days, then redubbed WRCA, was telecasting on Channel 4. My job was "stage manager," meaning that I passed to the on-air talent cues that had been given to me by the director in the control room and generally oversaw the broadcast and the studio while we were on the air. I was the one, for instance, who would call out, "Stand by, everybody, we're going to commercial," and do the countdown, "Ten . . . nine . . . eight . . . seven . . . ," etc. This gave the impression—incorrectly—that I was in charge, whereas I was just acting as the messenger for the director. Where I ranked in the production hierarchy was signified by my paycheck: $66 per week—just enough, with Joan's take-home pay, to set up housekeeping in a $75-a-month Brooklyn apartment.

But I didn't mind my lowly position. I was too excited to be working in television. This was the era of live drama, of producers and directors like Worthington Miner, who, in 1948, had started *Studio One*; and Fred Coe, who brought us Paddy Chayevsky's *Marty;* and of consistently terrific shows like *Playhouse 90* and *Omnibus,* hosted by Alistair Cooke, which brought us the performing arts on Sunday afternoons. Whole hosts of entertainers entered our living rooms, many of them holdovers from radio and imports from Hollywood, but there were any number of newcomers too, like Steve Allen who, with his *Tonight Show,* started NBC's dominance over the late evening, which would hold for half a century, thanks to Allen and his successors, Jack Paar, Johnny Carson, and Jay Leno. There were only six channels in New York—CBS (Channel 2), NBC (Channel 4), DuMont (Channel 5), ABC (Channel 7), WOR-TV (Channel 9, owned by Mutual), and WPIX (Channel 11, owned by the *Daily News*)—and none of them yet broadcast around the clock. (How few of us still remember the sign-offs at the end of the evening's programming, at midnight or maybe one A.M., the image of the American flag and the playing of "The Star-Spangled Banner," followed by the channel's insignia!) The Corporation for Public Broadcasting wouldn't even come into existence till 1967. Color, although color TVs went on sale in 1954, was a very slow happening because we were all so used to black and white.

But for a kid like me, the idea of working alongside talents like Jinx Falkenberg and Tex McCrary was all I needed. Their *Tex and Jinx* daytime talk show, an outgrowth of their earlier radio program, had a great following and was a must-stop for anyone visiting New York, from Sammy Davis Jr. to the Indian foreign minister Krishna Menon. It amazed me that a local program could draw such notables, but that was television: Everyone wanted to be on. Herb Sheldon, another personality I worked with, had shows three times a day. It didn't matter that everything he did was phony or that his only ability was singing off-key to the accompaniment of a player piano. Within the corridors of 30 Rockefeller Center, he was feared—because he was popular on the magic box. I even got a personal taste of the medium's power myself while working a five-minute, weekday program featuring the commentaries of Leon Pearson, brother of syndicated columnist Drew. One day, Pearson asked my opinion of an exchange between Eisenhower and Nikita Khrushchev.

"Sounds like a lot of summitry to me," I said.

Before I knew it, Pearson was on the air, saying, "To use a term coined by our own Roone Arledge . . ."

Had I actually invented the word? Or picked it up somewhere? It would take a Bill Safire to determine that, but at the time, I thought it was original with me. In any case, wherever I went for weeks after that, I'd hear, "Oh, you're the guy who invented 'summitry.' "

That was the power of television.

In due course, I was promoted to unit supervisor, a position that entailed managing a variety of backstage personnel. Who was allowed to do what was a subject taken most seriously at NBC, and any deviation from union contract rules—say, allowing a cameraman rather than a stagehand to shove a chair out of the way—could produce an instant work stoppage and the filing of a formal grievance. Mostly, I went by the book. However, the book said nothing about monkeys, one of whom was to be featured swinging on a bar in a five-minute morning slot advertising a department store. No sooner had the beast arrived than there was a noisy dispute over who should dress it. With Solomon-like wisdom, I ruled the monkey a prop, not a performer, thus awarding the task to a stagehand rather than the wardrobe mistress. Peace proved short-lived, as once on set, the monkey answered nature's call, adding to the furnishings something not called for in the script. The question: Under whose jurisdiction did dung removal fall? The suddenly amenable stagehands were happy to yield to Jim, the custodian, but Jim was a by-the-book man, too. "Mr. Arledge," he said, "I don't know much about this, but it seems to me that if that monkey is a prop, then any part of that monkey is a prop. And the one thing I do know is that I certainly can't touch any props."

Who was I to argue with such logic?

It was only a matter of time, I was confident, before such perspicacity would be rewarded with a job I really wanted, which was producing. It was slower coming than I would have liked, until, one fine day, my luck changed. I was approached by a friend, Pat Ferrar, who'd been tapped to produce an upcoming local show called *Sunday Schedule*. The program was to begin with cartoons at seven A.M., then, as the morning wore on, move into an increasingly adult mix of talk, news, and song and dance. The whole Sunday-morning schedule, in fact. Finally, at noon, about the time senility presumably set in, we would yield to the network and *Meet the Press*. Pat was a little daunted by the prospect of putting together five eclectic hours of programming every week and asked if I'd help out as coproducer. I said I'd be happy to (ecstatic was more like it).

Would that we were an immediate, brilliant success. Well, *Variety* didn't think so. In my first review ever, they pronounced our debut program "an abdication of programming responsibility." We did get better as the months went along—almost all television shows do, if they're given the chance—but when the network hit one of the periodic slumps that are endemic to television, it began lopping heads.

Our program didn't make the cut, but I did. I was now a producer, and my next assignment was a one-hour Monday-through-Saturday morning program, for mothers and children, called *Hi, Mom!* It featured Nurse Jane, who held forth on children's medical problems, and Josie McCarthy, a first-rate cook and presenter, who did a recipe section every day. But its star was a pretty, diminutive Brooklyn rabbi's daughter whose ventriloquist's gifts had won national attention in a 1952 appearance on *Arthur Godfrey's Talent Scouts.* Her name was Shari Lewis.

How Shari made her sock-puppet pals Lamb Chop, Charlie Horse, and Hush Puppy come to wisecracking life was a mystery I was never able to plumb. During rehearsal, I'd stand only feet away from her, trying to catch her lips moving. But there wasn't so much as a quiver. Her abilities were almost spooky, as was her relationship with the puppets, whose celebrity she resented but whose presence she couldn't do without, to the point that she took them along on her honeymoon. Shari and I, in any case, got on splendidly. She was receptive to virtually all my programming suggestions, drawing the line only when I proposed that Lamb Chop join in interviewing guests. Shari refused. (This notion—which would become Shari's signature after both of us had moved on—appeared, at the time, to touch a nerve buried somewhere deep within her psyche.) But, even without Lamb Chop chiming in, *Hi, Mom!* won an Emmy, my first of many.

It was nice having the statuette on my bookcase. It would have been even nicer, I thought, had it been acquired for producing something meatier than a morning kids' show. While still a unit supervisor, I'd begun batting around ideas with my college chum Larry Grossman, who was then working as a junior editor for *Look* and living in Brooklyn a couple of subway stops away. We weren't sure what we wanted to do, except that it had to be cultural and worthy, on the order of Alistair Cook's *Omnibus,* the then quintessence of Sunday afternoon highbrow. After thrashing around possibilities for nearly two years, we put together a proposal for a ninety-minute anthology that would tell the stories behind great works of art, music, and literature, modestly entitled *Masterpiece.* For the proposal, we chose Michelangelo's battles with the pope during the creation of the

Sistine Chapel; a study of how Beethoven's growing deafness and disillusionment with Napoleon combined in the *Eroica* symphony; and—a Larry favorite—the story of Walt Whitman's revulsion at the Civil War as expressed in *Drum Taps*. To these, we appended fifty other ideas for future subjects.

Joan typed up the final presentation, and we sent it off to the office of Pat Weaver, already the driving force behind NBC. Whether Weaver, whose daughter, Sigourney, would make a mark as well, actually looked at it I can't say, but it ended up in the hands of a senior minion. His letter to us read more or less as follows: "If you guys are so smart, how come you don't have a pilot?"

That, of course, is what we wanted NBC to make! Faced with a catch-22, we took our wares to CBS, where by now Larry was working in the public relations department, but CBS gave us a similar answer and our dreams of glory ended then and there. But not our friendship. When Larry was named president of the Public Broadcasting Service in 1976, I sent him a cable from Innsbruck, where I was producing the Winter Olympics: CONGRATULATIONS ON PBS JOB. HAVE A GREAT IDEA FOR A DRAMATIC SERIES BASED ON GREAT WORKS OF ART, MUSIC, LITERATURE. Larry cabled back: I HAVE PERFECT TITLE. LET'S CALL IT "MASTERPIECE THEATRE."

Meanwhile, back at WRCA, Shari was getting restless. She had always been haunted by the idea that people would think of her as only a ventriloquist. With shows starring the likes of Dean Martin and Andy Williams the current network rage, Shari, who could sing and tell jokes, didn't see why she shouldn't have one too. When she didn't get it, her contract demands began to escalate, as did her prickliness on the set. Eventually, both exceeded a level NBC deemed reasonable. The result was Shari's departure, and after a several-year absence from television, followed by a stint on the BBC (where Lamb Chop interviewed Queen Elizabeth), she reemerged as a national star on PBS.

I was left working for a short period with an affable gent named Jimmy Weldon, who'd seemed hilarious while filling in for Shari during her final vacation. Jimmy also had a puppet sidekick, a duck christened Webster Webfoot. But there Jimmy's resemblance to his predecessor ceased. He didn't sing, he didn't dance, and jokes that had seemed so funny during the two weeks he'd pinch-hit turned out to be about the only ones he knew. Jimmy also wasn't much of a ventriloquist. In fact, he wasn't a ventriloquist, period: Webster Webfoot "spoke" only through the magic of deceptive camera work.

That's where I came in, courtesy of a money-saving edict from NBC that producers take on directors' chores as well. After all, the executives must have said to each other, how hard could it be to sit in the cool dark of a control room, calling up shots? The answer was plenty. Cameras were the size of refrigerators then, and simply getting them around a stage floor snaked with thick cables was tricky. Once they were in position, a director had to keep his eyes on three or more monitors at once, all the while thinking of what was coming next and how best to capture it. To do this well—which is to say, so seamlessly that the viewer wasn't aware of the process—required quick wits and more than a little art. I learned my lessons from a master, Mike Gargulio, who at one time or another directed just about every game show that ever aired. With Mike's patient schooling and a union card from the Director's Guild (both invaluable, then and later), I set out to fool the children of New York.

When Webster Webfoot talked, I kept the camera focused tight on him, so viewers wouldn't see Jimmy's mouth blabbing away. Only when Jimmy was talking to Webster did I take a two-shot, showing the pair of them, Jimmy talking and Webster listening. Every line and move had, therefore, to be scripted, for the sake of preserving children's wonder, not to mention our jobs.

It worked, and my reward was being given the opportunity to produce and direct a live-remote: the 1959 lighting of the NBC Christmas tree. The Super Bowl it was not, but it brought me an introduction to a remarkable performer, Olympic gold medalist Dick Button, whose figure skating across the Rockefeller Center rink was to be a major highlight. The afternoon of the telecast, the weather was bitter cold, but Dick was wearing only cotton pants and a silk shirt.

"Aren't you going to freeze?" I asked.

Said Dick: "I'd rather look good than be warm."

He did look good, but there was an awful glitch, thanks to NBC's insistence on feeding its own audio and bypassing Rock Center's PA system. (This was also my first of many battles with audio engineers, for our technical problems and screwups in the years ahead were almost always on the audio rather than the video side.) Dick started off his routine to the music he'd chosen, the overture to *Miss Liberty,* but partway through, for reasons unknown, the feed to the rink system went dead. Ninety-nine out of one hundred performers would have stopped right then and there, wrecking the show in the process—this was a *live* broadcast—but not Dick Button. He kept right on skating in total silence, hearing the music in his head and gliding and spinning flawlessly. Only people on the spot knew what had happened. Those watching at home continued to hear the music and wouldn't have had the slightest idea that anything was amiss. Skater and overture finished impeccably in synch, and those few of us who witnessed it could only marvel at the incredible sangfroid and talent of this great performer. Years later, when ABC needed a figure-skating commentator as cool as he was well-informed, I knew exactly who to call.

Undaunted by the fate of *Masterpiece,* I ran a new proposal up the NBC flagpole, this one for a program to be called *For Men Only* and based on an amalgam of the men's magazines that were so popular at the time— *Playboy, True, Sport, Field & Stream,* and so on. NBC was sufficiently intrigued to make a stage and crew available, and production of a half-hour pilot commenced. One segment featured a performance by a jazz trio. Another had *Sports Illustrated* artist Robert Riger showing his evocative line drawings of Carmine Basilio's most recent battering at the hands of Sugar Ray Robinson. In yet another, Marty Glickman, a New York sports-announcing institution, narrated a film on track and field, a subject on which Marty was expert. We even had two pretty, bathing-suit-clad damsels whose role was to parade three or four times across the set with poster boards announcing upcoming attractions. As emcee, I had a Steve Allen look-alike in mind, Pat Hernon, the WRCA weatherman, who also had the considerable advantage for us of working for free.

For Men Only wasn't half bad, and it was with high hopes that I presented the finished kinescope to George Heinemann, WRCA's program director. George, however, was not in the habit of climbing out on programming limbs. He passed, concluding that *For Men Only* was "a little ahead of the awareness line"—too far ahead for NBC.

Another day, another defeat. But Pat Hernon had an idea. During his last job at the NBC affiliate in San Francisco, he'd gotten to know an ex-ad man who'd moved into television, packaging sports programs. His name was Ed Scherick, and, according to Pat, he was now in New York doing something or other for ABC. Whatever it was, Pat judged Scherick a risk taker. Who knew? Maybe he'd gamble on us.

Pat arranged for Scherick to come over the following week. In the interval, I repaired to the NBC clip library to learn everything I could about my putative savior.

Edgar Scherick. He'd also grown up, as it turned out, on suburban Long Island. After graduating from Harvard, he'd gone to work for an ad agency, where one of his clients had been Falstaff beer. Scherick put Falstaff together with the Chicago Bears and the then Chicago Cardinals, whose pro-football games were being televised on an ad hoc network of ABC affiliates in the Midwest, where Falstaff had most of its sales. The marriage was a success, and Scherick next took Falstaff into baseball, with the "Game of the Week."

After a brief tour with CBS, putting together their coverage of the suddenly popular National Football League, he struck out on his own. Sports Programs, Inc., as he called his company, offered a broadcaster one-stop shopping: It acquired the air rights, sold the commercial time, and supplied everything a telecast needed, down to the producers, directors, and announcers. He was currently doing most of his business with ABC, which lacked a sports division of its own, putting together an entire sports schedule for them. Bowling, baseball, boxing—Scherick had them all, and, as I soon found out, he'd also been hot on the trail of NCAA football and the fledgling, just-formed American Football League.

No wonder, I thought, the guy had been Phi Beta Kappa. This was sheer genius.

Scherick came over to the NBC screening room, which we'd booked for the occasion, to see *For Men Only.* Stocky, a little disheveled, pure New York in his speech, he also wore an impatient frown. That, I would learn, was typical. The man could barely sit still.

Pat introduced me, but Scherick didn't seem to notice. "Let's see the thing," he growled.

As the kinescope unwound, he rocked back and forth, his only reaction an occasional pursing of the lips.

"I don't have any use for this," he said when the screen went blank. "But I'd like to meet the guy who produced it."

I piped up, "That'd be me."

Scherick studied me for a moment. Maybe he was debating if I was telling the truth.

"Ever produce sports?" he asked.

"Sure," I said, not mentioning that the one "sport" in question had been a segment I'd done on the WRCA Citywide Marbles Tournament.

He handed me a card.

"Come over to my office tomorrow," he said. "We'll talk."

I didn't have time to say yes or no, much less inquire about what he wanted to discuss. Scherick was gone.

After my morning duties were finished the next day, I said I was taking an early lunch and instead hopped a cab to a Forty-second Street address, just off Times Square. A creaky elevator conveyed me to a two-room office that looked more like a bookie joint than the headquarters of Sports Programs, Inc. Everything about it was shopworn, including the paper-strewn warren where Scherick sat. He waved me to a battered chair, and, as I settled myself around a protruding spring, my eyes went to the photographs of sports figures that lined the walls.

The rest was sheer luck.

"Who's that?" said Scherick, catching my gaze. He pointed to a picture of a baseball player sliding home.

"Willie Mays."

"And that?" he said, gesturing at another photo, this one of a pitcher in mid windup.

"Sal Maglie. The Barber. Best there is."

"Why do they call him The Barber?"

"Because he likes to give batters 'close shaves.' "

"And him?" said Scherick, directing me to a quarterback cocking a football alongside his ear.

"Johnny Unitas, Baltimore Colts."

Thank God the ones he'd chosen were ones I recognized. Many others I didn't.

Saying I seemed "bright enough," Scherick tilted back and launched into a description of what Sports Programs, Inc. and ABC were up to, and how it had all been brought about by razor blades. Specifically, those manufactured by Gillette, which for years had urged men to "look sharp" and "feel sharp" on the *Friday Night Fights* on NBC. NBC, however, thought boxing had run its course, which prompted Gillette to the conclusion that NBC and Gillette had run their course. Gillette was bringing all its business to ABC, which not only meant the fights, but enough additional advertising dollars to go after a whole sports schedule.

Scherick glanced over to see if I was impressed.

I was.

"Which brings us," he said, "to college football. You know, of course, that the NCAA package is one of the most valuable in all of sports."

Yes, I did.

"And that NBC has had these games forever?"

Again, my head bobbed.

"And you certainly must know what a sorry outfit ABC is."

Everyone in television was aware of the woefulness of ABC, which had come to life back in the forties only because the government decided that NBC's two radio networks were one too many. The lesser of them was spun off as ABC, which had been trying to play catch-up with its broadcasting big brothers ever since, failing dismally every year. All manner of travail, economic and otherwise, afflicted ABC, which was headed by an ex-Paramount Theaters lawyer named Leonard Goldenson. Goldenson was determined to make ABC a contender. But with a fifth fewer stations than NBC or CBS, and many of its affiliates hard-to-tune-in UHF channels, it was going to be a helluva trick. NBC sure wasn't worried; at 30 Rock, ABC was referred to as "the Almost Broadcasting Company."

"I know all about ABC," I said.

"Then," said Scherick, "you realize what I was up against with the NCAA. The impossible. And you know how I beat it?" He tapped the side of his head. "With the most important thing in this business, Arledge—smarts."

As he told it, swiping college football from under NBC's nose had also involved a fair amount of monkeyshines. They started with Scherick collecting intelligence about the enemy, NBC Sports director Tom Gallery, a man revered by the National Collegiate Athletic Association. Whenever his NCAA friends put the television rights for football up for bid, Gallery, Scherick learned, came to the session with two envelopes: one containing a low figure (usually, 10 percent more than what NBC was paying on the current contract), the other, a blow-away-the-competition number. If Gallery spotted a representative from one of the other networks, he turned in the envelope with the higher number; if he didn't, the lower. Scherick knew that ABC couldn't come close to beating what was inside the big-figure envelope, so the key was in making Gallery believe he had no rivals. But how to conceal ABC's presence? Scherick's solution had been to send someone Gallery wouldn't recognize, a figure so bland he'd fade right into the wallpaper. In an ABC financial executive named Stanton Frankle he found the ideal candidate.

The day of the bidding, the plot went like silk. Stationing himself in a corner and speaking to no one, Frankle, per Scherick's instructions, waited until Gallery completed his inspection of the room and lay down the low-bid envelope. Frankle then stepped forward, announced himself as the emissary of the American Broadcasting Company, and with that, whipped a trumping bid from his breast pocket. For $6,251,114, ABC had won a two-year contract for college football, and a chance at respectability.

"Why the $1,114?" I asked.

Scherick grinned from ear to ear. "I didn't want to seem chintzy," he said.

I laughed, and Scherick said I still shouldn't bother calling ABC to ask for the sports department. There wasn't any; he was it. But everything was changing, he insisted. If it weren't, he wouldn't have been hired, and if it weren't, he wouldn't be hiring me.

Did that mean he was making me a job offer?

You bet he was, right there on the spot.

Scherick clearly wasn't the type to leave things dangling, and I had the feeling that if I got up and left, saying I wanted to think it over, that would be the end of it.

I thought a long, long moment. I'd been at NBC for six years. Working there was like working for a bank, all safe and secure and a little dull, and maybe, just maybe, if I was very lucky, I could end up a vice president of something or other before I retired, just like people who survive in banks. Now this wild man I hardly knew was asking me to give it all up for no security, no guarantees, nothing, maybe, but the possibility of doing something great. I mean, the guy was offering me *sports!* Imagine being paid for that!

But I had personal responsibilities, including a family in the making. We would end up with four kids, three girls and a boy.

So?

So I was twenty-nine years old—which seems a very advanced age when you're twenty-nine—and if I didn't take a chance now, when was I going to?

"It's a deal," I said.

Except for Joan, who knew how frustrated I'd become at NBC, everyone who heard the news thought I was crazy. *Work for ABC?* ABC was a place you tried to get out of, not go to work for! Whatever had possessed me?

My last day at work, I made the good-bye rounds, ending with Bud Rukeyser, NBC public relations man and an old friend from the army. When I walked into Bud's office, someone else was sitting there. I said I'd come back, but Bud said not at all, and he introduced me to this other guy, whose name didn't even register.

"I'm here to say good-bye, Bud," I said. "I'm off to ABC."

"What are you going to do there?" Bud's friend asked idly.

"Actually," I said, "I'm going to work for the guy who produces sports for them."

"What sports do they have?"

"Well," I said, "for one thing, I think they just got NCAA football."

"What have you been doing here?" the guy asked me.

"I produce and direct *Hi, Mom!* for WRCA."

End of a pleasant, in-passing conversation, and upon leaving Bud's office that day, I thought no more of it.

Until one week later when the roof fell in.

NCAA Football

Arr-ledge, get in here!"

It was day three of my employment at Sports Programs, Inc. I'd just returned from lunch.

"Yes?" I said, sticking my head around the door jamb. Scherick, who had his back turned, spun around. His face was crimson, and a paper was clutched in his hand.

"Are you out of your fucking mind?" he bellowed. "What was going on in your head?"

"I don't know what you're talking about," I said, feeling my cheeks go hot.

"*This!*" Scherick shouted, shoving the paper at me.

It was the latest edition of the trade paper, *Anny,* and on the front page was an item circled in red:

"Unknown twenty-nine-year-old freckle-faced kid named Roone Arledge," I read, not believing the words, "who produced a local kiddie show for NBC, to produce NCAA games for ABC."

"You know where I've been all morning?" Scherick said. "At ABC. They're going nuts. And Gillette is bouncing off the walls. What kind of lunatic are you?"

I was more stunned than Scherick. At first, I couldn't make sense of it. Was this somebody's idea of a joke? But then it came to me that the guy sitting in Bud Rukeyser's office and the *Anny* reporter were one and the same. But what had I said to him? Only that I was going to work for Scherick and that he and ABC had landed the NCAA games. And that I'd produced at NBC. But I'd never connected the two! I hadn't been hired to produce at Sports Programs, Inc.!

Scherick wasn't interested in explanations. Great damage had been done to ABC's hard-won relationship with Gillette, he said, and I—an idiot for saying *anything* to a reporter—was responsible. Now, he had to clean up my mess. So as soon as he finished with me, he said, he and Tom Moore, ABC's programming chief, were flying to Boston, where Gillette had its corporate headquarters.

"Tom's the guy who put together this deal," Scherick said, "and he's livid. So you know what we're going to do tomorrow morning when we see Gillette? Formally disown you. Until I get back, you don't talk to anyone. You don't even breathe. You just hope we can calm them down. 'Cause if we can't, it's your ass."

On the train home that night to Westchester County, where Joan and I had recently relocated, something I'd learned in a European history class at Columbia kept running through my head. It was a quote of Napoleon's foreign minister, Talleyrand, and it went: "It was worse than a crime, it was a blunder."

Scherick returned from Boston late Friday afternoon. He reported that Gillette had been mollified and that I would not have to begin collecting unemployment just yet. That same night, I was off to Yankee Stadium, where we were televising the rematch between the heavyweight champion Swedish boxer Ingemar Johansson, and Floyd Patterson, the former title-holder he'd knocked out one year before, for a closed-circuit-theater audience. It was a big deal for us—ABC had the radio broadcast, too—and my job was to be of use to anyone on the team who needed things done.

Little did I know.

At the eleventh hour, Johannson, the champion, whose word was therefore law, decided he didn't want a certain prizefighter to get his promised pre-bout introduction and promotional bow. Moreover, he was threatening not to step into the ring if he did. The about-to-be-disappointed pugilist was none other than Sonny Liston, a notoriously bad-tempered soul who'd done a stretch in the pen for murder, and was also to get a shot at the winner of this bout.

In one of those key kid-go-tell-Sonny orders, I was dispatched as the bringer of bad tidings. It was kill-the-messenger time. The first thing I noticed was the ill-fitting bowler perched atop Liston's shaved skull. On anyone else, it would have been comical; on Sonny, it only added to the menace. The second was his size. The third, when I held out my hand and introduced myself, was his fists: They were the size of frying pans. Big, black, cast-iron ones.

I withdrew my hand.

"Mister . . . ah . . . Liston," I managed.

"Yeah," he growled.

"Well, sir," I coughed, "it seems we have a small problem."

I fumbled through some excuse. We were running late, they'd had to cut down the pre-fight appearances, he wouldn't be going on. Sonny wasn't just angry, he was vesuvial and, I thought, ready to take on both fighters at the same time. Fortunately, he paid no further attention to the messenger, and as soon as I felt I prudently could, I beat a hasty retreat to the opposite side of the ring. There, a radio announcer had just finished his pre-fight commentary. Now, in tones that suggested a happening the equal of the Second Coming, he was doing a commercial for the *The Horse Soldiers*, starring Bill Holden and John Wayne, which was one of the sponsors of the bout. The announcer's singsong, nasal cadences sounded just like Eddie Bracken, and I wondered why we had hired the old movie comedian to call the fight for ABC radio. No, I was told, it wasn't Bracken, just a smart-ass from the local station. After Patterson put Johansson down for the count in the fifth round, so utterly I thought the Swede was dead, I jotted down the announcer's name: Howard Cosell.

The next few months, Scherick kept me on a tight leash, in the bullpen outside his office that functioned as the headquarters of ABC Sports. Four of us shared the space. Jim Colligan, Ed's all-purpose factotum, was a stenographic whiz who'd learned his trade from Billy Rose, the Broadway showman, and, I was startled to learn from Jim, winner of the 1938 World Shorthand Competition. Lest I forget either, Jim reminded me every day. Jack Lubell, who sat at the desk next to mine, was an ex-Marine who'd met Scherick while producing and directing sports at CBS and had been with him ever since. Around the industry, Jack was known as the "Iron Major," partly for his physical conditioning, partly for his pre-bedtime habit of ironing the crease in his pants and aligning his spit-and-polish shoes in perfect rows. Like Ed, who expressed annoyance by throwing his watch against the wall, Jack was also known to possess a temper. Scherick himself got a taste of it one day when, having pissed Jack off about something, he was seized by the neck and jerked into the air. Tongue out and gurgling, he hung suspended there till Jack cooled off and put him down. The sanest of my office mates was Ed's second-in-command, Chet Simmons. About my age, Chet had also come out of the ad biz and was not only superbly organized but unfailingly nice—the latter a quality not necessarily common in that office.

Then there was me. I happened to have landed there at a most fortuitous moment. Scherick's very success, the furious pace at which he was rounding up licenses for ABC, was creating chaos. To boxing, bowling, and baseball, he'd quickly added not only NCAA football but the American Football League, still embryonic and with no games yet but about to launch a full schedule. Even the NCAA schedule was more demanding than it looked, for, every third week or so, the telecast went regional, with three games to produce instead of one, and that meant not only three producers and directors and announcing teams but all the crews and equipment that went with them. My job was to keep track of all the production talent that *wasn't* tied down by other network commitments, to interview and line them up for Ed to either land in deals or dismiss. It was a strictly managerial task, but doing it, I came to know virtually all the people then involved in sports broadcasting.

Every so often, Scherick apparently judged it safe to let me out in public, and early that summer I was sent out with Jack Lubell to San Francisco for the *Baseball Game of the Week,* Giants versus Dodgers. Jack was to direct, I was to help on the pregame survey, checking camera positions and technical facilities. It was my first flight across the country (one of my first *anywhere*), and we had crystal-clear weather all the way across the continent. I gaped at our country while Jack, who'd made the trip dozens of times, snoozed. It was one remarkable sight after the other, from the Great Lakes to the glimpses of the big cities of the Midwest to the snow-capped Rockies in all their splendor.

We checked into a motel out near San Francisco airport—a far cry from the better downtown hotels where most of the media stayed—and went directly to Candlestick Park for the Friday night game to get our bearings and scout out our positions and facilities for our Saturday-afternoon telecast. After the seventh inning, Jack had had enough and we found a taxi to take us back down U.S. 101, toward our motel. The next thing I knew, Jack was cussing out the cabdriver. We'd just missed the freeway off-ramp to our motel—deliberately, Jack was convinced—and, ordering the driver to pull over, he threw some money at him and got out, with me behind him.

"C'mon!" he shouted at me. "Let's run for it!"

I couldn't believe him. But off he went, miraculously finding what must have been the one break that whole evening in the whizzing traffic. Eight lanes of it, mind you! I could barely watch, but I saw him emerge on the far side and head off.

There was no way I was going to try my luck. Instead, I walked on down, parallel to U.S. 101, until I got to the airport itself. There I crossed over on a transverse, still on foot, and found a taxi that took me back to the motel.

As for Jack? The next time I saw him, he said I'd never get anywhere in television being a chicken.

At Candlestick Park the next day, our cameras had been set up in fixed, static positions on the mezzanine behind home plate, and along the left- and right-field stands. From these sites they were to capture all the action, on the field and off, in a stadium that held 50,000. That was the way it was always done. "The view a fan gets at home," baseball commissioner Ford Frick had said, "should not be any better than that of the fan in the worst seat of the ball park."

Instinctively, I knew that was wrong. What television ought to be striving for was to give the fan the best seat in the house, with intelligent commentators describing and explaining what was going on. I finished my preliminary work that day with several hours to kill before "Play ball!" and began wandering the stadium, imagining camera angles from center field, the upper deck, the seats behind home plate, and along the first- and third-base lines. At every stop, I held my hands out, using my fingers to form a television screenlike box. I sat in different sections, at different heights. What if I could have *any* seat? I wondered, what would I want to see? What would be going on around me? I thought of the ballparks I'd been to with my dad: the peanut and hot dog vendors, the fans who knew every statistic and could pick apart every play, the kids who came out for batting practice with autograph books. I remembered the sucked-in breaths as a foul ball arced into the stands, the mad scramble after it, then the cheer when the lucky one held up his prize. That was the game, as much as a home run or a diving catch. They were all part of the piece.

By the time I got outside to the production truck, the grounds crew was smoothing the infield and Jack was wondering whether I'd gotten lost. I said I'd been double-checking some things, then took a seat in the last row behind the console. I have no memory of who won the game, but Jack Lubell was clearly uninterested in anything that happened *outside* the chalk lines. In fact, I recall, whenever a foul pop drifted into the crowd, Jack chose a crowd shot all right, but *not* one that followed the scramble for the souvenir!

No matter. Jack headed back home immediately after the game, but I stayed on an extra day or two to see San Francisco, and I fell in love. Not with a woman, but with a city. I rode the cable cars down to Fisherman's Wharf, took a boat ride that showed me Alcatraz as well as the Golden Gate Bridge, rode an elevator to the Top of the Mark, saw the Coit Tower, toured Chinatown, and hung out, in those pre-hippie days, in North Beach, which the beats made famous. I took it all in. I practically inhaled it. Without wanting to make too much of it, I'm pretty sure that one of the hallmarks of our future sports telecasts was born right then, that magical weekend: showing the place—the campus, the town, the terrain, the city, the people—as a setting for the sporting event. And why not? Wasn't part of the pleasure of seeing a ball game in Candlestick Park visiting the magic city of which it formed a part?

My friends back in New York couldn't understand what I was up to. Here you are, they'd say, a well-educated fellow who knows which fork to use, discusses poetry without embarrassment, and can hold his own when chat requires multisyllables. And what are you doing? (Pause, roll of the eyes.) *Sports*. Where was the value in it?

It didn't change many minds, but I had an answer: Sports were life condensed, all its drama, struggle, heartbreak, and triumph embodied in artificial contests. To play a game well, endless practice was required, just as it was in mastering life. Sports always contained the unexpected—a catch that should have been made and wasn't, a bar that shouldn't have been leaped and was. So did life—chaos intruding on the orderly patterns of civilization. Sports could bring tears or laughter, in wonderment over its sometime absurdity.

Television could capture it all, and in the 1960s, there was a chance to do it creatively. I wanted to make the game more intimate, and a lot more human. Bob Riger did it in *Sports Illustrated* with his photos and line drawings. His classic of Giants quarterback Y. A. Tittle kneeling on the turf—head down, helmet off, uniform smeared with dirt and blood—summed up defeat better than any box score could. We could create the same images with our cameras. They didn't have to be fixed, like lighthouses. They could move in, hunt around, seize the unexpected, just like the new, portable "creepie-peepies" had at the recent national political conventions. The new videotape machines were getting better, too. Well, what if we used them at halftime to review the big plays? No one had, yet, but that was all the more reason we should.

Scherick, of course, didn't need persuading. Maybe it was my enthusiasm, or maybe the fact that I was around the office the most, but after the San Francisco trip, he started asking my opinion about coverage: baseball first, then, as the season approached, football. I said I thought there were a lot of things television was missing and told him about taking Joan to a Notre Dame–Army game in Philadelphia a couple of years before. With thirty seconds to go, and the cadets lining up to kick what would be the game-winning field goal, she asked to use my binoculars. "Great," I thought, "she's getting into it." Then Joan said, "The Notre Dame band has gold tassels on their hats." In other words, she didn't give a damn about the outcome of the game, but she was smitten by the event.

Ed nodded in sympathy.

The point, I said, was that there were millions like Joan, people who weren't sports fanatics but did like a good show. And we could make them part of our audience by giving them one—not just the scoring drives, but all the color and pageantry that accompanied the big games. As it was now, I said, we just opened our cameras and waited for something to occur in front of them, ignoring everything else that was going on. It was, I said, like looking out on the Grand Canyon through a peephole in a door.

Would we get flak for doing things differently? Sure we would. Television treated sports as sacrosanct. But where was it written that God created a football field 100 yards long and that television cameras had to be riveted around it in fixed locations? Everything about sports was made up, including the rules, so why not add some artifice of our own? Besides, the times were changing. The explosion of the NFL since "the ultimate game"—the Colts overtime victory over the Giants for the 1958 championship—proved that. Around New York, the Giants had become the hot ticket on Sunday afternoons, even when it got cold and the wind blew so hard they had to hold the ball for kickoffs. We'd better change too, or we'd be left behind. And the place to begin, I said, was seeing the game as a story we were uniquely equipped to tell.

I didn't know where all the talk was going, since Ed had already appointed Lubell to produce the NCAA games, and innovation wasn't part of Jack's repertoire. But one midsummer Friday afternoon, Scherick called me into his office. ABC, he told me, had been marketing the hell out of NCAA football, and they were doing it right. Almost all the commercial availabilities had been sold. ABC had also been using the games, which were like religion in many parts of the country, to poach affiliates from NBC and CBS. More than a score of new stations had come aboard, including several in major markets where, up till now, the initials *ABC* had stood for mud. In short, Scherick said, the network had a huge bet riding on NCAA football. If the games were a success, the network could begin to climb out of the hole; if they weren't, it was back to the Dark Ages.

"I want you to write a memo over the weekend," he said, "laying out all this stuff you've been talking about. It's been decided that more of the same won't do. Do it like you're pitching a whole new concept and like we're out to stand the country on its ear."

He wanted it by Monday, in time for meetings he had the next week.

"Oh, and Roone?" he called after me.

Don't fuck it up, I expected him to say. But he didn't. Instead:

"Make it detailed. And, remember, this is television. Don't be afraid to hype."

I went home to Armonk that night, told Joan I had work to do over the weekend, but then spent much of Saturday thinking about what I wanted to say and generally procrastinating, as is my wont when something big is in the air. I putted on the golf course and puttered around the house. Finally, around two o'clock on Sunday afternoon, I grabbed a beer from the fridge, sat down, and began to type.

> Heretofore, television has done a remarkable job of bringing the game to the viewer—now we are going to take the viewer to the game!
>
> We will utilize every production technique that has been learned in producing variety shows, in covering political conventions, in shooting travel and adventure series to heighten the

viewer's feeling of actually sitting in the stands and participating personally in the excitement and color of walking through a college campus to the stadium to watch the big game. All these delightful adornments to the actual contest have been missing from previously televised sports events. . . .

To improve upon the audience . . . we must gain and hold the interest of women and others who are not fanatic followers of the sport we happen to be televising. Women come to football games, not so much to marvel at the adeptness of the quarterback in calling an end sweep or a lineman pulling out to lead a play, but to sit in a crowd, see what everyone else is wearing, watch the cheerleaders, and experience the countless things that make up the feeling of the game. Incidentally, very few men have ever switched channels when a nicely proportioned girl was leaping into the air or leading a band downfield. . . .

We will utilize six cameras for our basic coverage of the game, but each man will have a complete schedule of additional assignments that will allow him to cover all the other interesting facets of the game when he is not actually engaged in covering a game situation. In addition to our fixed cameras (using the term advisedly) we will have cameras mounted in Jeeps, on mike booms, in risers or helicopters, or anything necessary to get the complete story of the game. We will use a "creepie-peepie" camera to get the impact shots that we cannot get from a fixed camera—a coach's face as a man drops a pass in the clear—a pretty cheerleader after her hero has scored a touchdown—a coed who brings her infant baby to the game in her arms—the referee as he calls a particularly difficult play; a student hawking programs in the stands—two romantic students sharing a blanket late in the game on a cold day—the beaming face of a substitute halfback as he comes off the field after running seventy yards for a touchdown, on his first play for the varsity—all the excitement, wonder, jubilation, and despair that make this America's number one sports spectacle, and a human drama to match bullfights and heavyweight championships in intensity.

In short—WE ARE GOING TO ADD SHOW BUSINESS TO SPORTS!

In addition to the natural suspense and excitement of the actual game, we have a supply of human drama that would make the producer of a dramatic show drool. All we have to do is find and insert it in our game coverage at the proper moment. And this we will do!

The moment we take to the air, we will start making the viewer feel he is at the game. Instead of the hackneyed slide to introduce the telecast, we will attempt to videotape a college cheering-card section or a great college band spelling out "NCAA FOOTBALL" on a football field; and after our opening commercial billboards, instead of dissolving to the usual pan shots of the field, we will have pre-shot film of the campus and the stadium so we can orient the viewer. He must know he is in Columbus, Ohio, where the town is football mad; or that he is part of a small but wildly enthusiastic crowd in Corvallis, Oregon. He must know where in the country he is, what town, what the surrounding country and campus look like, how many other people are watching this game with him, how the people dress at football games in a particular part of the country, and what the game means to the two schools involved. While the color man is setting the scene, we will see people parking cars, possibly a group picnicking on the back of a station wagon before entering the field, and possibly others getting their programs from the student usher at the game.

Then the viewers must meet the players—but he will meet them as he would if he were at the game. This will be accomplished by using a blowup of the cover of the actual game program and introducing the actual players by means of pictures of them in their normal street attire. These are enthusiastic college kids—the pride of America, not hard-bitten pros—and we want everyone to know this.

The cameramen who will be using long zoom lenses will have wide-angle lenses attached for the pre-kickoff color and scene-setting shots. They will have time to get back to their game lenses before kickoff. This will be an enjoyable show to work on, but it will not be the place for lazy cameramen, directors, stage managers, or anyone trying to accomplish his job the easy way. The announcers will be familiar with the college town, the players on the two teams, the relative merits of the teams involved, the traditions surrounding the game, and the type of people involved in it as the most enthusiastic undergraduates actually present at the game.

We will use video recorders to enable us to replay the decisive plays of the first half at the halftime break . . .

The audioman must know just when the referee is liable to speak so that he can open the pot from the remote mike we will try to have him wear.

After some two hours pounding away, I finished with, "The personal satisfaction in such an undertaking will be great. We will be setting the standards that everyone will be talking about and that others in the industry will spend years trying to equal."

I believed every word of what I'd written. The question was whether Scherick could convince ABC, Gillette, and the NCAA to believe in it, too.

The first returns came in Monday afternoon. Ed said he'd just gotten off the phone with Tom Moore, who'd received a copy of the memo that morning. Tom had read it, and sent congrats: full steam ahead. Later that week, the NCAA weighed in, dubious in the extreme. Not surprising from a hidebound organization with a keeper-of-the-sacred-flame mentality, but there was nothing in our contract with them that could prevent us from trying. Besides, we had support from within. Asa Bushnell, head of the NCAA's TV committee at the time, said he could do without the coeds carrying babies—not exactly the image their member colleges wanted to project—but otherwise he thought it was terrific.

The powers at Gillette were the last to reply, and the most negative. It wasn't the proposals in the memo that bothered them; those, they thought, might produce a bigger bang for the advertising buck. But there was something else afoot, and I didn't get it until Ed Scherick called me into his office and told me to close the door, and even then it hit me like the bucket of iced Gatorade they dump over the coach these days when the big game is won.

"They're all buying it," Scherick said, "but there's a problem."

"What problem?" I asked.

"You," he said. "Tom Moore's amenable, and the NCAA won't get in the way, but Gillette's been pressuring me to reconsider."

"Reconsider what?" I said, not getting it.

"Reconsider you."

"What do you mean?"

"You're going to produce."

"Produce what?" I said, feeling my brain start to wobble.

"The games!" Ed said. "You're going to produce the games."

I couldn't say anything right away.

"But Gillette doesn't like it. They found your résumé a little skimpy. The *Anny* business didn't help either."

"What did you tell them?" I asked.

Ed looked out his office window for a long moment before replying. I think he was loving keeping me hanging.

"I told them you were our choice," he said finally.

Jesus Christ.

I could have kissed him, as unlikely a prospect as that was. Instead, I think I managed to thank him. Then I turned to get out of there before I jumped out of my skin.

"Oh, Roone," he called after me. "One other thing."

I looked around.

"Don't fuck it up."

My plan was that Jack Lubell would direct. In assigning producers and directors to our various programs, I'd gotten into the rhythm of mixing and matching novices with experienced hands. But Jack, blaming me for his being pulled as producer, wasn't about to. Find yourself another director, he told Scherick, he wasn't working with "that kid."

If Lubell was counting on Scherick to buckle, it didn't pan out. Ed put him on the AFL games, while I took Bill Bennington, a veteran we'd hired away from NBC to do the AFL. There was no fuss in lining up the announcers. We simply hired the two best: Curt Gowdy for the play-by-play and Paul Christman for the color. Gowdy had cut his broadcasting teeth at Oklahoma with Bud Wilkinson and had worked with Mel Allen, the "voice of the Yankees." Christman, a former All-America quarterback at Missouri, had been broadcasting the games of his old pro team, the Chicago Cardinals. After some arm-twisting from me, Scherick also signed a third announcer—Bob Neal, who did the Cleveland Browns games—to roam the sidelines for interview targets of opportunity. No one had ever done that before, but I had a hunch we'd come up with interesting stuff.

The last personnel matter was a production assistant. Ed said I could have my pick of two new kids who'd come into the office: Jim Spence, a quietly intense hard worker who'd been sports editor of the student paper at Dartmouth; and Chuck Howard, a booming-voiced Duke graduate and a refugee from the management training program at Chase Manhattan. They seemed a toss-up in savvy, but there was something appealing about throwing a would-be banker into the middle of a football game. I took Chuck, and Jim went to work on our bowling show. Both would be indispensable at ABC Sports for the next quarter of a century.

In early September, we flew to the site of the first game: Legion Field in Birmingham, Alabama, where Bear Bryant's Crimson Tide was hosting a Georgia squad led by a scrambling quarterback named Fran Tarkenton. Unless the Almighty had a grudge against the Bulldogs, Georgia, which had won the last Orange Bowl, was going to crush Alabama, which had lost the last Liberty Bowl. So long as there was drama in the crushing, that was fine with me. Given the story I hoped to tell, the numbers on the scoreboard were almost incidental.

"Hoped" was the operative word. Gowdy had never worked with Christman, I'd never produced a football game, and my laundry list of new techniques had never been tried. The Gillette people, who were there in force, were in a state of high anxiety. At a minimum, we needed a rehearsal, and I arranged a run-through, using a Friday-night high school game. Inevitably, a driving rainstorm washed out the game. Coach Bryant, though, had graciously invited us for an early dinner. "Least I can do," he drawled, "seeing how my po' boys are going to embarrass themselves on your first show and all."

In extremis, as soon as we knew the high school game had been canceled, I'd gotten us an auditorium for that evening so that all of us—crew/cameramen/announcers included—could show-and-tell our Gillette friends what we were going to do. The ABC brass were there as well, and so were the NCAA people. I was deep into our presentation when, in a momentary lull, Paul Christman, who was standing with a group of Gillette executives, sang out loud and clear, "I sure hope in the middle of all this stuff you get around to showin' some football, too." The line brought down the house and all but brought me to my knees. I wasn't used to being the butt of someone's joke, not in a crucial meeting. But I stuck to my guns, got through it somehow, and Ed, who was staunchly on my side, shouted down our critics.

And then it was Saturday. When I arrived at the production truck late the next morning, it was already packed, the din a hair less than that in the stadium. Tom Moore, who'd brought a passel of relatives from next-door Mississippi, was there, along with people from Gillette and its advertising agency and a couple of young women I guessed must be overnight girlfriends of the crew. But the source of most of the ruckus was Scherick, who, at the top of his lungs, was impressing on everyone present the life-or-death nature of what was about to commence.

I slid into the seat next to Bill Bennington, flipped open my production notebook, and, as the minutes ticked down to showtime, slipped off into a Zen-like zone. I was aware of the noise and commotion around me, but only dimly. It was as if I were sealed off in a bubble where the only reality was the monitors in front of me. "Roll film," I heard myself say as the console clock hit 1:00:01. "Cue Curt."

The next three hours had their share of bumps. Our major problem was that we'd made the mistake of believing all the advance notices, including Bear Bryant's. Georgia was going to romp, and our cameras were trained on all the hoopla and whoop-de-do we anticipated on the Georgia side of the field. Wrong. By halftime, though, Bear's "po' boys" were well on their way to an upset rout. The game was as good as over, and all we'd shown were glum faces. Still, for a first outing, it went better than I dared to expect. We had shots of cheerleaders and fans and anguished players; we explained a setting and a university and a coach and put a rivalry in context. However imperfectly, we used the violent meeting of twenty-two young men to do something television sports wasn't in the habit of doing: tell a story.

We did it better the following week, at Pittsburgh. The Pitt Panthers and their future NFL Hall of Fame linebacker Mike Ditka were playing Penn State, a contest that in Pennsylvania is on the order of Armageddon. How better to herald it, I thought, than with a shot approximating God looking down. Goodyear blimps weren't yet routine features at televised sporting events, so I had one of our cameras lugged to the roof of a hospital adjacent to the stadium. The show opened, and, wham, there it was, like the colosseum in Rome when the lions were about to be let loose.

The only problem was controlling Scherick. Just as during the Alabama game, he was all over the truck, shouting, "Cheerleader on the twenty! . . . Fan in section eight! . . . Catch that waterboy! . . . Get 'em, get 'em, get 'em!" When he wasn't driving us crazy, he was in the announcers' booth, barking at Gowdy and Christman. They'd had it, especially Christman, who was saying one more week with Scherick and he'd be back in Chicago. "Ed," I pleaded, "please, stay home. You can do more good telling us on Monday what we did wrong."

Ed promised he would, but the following week, Colorado at Kansas, there he was. By this time, though, I'd had it.

"Get out of here," I said, ordering him from the truck. "We can't do the show with you around."

I'd made arrangements ahead of time for Scherick to have the use of the Kansas University president's office during the game, and that's where he repaired, to watch the proceedings on television. I'd also routed a special phone line to him, but he had very few suggestions to make, and after that week, he mostly stayed home.

We managed to do fine without him. Some of our college hosts, however, regarded us as an economic threat. If a fan could get a better view of the game sitting at home, their argument went, watching for free from a cozy couch, why would he or she want to pay for a bad seat on a hard wooden bench in a stadium unprotected from the elements? I got my first inkling of the enmity when we were preparing to telecast from the University of Michigan, where the athletic director, Fritz Kreisler, was decades into his job and as crotchety as he was long serving. As we surveyed potential camera positions, one of Kreisler's aides blurted out, "You guys seem all right to me, but Fritz told me not to give you everything you want." I thereupon added to my list of technical needs a number of items I didn't want; they were exed out, and things were fine.

Meanwhile, Tom Gallery of NBC was fanning the flames. Humiliated by having been mouse-trapped by Scherick, he was sending a catalog of perceived ABC slips each week to Gillette and the NCAA. Gillette ignored him, but Gallery had an eager listener in the NCAA, whose receptivity to change was on a par with the Amish. Perhaps by coincidence, perhaps not, we suddenly had to struggle to televise big-ticket games. Instead, the NCAA began pushing us for the likes of Brown versus Dartmouth.

"People would love to see the Ivy League," I was told.

No comment.

The ratings, meanwhile, said we were on the right track. But there was so much more to be done—with the right technology, the right imagination—so many ways to make the images on the screen more immediate and real.

The following August, I went to Tokyo to acquire the rights for the Japanese All-Star baseball game. Between the conclusion of one fruitless meeting with a bureaucrat and the onset of another, I decided to take in a movie. The film was a samurai epic of some sort. I couldn't understand the dialogue, needless to say, or follow the plot. But one scene fascinated me because it was filmed in slow motion.

I came out of the theater thinking: What if we could do the same with football? What if there were some mechanism that allowed us to rerun a play at half or quarter speed or even slower? If a ref made a wrong call or a receiver stepped out of bounds, we'd know it. If a back miraculously broke through a line, we'd understand the wonder. We could view the whole game differently.

Three days later, having accomplished a minor miracle of my own by tracking down a bureaucrat with the authority to say yes, I flew eastward, across the Pacific. All the way across, I couldn't get the idea out of my head. I stopped off in Los Angeles, where we were producing a boxing match, to survey the Coliseum where, in a few weeks, we'd be televising a Southern Cal game. I went through the stadium with Bob Trachinger, one of ABC's West Coast engineers, an enterprising guy, something of a maverick, who was always at odds with management. The afternoon was blistering, and after we finished, I asked Trach if there was any place close where we could have a beer. He said there was, a little place called Julie's.

Over cold ones, I told Trach about the Tokyo movie and, excitedly, what I thought slow motion could do for football. Trach said he'd wondered about the same thing. He even had some ideas. He sketched how it might work on the bar napkins under our drinks. The drawings were smeary, but I got the gist: We'd tape the action, and as it replayed on an orthicon camera tube, tape it again with another camera running at half speed. Voilà, we'd have slow motion!

With my encouragement, he put some people to work on it. Whenever I saw it, though, the picture flickered too much, and lines ran through it. Trach's local bosses weren't happy either; they said we were wasting money and put the kibosh on further experiments. That didn't stop Trach. He could always find a way to find money, he kept tinkering, and I kept viewing the results. It took nearly three months, but he finally got rid of most of the bugs. When Texas played Texas A&M for its traditional game, Thanksgiving Day, 1961, I decided we'd give "slo-mo" its debut.

The game had all the excitement of watching pigskin cure: one field goal after two quarters. But, just to prove we could do it, at halftime I re-ran the only score. A videotape machine in New York clicked on, and, oh so slowly, the center snapped, the kicker connected, and the ball oozed over the crossbar. The picture still had some flicker, but we showed something that had never been seen before. The following weekend, when Boston College quarterback Jack Concannon broke loose for a seventy-yard scoring run against Syracuse, we showed its potential. At halftime, once more we showed Concannon scoring in slo-mo—with dreamlike grace this time, Paul Christman explaining every juke and jink. Watching, I saw the future open up before me.

We used the feature in all our productions from then on, and now we weren't the only ones. Two years later, after CBS director Tony Verna refined Trach's process, action in the Army-Navy game was shown again immediately after it occurred. What had begun over beers at Julie's was on its way to getting a name. It came, ironically, from NBC, which was so far behind us in technical innovations that they weren't even in the game. So we will give them credit for the words only: instant replay.

Alas, we were out of the college football business by that time, hoist by our own success. The techniques we'd introduced had jacked up ratings—and the bid price on the next NCAA contract. Leonard Goldenson judged the new figure too rich for ABC, and CBS took over, adopting much of what we'd accomplished and, once upon a time, been lambasted for by the august NCAA.

By then, I was deep into a new program that I'd been working on for many moons. I remember once, during the process, writing ideas for it on a lined yellow pad, late one night in a motel room I was sharing with Curt Gowdy. That afternoon, we'd televised the final game of the first NCAA season and gone out for a long, sodden celebration. It was well past midnight when we got back to the motel, and Curt, lying whipped in the next bed, asked what I was doing. I told him about the show, how every week it would travel the world for sports rarely, if ever, seen on U.S. television—some of them sports that Americans didn't even know existed.

"That's the craziest idea I ever heard of," said Curt, rolling over to go to sleep. "It'll never work."

Chapter 4

Wide World
of Sports

The show I told Curt about that night was *ABC's Wide World of Sports,* and it would become the longest-running, most influential sports program in history. It would also come within eight minutes of never getting on the air.

It got started because of a void. The college football season culminated in the bowl games on New Year's Day. By the time major league baseball opened in April, the weekend sports momentum we'd built with our NCAA coverage would have dissipated and there was no way we could hold it with *Saturday Night Fights* and *Make That Spare* (bowling). Even baseball, at the time, was limited by the fact that the major league owners, in their wisdom (?), insisted on blacking out the major league cities! We had one package, featuring the Giants and the Dodgers, but CBS had the better one, because they had the Yankees. As far as January to April was concerned, we were shut out of the basketball business, and ice hockey, in those pre-expansion years, had no national appeal whatsoever.

Nor was ABC the only network faced with the problem. CBS was using the name *Sports Spectacular* to cover a few disparate specials. They lacked cohesion of any kind, and they didn't run every week, but some of them were good: an AAU event, a documentary on the birth of an expansion team in Major League Baseball, a figure-skating competition from start to finish. Ed, Tom Moore, and I, along with others at Sports Programs, Inc., were intrigued by what we saw, and Ed and I worked our way toward the idea of a regular weekly program based on sporting events the world over. There were competitions that took place all over the globe that people either paid a great deal of money to see (like the soccer cup finals in all the European and South American countries, where crowds of 100,000 were the norm) or went to a great deal of trouble to get to (like the Tour de France bicycle race that circled France for the whole month of July), and that were almost totally unknown in the United States. The television rights for America, we assumed, could be acquired easily because no one had ever sought them. At least in some cases, we could probably buy the national coverage from the BBC in England, ORTF in France, and so on. It didn't even matter if some of the taped events were shown days or even a week later in the United States, because with the exception of scattered die-hard fans, our viewers would be unaware of the outcomes. We'd have competitions only. We'd run on a weekly basis, and if it worked, we'd go the year round, bringing ABC one step closer to being the network people tuned to for sports.

The credit for inventing the program has been attributed to several people, myself included. The truth is that no one of us *invented* it. The concept evolved. It was I who put it together, Ed and Tom Moore who took it to Leonard Goldenson, ABC's chairman, and convinced him to give us a shot, Saturday afternoons for twenty weeks. Once we had the okay, I was the one who planned it, shaped it, acquired the licenses for the events, found the host and the crews, and masterminded the shows themselves. And it was Ed, as I will relate, who later—with eight minutes left on the clock—saved the day.

We got the go-ahead from ABC at Christmastime, after which Ed left me pretty much on my own—for the very good reason, as I only later found out that he was preoccupied with selling Sports Programs, Inc. to ABC. I knew I had a late-April launch to make, and the rest was up to me.

The rest?

In a way, the concept was the least difficult part, and it was very easy to explain to people. The harder part, I knew from the beginning, was going to be to give it shape and style and a feel of importance above and beyond the particular calendar of events for any given Saturday. Inevitably, in the early days, we'd be offering a few major events if I could land them, sprinkled among lots of minor ones. Consequently—and this was truer of this program that it was of any other I ever developed—the whole had to be bigger than its parts and sports had to be defined as never before on television.

With no time to spare, I started to assemble the parts.

My first stop—in fact, that same Christmas week we got the okay—was just a few blocks away, at the New York Athletic Club. That was where the AAU was holding its meeting. The Amateur Athletic Union, in those days, controlled track and field, swimming and diving, and gymnastics among others, and they were a very powerful organization in American sports, often fighting with the NCAA for supremacy. But as Ed and I had surmised, there was no competition for the television rights to their events and they were delighted by our interest. For a token option fee against a final payment of $50,000, they awarded ABC exclusive television rights to all AAU competitions in the coming year—including the U.S. national team's annual track and field meet against the Soviets, which turned out to be the gem in the package. It was being held in Moscow in late July, and had never been previously televised.

With NCAA football, though, I'd at least started with the frame of a house in place. On this project, I had barely an architect's sketch. I'd never been outside the United States, and I didn't have anything resembling a guide to the international events we'd so airily described. Nor was there any use inquiring at ABC; they were lucky to have a phone book.

But the *New York Times* covered everything. All we'd have to do was go through back issues for the last year or two, record every sporting event that was off the beaten track from television's point of view, and we'd have a road map of possibilities. As luck would have it, when I'd worked at NBC, the corporate library was on the same floor as my office, and I knew they had the *Times* on microfilm. I was too familiar to people at NBC to go myself, but I sent Chuck Howard over to 30 Rock (we ourselves had recently moved into the Time-Life building), and forty-eight hours later, he put a compendium of worldwide sporting events, with their dates and locales, on my desk.

Tucked somewhere in the world of automobile racing, between the brickyard of the Indianapolis 500 and the winding courses (mostly in Europe) of the Formula One Grand Prix circuit, was an utterly unique, extraordinary, once-a-year event known as the 24 Hours of Le Mans. I'd heard of it. Most of us had. A great test of endurance and perseverance, human as well as mechanical, it drew crowds in the hundreds of thousands to the small provincial French town every June, and I thought it could capture the imagination of a much more general American public. The 24 Hours wasn't defined by distance, like the Indianapolis 500, but by time. Pairs of drivers took turns driving a car, literally for twenty-four hours, around the famous Le Mans circuit, all night long, all day long, and the car that went the farthest in the twenty-four hours was the winner.

Through the good offices of the tiny ABC news bureau in Paris, which rented space in the *Paris Herald Tribune*'s offices on the rue de Berri, I made contact with the *directeur adjoint* (the number-two man) at the Automobile Club de l'Ouest, which organized the race, and off I flew to Paris. I spoke almost no French, and in fact had almost no money to spend. No matter. I believe I was the first American ever to make a pitch for television rights, and the words "American Broadcasting Company" in this instance worked wonders. (How little did they know!) On the one hand, the words sounded important, not like the mom-and-pop shop that at the time was closer to the reality of the network. But on the other, they echoed the BBC—the British Broadcasting Corporation—which, as everyone knew, was as prestigious as it was parsimonious. I think it was this combination, in addition to my undeniable charm, that encouraged the *directeur adjoint* to award the United States rights to the 24 Hours for—ahem—$10,000.

There may well have been another reason too, as I'll relate in a moment.

I strolled up the Champs-Elysées toward the Arc de Triomphe that night, sure I had the best job on the planet. I was actually being *paid* to be in Paris—it was amazing—and I had my pick of where in the world to go next. I was the representative of—as one of my new French friends had put it—"ze *great* American Broadcasting Company." I spotted a wonderful book in a bookstore window and bought it. *Paris Bistro Cooking,* it was called, and it became a gastronomic guide not only for my few days in Paris but when I returned to America, too. It featured the best bistros in the city, with their stories, and, more important, recipes from their kitchens, which I would put to good use over the years. I was still thumbing through it, outside the store, when I saw an extraordinary sight. A young couple had just emerged from a café and was mounting a motorcycle. He was in a tux, she was in an evening gown, and both were wearing crash helmets. As they roared off, the image froze in my head, distilling how exotic and alluring the world suddenly seemed. That's what I had to communicate with our new show: the feeling I had at that moment of witnessing the unexpected, the thrilling, and the new in faraway, exotic places.

The next day, however, brought me up short. Now that I had my $10,000 deal, I wanted to buy coverage of the 24 Hours from ORTF, the French national network, because ABC could never afford to send over the requisite crew and equipment. I found myself talking on the phone to a Monsieur Georges Croses at ORTF, who, though he spoke fluent English, didn't quite seem to understand what I wanted.

"The images, yes," he said, "we could provide those, but what about the rights? Don't you have to secure the rights first?"

"That's not a problem," I said confidently. "I've already obtained the rights."

"Oh? But how can that be?"

I explained to him about my meeting the day before with Monsieur Mordret at the Automobile Club de l'Ouest.

"I see," he said. "But it would have been simpler if you'd come to me first. You see, *le Club* doesn't own the rights. They belong to the ORTF."

It was my turn to ask how that could be.

Georges Croses didn't tell me to get lost. He asked, most politely, that I wait where I was for a few minutes and he'd call me back. The call, though, when it came, was from Monsieur Mordret, the *directeur adjoint* at the Automobile Club de l'Ouest. He was very sorry, but the rights he'd sold me weren't, in fact, the club's to give. I would have to deal with a Monsieur Georges Croses at ORTF, on behalf of Eurovision, which was the continent-wide broadcasting consortium.

This was my first—but far from last—mishap in dealing with the bureaucracies of Europe and the sinuous question of who owned rights. And as was often the case, what seemed bright and clear one minute became murky and impossible the next. But as the old French expression, "Rien n'est simple, mais tout est facile," ("Nothing is simple, but everything is easy") has it, in this instance, what made it easy was Georges Croses himself. Not only was he happy to cede us the rights and the coverage, for minimal money, but we became good friends. And not only did we become good friends but, some years later I hired him at ABC Sports and in time he became our first European vice president.

My expeditions during the next two months adhered to the Paris pattern. I'd select an event that intrigued me, immerse myself in its lore, and fly off to acquire the rights. To be sure, none of our competitors had ever gone prospecting for these rights, but I walked away with options on the Football Association Soccer Championship in London, the International Golf Championship in Puerto Rico, the World Professional Tennis Championship in Mexico City, and—a contest I dreamed up myself—a special winner-take-all match between Arnold Palmer and Gary Player on the hallowed Old Course at St. Andrews, Scotland.

(As a footnote to the latter, what I'd originally wanted was to bring together at St. Andrews the winners of the four premier events in golf, two of which had been won the previous year by Player and one each by Palmer and Billy Casper. But Mark McCormack, a new force in American sports and the agent for both Player and Palmer, didn't want any part of Billy Casper, so we ended up with just Gary and Arnold in the deal.)

"American Broadcasting Company," needless to say, didn't cut the same ice in the States, but there were any number of events our competitors had ignored, and I went after them: the 500 Time Trials in Indianapolis, the Firecracker 250 in Daytona; the World Water Skiing Championships in Long Beach, the World Hydroplane Championships in Seattle; the PBA World Championship Bowling Tournament in Paramus, New Jersey; the Men's Softball All-Star Game in Clearwater, Florida. I even landed one of the great rodeo championships—the famous Cheyenne, Wyoming, "Frontier Days." Pretty good, I reckoned, for a first, hurry-up season.

There'd been other developments at the same time. I was on my way back from my trip to Japan to get the Japanese All-Star game for us when, stopping off in Los Angeles, I heard rumors that Ed Scherick had sold Sports Programs, Inc. to ABC. Indeed he had, and at the same time, he'd moved into one of the most important jobs in the corporation, vice president in charge of Sales for the network. Those of us in the old company were now officially ABC's sports department, with Chet Simmons, who reported to Tom Moore, in charge.

I thought Ed would do wonderfully well in Sales. He could have sold refrigerators to Eskimos. But, as I learned when I got back to New York and called Ed, my as-yet-untitled show was having a tough time attracting advertisers.

The reaction from most of them had been the same as Gowdy's: crazy idea, couldn't work. It wouldn't even have the chance to work unless something happened soon, since ABC simply didn't air shows that weren't pre-sold, and so far, only Gillette had bought significant commercial time. I began to worry about the danger of losing our options. Most ran out after a fixed amount of time, and what if I couldn't renew them? Already I'd heard rumors that CBS was waking up to what we'd been doing, notably the Time Trials at Indy, and suppose, as my options began to run out, they started making offers?

"I'm running up the red flag!" Ed proclaimed over the phone. That was his way of saying he knew we were in an emergency situation and he was about to pull out all the stops.

This was the situation in late March, a month before our scheduled debut, when on a Friday afternoon I went to see Scherick. There was one ray of hope. L&M cigarettes, a major sponsor of NCAA football, had recently switched ad agencies, and the new agency, intent on showing that they were different, had dropped L&M's quarter share for next fall. This was now, according to Ed, being lusted after by two other tobacco companies. He said he'd told both that, in order to get it, they had to take a quarter of the commercial time on our new show, too.

He was now waiting to hear.

I sat in Ed's office, waiting with him in what turned into one of the most harrowing afternoons of my life. I jumped at every phone call, and Ed took them all, not seeming to share my anxiety one bit.

Then Brown & Williamson's ad agency called. They said they'd take an eighth of my program, but Ed turned them down. He insisted it had to be a quarter or bust! Then Ollie Treyz, our president, called in, wanting to know what was happening. I heard the conversation only from Ed's side, but the gist of it seemed to be that Ollie called him a moron—or worse—for turning Brown & Williamson down, and he then carried on for a good minute while Ed listened.

"He thinks your show is stupid, too," Ed said after he'd hung up. "Anyway, I'm waiting on an answer from R. J. Reynolds, so don't give up hope. By the way, Ollie's given us till the close of business today to sell the quarter or the program's kaput."

"*Till the close of business today?*" I exclaimed, astonished. I glanced at my watch, then stared back at him, appalled. "But that's just thirty-two minutes from now!"

"You got it," Ed said.

This rendered me totally speechless. As for Ed, he just kept rocking in his chair, staring at the phone.

The minutes dragged by. More calls in between.

Adieu, Paris, I thought; good-bye, St. Andrews.

Then the phone rang again.

God Almighty.

He picked up the receiver and nodded at me. It was R. J. Reynolds's ad agency.

Ed kept a perfect poker face during the conversation. It was a short one, and mostly one way—a no from Ed here, a yes there, punctuated by grunts—but from his expression I couldn't get an inkling of their decision.

"For God's sake!" I exclaimed when he put down the receiver. "What did they say?"

"They said they didn't want it—"

I sagged in my seat. Probably I looked as if I'd just fainted.

Scherick rolled his eyes.

"Let me finish, Roone. They said they didn't want it, but since that was the only way I was going to let them have football, they agreed to take it."

I let out a whoop, and as Ed dialed Treyz, glanced at my watch: 4:52. We'd made it—with eight minutes to spare.

An eight-minute margin—for a program that was to last for forty years!

All I had to do now was make the program.

A group of us, Ed, Tom Moore, Chet Simmons, and myself, celebrated at Tavern on the Green, and began batting names around, something we hadn't done till then for fear we'd jinx it. I proposed "Wonderful World of Sport," but Tom said that was too close to "Wonderful World of Disney," one of ABC's few entertainment hits. How about "The World of Sport"? Chet offered. Nah, Scherick said, *Sports Illustrated* was already using that as a section heading. "How about this?" I said. "*Wide* World of Sport."

People thought "Sport" sounded too British.

"Well," I said, "make it Wide World of *Sports.*"

It didn't exactly bring down the house, but nobody dumped on it either.

Ed had one change. "Put 'ABC,' in front of it," he said. "If the thing flies, it'll help sell the network."

I agreed. And so we became *ABC's Wide World of Sports*.

But now we needed a host, someone who'd bring credibility to the venture. Chris Schenkel would have done that instantly, but because he and the New York Giants telecasts were so immediately identified with Marlboro and it was R. J. Reynolds who'd bailed us out, I didn't think it fair to approach him. Curt Gowdy was another obvious candidate, but he was tied down calling the Boston Red Sox games. We were drawing blanks on anyone else when one of our producers, a Brit named Hugh Beach, suggested, "Why not Burrhead?"

Burrhead?

"Jim McKay," said Beach. "Real name's Jim McManus. The 'burrhead' comes from his crew cut. Shortest you've ever seen."

We had talked to McKay a number of times about doing various things for us. Ed, I seemed to recall, had said that McKay had worked with Schenkel on Sports Program, Inc.'s first-ever event, the opening of a local harness track. He was an ex–newspaper guy in Baltimore who'd started at CBS in 1950 as host of a late-afternoon New York show called *The Real McKay*—a play on "The Real McCoy"—and some jerk of a network executive at the time had insisted he go by that name. So McManus had become McKay. I'd seen and liked him on the local news—CBS at the time had the best—and he'd also hosted a recently canceled afternoon network show, *The Verdict Is Yours,* that was the granddaddy of all today's courtroom shows.

I knew him to be smart, literate, and quick on his feet—and there wouldn't be any need for someone to write his copy. He was our man—if I could get him.

He was currently in Augusta, announcing the Masters for his network, but from my point of view, the days were slipping away. We had a press conference scheduled for the following Sunday to announce the show. So, with Chet listening in, I called the tournament pressroom and got Jim on the line.

"We're doing a new program, a summer replacement, twenty weeks guaranteed," I said. "It's called *ABC's Wide World of Sports.* We'll be covering a number of sports not normally seen on TV."

"Sounds interesting," he shouted back.

"How'd you like to be host?"

"Sounds very interesting!"

"It will require a certain amount of traveling," I said, the understatement of the year.

McKay said that would be okay with him (although I didn't know it then, he had no assignments on tap after the Masters). When I raised the question of money, though, he asked if that couldn't wait till he got back to New York. His wife, Margaret, he explained, usually did the negotiating for him. I said it really couldn't. Several phone calls later, he named his figure—a thousand a show for the run of it, plus all expenses—and we were in business.

Would that it were always that easy!

The next couple of days were a blur of exercising options and recruiting production staff. Everything came together, and Sunday, which was the final day of the Masters, we scheduled a press conference to announce *Wide World*'s debut.

Two weeks later, April 29, 1961, a camera opened up to show a short man with a crew cut and a pleasing face standing in the rain at Franklin Field in Philadelphia, site of the Penn Relays. Jim always liked to call himself "a man of average height," but, short or not, he introduced us with a flourish. "Today's exciting show launches *ABC's Wide World of Sports,* a new and exciting global concept of sports. Each Saturday for the next twenty weeks, we'll be taking our cameras to the scene of famous sports events all over the world."

We covered two track meets live that same day, the Penn Relays from Philly and the Drake Relays from Des Moines, Iowa, and it all came off tolerably well, even if the overnight rainstorm had kayoed three of our six cameras at Penn. But when we made our first trip abroad, to London's Wembley Stadium for the Football Association Cup the third week of May, we began to find our footing

Soccer then was all but unknown to American television viewers, and after doing my homework, I could understand why. The games were low scoring in the extreme, often ending in a tie, or, as the Brits called it, a draw, or one-nil, this after two hours of running back and forth by grown men in shorts who were forbidden to use their hands and arms except for throw-ins. Not exactly the stuff of which television ratings are made. Our first order of business, as I saw it, was making the contest comprehensible—such as explaining that "nil" meant "zero." I therefore engaged the services of Ken Wolstenholme, a top soccer announcer for the BBC, to call our play-by-play. Jim McKay, who'd never been to Europe before or witnessed a soccer match, would do the color—and I planned to have a ton of it. Maybe I couldn't get U.S. viewers to care that much about the sport, but with the right program, they might come to understand why so many other people in the world did.

The flight to London was the first extended chance I'd had to talk to Jim, and it was nice to hear that he shared my ideas on coverage: We had to emphasize the human dimension, the fans' eye view. The emotional impact always came first. It was also heartwarming to discover that when I talked about things like hanging cameras from 100-foot cranes or on the cowcatchers of trolleys, he didn't think I was nuts. But I knew I'd lucked into the perfect host when Jim began describing the scene at the Masters he'd just done—not the great shots or the ritual of last year's winner slipping the green jacket onto this one's, but the tiny, telling moments that gave the event its texture: the particular way Arnold Palmer hitched up his pants; the downturn of Jack Nicklaus's lips as he lined up a putt, the stare of the black caddies at the all-white field.

One other thing the flight brought out: Jim McKay was never at a loss for words, or curiosity. Why did the uniforms of the BOAC stewardesses seem more stylish than TWA's and PanAm's? Where did the accent of the captain put him in the spectrum of the English social classes? Why was England so class conscious? Only when we were descending into Heathrow was there a pause.

"What are you looking at?" I asked, seeing his nose pressed against the cabin window.

"Rooftops," Jim answered soberly. "Imagine all the guns that must have been on them twenty years ago."

Gazing down, I'd been thinking just that, and what it must have been like at night when the waves of Luftwaffe bombers flew over England.

Game-day morning, the streets around Wembley were jammed with 100,000 mostly working-class folk. I had Jim and a camera crew positioned at ground zero for F.A. Cup devotees, the Green Man Pub—where, he informed our audience, the beer was always warm and the patrons always stood. "Old boys" from FA Cup finals gone by provided historical background and tales of glories past. Then it was out to the street to buttonhole fans, their allegiance, Jim pointing out, always identifiable by the color of the rosettes on their lapels: blue and white for London's Tottenham Hotspurs, red and white for the underdogs from Leicester City. "Hotspurs," McKay reflected. "My, what a name to conjure with." The true diehards entered the stadium early to get the best standing places on the tiers of their respective end zones, for less than half of Wembley had sit-down seats. (I wondered how they managed to control themselves, for they couldn't go to the bathroom without running the risk of losing their spot, but nobody I ran into could give me a satisfactory answer!) And they started singing early, those chants and songs of the multitudes that char-acterize all European soccer fans, but the British in particular. All this going on before the match in soccer's Runnymede, its hallowed turf, an altar cloth of green reminiscent (to us former Colonials) of Yankee Sta-dium just before game one of the World Series.

Although the rather austere coverage of the BBC, which we used for America, left something to be desired, Jim and Ken Wolstenholme were in fine form. And what American heart did not go out to gritty Leicesterman Len Chalmers? A vicious hit had broken his leg toward the end of the first half, but professional soccer in those days did not permit substitutions. So, for the sake of his losing mates, Chalmers played on for the entire game. "Poor old Chalmers," Ken Wolstenholme kept saying, as he limped along. "Poor old Chalmers." Years later, strangers would come up to Jim in airports and ask, "Whatever happened to 'poor old Chalmers'?"

I'd hoped for a story that would carry across the Atlantic, and thanks to Ken and Jim, we got it.

June brought us to Le Mans, and the start of a relationship with Stir-ling Moss, then the most famous racing driver in the world, maybe the best driver ever, and British unflappability personified. Half a dozen times he'd been in crashes that should have killed him, and one that nearly did. Carted off to a hospital, both legs shattered, he was told he'd never walk again, certainly never drive; instead, day and night, he pushed his feet hard against the bottom of the bed, and two weeks later, he was back at the wheel.

I'd heard that Moss was everything a Grand Prix racer ought to be: cool, dashing, devil may care, lionized by men, adored by beautiful women. Five minutes in his presence made me a believer, and Stirling became *Wide World*'s expert commentator for the 24 Hours of Le Mans. The night before the race, we met for dinner to work out details. I hung on his every word, as I later found myself doing for all Grand Prix drivers on the eve of a race, men who were so exposed to danger, who took such fantastic risks, that it invariably occurred to me when we met that I might be talking to them for the last time.

Stirling himself, partnering with Graham Hill, was also competing at Le Mans, a circumstance that made him a wee bit pressed the next morning when Jim McKay sought his insights as he was about to climb into his machine. They did one take, then another, and another. Stirling was fine, not so the line feeding the picture to Paris for videotaping. It fouled up again at take four, and gendarmes on motorcycles, by this time, were moving in to clear the track. "*Un moment, monsieur,*" Chuck Howard pleaded, exhausting his French. Take five went swimmingly, until "God Save the Queen" began booming from the loudspeaker. When the English anthem played, it didn't pay to be standing near Stirling. He stopped talking in mid-sentence, and his whole body snapped to ramrod attention. As take six commenced, the "Marseillaise" was struck up, prompting the chief cop to whip out his pistol and point it at Chuck, who pretended not to get the message.

Stirling, meanwhile, kept talking; we got the segment; Chuck wasn't shot.

Moments later, the drivers did the famous run from one side of the track to leap into their cars on the other, a feat Stirling had practiced assiduously, twenty repetitions at least, in front of the cheering crowd—and just for the panache of it, because in a twenty-four-hour race it hardly mattered who got off to the early lead.

But even more special, to me, about Le Mans were the huge crowds and the festival ambience. Nobody slept. All night long, bands played and people danced and paraded in the surrounding streets, playing carnival-type games, eating carnival food, in an atmosphere that was maybe three-quarters the running of the bulls in Pamplona, Spain, and one-quarter Las Vegas. And the cars kept running, the drivers switching and their engines vroom-vrooming as they roared past in the darkness. They brought the dawn with them. Amazingly, a Catholic mass was conducted right next to the track shortly after the sun rose, it too punctuated by the vrooming of the passing engines.

And we caught it all. All in all, I concluded, it was a broadcast triumph.

The turning point in our acceptance as a show, though, was Moscow, the Soviet-American track meet.

Only someone forgot to tell the AAU to pave our way.

Amazingly, they had neglected to inform their Soviet counterpart that a U.S. television network would be arriving with tons of equipment and fifty production people. Jim and I and Tom Moore had already gone through the Cold War drill of landing in Moscow, where our Aeroflot plane was taxied to the far end of the runway, about as far as you could get from the terminal building, and a soldier with a submachine gun slung over his shoulder went up and down the aisle of the plane, demanding to see and then taking all our passports. We then shortly learned that the plane carrying our people and material was stuck in Amsterdam because the Russians were refusing to let it land on Russian soil without proper documentation.

Thank God for Roman Kislev!

Roman Kislev was our guide, our fixer, our key man in navigating the strange and sinister byways of Moscow. Not only was he a big shot in Russian athletic circles, but he was apparently as big a shot in politics. "Never mind," Roman said, apropos of our passports, "you'll get them back when you leave the country"—not the most reassuring news in the Cold War atmosphere. On the way into the city, aboard a wheezing Intourist bus, we passed a tank trap that had been converted into a memorial marking the farthest point of the Nazi advance. "It was the cold of the winter that stopped them, wasn't it?" one of our people asked him. "Yes, that," Roman replied, "but much more, it was the warmth of their reception."

Everywhere we went there were reminders of being far, far from home: the "authentic" Russian restaurant, with its factory-cafeteria decor (worker chic was in fashion that season), but where the "authentic" Russian orchestra struck up "It Happened in Sun Valley," a Glenn Miller tune by then a quarter of a century old! And then there were the crowds packed ten deep to gape at the wonder of our cheapest model Chevrolet and the paranoid disbelief of the Intourist driver when our announcer, Bill Flemming, showed him a photograph of his own Piper Cub. An individual own an airplane? The driver's face betrayed his conviction that any American who so claimed had to be an arrant liar or the devil incarnate, and he never spoke to us again!

This, mind you, was the grim height of the Cold War, the Khrushchev era when Americans in Moscow were few and far between, and when no one had ever done what we were about to do, that is, televise an athletic competition between our two countries.

Between setups at Lenin Stadium, 90,000 capacity, we looked for photo opportunities among the tourist sites, including visiting Lenin and Stalin's tomb. As visiting VIPs (Roman's doing, I imagine), we were obliged to wait only half an hour in line, unlike the rank-and-file comrades who'd been there since dawn, but it was a remarkable moment, witnessing the twin authors of so much murderous history stretched out as if for a nap. Stalin looked so incredibly alive! Not too long after, Khrushchev had Stalin's body removed from its preeminent position, and, on a subsequent trip to Moscow and another visit to the tomb, it was Jim McKay who got off the memorable line. As we shuffled by Lenin's now solitary catafalque, he whispered to me, "But we saw it when. It was like seeing *My Fair Lady* with the original cast."

Our own cast was primed for the competition, which we were capturing on state-of-the-art video recorders. Ampex, their manufacturer, was fearful the Soviets would steal the technology and had allowed us to bring the machines only after we'd promised to lock the recording heads in the U.S. embassy safe every night. I'd thought the precautions foolish. But when we set up our control room underneath the stands of the stadium and the crowd swarmed around our monitors, they were stupefied that the action they might just have seen could be witnessed again on a little screen. For the Russians, who had no video machines, it was as if we'd invented fire.

In the production truck, I cued McKay, a fanfare blared, and a moment later, parallel lines of American and Soviet athletes began appearing from the tunnel at the north end of the stadium. It was an extraordinary sight—side by side they came, representing the Cold War enemies—very unlike an American stadium where the teams emerge separately.

"Mike," I said into the microphone to cameraman Mike Friedman, who was on the field with a creepie-peepie, "lie down between them." Mike did, and the image Americans later saw in their homes was palms passing overhead, Russians and Americans side by side in friendship.

There were other special moments during the next three days, like Wilma Rudolph, the black girl from Tennessee who'd beaten polio to become an Olympic champion, sprinting to victory as Tom Moore, son of cracker-country Mississippi, shouted after her, "Run, sweetheart, run!" Or the chilly and rainy night when Valery Brumel, the Soviet high jumper, did his soon-to-be-famous number. Having failed on his first two attempts for a world record, he dramatically walked up to the bar, which was far above his head, stretched his arm as if in measurement, then retreated and launched himself into history, just barely clearing, to the tremendous roar of the crowd.

Television had shown other records and other wins, but never from the capital of our Cold War enemy, and never as we showed them. Inevitably, U.S. officials had a hassle with their Soviet counterparts as to who won. At this meet, and every one we attended, the same argument took place. Because the Russian women, in that era, were so far superior to ours, the Russians wanted the men's and women's results mixed together, which was also the custom in their country. This, of course, would make them the winners. The Americans wanted them kept separate, so that our superior men would win even as the women lost, and this was the custom in our country. Both sides were right, but they would argue bitterly as to which was fairer until, at the last minute, the Russians would agree to do it our way. Then, all during the meet, their scoreboard would keep the score totals separate. But the minute the final event was over and the results tabulated, repressed nationalism would win out. For there on the scoreboard would flash the one united score. Russia rules!

I realized I was experiencing the Cold War in microcosm, and that this kind of obdurate, uncompromising dispute, in which both sides in their own environment were right, characterized what went on in much more important spheres.

This historic meet, however, put us on the map, and more people began watching on Saturday afternoons. We were noticed again at the National Women's AAU Swimming & Diving Championships in Philadelphia three weeks later.

"What," I remember asking myself, "would I want to see in a swimming meet that I've never been able to see before?" Critical in any swimming competition were the turns, which took place largely underwater. And so we placed an underwater camera at the bottom of the pool and brought a new dimension to our viewers.

It was the same for the last show of the season, an exhibition game between the San Diego Chargers and the Buffalo Bills of the American Football League. I had asked the AFL to let us introduce both camera and radio mike inside the huddle, something I'd longed to do, and they were happy to comply. Thus, we had Mike Friedman dashing out with his camera to the Buffalo huddle between plays, then dashing back to the sidelines when the huddle broke; simultaneously, we hitched a mike ride, so to speak, on the Bills' quarterback, a well-spoken young man named Jack Kemp. Jack and the mike took a beating, but, apart from hearing plays being called *after* the Bills had broken the huddle and were lined up to run them (the consequence of a few seconds' tape delay to screen out obscenities), the scheme worked well. Even the hard-to-please Red Smith, famed sportswriter of the *New York Herald Tribune,* commended the effort in his column.

Leonard Goldenson put *Wide World* on the schedule the next season for a full fifty-two weeks, once NCAA football was over, and we never looked back. As the ever witty McKay once put it, "Do you realize, Roone, that we spend more time together than we do with our wives?" *ABC's Wide World of Sports* would travel to 53 countries and 46 states in the nearly four decades that followed, televising 4,967 events in more than 100 different sports—from cliff diving in Acapulco to wrist wrestling in Petaluma, California, to surfing in Waimea Bay, Hawaii, to ski flying in Falun, Sweden, to figure-eight demolition derbies in East Islip, Long Island, and the Little League World Series in Williamsport, Pennsylvania. There would be championships in tennis, volleyball, golf, boxing, billiards, and karate; weight lifting, tobogganing, skateboarding, hurling, and target diving; figure skating, speed skating, roller skating, and Australian surf lifesaving. In, on, aboard, or athwart bobsleds, bicycles, dragsters, stockcars, sprint cars, motorcycles, powerboats, sailboats, airplanes, and thoroughbreds, there would also be races. And just about any competition the mind could devise, including firemen running up ladders in Rochester, New York, and lumberjacks chopping through tree stumps in Hayward, Wisconsin.

Some thought events such as barrel jumping on ice skates should be called stunts, not sport. We treated them all with respect. Henny Lebell's breaking the supposedly unbreakable seventeen-barrel barrier at Grossingers in the Catskills in 1962 was as important to him, his weeping wife, and his sport as breaking the four-minute mile in 1954 had been to Roger Bannister and track and field. *Competing* was the yardstick I always used when selecting events for *Wide World*. And competition in all its aspects was the idea behind a credo I worked on during a flight home from London the first season.

> *Spanning the globe to bring you the constant variety of sport . . .*
> *The thrill of victory and the agony of defeat . . .*
> *The human drama of athletic competition . . .*
> *This is* ABC's Wide World of Sports.

The words expressed as best as I could the themes I mentioned earlier—that the whole was indeed greater than the parts, that competition was what we were after, whatever the events, that the exotic and the far-flung counted, and that the style and feel of our program was what most set us apart from the rank-and-file presentation of sports on television. These lines opened every *Wide World* from then on, and so did our selling of the title every time we went to a station break or a commercial: "We will return in a minute to *ABC's Wide World of Sports*."

There were many "thrills of victory," to be sure, on *Wide World*, but plenty of "agonies of defeat," too. None was more spectacular than the pinwheeling ski flier who illustrated the phrase every week. He looked like he'd just killed himself in this daredevil variation of ski jumping. But his only injury was a mild concussion. The skier's name was Vinko Bogataj, and when he was introduced at *Wide World* banquets, he was greeted invariably with the loudest applause, much louder even than the acclaim for Ali.

Wide World had its own victories and defeats. On the way to winning thirty-six Emmys (and the prestigious Peabody Award for Jim, the first sports announcer so honored), we were the first network sports show to go to Havana (for U.S.-Cuban volleyball in 1971); the first to North Korea (for the world table-tennis championships in Pyongyang in 1979); the first to televise live the British Open, the World Cup Soccer Final, and the Indianapolis and Daytona 500s. And when "Ping-Pong diplomacy" began between the United States and China in April 1971, it was *ABC's Wide World of Sports* that carried the match from Beijing.

But there was also the young woman we tried to smuggle out of Czechoslovakia in the back of our production van. She said she was assisting at the World Figure Skating Championships in Prague, said she yearned for freedom, but at the border, she turned out to be a Communist agent. Technology could be other than advertised as well. In April 1965, I arranged for *Early Bird,* the first commercial television satellite, to transmit the first satellite-delivered sports program from Europe: the annual Le Mans race. At the appointed moment, we began televising; *Early Bird* didn't. For the next hour, all viewers got was Jim McKay's and Phil Hill's voices over a slide that read "Temporary Technical Difficulty." The instant we signed off, *Early Bird* started to tweet. On another occasion, the tape of the World International Target Diving Championship was accidentally erased; on yet another, a rodeo wound up as part of *The Dick Van Dyke Show;* on still another, a CBS program wound up on us. And then there was the British Open, when Phil Rodgers missed a crucial putt on the eighteenth hole, which made New Zealander Bob Charles the winner. Or so we announced, a little surprised, perhaps, as we signed off, that the result brought only mild polite applause. We'd been using the BBC's scoring (from then on, we only used our own), but somewhere in the process there'd been a screwup and we had gotten the scores wrong. The missed putt had in fact brought about a tie and an eighteen-hole playoff the following day! As is so often the case in broadcasting, this one gaffe led, inexorably, as though by fate, to a series of others, ending with us trying frantically to mix and match lost tape with saved audio, resulting in noiseless drives off the tee and a putt making a whopping sound, like a wedge out of deep rough.

And then there was the time, early in *Wide World*'s run, when Jim McKay and I checked into Ricky's Studio Inn in Palo Alto, California, a few days before the next U.S.-USSR track meet, held at Stanford University. That establishment was so sprawling that guests were ferried to their rooms aboard golf carts. On the way over, our driver, an eager Stanford student, asked if we were with ABC. When we said yes, he exclaimed, "Golly, I'd do anything for a chance to work in television sports."

I remembered what had resulted for me years before from serving a hungry man and his family late one night at the Wayside Inn.

"Okay, come over to the production truck outside the stadium Friday morning. We'll find something for you to do. It'll give you a foot in the door."

"Friday?" he said. "Gee, I can't. I'm going water-skiing."

When he dropped us off, Jim said, "That kid will go through the rest of his life saying, 'I could never get a break.' "

There were literal breaks on *Wide World,* as when Evel Knievel fractured his back and pelvis trying to jump his motorcycle over the fountains at Caesar's Palace. And determination, as when Julie Moss, leading the Ironman Triathlon in Hawaii in 1982, collapsed, exhausted and delirious, with only yards to go. And as others ran by to claim her prize, she crawled, inch by agonizing inch, to the finish line. And skill, as when George Willig climbed rock faces for us after having illegally scaled the World Trade Center. And wonder, as when Pelé, the great Brazilian soccer star, stood in the middle of Giants Stadium in October 1977, on the day of his retirement, and said to the crowd, "Please say with me three times the word 'love.' " And as one, 70,000 New Yorkers did.

ABC's Wide World of Sports has transmitted countless such images in the four decades it's aired as a weekly program, but one has stayed with me more than any other.

This was in June 1963, barely half a year since the Cuban missile crisis, and we'd gone back to Moscow for another U.S.-Soviet track and field meet. It was a crazy time in Moscow. There was a film festival going on and we'd flown over in the same plane with Elizabeth Taylor. And the veteran U.S. statesman Averell Harriman had been there all week, negotiating the nuclear-test-ban treaty with Nikita Khrushchev on President Kennedy's behalf.

The final evening of our competition, Valery Brumel—who else?—was to try one more time to better his world record in the high jump. The air was cool and a light rain was falling, just as it had been two years before. In the dignitaries' box, Khrushchev was sitting alongside Harriman, who'd dealt with Soviet leaders since Stalin and World War II. Now, Lenin Stadium hushed as Brumel prepared for his third and final attempt. Again, his outstretched arm measured the height, and once more, he pounded down the approach and threw himself into the air. The bar trembled an instant, then he was over and clear, and a roar went up from 90,000 throats.

On the monitor in front of me, I was focused on a stocky Russian peasant, now leader of his country, and the slim American aristocrat-turned-diplomat. Their nations had come to the brink of annihilation, and it wasn't too much of an exaggeration to say that they'd had the fate of the world in their hands all that week.

But now, because of the simple feat of a man jumping over a bar, they were hugging each other close, and they were cheering.

That, for me, was *ABC's Wide World of Sports*.

Taking Command

I came to ABC warned to watch my back.

These were sharks, I was told, and they didn't play by gentlemen's rules. At General Sarnoff's NBC and Bill Paley's CBS, at least you knew where the minefields lay and who your boss would be Monday morning. At ABC, friends said, your pal today might slit your throat tomorrow and be gone the day after.

Maybe it was simply being out of the office so much on location, but I hadn't found this to be true. Ollie Treyz, the president, was clearly someone to be wary of. He was a super salesman, but one with a reputation in the industry for reneging on his promises, and if he told you the time, you were wise to look at your watch. *Variety* once ran a headline that went, "But, Ollie, You *Said*..." However, Tom Moore—who'd come into Entertainment (or "Programs," as it was originally called) by way of Sales, had gotten the responsibility for Sports because no one else at the network wanted it—was just as obviously an ally, partly because he was a huntin' and fishin', football-lovin' good ole boy; partly, I suspected, because he saw a successful Sports schedule as a path to bigger things. It certainly had been for Scherick, who'd sold his company to ABC and joined its executive ranks as head of Sales. That, I figured, gave me a friend—I *hoped* a friend—at court. I had less to do with Leonard Goldenson, but I did know him and he was far from invisible. My first and only encounter with General Sarnoff had come about because my wife was one of his secretaries, and we happened to bump into him at Toscanini's last concert. Sarnoff, I must add, was kind enough to give us a pair of extraordinary tickets on the spot, far better than the rafters' ones we'd arrived with, and so we experienced in grand style one of the great moments in twentieth-century cultural history. But with "Leonard" (as he insisted I call him), our first meeting took place when I was a scant six weeks on the job, at a Sales party at which the chairman and chief executive officer of ABC showed up wearing a sweater and jeans.

I liked this smart, unpretentious, lawyerly man, as nearly everyone at the network did. I also liked working at a place where someone still on the apple-cheeked side of thirty was entrusted with two valuable programs. I was a man of responsibilities now, with three daughters already on the team (Betsey, Susie, and Patricia, whom we called Tatty) and a son (Roone III), whom we called Boss, to come in 1964, but there was a looseness about ABC, an emphasis on youth and a willingness to risk, and I was living proof of both. If NBC was like a bank, all marble and glass and stiff collars, ABC resembled a delicatessen, so arms, elbows, and emotional you could almost smell the pastrami and potato salad in the halls.

Because of the constant travel for *Wide World* (twenty-three trips to thirteen countries on five continents in 1962), and the unbroken weekends and late nights spent show planning, I saw a lot less of my family than I'd have wished. But I was too caught up in the demands of ABC Sports—too obsessed, too committed—where the latest baby bird begging to be fed was the American Football League.

If ever a sports enterprise owed its existence to television, it was the AFL, which came into being in 1959 when Texas oilman Lamar Hunt, unable to land an NFL franchise, organized a group of fellow millionaires to form a competing league. It had a well-known commissioner in Medal of Honor winner and former South Dakota governor Joe Foss, innovative touches such as players' names written on the backs of their jerseys—but zero chance of taking to the field without a network contract. CBS and NBC passed, leaving ABC the AFL's last hope, a fact not lost on Tom Moore and Ed Scherick, who struck a five-year, fire-sale deal.

You could say we country cousins deserved each other. As hard as it may be to realize now, forty years ago, ABC was like a high school team playing with the pros when it came to the competing networks, and ABC Sports had few stars, either on the field or in the announcers' booths. And the first AFL games were a lopsided kaleidoscope of rarely completed hail marys, flung downfield in ramshackle stadiums before crowds so sparse they could easily have been seated in one of the Rose Bowl's end zones. But we knew we needed each other, and for ABC, the AFL was nothing if not accommodating. When a game featuring Hunt's Dallas Texans got under way while the network was in a commercial break, Jack Lubell, who was producing, raced onto the field, grabbed the ball away from an official, and stuck it into the chest of the referee. "You bastards!" he shouted. "*Never* again kick off until I say you can! Now go and do it again!"

In the announcers' booth, Jack Buck described the ruckus with characteristic aplomb: "Ladies and gentlemen, we're back live at the Cotton Bowl in Dallas and, unfortunately, an irate fan has run onto the field and is creating a disturbance."

The referee, needless to say, complied.

My own experience with the AFL's eagerness to please can be traced back to our getting permission to mike quarterback Jack Kemp for *Wide World*. But it wasn't until 1963 that I produced my first regular season game. We'd lost the NCAA by then, and the AFL was great for us. Not only was it the only football we had, but we were free to experiment with it, which would give us a leg up on our competitors in the years ahead. I'd started my own experimenting in the preseason—partly out of necessity. The game I'm thinking of pitted Hunt's Dallas Texans against Barron Hilton's Los Angeles Chargers (so dubbed because Hilton Hotels owned the Carte Blanche credit card); the venue, the Los Angeles Coliseum; the crowd . . . well, what crowd? As kickoff approached, fewer than 10,000 fans were scattered in the vast and otherwise unoccupied tiers of the stadium. I didn't dare show that picture; ABC was having a tough enough time selling ads. My solution: provide the *appearance* of a reasonably full house by bunching everyone near the fifty-yard line and censoring any shot that tracked the long flight of the ball, as on a kickoff or punt, because to do so would reveal endless rows of empty seats. Instead, we focused cameras tight on the kicker, then cut to the receiver as he caught the ball and ran up the field. Alternatively, when circumstances called for it, we panned along the ground.

Thereafter, such legerdemain, which we also used when *Wide World* covered particularly rinky-dink events, became known in the trade as "AFL coverage." I can recall at least one instance, many years later, when it was used in a reverse sense. When Pope John Paul II first visited his native Poland, to the surprise and immense chagrin of the Polish Communist party crowds in the millions gathered to greet him. But you'd never have guessed it from the feeds we got from Polish TV, which focused tight on the pontiff's smiling face and successfully censored out the joyful masses.

Pete Rozelle recognized it right off the bat. "That's AFL coverage!" he quipped.

Televising the AFL in those early days offered us a veritable production laboratory on the field and the freedom to experiment. We spotted our cameras and mikes all over the stadium and on the sidelines, giving fans at home immeasurably better and more varied looks at the action than they ever got watching the NFL on CBS. As mentioned, we wired a quarterback for *Wide World,* only to think better of it when a lineman in the huddle could be heard, loud and clear, bellowing, "Shee-it!," about a chop block the refs had failed to call. We also set out to make our stars familiar to our viewers. When, say, wide receiver Don Maynard of the New York Titans caught a pass, his name, position, and stats would appear immediately on the screen, followed, later on, by replays of other catches he'd made, either earlier in the game or the previous week—all of which became standard practice in football coverage.

For several years, the AFL had to struggle with second bests, making its own stars out of players only the most devout fans had heard of. All of this would change in time, thanks in good part to a gimpy-legged quarterback from the University of Alabama, soon to be known to the world as Broadway Joe. But as for the innovative and perfectionist young producer from ABC who was growing in confidence just as the league was, well, Mrs. Arledge's son was about to get his first harsh lesson in the network jungle.

In 1963, Harry Wismer, cofounder of the AFL and owner of its New York entry, the Titans, got tired of losing money and offered to sell the team . . . to ABC! There was nothing wonderful about Wismer, an ex-broadcaster and flamboyant boozer. Nor was there anything glorious about the Titans, who played their usually losing home games in the nearly deserted precincts of the Polo Grounds. But there was no beating the price: $1 million for a pro football franchise in the biggest media market in the country.

Leonard Goldenson wanted to do the deal. But Ev Erlick, ABC's chief counsel and a master at devising reasons to say no, turned thumbs-down. The purchase, he feared, would violate antitrust statutes. When, not long after, CBS purchased the New York Yankees, there was nary a peep from the feds, but Leonard, before that, listened to Ev, and ownership of the Titans passed instead to a group fronted by Sonny Werblin, an extremely shrewd veteran agent from MCA and a very good friend, as it happened, of both Robert Sarnoff and Robert Kintner, president of NBC and a former president of ABC. (Years later, it's worth noting, in January 2000, the Jets were sold by the estate of Leon Hess to Robert Wood Johnson IV for $635 million!)

Sonny began talking to Bob Kintner, and Bob—who'd been fired by ABC and thus had a score to settle—wound up offering $35 million for five years of AFL games, commencing in 1965. ABC's contract with the league contained a right-to-match clause, but NBC's number was more than five times what we had paid in the original deal and we, as usual, were hard up for cash. Instead of matching, we actually sold our final AFL season to NBC, and that, dear reader, left us suddenly with no football whatsoever.

The rest?

Well, Sonny Werblin changed the name of the Titans to the Jets, and, in the spring of 1965, signed the quarterback from Alabama, Joe Namath, to an unprecedented $400,000 contract. Numerous other high-profile signings followed, and the level of AFL play improved dramatically, as did the ratings. In June 1966, the NFL and its suddenly thriving rival merged, ending their own version of the Cold War. This led to championship games between the two realigned conferences that would evolve into the single-most-watched sporting event in the United States, the Super Bowl. Three Super Bowls in, Broadway Joe delivered on his "guarantee" that his upstart Jets would beat the Baltimore Colts.

And so it came to pass.

And I got to watch it all—on NBC and CBS.

Some events define who you are professionally; the ten Olympics I produced did just that for me.

I'd gotten hooked in 1960, watching the Winter Games in Squaw Valley—the first time the Olympics were televised. Thank the good Lord I was still a few months away from being hired by Ed Scherick, because ABC, which had bought the rights from the Squaw Valley organizers for all of $50,000, had subsequently backed out. In the aftermath of that embarrassment, CBS had picked up the Games, not out of any love for the

Olympics but as a favor from Bill Paley to Walt Disney. You had to be alert, though, to catch the network's broadcasts, which ran all of fifteen minutes a night. The Games themselves—mounted on a budget so tight there hadn't been the money to build a bobsled run—were threadbare and haphazard, but I got caught up in them. There was magic in seeing the divided world come together in sport. And edge-of-the-seat competition to witness too, like the U.S. hockey team scoring six final-period goals against Czechoslovakia to win its first-ever gold medal. And something else that I spotted: the dimensions of the rink, the spotlight on single performers, the limited time spans, and the suspense of waiting for the judges' decisions— all these plus Carol Heiss—made figure skating a made-for-television event.

This was programming I wanted to be part of.

Badly.

Given the fiasco of that 1960 contract, it seemed highly unlikely I'd get the chance as long as I worked at ABC. But the itch didn't go away, and by 1962, two years before the start of the Winter Games in Innsbruck, Austria, Chet Simmons and I convinced Tom Moore that the future of ABC Sports—indeed, of the network itself—rested on a successful Olympic bid. Tom, in turn, convinced Leonard, and a cable was dispatched to the famously curmudgeonly chairman of the International Olympic Committee, Avery Brundage. He wired back that we should get in touch with "Wolfgang." It took some doing, but I finally determined that Wolfgang was Dr. Friedl Wolfgang, a university professor who doubled as head of the Innsbruck organizing committee. With no further ado, Chet and I boarded a flight for Munich, the closest international airport to Innsbruck.

The trip was to give us a chance to look around and get a feel for Herr Professor's financial parameters. Never having been to Austria, I was as excited as could be, but Chet barely spoke on the flight.

"I gotta tell you," he said as we arrived on foreign soil, "deep in my Jewish bones, I feel one hell of a chill."

Nothing I could do or say could allay his anxiety, nor did our driver, one Kurt Fuchs, who turned out to be a Russian-front veteran of the Wehrmacht. Kurt, who spoke English with a strong German accent and had somehow managed to come by passports from three different countries, was a jovial type who delighted in pointing out the passing Bavarian sights, including, much to Chet's discomfort, the road that led to Berchtesgaden.

It was well past midnight when we reached our shared Innsbruck hotel suite. Chet immediately tumbled into bed, but I, jet-lagged and restless, got up in the middle of the night and decided to shower and shave. In my addled state, I inadvertently dropped my razor, and it, with unerring accuracy, slashed into my foot, penetrating an artery and sending a geyser of blood across the bathroom. I bound the wound with a towel, and toddled back to my bed, too beat to notice the trail of bloody footprints I left as I went.

Someone else did, though.

It was Chet.

"Roone! Roone!" he shouted, shaking me.

"What the hell is it?" I croaked back groggily, trying to wake up and go back to sleep at the same time.

"Oh, my God!" The lights were on. His face was as white as a ghost's. "Thank God, you're alive! For a minute I thought they'd *murdered* you!"

I stared up at him in bewilderment—until I realized who the "they" were.

Patched up, I toured the city with Chet the next day, discovering its enchanting Old Town, filled with half-timbered houses and shops, some dating to medieval times and the reign of the first Hapsburg emperors. Walking the narrow, twisting streets, you could almost hear the tinkle of sleigh bells and the laughter of parka-clad couples, as arm in arm they ducked into *bier stubes* for a warming tot. This was the Olympic image we'd be sending home.

It also wasn't hard to figure out the show opener: the Alps, of course. I'd seen mountains from Steamboat Springs to Garmisch-Partenkirchen, but none like these. Towering, snow-capped peaks literally encircled the city, humbling everything in their shadow—including a pair of American TV guys.

"God," Chet kept saying. "God Almighty."

"And what sort of music do you think the good Lord would like to hear?" I asked, still thinking of how we would open.

Chet laughed, but the question would echo in my mind. In the course of things, ABC commissioned a series of thirteen pre-Olympics programs, complete with a fancy intro that was supposed to become a kind of logo or trademark to be used to introduce our telecasts, too. We had nothing to do with them, but when I finally got around to looking, my feelings about the intro music grew in a crescendo from mere distaste to outright loathing. Well, I had plenty of other things to occupy my mind, but at the eleventh hour—I'm literally talking about a day or two before we left for the games—the loathing spilled over.

I called Jack Kelly into our office—he was one of our sound engineers—and I laid it on him.

"I really don't like the music," I said. "I can't stand it. We've gotta do better. You've gotta find me something." Then, seeing his reaction—he looked utterly incredulous—I began to expand on this. "Come on, find me music that says the Alps. I want it to say Alps. I want it to say majestic mountains, major, major event. It should be a hymn, almost. Divine. The whole world coming together in sports." And I was on my feet, gesturing to match, my arms in circles above my head.

And off he went, doubtless muttering about the craziness of bosses in general, and Arledge in particular.

Picking music—theme music I should say—is a little like finding a title for a show. Sometimes, if you're very lucky, the title's right there, jumping into your mind almost before you start thinking. But more often it's sheer torture, involving endless meetings and lists of possibilities, each worse than the one before, and suggestions from everyone you can think of, including your most distant relatives, and desperate climbing-the-walls frustration.

Only this, as I say, was the eleventh hour.

I can still see Jack Kelly coming back into my office, a stack of LPs under his arm.

You're not going to believe this, but it's absolutely true. The very first LP Jack played raised gooseflesh on the nape of my neck. Whatever thoughts he harbored about his boss's sanity were surely confirmed when I told him to take the other candidates away. Didn't I want to hear them? No, there was no need. This was what I wanted—everything I wanted. It was a wonderful fanfare of trumpets, by a composer named Felix Slatkin, which he'd titled "Bugler's Dream." I want you to close your eyes now and imagine the linked rings of the Olympics symbol. You can hear it, can't you? It's now universally referred to as "the Olympic Hymn" because its been the opening theme for every Olympic telecast produced by ABC to this day, and when NBC took on some of the games, they used it, too.

Back to Professor Wolfgang.

He greeted us most cordially, and he was delighted to hear of our interest in obtaining U.S. television rights. (Though we didn't know it at the time, CBS and NBC had none.) However, as he reminded us, all the financial dealings would have to be with an advertising agency that had been deputized to negotiate television contracts. This we already knew, but there were any number of other issues that had to be negotiated in Austria. Language loomed as a problem. Wolfgang's English seemed a little wobbly, and our German was nonexistent. Chet looked at me and I looked at Chet: "Kurt," we said at the same time. Pledging to each other we'd never tell Leonard, we brought Kurt Fuchs in to do battle for ABC. It was as if the Austrians were negotiating for the rights to the World Series, using the cabdriver who'd brought them in from JFK. But it worked, sufficiently, in any event, for us to return to New York ready to go forward.

The board in those days had to approve any expenditure over $100,000, and it wasn't happy at all about paying $500,000 for the rights, a tenfold multiple of the original price for Squaw Valley. And it was made unhappier still by the Austrians' insistence through their ad agency that the network, precisely because of Squaw Valley, post a bank guarantee. But Tom, Chet, and I persevered, and amid squawks from Leonard's finance man, Si Siegal, who opposed sending a pfennig to Hitler's birthplace, the board went along with us.

I made several more trips to Austria in the months that followed, the last with senior engineering staff for a detailed survey of our needs. A lot of it was technical stuff—electrical power, the compatibility problems in using American equipment, the placements we needed for our cable runs, lumens and luxes for the ice-skating arena, and so on—and we needed special permission for everything, from camera positions to the interview stands to the interviews themselves. We'd arranged to meet for a working dinner, and Dr. Wolfgang, who'd brushed aside my suggestion that we bring along a translator, was cordial and agreeable to everything we brought up. "*Ja,*" he said, nodding his head to each and every request or stipulation or specification, even the most arcane, and making notes to himself, and "*ja*" and "*ja*" and "*ja,*" item after item, and I remember thinking that if only it were always this easy. Still, my list was long, and it was after eleven at night when I finally got to the end of it.

And then came the punch line.

Professor Wolfgang pushed back his chair and stood, smiling his most cordial smile.

"I see by my watch is late," he said. "So I must say *hello*."

Our good host, it turned out, hadn't understood half of what we'd said all day!

Eleven and a half months later, the XIX Winter Games got under way. So did the screwups, courtesy first off of an Austrian army truck that rolled over and severed the cable leading to Jim McKay's ABC monitor just as the Parade of Nations was beginning. We in the control room didn't even realize at first what had happened. Jim was describing stuff he saw on the monitor, but the images came from Austrian television's feed to Eurovision. Often we used those same images, but sometimes we cut away, or digressed, or focused in on a detail of our own choosing—an athlete, a flag, God knows what. But finally I realized that Jim was describing stuff we weren't showing. It was all out of sync. The Eurovision image, for example, might be showing Germany entering the stadium while ours was focused on the Canadian flag bearer! To appreciate the horror of what had happened, picture Jim sitting with headphones over his ears, describing the passage of forty-five national contingents when he only knew what was being shown on the screen through my whispered voice!

But he pulled it off—a truly extraordinary tour de force.

That was Jim McKay. He had the ability, as rare as it was little appreciated, to focus totally on the task before him when things all around him were going to pieces. I know few sportscasters who could have conquered their own panic in such circumstances, but I'm sure Jim didn't allow himself even a moment of panic. Not only did he wing it, he winged it with complete sangfroid.

Another huge problem at Innsbruck was getting our programs back to the U.S. Telstar, the sole television satellite at the time, was not only hideously expensive but passed overhead a mere twenty minutes at a time and on an orbiting schedule that had no synchronicity with our key events. Instead, we had to rely on a jet-age version of the Pony Express. Every night at three A.M., we'd load the previous day's videotapes into a station wagon for a slippery trip over the mountains to Munich. There, the tapes would be put aboard a plane to Frankfurt, where they'd be transferred to a flight that stopped in London. From England, there was a direct satellite feed to Andover, Maine, and on to New York and the network. Fulfilling my prayers, said nightly to St. Andrew, patron saint of Scotland, they always made it.

It didn't matter that the United States won only one gold medal to the Soviets' eleven, or that ABC ran the programs in the worst possible time slots: The more they aired, the bigger the audience grew. It turned out that viewers were hungry for Olympic excellence, and we fed that hunger with stories like that of Terry McDermott, a small-town Michigan barber who came from nowhere to triumph in the 500-meter speed-skating event, wearing borrowed skates on a slushy track. A tragic story from the recent past—the death in a plane crash, two years before, of the entire U.S. figure-skating team—became the springboard for the emergence of fourteen-year-old Scotty Allen from Smoke Rise, New Jersey. And who could resist the image of the fifteen-year-old daughter of a newspaper pressman pirouetting across the ice in a costume sewn by her mother? I couldn't, and I didn't care that Peggy Fleming finished sixth.

Carol Heiss, our women's figure-skating commentator and gold medalist at Squaw Valley, introduced us, and I became Peggy's unofficial chauffeur. She insisted on calling me "sir." I didn't care about that either; I knew I was driving a future champion. I later discreetly helped her by arranging for *Wide World* to pay a larger than normal fee to a Seattle ice club so that they would help finance coaching lessons Peggy could other-wise not afford. She never knew that and neither did the International Olympic Committee. Whether it was on the complete up-and-up, I made a point not to check. All I know is that, in 1968, flashing sensationally and stunningly across the ice in her mint-green costume, Peggy Fleming won gold at Grenoble.

As Innsbruck wound down, I took to going to the top of the ninety-meter ski jump whenever I had the chance. I was in an exalted state. The view of the city staggered me from that vantage point, and I realized up there to what extent I'd been swept away by the events. Even though my view of them had been from a cold and dusty control room in the base-ment of the ice arena, an adrenaline rush had kept me going on three hours of sleep a night for two full weeks. I felt like a kid in a candy store. I wanted it all—every sight, sound, experience, and taste. Tell me about luge! Explain the triple axel! Who thought up the biathlon?

Could we do this better next time?

Yes, you're damn right we could. I was already planning it. More personalizing of competitors. More sense of place. More innovative shots. More communicating of what I felt watching moments like the one when Scotty Allen beat figure skaters twice his age. I hummed from my exalted summit, considering the possibilities, the same melody I'd been humming for days: Rachmaninov's *Rhapsody on a Theme of Paganini.* I couldn't get the music out of my head; it was what Ludmila Beloussova and Oleg Protopopov had skated to, winning gold in the pairs even as they brought ballet to the ice.

Homecoming in New York lasted only a few weeks. Then I was on a plane for Africa to produce an installment of a new Sunday program to be called *The American Sportsman,* the impetus for which came from an Argentine troutfishing competition I'd staged for *Wide World.* As to the latter, Curt Gowdy, angler nonpareil, had been segment host and one of the contestants, and I'd appointed myself producer because I like fishing and Curt's company. I'd also been curious about Argentina, although, as it turned out, everything that could go wrong on that particular expedition did. It took innumerable airplane flights and hours of traversing unpaved ruts to get to our destination: the waters of Lago General Paz, near the Chilean border. At 11,000 feet in elevation, the lake was freezing; Curt came down with the trots ("Avenida de Gowdy," we christened his papered route to the woods); a park ranger threatened us with arrest near the Chilean border; trout was the only menu item for breakfast, lunch, and dinner; our boats nearly capsized in a windstorm; and on the way back to civilization many overdue days later, the steering wheel came off while our Jeep was doing fifty, sending us careening down a forty-foot embankment. But we had a great time and we got a fabulous show out of it.

But now, on the heels of Innsbruck, I was off to Kenya for big-game hunting. Tom Moore came along too, then and on subsequent shows, for the simple reason that he liked hunting, too. Our celebrity guest that particular time was the actor Robert Stack, but our most regular guests in the future would be none other than Bing Crosby and his irrepressible friend Phil Harris.

Bing was an ABC fixture, with his annual pro-am golf tournament at Pebble Beach and guest-hosting the variety show *Hollywood Palace.* Phil's ticket was being Bing's friend and never being at a loss for a joke. Both were good shots and even better sports.

I well remember an *American Sportsman* that went trekking into the bush with Bing and Phil, Teddy Roosevelt style—and our crew, and our native bearers. We were also accompanied by a prototypical white hunter, whose intimacy with our quarry was attested to by the claw marks on his back. "It's usually not the bite that kills you," he said. "It's the gangrene. Beasts have filthy paws."

I filed the information away, trusting there'd be no use for it.

We pitched our camp this one time at what was deemed a promising spot. Bing, who was a quirky and sometimes superstitious gent, had particular ideas about sleeping arrangements, be it in hotels, where he always wanted to be separate from everyone else, or in the wild. He promptly ordered his tent set up well away from the one I was sharing with Phil, and after dinner, that was where he repaired. Proximity to other humans, however, lends a certain comfort in the safari night when the wildlife takes over the neighborhood—most audibly. And it turned out to be the same for Bing. He showed up at dawn, ash-pale, not having slept a wink, with the request that his tent be moved closer. Much closer.

As for me, I didn't mind the ominous nocturnal noises or the discovery made that morning in one of the supply tents of a very cross spitting cobra. I was drinking in Africa, and getting more intoxicated by the hour. My own favorite spot was a rocky hill some distance from camp. When the day's shooting was done, I'd climb up, find a boulder to sit on (just what I *shouldn't* have been doing, our hunter guide later informed me, for poisonous snakes enjoy shading themselves beneath the rocks), light up a pipe, and watch the sun set over the savannah, not thinking of anything except how blessed I was. My great frustration, though, was that I'd been able to do precious little hunting myself. After all, I was being paid to produce a television show, and that was a full-time job, whether I did it sitting in a control room in Innsbruck or a Land Rover in the wilds of Masai country.

The only time to change this was in the downtime from making the show. That meant going out at night, when you could track the animals by sound, if not sight, and as foolhardy as it now sounds (and undoubtedly was), I was determined to give it a try. So it was that, in the middle of one night, I took off from camp with a Winchester in the crook of my arm and a young man in his late teens as my guide, who, even though he'd been assigned to go with me, was as inexperienced as I was. We tracked for what seemed like an eternity, following sounds, stopping from time to time to listen, then advancing slowly forward. Then shortly before the dawn came, when the light was still dim and the African continent was just on the verge of taking on color, I saw a lioness bound from the cover of thick brush. She was maybe a hundred yards in front of us. Seconds later, when her big-maned mate, or would-be mate, did the same, I was ready for him. I steadied, aimed through the scope, and fired, and I saw the creature stagger before it leaped away into the concealment of tall and heavy grass.

Okay. Deep breaths now.

One of the first things every hunter learns—and I had indeed been taught it in childhood—is the danger of wounded animals. If you encounter a predator in the wild, the chances are it's going to give you a wide berth without your even knowing it's there. But a wounded predator, unable to escape, is instinctively going to strike and try to kill any creature that comes close. Including a man with a gun. In addition, the cumbersome scope on my rifle would have made it impossible to aim at close quarters. From this point of view, the most sensible thing to have done would probably have been to give the young man a few dollars to keep his mouth shut and head back to camp.

But there is another code among hunters, and even if I'd learned it from reading Robert Ruark and Ernest Hemingway, I suspect it goes back atavistically, way, way back, into the human collective memory. You don't leave another creature to die. You just don't. There's a practical aspect to this, sure: Other creatures, even members of your own human tribe, could be killed by your inaction. But there's something else, too. A kind of male code of conduct, if you will. A testing. I hesitate to use the word, but I'd call it moral.

I got down on my haunches and pulled out my pipe.

"We wait," I told the young man. This was another bit of hunter's law. A wounded animal, forced to lie low, will stiffen with the passage of time and be less able to spring.

And so we waited. Half an hour dragged by. The sun rose fully, and the world became gloriously bright and alive. Finally I got up, and summoning whatever bravado still lingered inside me, I led us forward to where I'd seen the lion disappear. Slowly, however. Stopping, looking, listening. Step by step.

Until we came upon him, lying on his side, a single, neat hole where his shoulder met his neck.

God Almighty.

It wasn't long afterward, back in New York, when Tom Moore summoned me to his office. It was to give me a raise—always good and particularly welcome to someone with a growing family—and also to announce a reshuffling of the organizational cards. Tom was keeping the sports portfolio for himself—"Do you think I'd let you go to Africa without me?"— but that was really pro forma stuff.

"We're going to have a real sports division," he said, "and a real vice president is going to run it."

"Great," I said. "When does Chet take over?"

Tom smiled. "He's not going to," he said. "You are."

I stared at him, bewildered. Not only was Chet Simmons already a VP, but he was older, had been at ABC longer, and, God knows, had a lot more management experience than I did.

"*Me?*" I heard myself sputter.

"Yes, Roone," Tom Moore said, "*you.*"

Sports Prez

Is *this* how you intend to run Sports?" Tom Moore exploded at me over the phone. "Losing the most important piece of manpower you have?" I tried to say something but he wouldn't let me. "How the hell could you have let this happen, Roone? I'm holding you responsible!"

Before I could answer, the phone banged in my ear.

Chet Simmons had just announced his departure, and in the time-honored tradition of bosses, Tom was furious. If anyone was to blame, though (as, once he cooled down, he had the good sense to realize), it was Tom himself. Chet had worked hard in the trenches for years as Ed Scherick's number two, and while he was no producer, the only other thing he lacked in terms of being named vice president, Sports, was being well known by Tom Moore. His subsequent career would attest to his considerable managerial talents, for he was named president of NBC Sports in 1973, then commissioner of the United States Football League, and, later still, head of ESPN.

So there I was, alone at the top. This meant, among other things, that I was going to have to cut back on producing, which was the fun part of the job for me, in order to find events for us to produce. The good news was that I was starting from nothing, and so had little to lose. But that was the bad news, too. Early on, I drew up a list of fourteen must-have, marquee events—things like NFL football, the four great tournaments of golf's Grand Slam, horse racing's Triple Crown. Not a single one was owned by ABC. All were currently locked up by our competitors, and most had been for years, in some cases, decades. Looked at this way, we were like the hungry little kids in the old movies, staring through the windows of restaurants at the nabobs stuffing themselves. We weren't even in the game. Nor was money alone the answer, even though far more than ABC was used to spending would be required. Sports broadcasting in those days—and to a fair extent it's still true—was like an insider's club. You couldn't just buy your way in, you had to have connections, ambassadors, people who knew the right people who controlled what you wanted. Today this is called networking, but I'm not talking about networking with just anybody. We needed stars—important media people who had instant access to other important media people—and when I took over ABC Sports, we had none.

This kind of thinking led me to Chris Schenkel, whom I will come to in a minute, but it also made me reach out for the likes of Jim McKay. Jim had begun his career as a journalist on the *Baltimore Sun,* and to me, he had a poet's eye and an essayist's skill with language. He became a master, if ever there was one, at finding and dramatizing the miniature story in the huge panorama of an event, a skill, in future years, that would make him so valuable when we began introducing "Up Close and Personals" in our Olympics coverage.

The one problem with Jim—if it was a problem (looking back, I have my doubts)—was that he didn't come across to the public as a star in his own right. When you ran down lists of the best sports announcers on television, he'd often get left out, even though the moment you reminded people of him, they'd invariably say, "Oh sure, Jim McKay. He's tops!" I used to work him over about it, telling him he had to get around more, spend more time, for example, in the watering holes of the New York sports beat, and I remember Jim one time—this was after we'd done the Innsbruck Olympics—telling me about how he'd had occasion to revisit Innsbruck and how the bartender at the Hotel Tyrol, the minute he walked in, had said, "Ah, Mr. McKay, *guten abend,* would you like the usual?"

"But that's Austria," I argued with him that time. "I want them to recognize you in New York City, too!"

"Well, they do, Roone," he countered. "I think you're making a big deal out of nothing."

"Come with me," I said, and, grabbing my coat, led him from our offices, which were on Fifth Avenue at the time, to the bar at Toots Shor's.

Sure enough, the bartender, when we walked in, said, "Hi, Mr.

Arledge, what'll it be?" After which, he turned from me to Jim, whom he obviously didn't recognize from Adam, and he said, "And you, sir?"

And I turned to Jim, saying, "I rest my case."

Jim never filled that ambassador's role I mentioned, but he became a mainstay of ABC Sports, one of our great and truly classy professionals, and I will touch on some of his finer moments later.

And then there was Chris. In fact, had it not been for his association with Marlboros (sponsors of the Giants) and the fact that L&Ms had bailed us out by buying half of *Wide World* when no one else wanted it, I'd certainly have used Chris Schenkel ahead of Jim McKay on *Wide World of Sports*. At the time I'm talking about—the early sixties—Chris was to sports broadcasting what Walter Cronkite was to television news: the platinum standard. No one in the field had more clout or carried more weight. He was the voice of the New York Giants, the most important franchise in what was, from television's point of view, the most important sport. He did baseball too, and horse racing, auto racing, golf. He knew everyone. Pete Rozelle, commissioner of the National Football League, was an old, dear friend; so was Cliff Roberts, the head of Augusta National; and Tony Hulman, owner of the Indianapolis Speedway, and Wathen Knebelkamp of Churchill Downs. Chris Schenkel shook hands with milkmen in his native Indiana as well as headwaiters at Toots Shor's and "21." He was universally admired and well liked, a very classy guy. Get Chris Schenkel on your team and you'd have an instant ambassador.

Easily said.

I found out that CBS was paying Schenkel $175,000 per—great money in the normal world of 1964, but bargain basement for all he brought to the network. You didn't, however, land a Chris Schenkel with dollars alone any more than you landed one of those sacred franchises on my secret list. First you had to build a relationship, and that's precisely what I set out to do. So began a long romance—my first, really, in a career that became known for the courtship of media stars, a practice that reached its peak years later when I was able to lure Diane Sawyer away from CBS. Lunches, dinners, schmoozing phone calls, little thought-this-might-interest-you notes of appreciation. A full-court press, as they say in basketball, but one that grew from the opening whistle on. Chris Schenkel undoubtedly knew what I was up to, and why, but even stars are flattered by the attention of upstarts, and all too often, their employers start to take them for granted in the day-to-day whirl.

Of course there was the money question, too. For $200,000, I calculated, I might eventually be able to lure Chris into negotiations, then settle for something like $225,000—still cheap for all he could do for us. If I let that happen, though, CBS was bound to find out. Then they'd make a counteroffer, touching off a bidding war that, despite all my charms and blandishments, ABC was almost certain to lose. When the time came to pry Chris loose, I figured, I would have to make the proverbial offer-he-couldn't-refuse.

That time came. By then, Chris knew full well how much ABC thought of him, how in our firmament he could become an even bigger star than he was at CBS, and in that sense, the money had become an almost secondary consideration.

Almost.

"We love you, Chris," I told him, "and we need you. Please know that. But it's because we do that I'm making you an offer that will assure your family's financial security."

I named the figure: $250,000.

He gulped. I waited, holding my breath.

"What's my first assignment, Roone?" he said smoothly.

"Bold," the trades called Schenkel's hiring (with a little stirring of the PR pot). "Look out, NBC and CBS."

But they should have said, "Look out, Arledge."

Because even as Chris Schenkel walked in one door, the Orange Bowl, unbeknownst to yours truly, was walking out the other.

This is what happened.

The Orange Bowl—at the time one of the four major bowls, all of which were played on New Year's Day—was ABC's last significant piece of the football pie. It had been Tom Moore's deal, and Tom, who'd been riding high at the company, had simply neglected to obtain board approval, which was required for any commitment over $100,000. Si Siegel took great umbrage at this. Si was our resident cost-control guru and Leonard's number two and close friend, and Si also controlled the agenda for the board meetings. When the Orange Bowl renewal came up, he decided it was time to teach Tom a lesson. The board flatly turned it down. Even though the decision was later papered over as a "fiscally prudent response to low ratings," it was clearly a slap at Tom and—no two ways about it—a sign of trouble looming on the horizon.

Meanwhile, totally unaware of what had just transpired, ABC's freckle-faced red-headed vice president, Sports, Roone Arledge, was lunching at the New York Athletic Club with a visiting, likewise ignorant delegation from . . . you guessed it, the Orange Bowl! They, on their side, were waiting for ABC's offer, which they assumed I was bringing to them, while I, supposing that Tom had already taken care of it, was laying one of my pet ideas on them with all my powers of persuasion. The Orange Bowl, in the New Year's Day tradition, always aired head-to-head with the Cotton Bowl, and, as a result, usually came out second best in the ratings. Well, I had come up with a surefire way to beat that. What if we simply moved the game to New Year's night?

They seemed to find the idea interesting, but somehow, in the course of the lunch, I realized I was losing them. The atmosphere had turned from conviviality to awkwardness, and I had no idea why. It was only when I got back to the office that I found out the dreadful news.

And guess what?

After they left me that day, the Orange Bowl delegation took their business down the street, as it were, to NBC. And when the smoke had cleared and the Orange Bowl rights, to my huge but helpless mortification, went to NBC, guess what the network did? Well, they moved the game to the nighttime—what else?—transforming it thereby into a cash spigot and, until very recently, the most highly rated event of the New Year's bowl program.

And then there was Porky Pig.

It is a story hardly worth telling, and embarrassing to boot, but it illustrates what we sometimes ran into toiling for a struggling network that still employed as many small-minded functionaries as our bigger competitors. In 1965, we figured out a way to use Telstar—the broadcasting satellite—to bring in three events, live, to American audiences. The three, I thought, represented a coup for ABC and, further, constituted a landmark in broadcasting history. The first was a full hour of the celebrated road race, the 24 Hours of Le Mans. The second was the Irish Sweepstakes. And the third, one Saturday in July, was the U.S.-Soviet track meet to be held in Kiev and which, at the height of the Cold War, would be the first sporting event ever transmitted live from the Soviet Union to the United States.

The hitch? That's right, the hitch was the pig. Because of the time difference, the track meet would have to preempt our regular Saturday-morning programming. And our regular Saturday-morning programming, as I was informed by an ABC cost-control guy, included the animated adventures of Porky Pig, which brought in $50,000 in ad revenue.

I won't embarrass the cost-control guy now by giving his name. At first, I couldn't believe him. Was he really measuring the umpteenth rerun of a Loony Tunes cartoon and $50,000 in revenue against an historic telecast? Yes, it turned out that he was. Didn't I realize that Saturday-morning programming was serious business at ABC? He dug in his heels. Days of disputation and acrimony followed, but the cost-control guy refused to give in and, in the end, it took the intervention of—yes—our CEO, Mr. Goldenson, to settle the issue. Thank God, Leonard decided in favor of history!

But it was never easy inside the company, in those early days. One of my first targets was golf, which had the untouchable Masters; the Professional Golf Association championship, or PGA; and the two opens, the United States and the British. If you wanted to be a player in televised sports, you had to have golf, and we, needless to say, weren't players. But when I did break through in 1965, securing the rights to the PGA by topping CBS's bid by a slim $10,000 and thereby capturing the plum from the network that had aired the event since time immemorial, there was hand-wringing over how much I'd spent, and the hand wringer in chief, as he'd been before, was Si Siegel. Tennis, at the time, was no big deal on television, granted, but Open tennis was clearly about to happen. Nonetheless, in a moment of corporate austerity, and all because of a $5,000 loss on the event the previous year, we tossed aside what would become a huge future earner for our competitors, known forevermore as the U.S. (Tennis) Open.

Still, as our revenues steadily increased, so did our victories outnumber our defeats. In 1965, ABC became the first network to televise the Indianapolis 500, largely thanks to door opening by Chris Schenkel. That same year, we managed to snatch NBA basketball away from NBC, partly to counter *CBS Sports Spectacular,* which was belatedly trying to undermine *Wide World. CBS Sports Spectacular* soon disappeared, but ABC Sports gained a franchise that, thanks to the amazing rivalry of Wilt Chamberlain and Bill Russell, was about to take off. I gave the games *Wide World* treatment by spotting cameras throughout arenas and personalizing players in sixty-second mini-clips, and I also put a new emphasis on explaining strategy by installing as expert commentator Bob Cousy, the former Boston Celtics star.

I hadn't met "Cooze" before hiring him, and I didn't scrimp on superlatives in our first encounter.

"Bob," I said, "I can't tell you how excited I am. We're about to start a whole new era of NBA basketball. We're going to show America what a great sport it is, that it's more than just a physical thing, that there's an intellectual dimension only a great player like you can describe. Through your ability to articulate, we're going to open the eyes of the world to the NBA."

To which Cousy replied: "Thanks, *Woone.*"

God. Research had somehow missed the fact that Cousy, having grown up in a French-Canadian household, had trouble pronouncing English *r*s. It's a common ailment of the French, I've noticed since, who seem to be gargling when they do their own *r*s, but I came up with a quick fix. I asked Chris Schenkel, who was to call the games with Bob, to make him repeat, as rapid-fire as he could, "Russell and Robertson rebound rapidly."

After a week, Bob Cousy was performing flawlessly—or so Chris reported.

Well, he did know a lot about basketball.

As for me, who couldn't tell the difference between a screen and a pick and roll, my own expertise, such as it was, centered on golf. The tutelage was begun by my father, who regarded golf as Baptists do religion, continued into adulthood with playing-partner debates over arcane regulations, and assumed the dimensions of a Ph.D. dissertation when I went in quest of the Holy Grail: the U.S. Open.

To the purist, no event, including the Masters, is more hallowed than the Open, no organization more sacrosanct than the United States Golf Association, which is the governing body of the tournament and safeguards golf's traditions. The network that carries the Open bears the USGA's imprimatur. CBS already had the Masters, and the Masters refused to allow its broadcaster to carry the Open. That left NBC, which, I knew, was not going to part willingly with a prize it had possessed for twelve years. That made me all the more determined to get it.

I knew, though, that the august USGA would never transfer its seal of approval for mere lucre. A Lancelot would have to prove his honor. Accordingly, I began attending USGA events whenever possible, in demonstration that I cared as much about the sport as the television rights thereto, which approximated the truth. I also steeped myself in golf's legend and lore, to the point where my knowledge of the game was in inverse relationship to my skill in playing it. Finally, long before NBC's contract was to expire, I started to drop by the USGA's Thirty-seventh Street headquarters for informal chats with its executive director, Joe Dey.

Joe Dey was Mr. Golf in those days, the quintessential keeper of the flame. A former divinity student, he was also a devout Christian, balking at attending the Masters when it was held on Easter Sunday. We never discussed commercial concerns during my visits to his office, but focused rather on such matters as Bobby Jones's record victory string during the 1920s and technological developments in the manufacture of clubs and golf balls, which Joe tended to deplore. Sometimes our conversations waxed into the evening hours, and I grew to like the man immensely. I thought the feeling was mutual, but I wasn't sure until he invited me to lunch at the Union League Club, on Thirty-seventh and Park. He introduced me that day to a Scotsman who, although affable enough, made no great impression on me until, some time later, Joe solemnly informed me that I'd been accepted into the Royal and Ancient Golf Club of St. Andrews, the holy of holies on the other side of the ocean. He then confessed that the Scottish gentleman at the Union League that day had been there to check out my suitability for membership!

At that point, I knew the contract for the U.S. Open could be mine as soon as NBC's expired. And so it came to pass—a moment Joe and I celebrated by going to a hotel bar across the street, where my benefactor actually ordered a sherry!—and just in time for ABC's cameras to capture another great sports rivalry, that between Arnold Palmer and Jack Nicklaus.

But this left football. Without football, ABC would never be a sports power, and without Pete Rozelle, the NFL's commissioner, we would never have football.

If Pete, once he had the job, turned out to have been an inspired choice, at the time, he'd been a compromise when the owners, like the kingmakers of the old political parties, failed to agree on a candidate. The former PR man of the L.A. Rams, he was smart, quick, stylish, and oh so smooth. I first became acquainted with his methods in 1964, when, after a long and cozy association with CBS, the NFL put its television rights up for open bid. Financially, I knew ABC would be outgunned, but in studying the fine print in the League's bidding specifications and conditions, I thought I spotted something that would permit us to televise *two* games every Sunday. If I was correct, and as long as we could keep CBS and NBC in the dark on the issue, we could afford to make a bid that would guarantee us the contract. Unfortunately, ABC insisted that a lawyer call Rozelle's office. At least this confirmed my interpretation, and suddenly the powers that be at ABC got excited. Leonard took it to the ABC board and got them to authorize a $13.2-million bid for each of two seasons—the largest rights offer in the network's history. After the vote was taken, one of the directors, a South Carolinian named Bob Huffines downed a double bourbon, proclaiming, "I want the minutes to reflect that I just voted to spend more money than we paid for the whole network a couple of years ago."

By bid day, we were all nervous wrecks, Leonard first and foremost, to the point that he insisted I and Alan Morris, our lawyer, ride to NFL headquarters over on Park Avenue in separate cabs. If one of us was in an accident, at least the other would get through to deliver ABC's bid! Needless to say, we both made it, and along with the bid I made an impassioned, if rather bowing-and-scraping, presentation to Pete and his colleagues about the new ABC, complete with reviews of our accomplishments and the ratings of our sports programming, all to prove how capable we were and worthy of carrying NFL games.

Rozelle & Co. heard me out. If they didn't seem altogether convinced by my passion, well, I was. I figured we had a winner. We'd caught our competitors asleep at the switch, and whether Rozelle thought we were up to their level or not (I knew he didn't think so), our money was just as good as theirs. Besides, with NFL football on our roster, we *would* be up there!

Hey, guys (I felt like shouting out to the complacent NFL brass), we've arrived!

We're *players!*

And then, with a shocking *fzzzzzz-zzzz,* the air went out of the balloon.

The bid from CBS topped ours by $900,000 per season.

I know, you win some, you lose some—that's what we kept telling each other at ABC. But I don't like being snookered. I couldn't prove it, then or later, and Pete Rozelle vociferously has denied it, but I was sure he'd leaked my "double-header" discovery to Bill MacPhail, a long-time crony of his with whom he shared a Long Island summer house and who just happened to be the president of CBS Sports.

Once again, we were without football, and it made me nuts. Somehow, we had to change the bidding balance of power, and that, among other things, meant a long-term campaign of cultivating Mr. Rozelle. An iffy proposition, I thought. I liked Pete, and Pete, I thought, liked me, but I was the new guy on the block and ABC, from his lofty point of view, was strictly a minor-league operation.

Time went by, a year, more. But then, one rare morning—I remember I was standing in the shower, planning and plotting even as water sluiced over me—I had one of those *Eureka!* moments.

"Dummy," I heard my inner voice shouting, "you're forgetting about Walter!"

Walter was Walter Byers, the all-powerful executive director of the NCAA, and a figure unequaled in his detestation of professional football. Rumor had it that Walter's loathing had to do with his having been raised in Kansas (where he'd moved NCAA headquarters from sinful Chicago) and with pro owners being for the most part city slickers. Whatever the reason, Byers regarded the pros not so much as competition but as a plague upon the land. And, therein, I realized, lay the means of turning weakness into strength.

Because ABC had no professional taint. Ergo, Walter had to love us, especially with the inducement of a good deal when his current television contract with NBC expired.

Mind you, I didn't want the NCAA as badly as I wanted the NFL, but we had to have football. By the luck of things, the NFL's last agreement with CBS would come to an end almost simultaneously with the NCAA's with NBC. NBC, I figured, was unlikely to bid for the CBS package. That left CBS and us. In order to jack up the price, Rozelle needed to play us against CBS. But I wasn't doing that again when ABC was sure to be a loser. I didn't intend to bid on anything. Instead, I was going to play Walter against Pete.

I called Rozelle. ABC, I said, was most interested in obtaining the NFL's television rights, but we had no appetite for another bidding war. At the same time, we had to have football. We'd decided therefore to negotiate directly with both the NFL and the NCAA, and we would go with whoever was first to offer us an acceptable deal, leaving the other out in the cold.

"Name a number," I said. "If it's in the ballpark, we can draw up a contract right now."

Pete politely demurred, as I knew he would, but he didn't hang up the phone. Instead, he advised me to take up my proposal—my "novel proposal," he called it—with Art Modell, owner of the Cleveland Browns, and a major voice in deciding the League's television affairs.

"Enjoy Cleveland," he said, as affable as ever.

Alvin "Pete" Rozelle was clearly a poker player.

But I had some face cards of my own, one being the services of Barry Frank, a Harvard MBA and ex-J. Walter Thompson exec who'd worked with Ford, the largest television sports advertiser. Now my director of planning, Barry knew NFL economics forward and back. He also had a good fix on Modell, with whom I'd crossed paths years before when I was producing Shari Lewis and Art was producing *and* owning a rival cooking show.

Mr. Modell, we agreed, was a formidable customer, with a flair for our business that, at least on this particular occasion, bordered on arrogance.

He was all charm, though, when he greeted us at his Cleveland apartment. To this day, I can still see its most notable furnishing—a pink football. I never plumbed the pink football's significance, though, and as our conversation, once I'd made my presentation that day, was exceedingly brief, I never got around to asking.

"You're telling me you'd walk away from the NFL for *college football?*" Art snorted, when I finished. "You've gotta be out of your head!"

"Maybe so, but we can't end up empty-handed," I countered. "If that's the only way I can guarantee ABC'll have football, yes, that's exactly what I'll do. One way or the other, someone's gonna wind up a network short."

Modell burst out laughing. "Well, I've heard of crazy negotiating ploys, but this one beats 'em all. I appreciate your coming all this way, gentlemen, but I suggest you get back to us when you decide to stop playing games."

Did I say "arrogance"?

"Now what?" Barry Frank asked as we rode down in the elevator.

"Well," I said, "now we show we're not kidding."

I'd like to say I phoned Walter Byers from the airport—that's how they'd do it in Hollywood—but it didn't happen quite that fast. Not all that long afterward, though, I began pitching Walter.

The NCAA, at the time, had a cozy deal going. Walter organized his favorite athletic directors (meaning everybody except Notre Dame, it sometimes seemed) into committees, and the committees got to go off on junkets to decide the important things, like the next season's schedule, and television paid handsomely for all of it. Walter could hide behind his committees on the one hand, and manipulate them on the other, and he managed to do it successfully for a number of years.

But I knew I had compelling arguments.

"Walter," I told him, "I don't think you should even put the contract up for bids."

"It would take a huge amount of money to keep me from doing that," he said.

"You don't have to worry about that. We're ready to fill your pockets. But there's something more important than money at stake. You should negotiate directly with us, because if NBC or CBS gets your games, you know as well as I do that you'll be nothing but an afterthought to their pro broadcasts. You'll get their leavings—their second-best announcers, producers, their apprentice technical directors. With us, you'll be the main guys. That's a promise."

"Are you really ready to abandon the pros if we come with you?"

"Scout's honor."

"Are you ready to put that in writing?"

"Of course we are. The way the colleges have to look at it, Walter, it'll be like having their own television network."

Inevitably, he had to consult with his committee, but I think that last idea—that for the colleges it would be like having their own network—was what swung the day. Because the day did come when Walter and his committee people arrived in New York, ready to negotiate with us and us alone.

The offer we prepared was rich: $15.5 million for the 1966 and 1967 seasons—two million more per season than NBC's current deal. But in return, we asked the moon: no bidding, and a never-before-granted option to renew for two additional years at the same price. In other words, it was a four-year deal. The ABC board gave its go-ahead, and I left word with Rozelle's office that the NCAA train was pulling out of the station.

But the call wasn't returned; Pete, apparently, still didn't think I was serious.

On the appointed day, I trooped over to Walter's hotel along with Leonard, Tom Moore, and a clutch of lawyers. The atmosphere was serious, indeed momentous. On Walter's side, this meeting was what he and his negotiating committee lived for, and in exchange for a very strong deal, they were being asked for things they'd never before agreed to. But we worked our way through the terms and conditions in good style, and as cocktail time drew near, only one sticking point remained: Walter's insistence that they have announcer approval. CBS and NBC had always agreed to it, he argued, and I knew he was right. But it wasn't okay by me, not at all.

"Look," I said, "if I give that to you, I'll have to give it to every team owner and sports commissioner who comes along. So why don't we each tend to our own knitting? Let each of us do what we do best."

Without pontificating, I must say I believed wholeheartedly in the point. I wanted our announcers to report what they saw without fear of being tossed out. I wanted sports journalism, not the kind of bland and pandering words that all too often passed for it. I was all too aware of what went on behind the scenes, and to this day, I still remember the Masters getting Jack Whitaker removed from CBS for referring to the crowd on the links as "a mob."

"I hope you'll agree, Walter," I said, looking him straight in the eye. "Because it's a deal breaker for me."

He was just starting to flush when I was called to the phone. I excused myself and took the call outside the room. It was from the hotel desk, informing me that a "Mr. Roselli" had been leaving urgent messages.

The time had come to cross the Rubicon.

"The next time he calls," I said, "tell him I'm in a conference with someone who believes me." I could only pray that Walter did—about the announcer-approval issue—because I wasn't bluffing.

"Just for the sake of argument," Walter said, when I came back, "who were you thinking of having call the games?"

"Chris Schenkel and Bud Wilkinson."

"*Bud Wilkinson?*" he exclaimed. It was as if I'd just invoked the name of God. But to the NCAA in those years, the former coach of the Oklahoma Sooners was as close as a human being could come to deification.

I nodded solemnly.

"Then, Roone," said Walter Byers, "we've got a deal."

When Carl Lindemann, the vice president of NBC Sports, heard of the NCAA's first-ever no-bid contract, he called it "a discredit to amateur athletics," which gave me the opportunity to call my former employers crybabies. Pete Rozelle kept his own counsel. But the illustrious owner of the sole television station in Austin, Texas, an independent who was now facing competition from an upstart competitor, phoned Leonard from his temporary Washington residence to plead for NCAA football. Leonard said no. Unless, that is, the owner in question would agree to air much of ABC's entertainment schedule in the bargain?

Which President Lyndon B. Johnson promptly did.

It was heartwarming all around, and so would be the nineteen unbroken years ABC Sports televised NCAA football. But I wasn't done yet, far from it. The 1968 Winter Games in Grenoble were coming up, and I'd been tipped that Carl Lindemann had been spotted in Paris. I raced to the airport with my passport and, literally, $6 in my pocket.

By the time clothes and cash caught up with me, Lindemann had already treated the Grenoble organizers to an elaborate slide show, trumpeting NBC's televising of the Rose, Orange, and Sugar Bowls. My gear was more modest: a scrapbook of press clippings comparing—most unfavorably—NBC's coverage of the 1964 Summer Games in Tokyo with ours in Innsbruck. I also had $2 million to offer, and a detailed history of *Wide World*'s four visits to France.

To my immense gratification, it was no contest.

"I want to offer my congratulations," the head of the organizing committee said afterward, shaking my hand. "But, please, explain for me why NBC kept talking of their 'bowel games.' It was in very questionable taste."

Landing the '68 Summer Olympics in Mexico City, though, wasn't going to be such a piece of cake. A presumably wiser NBC would be in the hunt again, and word was that CBS chairman Bill Paley had won over the local Olympic committee. Mexico being Mexico, there was also an abundance of characters claiming to know somebody who knew somebody who could deliver the rights—for a fee. I escaped ethical pangs by being unable to determine the proper palm to grease. I did manage, however, to find some intermediaries who had the ear of the organizers, including a media baron whose only charge was flattery. This I dispensed lavishly.

The day before the contract was to be awarded, Barry and I found ourselves on the same Mexico City–bound plane as CBS Sports president Bill MacPhail. He was stretched out in first class; we were scrunched up in coach. During the flight, he sent back peanuts. But a funny thing happened in Mexico City. Believing there'd be multiple rounds of bidding, CBS and NBC opened with offers in the $2-million neighborhood, while we, on the basis of certain assurances we'd been given, opted to go with a single close-out bid of $4.8 million. Game, set, match, ABC.

Although the close-out bid was a tactic I liked to use in situations where I thought the seller of rights could be swept away by a major jump in dollars, it was at the same time a two-edged sword. On this occasion, I was absolutely certain from the soundings I'd taken that, given the chance, CBS and NBC would have bid well beyond their $2-million openers and that my $4.8 million would have been topped. A *Sports Illustrated* story even quoted Carl Lindemann as saying I'd bribed a Mexican colonel with a Maserati! (Not true.) But sure enough, when I got back to New York, my sidelines critics—the cost-control naysayers at the network— spread the word inside the company that I'd overpaid by $2.8 million! And technically, of course, I had! (No, I couldn't *prove* our competitors would have gone higher. I just knew it.)

It was this kind of mentality that, years later, would diminish the organization I helped build, but in the sixties and seventies, with Leonard running the show and supportive of the bold stroke as long as Sales could turn a profit on it, we were building a business and, in the process, a terrific profit center for ABC. The world had started to take notice.

And then there was Howard Cosell.

I can think of no other way to introduce him than to let him barge in, just as he barged into my life in 1965 when I hired him. He'd been off the network for five years at that point, blackballed by Tom Moore for being too New York, too loud, too pushy, too all the qualities that made Cosell

Cosell. Howard, who admitted to being "arrogant, pompous, obnoxious, vain, cruel, persecuting, distasteful, verbose, a show-off, and a hypochondriac," thought anti-Semitism was the actual root of his banning. I'd been following his ups and downs for years, and was well aware of the strange creature who'd wandered the nation's locker rooms with a thirty-pound tape recorder strapped to his back, interviewing anyone who'd talk to him. And most everyone did: Vince Lombardi, Ralph Houk, Jimmy Brown, Pancho Gonzales, Wilt Chamberlain, Tony Lima—you name the star, Howard Cosell, broadcasting nobody, got them. Furthermore, he asked questions I'd have answered with a fist to the face, but the athletes seemed to love him for it.

After Tom Moore's edict, Howard had been reduced to radio and local TV, and even the latter was terminated when Howard informed his listeners that Casey Stengel, colorful manager of the woeful New York Mets, was taking naps during his team's games.

But Cosell was not to be ignored, and in a mouthy Olympic boxing champion then going by the name Cassius Clay he found the perfect mate. Their pas de deux started in 1962, with Howard asking who would win the upcoming Floyd Patterson-Sonny Liston bout (both, Cassius predicted). The first of many contretemps came two years later when Clay upset Liston for the heavyweight championship and the next day announced himself by his new Muslim name, Muhammad Ali. Howard Cosell was the only media person who addressed the champ accordingly, which brought him sacks of mail calling him "nigger-loving Jew."

Over the next thirteen months, the Cosell-Ali act generated increasing broadcast heat, and my feelings about Howard grew from being amused and intrigued to acquisitive lust. But how to sneak him onto the air?

Stealth and slipperiness, I decided, was the answer. Tom had certainly told me of Howard's banning. Ed Scherick knew about it, too. But my mandate was to build the best sports schedule possible. A notable loser on that schedule was weekend baseball—a chronic problem over the years for all the national networks. With the addition of a pregame show—low profile, of course, but with a host who could deliver the biggest stars and get them talking—who knew what might happen? Wasn't it worth a try? Wasn't I only doing my network duty?

It wasn't under cover of night that I summoned Howard to my office, but for all the secrecy involved, it might as well have been.

"Roone," he said, when I told him what was up, "we are today witnessing an occurrence on the scale of Milo T. Farnsworth's invention of the cathode ray tube: the television rebirth of an acknowledged genius. You are to be congratulated, young man, on your sagacity."

"Howard," I said, "cut the crap."

At this we both burst out laughing and, in a way, we never stopped.

I knew Tom would be purple-faced when he found out, and he was. But by then Howard was already doing the show and causing a stir. Besides, Cosell, when he wanted to be, was irresistible: funny, self-mocking, bighearted, a person who owned a room simply by walking into it. And he and Tom grew to be quite friendly.

I always steeled myself in Howard's company. You never knew what to expect, the more so since among his many talents was a preternatural ability to extract the most intimate of secrets. Among his favored targets were busty airline flight attendants, whom he habitually seduced—not for the usual purpose (Howard was devoted to his guard-dog wife, Emmy), but, I always thought, to prove he could, even with looks only a proverbial mother could love.

"Watch this," he said to me once, as a most attractive crew member approached with drinks on a flight to a *Wide World* shoot. "My dear," he then said, kissing her hand, "you must forgive the little boy in me, but I am overwhelmed imagining the caresses you bestow with these feathery fingers." He drew her closer, the better to ogle her cleavage. "Is it possible for a woman to have more succulent lips? A more sensuous neck?"

I was ready to crawl under my seat, but the flight attendant was smitten, as Howard, in tones befitting a smutty Elizabeth Barrett Browning, described the pleasures of her swelling breasts and dewy thighs. By the time he was finished, she was telling him—I kid you not—of the dampness she'd experienced while riding a horse nude in Oregon.

Howard's professional feats were, if anything, even more otherworldly. He never used notes when recording his daily five-minute radio show, *Speaking of Sports,* never needed a second take. It was always perfect the first time through. He was the same when timing a piece. Ask him to deliver a report in, say, three and a half minutes and Cosell—never looking at a clock—did it to the second. I never learned how he pulled it off, or the source of the memory that allowed him to walk into any dugout and say, "Ah, so-and-so, batted .325 in Norfolk four years ago, but hams for hands.

Seventeen errors producing six unearned runs, two lost games." Except to check what was being written about him, I never saw Howard read the sports pages, much less the *Elias Sporting Guide*. The information at his fingertips was just spookily *there*.

The same went for his speech making. He never needed a note when addressing an audience. He had total recall. He wielded his voice like a musical instrument, now speaking so softly people had to lean forward to listen, now rising in decibels and conviction with an almost evangelical fervor. And even at his most controversial moments, when any audience he addressed was sure to include a preponderance of Cosell haters, he always, at the end, got a standing O.

Amazing man.

He had guts, too. Any number of incidents might illustrate the point, but on one occasion, when he was riding through Harlem in a limousine, he saw a crowd of people milling around on the sidewalk and a bloody street fight in progress. Ordering the driver to stop, Howard charged through the throng and separated the combatants, admonishing them, and ordering each—as it were—to a neutral corner. Any other white man who did that would undoubtedly have been mobbed, and few enough would have dared. But Howard, recognized by the crowd, was somehow able to wade in, stop the fight, get back into his car, and continue on his way unscathed.

But I most admired Howard for sticking by Ali after he refused draft induction in April 1967, and was stripped of his championship and his license to box. There was no career boost in remaining loyal to Ali, who wouldn't fight again for the next three years—quite the contrary, to judge from the column inches denouncing him for giving aid and comfort to the enemy. But Howard wouldn't be moved; as he saw it (and the U.S. Supreme Court ultimately agreed), injustice had been done and that was that.

I got to know Ali myself during this period, thanks in part to a classic Cosell moment. We'd been told to come to the Champ's hotel suite, which we did. This, I should say, was the heyday of Black Power and burning ghettos in American cities, and the idea of Black Muslims, of people like Elijah Mohammed and Malcolm X in their black suits and white shirts preaching against whitey, drove fear into the hearts of even the most liberal citizens. So when we came out of the elevator and onto Ali's floor and found ourselves in a place packed with Black Muslims, my pulse began to pitter-pat.

We were greeted by dead silence—which was broken by Howard Cosell bellowing, "All right, everybody who isn't white, get out!"

Again, a split second of dead silence. But then they got it—all at once—for the Muslims collapsed in hysterics.

Ali and I would end up on occasion in planes together, and while I remained in awe of what he was sacrificing by taking on the U.S. government in the name of religious principle, I could never quite figure him out. We'd be talking, and he'd begin fiddling with something in the seat pocket or staring out the window, and I'd be certain he hadn't heard a word. But six months later, when even I'd forgotten what had been discussed, he'd recount our conversation back to me. He was, on the one hand, a child, and, on the other, a shrewd and honorable man. The same, I'd come to learn, could be said of Howard Cosell.

I took flak, of course, for allowing Howard to be Howard, even for permitting him to call Ali, Ali. ("Somebody with the name Roone has no right to tell anybody what they can be called," was my rejoinder.) But it didn't compare with the fire that greeted my hiring Ali to be ABC's expert commentator at an A.A.U.-sponsored U.S.-Soviet amateur boxing tournament in Las Vegas.

Protests cascaded in. ABC's upper reaches were inclined to cave to pressure from Washington—after all, at the very heart of our business was the license granted to our stations by the FCC to use (and profit from) the public airways—and the U.S. State Department became somehow convinced that détente itself would be compromised if Ali went on. My bosses turned to me for reassurance, but I had nowhere to turn except to Ali.

He was well aware of the protests, which he lived with every day. Aware too, I'm sure, of the spot I was in.

"Will you call the matches without talking about politics?" I asked Ali. "Or your personal situation?"

"Sure," Ali said.

"It'll be just the boxing? That's all you'll talk about?"

"That's right."

Maybe I had some Cosell in me. I stuck by my guns, and so did my bosses, and the State Department, I suppose, found someone else to harass.

Oh yes, when we covered the tournament in Vegas, the Champ was as good as his word.

The 1968 Winter Games were Innsbruck cubed: three times the effort, three times the crew, three times the programming hours. Fifty tons of equipment had to be moved in, forty miles of cable laid—carefully, because we were doing Olympic things that hadn't been done before: televising in color, transmitting by satellite, airing events live on the same day. Grenoble was also the first time television created a national heroine overnight, and it did so via the first satellite telecast of a single figure-skating performance, start to finish. I'm talking about Peggy Fleming in her lime green costume, winner of the only American gold, and ABC's figure-skating commentator for years to come.

Mexico City, five months later, was a different story. Conviviality was altogether missing from these Games, which took place in the midst of student protests and rioting all over the Western world. The Mexican police had waded in with live ammunition. There'd been deaths as well as other casualties, and it was in the midst of a veritable armed camp that I produced the biggest Olympic extravaganza ever: 50 cameras (one hung from a 225 foot crane); 450 producers, directors, and crew; 44 hours of programming. We also introduced the very latest in technological gizmos, such as a wireless mike I'd placed in the Olympic torch to catch the *whoosh* of the flame being lighted.

Except for Jim McKay having to fill forty minutes when the control room died—thank God it was always Jim!—all went according to plan. There were thrills of victory (Bob Beamon leaping 29 feet, 3 inches in the long jump, a mark that would stand for nearly three decades), agonies of defeat (a boastful Mark Spitz shut out from swimming for the gold), and, despite air times seemingly designed to prevent viewing, record millions tuning in—including a very cross president of the International Olympic Committee, Avery Brundage.

It was 72 televised seconds that set him off—the 200-meter-dash medal ceremony. Americans Tommie Smith and John Carlos had placed first and third, and, as they mounted the victory stand, I started yelling in the control room. The two men were barefoot and their heads were hung. "Get in there!" I shouted. "This is Black Power! Get in on them!"

Then the extraordinary happened: As "The Star-Spangled Banner" began to play, Smith and Carlos raised black-gloved fists.

Bad enough, Brundage would say, that I'd aired the "nasty demonstration against the United States flag by Negroes." But did I have to compound "the shameful abuse of hospitality" by sending Howard Cosell in search of Smith? Yes, sir, you bet I did. This was a major news story, and, unlike the hundreds of other journalists on hand, Howard delivered. Learning from contacts that Smith had been expelled from the Olympic Village, he spent hours scouring the city before tracking him down in a hotel room. Smith was adamant about not talking, but one simply didn't say no to Howard Cosell, who brought him back to the studio.

"Are you proud to be an American?" Howard asked him on the air.

"I'm proud to be a black American," Tommie answered.

That exchange, shown and quoted worldwide, pushed Brundage over the edge. Smith and Carlos were sent home, barred from competition, and a short-lived investigation, aimed at taking away their medals, was launched. "Warped mentalities and cracked personalities seemed to be everywhere, and impossible to eliminate," Brundage said. Whether he was referring to Howard, the athletes, or the new president of ABC Sports, Brundage didn't say.

Yes, I did just say "the new president of ABC Sports." In fact, Tom Moore had christened me with the new title, along with a most welcome raise, before the Olympics. But now Tom was gone, victim of palace intrigue and low Entertainment ratings, and so was Ed Scherick (to Hollywood and success as a movie producer), and in Tom's place came Elton Rule, a movie-star-handsome executive who'd run ABC's station in Los Angeles. He was Leonard's favorite. It turned out that Leonard had been after him for some time to come to New York, but Elton would come only as Leonard's number two, meaning president of the network. Finally Leonard had said yes, and that had led to changes and shake-ups up and down the line—all par for the course in the what-have-you-done-for-us-lately pressure cooker of network television.

None of this affected me materially for the moment, but I was aware of other more subtle changes that did. Our very success at ABC Sports made it harder to operate beneath the competition's radar scope. It was also getting me mentioned in the press more—not always kindly. The next, post-Olympic brouhaha was over the art on the ABC Sports Christmas card, a Leroy Neiman painting I'd commissioned of Bill Toomey and his Soviet rival holding each other up at the conclusion of the Mexico City decathlon. I thought it the perfect and wonderfully appropriate distillation of "Peace on Earth, Good Will Toward Men." But in the columns, I was attacked as being a Communist sympathizer.

There was not much comfort to be had in Howard's getting far worse. Mexico City had brought him the full-blown notoriety that would be his trademark, and now every press hit, slur, or slander—real and imagined—brought me a middle-of-the-night phone call from Howard. I had a genuine celebrity on my hands now, insecure, insomniac, self-involved—but, I thought, well worth the trouble.

Because I had plans for Howard Cosell. Sixteen weeks every fall, he was going to have to keep his Monday nights free. But that is a story that's surely worth a chapter all its own.

Monday Night Football

Football. Professional football. Yes, we had the NCAA now, and that was the number two package at the time, ranked behind the NFL but still slightly ahead of the AFL. Great prestige, too. But ever since "the game of the century"—I'm talking about the Baltimore Colts' celebrated overtime victory over the New York Giants back in 1958—the pros on Sunday afternoon had been the action, and I wanted a piece of it so badly I could taste it.

Not that we hadn't tried other schemes, as well as my "double-header" discovery of 1964, which Rozelle spilled to CBS. Tom Moore had had the idea, once upon a time, of substituting an NFL game for our fast-fading *Gillette Friday Night Fights,* an albatross if ever there was one, and Pete Rozelle, who'd increased television revenues tenfold in four years as commissioner, was ready for more. So, in fact, was the Ford Motor Company, whose marketing manager—a promising fellow named Lee Iacocca—offered to be sole sponsor. But before plans could go further, the NCAA got wind of what was going on. Walter Byers rallied his troops, and before you could say Friday-Night Football, athletic directors from all over the country, even some university presidents, were lobbying their congressmen—not, mind you, because the NCAA was threatened but because Friday nights were when so many high school teams played their games. *High schools,* mind you. Clever man, Walter Byers. Congress passed a resolution banning pro telecasts on both Friday and Saturday nights when high schools played their games and Rozelle, who had antitrust exemptions to protect, declined to challenge it.

That took care of Friday and Saturday. Sunday was out because of the daytime telecasts, and Tuesday through Thursday were doubtful because they would wreck the rhythm of the teams' practice schedules. That left Monday. In any case, once I'd reclaimed NCAA football in 1966, the NFL was off-limits for us—for the time being. Pete nonetheless kept pushing for prime time and eventually got CBS and NBC to air an experimental handful of games, mostly preseason. The ratings were hardly noteworthy.

Fast-forward to 1969. We were then in the renewal period of our NCAA contract—a fact, as I shall explain, of some significance. Early that year, I got a call from John Fetzer, the wine-maker and Detroit Tigers owner, asking if I was interested in televising baseball on Monday nights. I wasn't, actually. Baseball, except for the All-Star Game and the World Series, had always been trouble in prime time for all the networks, ABC included. Our own *Game of the Week* had never been a winner either. Baseball may well have been "the national pastime," but the interest, I always thought, was local. In other words, people would tune in avidly to follow their hometown teams, but the Pirates against the Cardinals, say? If you lived in Atlanta? And in prime time?

The same wasn't true of football. For one thing, the schedule was limited to one season of the year, and teams played a limited number of games. For another, a fair number of them had developed national appeal—the New York Giants, of course, the Washington Redskins, the Chicago Bears, the Packers from Green Bay, the Colts, even the Cleveland Browns. (The Dallas Cowboys, at the time, could not yet claim the title "America's Team.") And football had the potential for drama and heroics and maybe—just maybe, if I could figure out how to do it—an appeal for viewers beyond the dyed-in-the-wool fans.

I hesitate to say it—even whisper it—but I was thinking about women. That other half of the viewing audience.

Plus, there was another reason CBS and NBC had failed in their weeknight dabblings and that was CBS and NBC. Their idea of televising a football game was to plant cameras on the fifty-yard line and call it a day, and that was fine for a hometown Sunday-afternoon telecast with no competition. But for a national game on a weeknight? Deadly. Prime time wasn't Sunday afternoon. Everything was different: audience, habits, expectations, program content, choices. You turned on your set at night wanting to be entertained. If you weren't, the channel got switched.

Football as entertainment. Football at night under the lights, helmets gleaming, uniforms dazzling. Even cheerleaders looked better under the lights. And so did the turf, whether it was grass or artificial, while shots from blimps overhead made the whole stadium resemble a jeweled oasis floating in the darkness.

From a production point of view, I was convinced we were already on to something. NCAA games on Saturdays had become a kind of laboratory for us. From a purely visual point of view, our telecasts were far superior to the Sunday guys.

But there was something else, too. The announcers. Since time immemorial, there'd been two guys in the announcers' booth—the play-by-play voice and the analyst, or x's and o's expert, who was more often than not an ex-jock. I'll mention no names—it wasn't altogether the fault of the announcers either—but was there any law that said games had to be announced as though they were being played in a cathedral?

My ideas—for turning a popular sport into a prime-time *event*—evolved over a long period of time. But their common denominator was to find ways of making people watch even if Lichtenstein was playing Andorra.

In any case, it took many lunches over the next eight months for me to persuade Mr. Rozelle that we weren't as bad as it seemed. In the eyes of the NFL brass, there were CBS and NBC, and then, way down somewhere near the bottom of the ladder, was ABC. Yes, there were jokes about our prime-time schedule ("How do you end the Vietnam war?" the latest went. "Put it on ABC; it'll be canceled after thirteen weeks."), and true, ABC continued to trail in number and quality of affiliates. But look at what we'd done with sports, I pointed out. And imagine what we could do with football on Monday night? A vast, untapped audience was out there for the NFL, and ABC Sports had the style and savvy to serve it up.

It was a long, charm-draining slog, but gradually Pete came around, and by July 1969, we appeared on the edge of beginning to talk deal.

Meanwhile, I had less success with my own network. Sales execs couldn't see the NFL's appeal to women no matter how much pizzazz we put into production. Some of the bigger affiliates loved it—the big cities were hotbeds of interest in the pros—but the small guys were worried that I was secretly plotting to dump the NCAA, and down in Tulsa, Oklahoma,

Texas was three thousand times more important than the Giants and the Bears. Leonard was supportive, but Elton Rule, our new president, didn't want football intruding on the prime-time schedule, however dismal the ratings.

I refrained from telling Rozelle what was going on, but Pete, as always, had other sources, and suddenly his lunch calendar became filled. Then, in late August, the other shoe abruptly dropped. In the course of a meeting, Bob Cochran, Pete's television coordinator, let on that they'd had some conversations with an ad hoc collection of stations being strung together by the Howard Hughes–owned Sports Network to air Monday-night football.

I couldn't believe it.

"You've got to be kidding!" I told Cochran. "That's not even a network, a real one. Pete's playing games."

I even got the impression that this ad hoc non-network might have been Cochran's own idea. His job was to stir up more revenue for the NFL in any way he could, and he'd always been disparaging about ABC.

There was worse. According to Cochran, any number of ABC affiliates were ready to dump the network and commit to Monday-night football! I could believe that. Our affiliates were the least loyal in the land—with good reason, for our Entertainment programming ran a consistent, and sometimes distant, third to CBS and NBC.

If Cochran's—or Pete's—idea had been to stampede me, it worked. I went to see Fred. Fred Pierce, former director of Sales, new president of the network, had always supported football in prime time, and he saw immediately the dangers of an independent network.

"We'd better take this to Elton," he said, and off we went to Rule's office.

"I'm here to brainwash you, Elton," was what I said for openers, "and I hope to hell I can, because if we don't get this football package, you can kiss a hundred affiliates good-bye on Monday nights. We'll be wiped out. We might as well go black."

"A *hundred* stations?" he exclaimed. "You've got to be kidding."

"I'm not," I said. "That's a minimum. And it includes Philly."

That's what Cochran had told me, and predictably, it knocked Elton back in his chair. Philadelphia was the most powerful of all our ABC affiliates. As it went, so went many of the others.

"I've gotta talk to Goldenson about this," Elton said.

I'd counted on Leonard being terrorized by the news. He was, and twenty-four hours later, I was back lunching with Pete. We didn't waste time dickering. I said we'd do a three-year deal for $25.5 million, he said that was fine with him, and that seemed to be that.

Only it wasn't.

Looking back on it, it was like one of those horror movies where you think the hero is safe and sound—at long last—and is about to live happily ever after . . . at which point the monster wraps his arms around him one more time. But while it's easy enough to be flip about it now, when I heard what Pete said next, I choked, gagged, and went ballistic.

Before a contract could be drawn up, Pete said blithely, established relationships demanded that he give NBC and CBS the right of first refusal. That meant the right to match my offer.

"You've got to be kidding!" I managed finally.

He wasn't.

"But we made a *deal!*" I shouted. "You can't just shop it!"

Yes, he could, and not only could, but was going to.

"But that's not *fair!*" I remonstrated. "Don't you see how unfair that is to ABC?"

Freckled and fair skinned, I redden easily when the blood starts to bubble inside. This time, I think I must have gone purple. Because it *wasn't* fair, I fumed. He'd never have pulled a stunt like this with NBC or CBS. It was because we were ABC that he thought he could screw around with us.

Etc., etc., etc.

I don't remember all I said. I was too irate. But Pete couldn't be budged and at the end of the day, there was nothing to be done. I myself couldn't walk on the deal. ABC needed Monday-night football, we had to have it. And though I thought we'd earned it fair and square, there was nothing left to do now but twist on tenterhooks . . . while Rozelle made his rounds.

CBS, which got first crack, passed: no way they were going to diddle a Monday lineup of *Lucy, Mayberry R.F.D.,* and *Doris Day.*

NBC, however, had only movies, followed by an easily moved *Laugh-In.* I was scared to death of NBC. But there was a hitch, thank God. They'd have to push back *The Tonight Show*—their biggest earner—if a game ran long. So weighty was the matter, Pete informed me, that Bob Sarnoff himself, the General's son and heir, was making the call.

The morning NBC's decision was due, I couldn't work. I went with Barry Frank to Rozelle's office to keep the death watch. It so happened that just that day, ABC's affiliates were winding up their annual meeting in San Francisco—a meeting I'd skipped because of what was going on in New York. Many of them were aware of it, and they had mixed feelings about it, but in order to allow me to make a nine A.M. announcement, West Coast time, Pete had given NBC a noon deadline.

At eleven-thirty, the phone rang. I watched Pete listen. I couldn't read his reaction at all. But when he hung up and turned to me, he was smiling.

"You owe a thank-you note to Johnny Carson," he said to me. "Bob decided they didn't want to piss him off. He didn't even make the call."

You win some. And then you *win* some!

I'd skirted something that now needed settling: announcer approval. It wasn't that same morning, but soon after. The NFL, I knew, had kept it with CBS and NBC. On the other hand, I didn't consider professional football a religious experience, and Pete was well aware that it was entertainment I was after, entertainment and innovation.

To my surprise, Pete had no objection at all.

"It's your show, Roone," he said.

Then I mentioned, kind of in passing, "What would you think if I put Howard in the booth."

"*Cosell?*" he'd said. Then he laughed. "Why don't you just dig up Attila the Hun?"

I let it go at that. With our first telecast still more than a year off, I wanted time to consider the possibilities. I had various schemes in mind, but secretly, Howard was a fixture in all of them. In any case, I had another, more immediate problem: When he heard of my Monday-night deal, Walter Byers blew his considerable cork.

I confess I'd seen this coming. That was why I'd done my homework.

I let Walter rage, and he raged. How I'd double-crossed him, violated their sacred trust, and how a torn-up NCAA contract would be my payback. I told him what I'd discovered, and he didn't give a damn about that, I'd still broken my word. The truth was that my no-pursuit-of-pros pledge covered only the two years of our original agreement. Our lawyers agreed with me. It wasn't specified at all in the renewal deal.

Well, that didn't mollify him much, nor did the formal letter I had to write him, but slowly we started to talk again. I had to make some concessions. He and his committee were afraid that I was going to use Saturday NCAA games to promote the hated pros. I committed us to not doing this. I also—their idea—committed us to promoting, on Monday nights, the NCAA games. I also swore—and put in writing—that I wouldn't tamper with the NCAA's A-list broadcast team, which included Chris Schenkel, or the crackerjack production teams that put on the games.

In return, Walter agreed to return to being only normally abusive.

The truth? I can say now that he had every right to be pissed. I'd gotten him on a technicality. But life went on, and before we were done, we had the NCAA package for nineteen years. And I gave it the tender loving care it deserved.

For example, that very year, as I saw in the advance schedule, Frank Broyles's Arkansas Razorbacks, ranked number one in the preseason polls, would be playing Darrell Royall's hated, second-ranked Texas Longhorns in October. It would be a terrific event—but how much more spectacular, I thought, if the national championship was at stake, and the game was played the last week of the season? I called Broyles, who had home-field advantage, and he agreed to the switch. Royall did too, though more dubiously.

"You really don't think Ohio State's going to be number one?" he laughed, referring to the national champs the previous year.

"The football gods have spoken to me," I said, fingers crossed. "I'm sure you and Frank aren't going to let them down."

They didn't, and Texas and Arkansas were still undefeated in November, heading into what we ballyhooed as "The Shoot-Out of '69." I wasn't going to be on hand to see it myself. ABC's board of governors was meeting in Hawaii that same weekend, and I'd also promised Joan we'd use the occasion to take our first vacation together in years. We badly needed to get away. Suffice it to say that I was so involved in my work that I'd had a run of prolonged absences from home, and Joan in particular looked on the trip as do or die for our marriage. Plans were carved in concrete: She would depart for Honolulu the Wednesday before the game, I'd follow Friday after seeing to final production details, and the next ten tropical days would be ours.

"You be there," Joan warned as I put her on the plane.

"Cross my heart," I said.

Then, the next day, the White House announced that President Nixon would be attending the Texas-Arkansas game.

A bit of background. This was 1969, and we were living in very anxious times. Not 9/11-level anxiety, perhaps, but just six years before, the president of the United States, John F. Kennedy, had been gunned down in Dallas before the eyes of the nation. That had been, for many of us, a watershed, the end of our innocence, a life-will-never-be-the-same happening. And a perennial sore point for ABC, at least in my mind, because the Sunday morning after the assassination, when Lee Harvey Oswald was led out in the basement of the Dallas jail, ABC News had already left the story to televise President Kennedy's memorial service at the Capitol. So, for that matter, had CBS, leaving only NBC's viewers to witness Jack Ruby pulling the trigger.

Six years had passed, yes, but closer to home, in 1968, Robert Kennedy had been assassinated in Los Angeles, and we'd seen the world go mad before our eyes at the Democratic National Convention in Chicago. Vietnam was the headline story night after night after night on the evening news, and the country was deeply divided, with a lot of rage out there. If all we were going to do was televise the game, I'd have left it to our production team. But with a highly controversial president now joining the spectators, in a big, open stadium, and with 45,000 fans expected . . . ?

Hey, nothing I could do could prevent an assassination attempt if it happened, but if it did, we were going to be the ones covering it and I didn't want anyone else making the decisions about how to do it.

In other words, there was no way I wasn't going to be in Fayetteville, Arkansas, come Saturday.

It was six A.M. Honolulu time when I tried to explain this to Joan. My answer was the sound of a receiver clicking.

Texas scored two fourth-quarter touchdowns to beat Arkansas 15–14, and as a then-record television audience tuned in, an unscathed Richard Nixon presented the national championship trophy to the winners in the Longhorns' dressing room. And my marriage came unglued.

Hard stuff. But as often happens in life, the loss brought me a gain—a close friend who was going through his own split at the time. His name was Frank Gifford.

We met at one of the black-tie affairs the television industry stages to congratulate itself; took an instant liking to each other while making small talk about Frank's sportscasting career since his retirement as a star halfback for the Giants; and afterward, poured out our respective marital woes over scotch at P. J. Clarke's. Like survivors clinging to the same life raft, we became all but inseparable, hanging out at Toots Shor's, golfing at Wing Foot, where we were both members, playing pool with Rozelle in the bachelor digs I soon moved into.

We talked about anything and everything, including his work at CBS, where Frank, a doting father of three, felt out of place in a boys'-club culture centered on late-night drinking and womanizing. His unhappiness, plus his stardom, plus his deftness at explaining the football inexplicable made me begin to wonder if I hadn't found the expert commentator I was going to need come Monday nights the following fall.

We flew down to the Masters together that April, where Frank was to pronounce the benediction of the tournament for CBS—one of those "due to the importance of this event" things, "CBS and the Masters are proud to announce that it will be presented in its entirety, with limited commercial interruption." And on the flight, I asked:

"What do you think of Howard Cosell?"

"Not much," Frank answered.

That was no surprise. Howard had taken public potshots at the broadcasting style of "pretty" Frank. Not that Frank should have felt singled out. Howard did that to everybody.

"What would you think if I had him as sort of a columnist on *Monday Night Football*?" I asked.

"Still not much."

"Well," I said, popping the big question, "what would you think about Frank Gifford being the expert commentator on *Monday Night Football*?"

Frank gaped at me.

"You're kidding me, aren't you?"

"Dead serious."

"Roone," he said, "I'd like that job more than anything in the world. But I can't take it."

The problem wasn't at all Howard. It may have been in part the year remaining on his CBS contract, which he felt honor bound to fulfill, but he could easily have gotten out of that if he'd wanted to. But, Frank being

Frank, and being the most loyal of friends, there was something else on his mind.

"I'll tell you someone who'd be great for you," he said. "And he really could use the work."

"Who's that?" I asked.

"Don Meredith."

I only knew Don from his press clippings, but they were impressive. All-American quarterback at SMU; holder of the college record for passing accuracy; nine seasons with the Dallas Cowboys; twice voted All-Pro; described as the 6-foot, 3-inch, 200-pound Texas version of Huckleberry Finn crossed with Mark Twain. What I particularly liked was his reputation of not being intimidated by the Cowboys' coach, Tom Landry, who made Vince Lombardi seem like the Welcome Wagon. If Don, who wasn't having any fun trying to be a stockbroker, wasn't awed by Landry, analyzing the performance of mere mortals would be a snap.

I asked Frank, who'd been his good friend since Giants days, to have him give me a ring.

That's when Don encountered a trait for which I was, alas, becoming notorious. Not returning phone calls. Then, as now, I offered various reasons: being swamped (which I usually was); avoiding Howard (believe it or not, at the time I had an answering service screening my home calls for precisely this purpose); believing that problems were best solved by the passage of time (not always true). I also confess to an acute aversion to having to impart bad news or, alternatively, to being put on the spot before I've war-gamed every in and out. Add to this an innate shyness of unplumbed depths, and the wonder is that I didn't communicate by carrier pigeon.

Unaware of this quirk—okay, call it a character defect!—Don left four messages in as many days, then took Texas-size umbrage and left a fifth, saying he was commencing negotiations with CBS. That got my attention, and with Frank's intercession, lunch was set.

I'd prepared apologies, but when Don turned up at Toots Shor's, he was not in a forgiving mood.

"The only reason I came," he drawled, "is to tell you to your face what a horse's ass you are."

I replied: "And that, sir, is the kind of candor I want in an expert commentator."

Don laughed, and after several hours together, I understood why

Frank was hooked. "Jeff and Hazel's boy from Mt. Vernon, Texas," as he styled himself, was smart, funny, disarmingly down-home (calculatedly so, I thought), and, in the wheels-within-wheels working of his mind, infinitely more complicated than the folksy act. His good looks and charm would be a nice counterpoint to anyone I put him with, particularly with the female audience I was hoping to attract. But while I'd been not returning phone calls, CBS had actually offered Don a contract to analyze regional Cowboys games at $20,000 a season—exactly what I'd planned to pay. Several scribblings on cocktail napkins later, we settled at $30,000.

"You know," I said as we shook hands, "this lunch cost me ten thousand dollars."

Don grinned. "It'll be the best ten thousand you ever spent."

"Right on!" I echoed.

And that was when I put in a call to Howard, whom I found in the postprandial phase of a liquid lunch at Jimmy Weston's.

"Get over here as soon as you can," I said. "There's something I need to talk to you about."

"Ahhhh," he said. "From the desperation of your tone, I can only conclude that the bon vivant who is Roone Pinckney Arledge is beseeching me to rescue the trifle he's devised for Monday evenings. Am I not correct?"

"As always, Howard."

"And you no doubt expect me to shoulder this Stygian burden without additional compensation."

"Yes, Howard, I do."

"I accept," he said.

Let me digress for a further moment about Mr. Cosell. I'd always had him secretly in mind for *Monday Night Football,* without knowing for the longest time precisely how to work him in. I tried out the idea here and there, with no takers. But the more people didn't like the idea, the more I was convinced Howard was the key missing ingredient. You could hate him, at times want to strangle him, but he wouldn't let you ignore him. He forced you to watch. I thought of it as the Kilgallen effect.

Dorothy Kilgallen had been a prominent, sharp-tongued newspaper columnist and the secret weapon, I always thought, of the *What's My Line?* phenomenon. Graybeards like me still remember that program, a simple quiz show where celebrity panelists had to guess the often-wacko occupations of the contestants, but it had run for years and years and years—in prime time! And one of the main reasons was Kilgallen herself. Where the other panelists were relaxed, tossed out gags and laughs, Dorothy played it to win! She pushed, she bored in, and if someone else guessed the answer first, before she did, she was visibly annoyed! I think a lot of people tuned in just to hear what was next going to pop out of her mouth.

Enter Howard. But the question was: How to pair him? And with whom? He could never be the play-by-play man, and he was far too opinionated to be the expert analyst. Relegate him to the sidelines? That made no sense either, I wanted him in the booth. But what, I realized, if we turned the announcers' booth into a kind of stage set, where an engrossing and possibly funny and certainly controversial drama might play out between the players?

Once I got that far, it was but a short step to the next question: Where was it carved in stone that there could be only two announcers in the booth? Why couldn't there be three? If you could have three, you could have a play-by-play man, Don Meredith as your expert analyst—and Howard Cosell as your gadfly. The Kilgallen effect. The iconoclast, the voice of truth.

Handsome Don and Nasty Howard. I realized the chemistry between them could be incredible.

That left the play-by-play slot, which was the least of my worries. My first thought was Curt Gowdy, who'd gone to NBC with the AFL package in 1964. He continued to host *The American Sportsman,* though, and we'd stayed in close touch. When I told him of plans for "the biggest thing in television sports" (no need to be modest when selling), he was ready to sign up, then and there. But his NBC contract still had two years to run, and the only person who could free him from it was Carl Lindemann, not an Arledge admirer.

Chris Schenkel I couldn't have either. In appeasing Walter Byers, I'd pledged his services exclusively to the NCAA.

When choice number three, L.A. Dodgers voice Vin Scully wisely declined, partly because of travel, partly because of Howard ("He's a roomful all by himself," Scully said), I realized I had another candidate right in our midst, the more so after I'd decided to alter the play-by-play role. Although I didn't tell them so, I knew I couldn't rely on Howard or Don to give viewers the facts of what was going on in the game. Keith Jackson was my answer. Keith was a rolling-voiced, Georgia farm boy I'd used on *Wide World* assignments, and he'd done stock cars as well as NCAA football. Among other attributes, he had a majorly impressive voice, and he was loud enough—and unflappable enough—to be heard over Howard.

I had another secret weapon—Chet Forte, the most gifted and innovative sports director I ever worked with. Another character too, I should say. Chet had been a first-string all-American basketball star at Columbia (named AP Player of the Year—at five-nine, mind you), and he was as addicted a gambler as I've ever known (which, years later, despite countless warnings, would oblige me to fire him), but he had a great and innovative flair for broadcasting sports. Among other things, he would later invent the reverse-angle shot, which is now commonplace in football telecasts. Chet would arm his *Monday Night Football* crews with handheld portables to roam the sidelines (there'd be eavesdropping parabolic mikes to go with them), and two others stuck mounted on top of field-level carts that would move with the action. We'd also have a second unit, with its own crew and production truck, dedicated solely to instant replays and slow motion. I wanted Chet to capture every grunt, groan, smack, and hit.

We used the Detroit–Kansas City preseason game as a full-scale dress rehearsal, and right away, Don had problems. He was talking in clichés ("Hello, football fans everywhere"), using ten sentences to say what could be said in three, analyzing the obvious ("Bango, look at those two guards pull out"), and, because he hadn't done his homework, having a tough time keeping track of who was whom and on which team. What was driving him crazier than anything, though, was Chet Forte sulphurously noting same.

"Fuck this," Don said, throwing down his earpiece. "These guys are crazy."

He was uncharacteristically down as we ran the tape the next day, going over everybody's mistakes. Unbeknownst to us, Don was flying home that night to attend to a personal family matter.

"Look, fellas," he said, getting up after another critique, "this really isn't my bag, and I don't even know that much about football. I only know the X's and O's Mr. Landry taught me in Texas. So ah'll just leave."

Howard caught him on the sidewalk, trying to hail a cab for Kennedy, and persuaded him to have a drink at the nearby Warwick

Hotel. There—this was according to Howard, mind you—he delivered a two-hour pep talk, concluding: "Look, Don, I know you're feeling down, but people are going to love you. And I'm going to have to suffer being the villain—the guy who is telling it like it is. I'll get all the heat, you'll get all the light, and in the long run we are both going to win. You'll wear the white hat and I'll wear the black hat. If you leave now, you're crazy. You can be a star!" To which Don replied: "By gol, Ha'ard, you're right. I'm with you!"

According to Don, the chat was closer to twenty minutes, and boiled down to Howard providing polysyllabic encouragement to keep his chin up. Whatever, Don was in the booth September 21, 1970, when we debuted in Cleveland, with the Browns playing the Jets, before a record crowd of 85,703.

Howard set the scene: "It is a hot . . . sultry . . . almost windless night here at Municipal Stadium . . ."

He brought out the opposing stars: "The extraordinary running back, number forty-four, Leroy Kelly of the Browns . . . the premier quarterback, number twelve, Joe Willie Namath, of the Jets . . ."

And *Monday Night Football* was off and running—with those dazzling, unforgettable images I'd always imagined, the helmets gleaming, the colors of the uniforms magically bright against the bright green carpet of the turf, and the cheerleaders, the fans roaring, the mysterious darkness of night beyond the brilliant stadium lights, and Keith's steady, intelligent commentary punctuated by the comic relief of the best pair since Gallagher and Sheen.

It all came off marvelously well. Howard modeled his black hat by narrating a tape of Don's worst Cowboy moments, and "Dandy," as Howard dubbed him, showed off his white hat by yucking along. There was teasing (Howard: "As long as Cleveland keeps possession, Namath can't score"; Don: "You got a point there, Howard"), and good lines (Meredith on pass interference: "I don't know what it is, but it's a no-no"), and artful camera work (replays in slo-mo and stop action; split screens to show receivers and defenders; contested calls examined in multiple angles), and one utterly memorable shot.

"Look at Namath!" I shouted in the mobile truck. I'd just spotted him on a monitor, right after he'd thrown a last-minute, game-losing interception. "Get it!" I shouted at Forte. "Look at Namath! Take it! Take it!" The air camera fixed on the figure standing frozen on the sidelines, head down, hands on his hips, shoulders hunched, a Goya of an athlete in defeat.

The critics loved the image, and most liked the show, which Pete Axthelm of *Newsweek* said had "more imagination and fewer clichés than any football telecast in memory." Howard was something else. "The master of the verbal cheap shot," they wrote. "Wretched prattle . . . Towering ignorance of football." Then the mail came in, sacks and sacks of it. Not letters that began, "In my opinion," but started, "We, the undersigned," and ended with three hundred names. More than one in three Americans who'd turned on television had watched *Monday Night Football*, and, in Howard Cosell, they'd found the man they loved to hate.

"You worried about all the controversy?" asked one of the reporters clogging the phone lines.

"*Worried?*" I said. "That's exactly what I'm looking for!"

The next call was from Leonard's secretary, requesting my presence in Mr. Goldenson's office.

He was with Elton Rule when I went in, and from their mien, congratulations were not on the agenda. Leonard reported that he'd just gotten off the phone with Henry Ford II, and that the network's leading advertiser was most distressed about my color man. "Get that guy Cosell off" had been his exact words. "He's hogging all the time. He talks so much I can't enjoy the football game."

I knew what was being asked for, but I wasn't going to give it.

"Howard's fine," I said. "It's only been one show. The audience needs to get to know him."

Leonard looked worried, but he didn't order me to fire Howard, I guess because he knew I'd refuse. At the same time, I decided not to tell Howard, who was already leaving hysterical messages, pleading with me to stop the "$180-a-week mediocrities"—his description of all sportswriters—from slandering him. Disclosing what Ford had said might make him quit. It certainly wouldn't improve his performance.

My concern about Howard's fragility was confirmed the very next week, when Kansas City played the Colts. Shortly before halftime, the Chiefs' running back Mike Garrett hobbled to the bench with an injury. "Dandy, there's little Mike on the sidelines," Howard said. "But he's a tough little cookie. He'll be back quickly."

"What if he doesn't come back?" I snapped into Howard's earpiece.

"People are laying for you, and that's the kind of thing that's going to get you in trouble."

By way of an answer, Howard stayed mute the rest of the night—something he did sporadically in the future. Whenever any of us criticized him, this was his way, however childish, of punishing us for it. He simply closed down.

The reviews that time—noting Garrett's failure to reappear—were as withering as week one, and at dinner with Don and Keith before the Bears-Lions game in Detroit, Howard announced he'd had it.

"*I'm* not coming back," he said.

Keith, mad about not getting more airtime, said he wasn't either. Not Don, though; a columnist had just called him "the brightest thing to hit TV since color."

"The ol' cowboy, he's coming back," he said. "I got nothing better to do that pays me so much."

There was no talk of quitting after Detroit, because everything that could go right that night, did. Howard was at his best again, we buried Bob Hope and Jack Paar specials on NBC, and Mr. Ford called Leonard again.

"I want to apologize," he said. "I like the patter that's going on between Cosell and Meredith."

Meanwhile a *TV Guide* poll pronounced Howard the most hated—and the most *liked*—sportscaster in the United States. At a bar in the South, patrons were chipping in to buy an old TV every week, then drawing lots; when Howard appeared, the winner got to blast the set with a shotgun. So many turned out for a "Why I Hate Howie" lunch at a Texas hotel, a second ballroom had to be opened. A Buddy Hackett joke made the rounds: "There have always been mixed emotions about Howard Cosell. Some people hate him like poison, and some people hate him regular." Even death threats started coming in; it was not unusual for FBI agents to show up in the announcers' booth because of them.

I was soothing Howard three and four times a day, but it didn't always work. In Minnesota for a Vikings game, he grabbed a Rozelle aide and denounced the NFL for his troubles. Then he collared me, and blamed ABC. Pete Rozelle heard and came to Howard's apartment to try to calm him. "Just have fun with the game," he implored.

Then, the following week, Baltimore at Green Bay, it was Meredith's turn again. "I'm going back to New York," he said to Howard, "and have it out with all of them," this after I'd probably criticized him one time too many. "I'm getting out of this thing."

Then, in Dallas, Texas, we all got back together again. I sat down with Don and told him this was his best shot, the one we'd all been waiting for. He knew the Cowboys inside and out. Many of them had been his team-mates. This—the Cowboys against the St. Louis Cards—was where we expected his insider knowledge and analytic brilliance to shine. And by the time he went on the air that night, Don was loaded for analytic bear.

But the Cowboys had a different idea. Without anybody anticipating it, they were on their way from the opening kickoff to one of the worst thrashings in their history, one utterly beyond explaining. And Don Meredith was absolutely magnificent, in a totally unexpected way.

"I don't know what the heck they're doing down there," he mourned, "but I've never seen anything like it in my life."

The worse it got for the Cowboys, the more Howard needled him, and the more Don moaned.

"Roger Staubach is now four for four in the passing department," he said, after an interception. "He's completed two to his team, and two to the other."

By halftime, it was 21-0, and Don was saying, "You don't know what trouble is till you're down 21-0 in the Cotton Bowl," and the crowd was looking up to the announcers' booth and chanting, "We want Meredith! We want Meredith!"

"I'm not going down there on a night like this," Don said.

The final score was 38 to 0, a blowout that should have had TV sets turned off coast to coast. Instead, we kept our biggest audience of the year, and beat a Johnny Carson special. Howard, the smart-aleck New Yorker, and Dandy, the aw-shucks cowboy who puts him down, were enshrined, and a principle was proved: The show was bigger than the game.

For an encore, Howard got pie-eyed on national television.

I knew he'd had a martini or two or three at the hospitality suite in Philadelphia before the Giants game; "my silver bullets," Howard called them. What I was not cognizant of was that chilling in the large fire bucket beside Howard in the booth was an entire bandolier bestowed by Eagles owner Leonard Tose. This only became evident early in the second quarter, when Howard began experiencing difficulty in completing sentences.

"What the hell is the matter?" I asked Chet, sitting a few rows in front of me.

He spun around. "The son of a bitch is drunk!"

Any doubts on that score vanished when, shortly before the end of the first half, Howard pitched forward and threw up on Dandy Don's brand-new cowboy boots.

I hoped a halftime cup of coffee would sober him up, but when Howard tried to announce the score after the weekly highlights package, Philadelphia came out "Full-aaahhh-dull-phhee-aaahhh." That was enough for me. I put him in a limo for New York, told him to go home and sleep it off, and in the morning, I had a statement put out that Howard had suffered a reaction to flu medication.

The press swallowed it, but Howard was not contrite. "*Drunk?*" he huffed when I told him that was the consensus of the overnight calls. Why, he'd never been inebriated a day in his life. A "virulent virus" had struck him, a malady so ferocious, Howard said, "I thought I'd had a stroke and was dying."

Not just a virus, I thought, hanging up. A *virulent* virus. Only Cosell could come up with that.

I hadn't planned to attend the next game, in Atlanta, but *Sports Illustrated* was reporting that Howard was about to be fired, and the flag needed to be shown. After the events in Philadelphia, Howard was also in need of handholding. He was convinced I was going to fire him, absolutely sure "they" were going to get him. I stayed glued to his side before and during the telecast, and shielded him from recurrences of the virulent "virus"; Howard had one of his strongest nights.

As the season wound to a close, the press filled with stories of *Monday Night Football* as a cultural phenomenon. Bowling leagues, it was reported, were switching their nights to Tuesdays, and PTAs were rescheduling Monday meetings. Restaurants were also closing Monday nights, and business at those that remained open was down 25 percent. The NFL was getting letters from women (40 percent of our audience, some weeks), thanking *Monday Night Football* for saving their marriages, and, in Miami, a community college was offering a course aimed at females entitled "Understanding and Enjoying *Monday Night Football*." The worst sick-out day in the auto industry, for decades Monday, was now Tuesday. New

York cops said Monday-night crimes were down 16 percent, because there were fewer out to commit them. For process servers, though, Monday night had become the busiest time of the week: Defendants were all at home. To counter nose-diving movie attendance on Monday night, theater chains were cutting prices and offering free snacks. A Seattle hospital even attempted to ban births between the hours of seven and ten P.M. on Mondays.

"It's all because of me," Howard crowed. I thought maybe a few others had made contributions, but Howard was feeling too good to say so. By the end of the season, his hate mail had trailed off, he was booked to do guest shots on *Nanny and the Professor* and *The Partridge Family* and in growing danger of being beloved. Don wasn't threatening departure anymore either. He had forty-seven after-dinner speeches to deliver in the next three months, and after that, an Emmy to accept for "Best Performance in Sports Programming."

This last made Howard absolutely nuts.

As for me, I believed we could be better.

Keith Jackson had done all I'd asked and more in the circumscribed role I'd imposed on him. But for Season II, I thought we needed a larger personality in a larger part. With all the dust Howard's comments about "dumb trades" and players' "God-given organizing rights" had kicked up among team owners, I also thought *Monday Night Football* could stand the addition of a respected member of the football establishment. A former New York Giant of my acquaintance whose CBS contract was up met the criteria.

It was a mark of Frank that he instructed his lawyer to accept anything I offered. It was a mark of the lawyer, Ron Konecky, that he told me so. Gifford took over expanded play-by-play duties, Konecky became my attorney.

Keith Jackson, I handled miserably.

He learned he was being dropped by reading about it in the newspaper, and he stormed into my office, furious. I hadn't talked to the reporter in question, but I'd procrastinated about informing Keith—no two ways about it—and word had leaked.

I did a mea culpa and apologized profusely. In fact, I had a far better fit in mind for Keith Jackson, one that I thought could—and did—make him much better known. That was lead announcer on NCAA football, and if I jumped the gun a bit, telling him that day, I'd already made up my mind. As it turned out, Keith became a virtual legend as a sports broadcaster because of his NCAA work, and the year he announced his retirement, his millions of fans protested—which brought him back for a season of encores. But the personal rupture between us was permanent, and all my doing.

In a way, though, I'd only compounded my troubles. Chris Schenkel had the job I was giving Keith. Chris and Jim McKay had been my first major hires at the network, all those years before, and no nicer a person ever worked at ABC Sports. But Chris's very decency had done him in. His determinedly noncritical announcing style, suited to a gentler era, was now making him the butt of jokes.

In Chris's case, I'd tried hard, even though I knew how much he hated the whole Howard Cosell school.

"You just have to change," I urged him during one of many conversations we'd had on the subject. "If somebody doesn't do something right on the field, you've got to say so."

"Sorry, Roone," came his answer. "I'm not about to knock some college kid just for dropping a pass or missing a block. They're just kids, like yours and mine. I can't change and I never will."

He was gentlemanly, as always, when I told him I was reducing his role, and he even thanked me warmly after I assured him that he'd continue to be indispensable to *Wide World*, the Olympics, and so much else. But the pain was in his eyes.

There are times when being a corporate manager in business really sucks. And if I say that fliply now, I do so simply to mask my own pain.

Onward.

Frank had had extensive experience on CBS's NFL coverage, but that had been as an analyst, not as a play-by-play man. He deserved a preseason toe-dipping before bathing in the Howard–Dandy Don cauldron, and the NFL Hall of Fame game in Canton, Ohio, seemed ideal for the purpose. It counted for nothing, occurred on a lazy August afternoon, was watched by few. The only unusual aspect of the 1971 contest was that Richard Nixon was going to be on hand to dedicate the league's new hall.

I'd already met the president two years before at the annual pre–Hall of Fame game banquet in New York. Bud Wilkinson had informed him of my travails on account of his visit to Razorback Stadium for the Texas-Arkansas title game, and, in recompense, I'd been invited to his suite at the Waldorf Towers.

I arrived that time to find a living room the size of an ice rink, but all it contained, to my astonishment, was an American flag, a presidential flag, and not a living human being. I was puzzling over the whereabouts of the more distinguished dozens I'd assumed would also be present, when Nixon walked in, pumped my hand, and launched into an immediate reprise of the 1932 Olympics in Los Angeles. He said he'd witnessed some of the events and even ticked off the winning split times in the quarter-mile. How considerate, I thought; he's trying to put me at ease. I began to wonder, though, after I asked about his China trip, when he started analyzing the Redskins instead and when urban policy, my next query, elicited a dissection of Jim Palmer's curveball. And so it went, for more than half an hour, until I realized, to my astonishment, that the stories of his insecurity were true and that all the Leader of the Free World wanted was to try to impress me!

Now, in 1971, I was alone again with him in Canton, Ohio, while Frank, who was about to make his *Monday Night Football* debut, was having makeup applied for a presidential interview.

"You know," Nixon said to me, "when Frank Gifford was playing with the Giants, I used to go to a lot of their games. And, after the games, Frank would have cocktail parties at his apartment, which was right near the stadium. I used to go there quite a bit. I was invited many times.

"I know Frank Gifford," he said authoritatively. "I'm sure he'll remember me."

Amazing!

Yes, Frank was indeed able to recall the identity of the president of the United States, and he did a fine interview. As nervous as I knew he was about his play-by-play debut, and aside from some player name and number fluffs, he nonetheless turned in a highly credible performance. Howard, however, was all over him, belittling every slip.

"Faultless Frank," he said after the telecast, was "an embarrassment," who owed employment to being part of the "jockocracy." When Howard volunteered to a reporter that it had been wrong to put Frank in Keith's place, I told him to knock it off or I'd run a reel of *his* mistakes. He complied—for a while, until he began complaining that, with my approval, Frank and Don were conspiring to make him look bad on the air!

In hindsight, I couldn't say which of them was the more insecure—Richard Nixon, president of the United States, or Howard Cosell!

Frank, mind you, had the ego strength to ignore Howard, while Don tried to jolly him into behaving. I simply got mad, even though I knew what was eating him. It wasn't Frank's stumbles, it was Frank himself: his ease and self-assurance, his status and connections, his appearance and grace. Everything Howard was not.

But the show was bigger than Howard's craziness too, and by the end of the second season, 30 million Americans were watching *Monday Night Football*—and the number was growing. Mayors and governors had begun staging parades when we came to town, and Howard Cosell was mobbed wherever he went. We had no competition anymore. CBS had killed *Mayberry R.F.D.* and moved Carol Burnett to a safer harbor; NBC was spending millions more on better movies but it didn't move their ratings. I had a tiger by the tail, and everything about ABC Sports was changing. Instead of finding Roone in the control room, there were "Roone Phones" everywhere, and they rang off the hook while I watched more shows on office television sets than in the mobile truck. We were hurtling toward Number One, and I found myself already missing some of the fun of the old days.

It was just as well then that another Summer Games was at hand to prepare for—our biggest and most elaborate yet. This was one event I wasn't going to miss. I'd produce every thrilling moment of it, and I couldn't wait for what they were already calling the "Olympics of Peace."

Any day now, I'd leave for Munich.

Munich

Growing up, I knew three things about the capital of Bavaria.

It was the place Hitler staged his beer hall *putsch,* where Neville Chamberlain negotiated "peace in our time," and where, every October, large-bosomed women in low-cut *dirndls* served many, many tankards of beer.

In 1968, I was about to learn a fourth: Securing the Summer Games of the XX Olympiad would not be so easy. Having just lost, at the time, the 1972 Winter Games to NBC—not a huge loss, mind you, for Sapporo, Japan, where they would be held, struck me as a good deal less magical than the Alps—I'd nonetheless resolved that my "child" would not be kidnapped again. Even before the rights to the Summer Games in Munich were put up for auction, I would make a preemptive $6.5 million strike—more than double the figure that had won Mexico City.

I called the Munich organizers immediately after the Mexico City Games—before I left the El Presidente hotel, in fact. But I was told to check back in a few months, as they were then preoccupied with planning facilities. Afterward, I learned that CBS—deterred by the millions NBC had dropped televising Tokyo in 1964—was passing on Munich, and that the chances of NBC itself making a bid were less than fifty-fifty. I began to think I might be able to shave a million or two from the $6.5.

Then, in early January 1969, as I was waiting for the elevator after one of Leonard Goldenson's monthly division-president meetings, Ellis Moore, the head of network PR, mentioned that he'd bumped into Carl Lindemann at a cocktail party the night before, and that Lindemann told him that he was leaving on a European trip in the morning.

"Carl say where he was going?" I asked, half interested.

"Yeah," Ellis said. "Munich."

I was amazed to find out so casually and easily. For my part, I was a nut on security, and if my opposite number at NBC had found out similarly where I was going, heads would have rolled at ABC.

I booked a flight that same afternoon.

Lindemann had come and gone by the time I arrived in Germany, but I wasn't overly worried. I doubted the rights would be sold before knowing what else was out there, and I thought I had a killer offer.

I was half right. The organizers were pleased to see me, but the blowing away had already been done by NBC with an offer of *$9.5 million.*

The good news was that the Muncheners had turned it down. The bad news was that they wanted bidding to begin at $30 million!

I knew they needed cash. Seeing the Olympics as symbolizing their reentry into the civilized world, the Germans were transforming the entire Munich cityscape. New subway and trolley lines were being laid, a Plexiglas-tented 80,000-seat stadium was going up, and, along with a welter of smaller, though no less shiny stadia and dromes, a state-of-the-art press center was being built, capacious enough to accommodate 4,000 journalists and 2,500 technicians. Presiding over it all would be a soaring TV tower. But the crown jewel was the Olympic Village, a terraced, lushly landscaped low-slung apartment complex, where 10,490 athletes from 120 countries were to be housed with their coaches and trainers. The total cost—including transplanting 3,000 half-century-old trees on the site, and relandscaping into an enchanting hillock park a giant trash heap of buildings destroyed by Allied bombing—was put at close to $2 billion. I admired the Germans' industry; I just wasn't going to finance it.

The next time around, NBC came in at just over $11 million, while I offered $10 million—the maximum we could spend, ABC's Sales department had calculated, without incurring a loss. But once again, the Germans sent us packing.

Back in New York, we simply had to figure out a way of pushing past the $10-million barrier, and it was Barry Frank who devised it: Expand coverage to sixty-seven hours, and for two plus weeks, take over *all* of prime time, where the largest loot was to be mined. Sell about 500 commercial minutes at an average cost of $48,000 each, and total revenue would be just shy of $24 million—enough to cover the cost of rights, facilities, and production, with a healthy profit left over.

With little to lose, given how our current prime-time schedule was then performing, Leonard approved the plan, and in April 1969, I flew to Munich for the showdown. NBC presented first, offering $12.5 million for rights and facilities, and advising the organizers to be leery of ABC. After all, hadn't we—the overall company—posted a $20-million loss the year before? Over lunch, I countered with the latest edition of Olympic coverage press reviews—we had scored consistent and quasiuniversal high marks—and noted that whatever my network's bottom line, ABC Sports had made millions in 1968. That seemed to satisfy the organizers, and I spent the rest of the meal amiably chatting with one of the senior officials on the organizing committee.

"Have you ever been to the States?" I asked him, congratulating him on the excellence of his English.

"Just once," he said. "I visited Bangor, Maine, and Texarkana, Texas."

"Gee," I said, "I wish you'd seen New York and California and the Rockies. How did you happen to choose such an odd combination?"

The official smiled. "At the time," he said, "I was a prisoner of war."

I nearly choked on my sauerbraten.

We toasted better days, however, and moved into the conference room to thrash out money. I said we'd reluctantly match NBC, but couldn't go a pfennig higher. The lead negotiator looked at his watch, announced he had a train to catch, and started stuffing papers into his attaché case. I tried to recall whether bluffing was a Teutonic trait.

"All right," I said. "Seven point five million for rights plus six million more for facilities. That's a million more than NBC."

The negotiator unsnapped his attaché case.

"*Sehr gut,*" he said.

The next three years were spent planning and building on a prime-time scale, which included augmenting coverage with the help of ABC News. I can't claim it was out of prescience, but I approached a young Canadian I knew whose reporting from the Middle East had impressed me, as had his reputation for having girlfriends from Baghdad to Benghazi. His name was Peter Jennings.

"How would you like to spend two nice weeks in beautiful Bavaria?" I asked, catching him at his Beirut apartment. "It'll give you a rest from Middle East politics."

Said Peter: "I could use the escape."

He talked to his bosses at News and got approval for the assignment.

The last detail, I remember, was testing the service at the newly built Sheraton Munich, where most of the senior staff, including Chris Schenkel, who'd be hosting, would be putting up for the Games. Associate producer Geoff Mason got the assignment of checking the wake-up calls, and he called the hotel operator.

"I'd like to leave two wake-up calls. One for seven, the other for seven-fifteen."

"Certainly, sir," the operator replied brightly. "And which would you like first?"

That aside, the Munich we came to in late August 1972, was new, fresh, sparkling, and what wasn't painted pastel was covered in flowers. Not a black boot was in sight; even the security officers were togged in cheery powder blue. The effect, Jim McKay said, was "more Hansel and Gretel than Hitler and Göring."

Jim, who'd be covering track and field and gymnastics, had brought along his teenagers Mary and Sean (Sean, I can't resist pointing out proudly, is now the president of CBS Sports), I had Betsey and Susie with me, and most of the ABC executives, including Leonard, had come with their wives. It was—or so my daughters said, while I dragged off to bed each dawn—the most fun Olympics yet.

And, from the start, the most eventful. Rick DeMont, a fifteen-year-old California swimmer, lost a gold medal in the 400-meter freestyle when testing detected a stimulant in his asthma medication. Bob Seagren, the American world record holder in the pole vault, had his favorite pole swiped on the eve of the competition—the result of, he said, a conspiracy to award the gold medal to East Germany. More unfortunate still was the plight of Stan Wright, an assistant U.S. track coach, who had to undergo a nationally televised interrogation by Howard Cosell. "Inquisition" would be a better word. Two of Wright's runners lost their chance at Olympic glory because Wright had misread the event schedule. "An American tragedy," Howard intoned, as he lambasted the hapless coach, an eminently decent black man who was stricken enough without Howard's help.

But then there was little Olga.

"You gotta see this girl," Doug Wilson, who was producing and directing women's gymnastics, said into my headset on the second day of competition. "There's never been a Russian like this. Hell, there's never been anyone like this!"

I punched up the monitor to see why Doug was so excited—and flying on the uneven bars, there she was, all four-eleven, ninety-two pounds of her, blond hair tied back with bright bows, eyes dancing like a teenager going to her first prom, impossibly big smile exploding from a pretty pixie's face.

"*Who* is that?" I asked Doug.

"Olga Korbut," came his answer. "Soviet Union. Seventeen-year-old. Last-minute replacement. She's hardly competed before internationally, but, God, look at her!"

She was an amazement—"like a little kid playing in the sun," Jim McKay said—and the crowd went crazy, watching her tricks.

"What do you think she'll get for a mark?" Jim asked Gordon Maddox, our expert commentator. Ten, I should point out, was the perfect score in gymnastics.

"I'd give her an eleven!" Gordon exclaimed.

"She's our story," I said to Doug, mindful too that, at the height of the Cold War, détente was in the air. "Follow her."

We did for three days, and the tight-focused images of Olga—beaming in victory, collapsing weeping into her coach's arms in defeat, three gold medals in all—made a previously obscure sport a television obsession and launched the gymnastics craze among teenage girls in America and, presumably, the world over.

Coverage Tuesday, September 5, ended at four A.M., Munich time, on Wednesday, September 6. The Broadcast Center cleared out quickly, and by the time I finished working my way through a stack of accumulated mail, I was alone in the building. Bone weary, I walked out the rear door, to the parking lot, where my driver was waiting to take me back to the hotel. The moon was up and gorgeous, and the stadium was still ablaze with light. Here and there, lights also peeked from the Olympic Village, directly in front of me. Parties still in progress, I smiled to myself.

"Have you ever seen a more beautiful night?" I said to the driver. "Let's just stay a little and take it in."

It was magical, I thought: the night, the scene, the idea that here, of all places, the world could come together in sport and peace.

It occurred to me to walk the perimeter of the lot. Good thing I didn't. Instead, I took a deep mouthful of air and then climbed into the car. As we turned out of the lot, our headlights swept over a grassy area and caught the lip of a shallow ravine in front of the fence that surrounded the Olympic Village. Not until later would I learn that hidden there at that moment were eight hooded men seeking neither sport nor peace.

I had told my daughters not to wake me till at least nine, and to hold the calls that had interrupted sleep three nights running. Once, it had been a Cosell hater, babbling the usual. Another time, it had been an Arkansas viewer, bitching that his local station was running the Olympics instead of a minor league baseball game. How they'd found me I have no idea. The night before, I'd picked up the phone to hear someone going, "Hello, Roone, *boo-boo be-doo*," a bad impersonation, I thought, of Bing Crosby. But it really was Bing, who'd wanted tickets so he could watch Mark Spitz go for his seventh swimming gold. I got him his tickets, but even Bing I didn't want to hear from on this night. No calls; no exceptions.

As I tumbled into bed, the men who'd been concealed in the ravine outside the broadcast center were making their way through the Olympic Village to number 31 Connollystrasse, headquarters of the Israeli team. Faces blackened by shoe polish, automatic weapons and grenades slung to their sides, they were members of Black September, a militant splinter group of the Palestinian al Fatah.

Shortly after four-thirty—that is, less than ten minutes after I'd been less than fifty yards away from them—the terrorists entered the building. In the ensuing melee, a handful of Israelis managed to escape, two—a coach and a trainer—were cut down trying to resist, and nine others, mostly members of the wrestling squad, were taken hostage, including David Berger, a Columbia Law School graduate from Shaker Heights, Ohio.

A cleaning woman who heard shots notified authorities, and within half an hour, battalions of police were cordoning off the Olympic Village. Several of the arriving officers went to the Israeli building, where a terrorist dropped a note from a window demanding the release of 234 Palestinian prisoners, along with Andreas Baader and Ulrike Meinhof, leaders of Germany's infamous Baader-Meinhof Gang. If they weren't freed by nine A.M., the note said, hostages would begin to be shot. To show they meant business, the terrorists brought a mutilated, near-naked corpse to the balcony and flung it at the policemen's feet.

The first ABC Sports executive to learn what had happened was European engineering-operations director Jacques Lesgards, who arrived at the tech bungalow at seven A.M. to begin readying the day's coverage. It was to be a light schedule. No track and field events were on, and Jim McKay was taking the day off—his first in four months. Jacques would be working as always, though. He was Mr. Able-to-Do-Anything, including get credentials for every Olympics, even a photo ID, for his "assistant," Bertrand—a twenty-one-inch stuffed rabbit that went everywhere with him.

At the door, Jacques was met by Jean Adami, an ABC telephone operator who'd picked up a mangled version of the takeover.

"Something terrible is going on," she choked out. "They say a Russian has been killed in the Olympic Village and a shot went through the German television people's cafeteria."

Lesgards calmed her down and gave a walkie-talkie to Dave McCabe, an American living in Munich who'd been hired as an assistant. Go to the Village, he ordered; find out what's happening. McCabe radioed in the truth a few minutes later, and Lesgards had Adami start to alert staff while he prepared the dispatch of a mobile "flash unit," a small van with one or two cameras that we'd decided to bring along—"Just in case of the unexpected," as I'd put it to Jacques. By the time the van was ready, though, police had sealed off the Village to the press. Lesgards spotted an ice-cream truck parked near the press center. What could seem more innocent? Three hundred deutschemarks got the flash unit plastered with signs advertising cold delights, and the cops waved it through the gate.

The AP wire, meanwhile, was reporting the killing of one, possibly two, Israeli athletes. Jacques ripped the copy from the wire machine and called the Sheraton barbershop, where Marvin Bader, ABC's Olympics logistics chief since Innsbruck, was having his daily shampoo. Marvin tore the towels from his neck and ran to his car. Jacques had already broken down the door to his office and was passing out credentials and high-powered Telefunken walkie-talkies when Marvin arrived.

"We need bodies," Lesgards yelled. "Start making calls."

Marvin dialed John Wilcox, one of our producers. "Find your crews," he said. "Get them over here." Then he called our suite, where Susie answered and dutifully relayed my instructions.

"Your father's gonna want this call," Marvin said. "Wake him."

"This better be good," I yawned, coming on the line.

"It's the worst fucking thing you can imagine," he replied.

Marvin told me as much as he knew, and what had been geared up thus far. I told him to find McKay first thing. I wanted Jim to host. And then Cosell and Jennings, and to get them into the Village.

"How about Schenkel?" Marvin asked.

"I'll talk to Chris," I said. "And one more thing, Marvin. Have Jacques call New York and book as many satellite hours as we can get."

I was putting on my pants when the phone rang again, Jacques saying we could have "the bird" starting at one P.M. I said I'd be over in twenty minutes, then called Leonard Goldenson in his hotel suite, where he'd been laid low by a high fever the day before. He gasped when I told him about the Israelis.

"I'd like to stay live till this thing's over," I said. "I'll need the network."

"You got it," he said.

I walked to the window and looked out in the direction of the Olympic Village, so peaceful just a few hours before. Now blue-light flashing police cars were streaming toward it.

At the Broadcast Center, Marvin greeted me with the news that the Germans had talked the terrorists into extending their deadline until eleven in order to give Golda Meir's government in Jerusalem time to consider their demands. The Germans, I knew, were just stalling; Israel never gave in to terrorists, and with Dachau nine miles up the road, it sure wouldn't here. I told Don Ohlmeyer to move two of the four studio cameras onto a pedestrian walkway just outside the broadcast center, where they'd have a straight shot at 31 Connollystrasse, then reviewed our deployments with Jacques and Geoff Mason.

Jim Flood of production services had sneaked walkie-talkies into the Village and was rendezvousing with Cosell and Jennings at the Plaza of Nations, a couple of hundred yards from where the Israelis were being held. Marvin's secretary, Gladys Deist, had told the head of the graphic arts department to start phonying up credentials, and was in the process of buying or borrowing all the Olympic uniforms she could get her hands on. Gary Slaughter, another American living in Munich hired as a temp, was carrying film and supplies in and out of the Village posing as a member of the U.S. track team. Gary had a good disguise: He was black, looked like an athlete, and his credentials—acquired while working with the U.S. runners prior to the Games—were the real thing. Dave McCabe, whose face was a map of Ireland, was having a tougher time; the only uniform he could find was from Pakistan.

"Anyone get hold of McKay?" I asked.

"We sent his driver over to the Sheraton to tell him he's on standby," Geoff said. "But that was more than an hour ago. I expected to hear from him by now."

A production assistant waved one of the console phones. "For you, Geoff. It's McKay."

"Tell him he's gonna anchor," I said, "and to get over here."

Jim turned up shortly. He'd taken a sauna and an icy shower and had just slipped on yellow swimming trunks for a dip in the Sheraton's pool when he'd seen a phone and, on impulse, had called in.

"Glad you did," I said. "You may have a long day coming up."

Actually, I doubted that. The hostage taking seemed like a bank holdup gone bad, and with Germany's image to the world now at stake, I figured the Germans would have the situation quickly under control. So I'd told Schenkel before coming over. Take it easy, I'd said to him on the phone, you'll be on in prime time, same as always.

As our reports came in, though, I started to wonder. Once again, the terrorists had pushed back their deadline, to one P.M. If Israel didn't accede to their demands by then, they vowed to publicly execute two hostages "so the whole world can see." It was now approaching twelve-thirty, and while there had been no public announcement from Jerusalem, rumors were spreading that Meir and her cabinet had voted to hold fast.

Our preparations were in place. The long lenses of the cameras on the rise brought the third-floor balcony of the Israeli quarters so close, I could almost count the buttons on the safari jacket of an Arab in a white hat—the terrorists' leader, I guessed—patrolling back and forth. In addition, we had the use of two cameras—one belonging to us, the other to German television—stationed on top of the 950-foot television tower in the middle of the Olympic complex. From there, they could peer down on anything that might happen on the roof of 31 Connollystrasse and the surrounding buildings. Cosell and Jennings were also in position. Howard, who'd gotten past security by stripping off his yellow ABC Sports blazer and claiming to be a Puma shoe salesman, was near an underpass that separated the Italian and Burmese buildings, across the street from the Israeli quarters, while Peter had charmed his way into one of the upper stories of the Italian building, where he'd hidden in a bathroom when the police swept the Village for reporters. And now he had a clear view of 31 Connollystrasse, as well as the street where German negotiators had been doing their talking all morning. He was also the only one among us who, thanks to his being stationed in Beirut, had detailed knowledge of the terrorist groups.

John Wilcox had the best vantage point of all. After being roused by Bader, he'd met up with Willi Schaeffler, our Bavarian-born film crew supervisor, and, in another life, head coach of the U.S. Alpine ski team. John had donned Willi's ski uniform, filled an athletic bag with camera equipment and a walkie-talkie, and gained entrance to the Burmese building by telling the guard he was an American boxer on the way to see his coach. He'd then gone to the balcony of an unlocked third-floor apartment. Directly across from him on another balcony not fifty feet away, a Black September terrorist cradling an AK-47 puffed on a cigarette. John had tiptoed back inside without being seen, and ever since had been radioing in reports that gave new meaning to "up close and personal."

The only question now was whether we would open coverage with a shot of two executions. I watched the clock tick down. Then Jim was on. I heard no shots. But I would be in his ear for the next fourteen hours.

The terrorists, convinced by the Germans that their demands were about to be met (in fact, Israel had rejected any prisoner release more than an hour before), had pushed back the deadline yet again. Zero hour now was three P.M.

Two more hours of waiting. Every producing instinct in me shrieked to fill the time with studio interviews and background reports, but I remembered that certain Sunday morning in November 1963, the one I've already mentioned when Lee Harvey Oswald was being led out in the basement of the Dallas jail and ABC wasn't there.

"Stay on the balcony," I instructed. "And don't leave it."

Jim Spence, who'd started as a production assistant with Scherick and was now my vice president of Planning and Administration, came in, saying that at the volleyball arena next door, the match between Germany and Japan was still going strong. I had all but forgotten about the Games. I assumed they'd been suspended.

"Are you sure?" I asked.

"I just watched a few minutes of it myself," Jim said. "Gotta be three thousand Germans in there, going nuts."

I guess I shouldn't have been surprised. For eighty-one-year-old Avery Brundage, who was taking his long overdue retirement at the conclusion of the Games, the Olympics superseded all—certainly a couple of dead Jews.

Meanwhile, Howard was calling in other odd happenings. Though the press was still barred from the Village, kids were scrambling over the security fence and hunting for athletes' autographs. A good number of the athletes themselves had turned out to watch the proceedings, and some of them were lazing and sunbathing outside. Sightseers were gathering and *wurst mit sauerkraut* vendors were doing a brisk business. ABC commerce went on as well. Marty Starger, head of the Entertainment division, had someone call to ask if I'd be attending the cocktail reception for advertisers that night!

I conveyed regrets.

The day slowly settled into a strange routine. Jim described events on the monitor while eating popcorn. Reports drifted in. The Germans, who lacked a rescue squad of their own, had turned down an offer from the Israelis to send in the world's most experienced. Brundage had told security officials that, as a Chicago native, he was expert on criminal matters and advised the use of the Windy City PD's instant knockout gas. (The Germans checked; no such gas existed.) After an expression of public outrage from Golda Meir, Brundage finally agreed to suspend competition—though not until late in the afternoon and only for twenty-four hours, retroactive to noon. There would be a morning memorial service at the Olympic Stadium, but the Games would resume afterward. Teams from Arab countries were heading home. Worried he'd be a target, Mark Spitz, the Games's most prominent Jew, had left already, with three German bodyguards.

I passed each new scrap into Jim's earpiece, following the pattern we'd developed over many programs: phrases, not sentences; soft, not loud; encouragement, not alarm.

Inwardly, though, I'd begun to be alarmed. The three o'clock deadline had passed, and there'd been no shots but also no announcement of a deal. I told Marvin Bader, who'd made many well-placed friends during the nearly three years he'd been in Munich, to work his sources. He called a contact in the Olympic press office. The Germans had promised something to get the deadline moved to five o'clock, but he couldn't find out what. He made another call, to a Lufthansa ticket agent he knew out at Reim, Munich's main airport. There was no sign that the terrorists were about to be flown out.

An hour and a half dragged by. Peter was relating the history of Black September on the air; how it had acquired its name (from the month, in 1970, when King Hussein drove Yassir Arafat's guerillas from Jordan); the number and location of previous attacks. The "commandos," in Peter's judgment, were unlikely to shed more blood.

I kept watching the monitor and the clock. At 4:50, ten minutes before the latest deadline, I saw movement on the roofs of the buildings around the Israeli quarters. Men in track suits were creeping across them. They weren't athletes; athletes don't carry sniper rifles. At 5:10, other men appeared, also in track suits, crawling toward the ventilator shafts of 31 Connollystrasse. They had short-barreled automatic weapons, the kind that are used for close, interior combat.

Jim narrated the action:

"One of the terrorists is at the door of the balcony . . . a balcony not too unlike the one Martin Luther King Jr. walked on and met his death. . . . His head is sticking out. You might wonder, why doesn't a sniper take off that head right now? Well, presumably his colleagues are inside and they would execute their hostages if that was done. Therein lies the problem. . . .

"There you see an athlete holding a canvas bag in which is obviously a machine gun. He's not an athlete, he's a policeman. And the bulletproof vest quite apparent there in the stiff-appearing front he has. There you see a gun being removed from its bag. . . .

"There's that head at the door again. It's become such a terribly tantalizing symbol. . . . What's going on inside that head? In that mind?

"A man on the roof in a red athletic suit. We now see just the tip of his head, he seems to be inching forward. See the arrow? We're placing that arrow superimposed in our studio over the live picture. It's just a little bit to the left of the point of that arrow. That man in the red athletic suit has a gun with him. It would appear that some sort of operation is under way very, very slowly and delicately."

Howard reported in: "More cars pulling up beneath the underpass . . . police getting out . . . submachine guns and pistols plainly visible."

Then Wilcox: "They can shoot the Arab guard dead, *at will*. He's an open target."

Then Peter: "I have a strong feeling this is going to turn out badly."

I heard a commotion in the back of the control room and turned around to see Geoff Mason arguing with a couple of German police.

"*Offenzie*," they were shouting, gesturing at the tower camera monitor, which was showing officers getting into firing positions on the roofs. Geoff, who'd picked up some pidgin German in his many Munich trips, was gesturing back and arguing. Suddenly, one of the cops stuck a submachine gun at Geoff's chest.

"*Offen-zie!*" he shouted.

The dispute was whether the terrorists inside the village could watch on television everything that was going on around them. I'd repeatedly asked that question myself and had been reassured that they couldn't. The Germans didn't care: they wanted the tower camera turned off altogether. In the end, after laborious negotiation, we reached a compromise: The tower camera could stay on but the feed to Europe was shut down.

Meanwhile, the police on the rooftops froze in their places, as if awaiting instructions. Marvin got word of a new deadline: six P.M.. At a quarter of, New York called. I listened, stunned, then whispered to Jim.

"We seem to have a technical problem," he told our audience imperturbably. "It looks like from now we're going to lose the satellite that is carrying these electronic pictures to you in your homes in the United States of this live, tense atmosphere. We will, of course, be recording whatever happens, and Peter Jennings and I will continue our commentary on ABC radio. This is Jim McKay in Munich, Germany, returning you to Lem Tucker in New York."

The unbelievable had just happened. All day long, it turned out, CBS had been pleading to share our Munich feed, and all day long an ABC News deskman had been turning them down. I'd long since sent back word that of course we had to give it to them—it was a breaking news story of national importance. But the deskman, unbeknownst to us, had held his ground: Why should we give up our exclusivity? Now, when we needed to be live most, CBS was paying us back by using their pre-booked satellite time to transmit . . . the tape of a day-old British soccer game!

The minute I found out about it, I overruled the desk and we gave CBS our feed, but in the interim, I held my breath against the worst. What if it were Jack Ruby time all over again? Then, moments before it seemed that the police were about to storm the building, the Germans told the terrorists that two helicopters would be provided to transport them and their hostages to Fürstenfeldbruck, an out-of-the-way NATO air base, where a Lufthansa 727 would be waiting to fly them to the country of their choosing.

We were back on the "bird," when, a few minutes after ten P.M., the terrorists herded the bound and blindfolded Israelis into a bus for the drive to the helicopter landing site on the far side of Olympic Village. Our flash unit caught the choppers as they rose into the air and turned in our direction, at the broadcast center. For once, I wanted to see history through more than a camera, and I ran outside to where I could hear the sirens, see the flashing lights, and watch them pass overhead, two, dark, terror-filled, insectlike shapes beating into the unknown.

New York was waiting for me in the control room. Time for the local evening news was coming up in the east, they said, and all our affiliates were screaming to go on the air with their biggest money earner. We had no cameras at Fürstenfeldbruck, of course, and we were only filling. The affiliates wanted the network back. If there was word during the next hour, we could break in.

I had Geoff radio Howard that he could take a break and tell Peter to grab a quick shower, then come to the studio to sit in with Jim, who'd now been on the air for ten hours—swimsuit still under his pants. As I took off my glasses to rub my eyes, Chris Schenkel turned up.

God Almighty. I'd simply forgotten about him. With everything that had been going on, I hadn't spoken to him all day.

"Is there room for me?" he said.

I knew I should say no, but I couldn't bring myself to.

"Of course there is," I lied. "I was just going to call. I want you in with Jim when we go back on."

He knew I was lying, and I knew he knew, and in my discomfort I pleaded need of a men's room. I ducked out into the corridor, and there—

to my absolute astonishment—I bumped into a lone man who was pacing back and forth. I'd seen his craggy face a thousand times before, but never so anguished. But what made the moment unalterably incredible was that here, in the heart of Germany, when the whole Olympic Village was like an armed camp, he had no security with him, no guards, no entourage of any sort.

"It must be a terrible day for your country," I said to him.

"It's a terrible day for the world," Willi Brandt, the chancellor of Germany, replied.

True to my métier, I got him to promise us an interview in the morning, after which I wished him good luck and returned to the control room to await developments. At 11:31, the Reuters machine rang five times—stop-press, flash.

"ALL ISRAELI HOSTAGES HAVE BEEN FREED."

No details, just that.

I hesitated. I wanted to call New York, but I wanted confirmation first. Jim, meanwhile, was taping an interview with Konrad Ahlers, spokesman for the West German government.

"As far as we can now see," Ahlers said, "the police action was perfect. Of course, it is an unfortunate interruption of the Olympic Games, but if all comes out as we hope it will come out or has come out, I think it will be forgotten after a few weeks."

Not long thereafter, though, the AP issued a more ominous report. It quoted an Olympic spokesman as saying that a gun battle had erupted between police and terrorists during a rescue attempt at the airport. Three of the terrorists were dead, another had committed suicide, and several others had escaped. A policeman had also been killed, and three others were wounded. The fate of the hostages was unknown, but the spokesman said, "We are afraid that the information given out so far is too optimistic."

I called New York immediately and said we needed air.

Jim opened with the latest:

"The word we get from the airport is that quote 'All hell has broken loose out there,' that there is still shooting going on. There was a report of a burning helicopter. But it all seems to be confusion. Nothing is nailed down. We have no idea what has happened to the hostages."

Jennings arrived, then Lou Cioffi, one of ABC News's key European correspondents, who happened to have been on vacation in southern Germany. I'd been told Cioffi had gone to Fürstenfeldbruck, but I hadn't heard from him all night.

"I thought you were at the airport," I said to him.

"I was. But I couldn't get near what was going on."

"Why not?"

"They've got the whole place cordoned off. The German military. I heard automatic-weapons fire, then an explosion—it was one of the helicopters—and you could see a column of white smoke."

"Is there still fighting going on?"

"That's what I heard on the radio, coming in. The roads are clogged. Everyone and their brother and sister is going out there."

"Why are you here?" I asked.

"I thought you'd want me on the air," he said.

For nearly two hours, mind you, I'd been trying to find out what was happening at Fürstenfeldbruck, and the ABC News correspondent who was there not only hadn't bothered to call in, he'd *left*. My face went a shade pinker, and I started picking at my shirt, as if looking for lint. My opinion of News had just gone through the floor.

"Okay," I said with measured softness. "You go on with Peter at the next station ID."

The phone buzzed, Marvin Bader saying there was going to be a press conference at Olympic headquarters. The time wasn't set but he was going over, and he'd radio in if he picked up anything.

Howard materialized, fresh from Marty Starger's cocktail party.

"I want to go on," he shouted, busting in on all of us. "Got to be part of this story. Put me on, Arledge, I'm the only one who can tell it."

He leaned into my face. Four silver bullets minimum, I figured. Maybe five.

"Dirty bastards," he intoned. "They already killed six million of us. What's a few more?"

"No, Howard," I said. "We're in the middle of it. There's no place for you."

"C'mon!" he insisted raucously. "Put me on the air! Gotta get on!"

"*No*, Howard," I repeated, escorting him toward the door. "Trust me. You'll be the first to thank me in the morning."

Typical Cosell. I'd just saved his ass—it would have been a disaster if he'd gone on the air—but years later, he still brought the subject up, with enormous resentment toward me for having deprived him of his moment.

On the other hand, he did leave.

An hour went by with nothing from Marvin, and our people on the air were reduced to thumb sucking. What would Israel do to retaliate? How come Duane Bobick, America's Great White Hope, had lost to the Cuban, Teofilo Stevenson, in the morning's heavyweight finals?

If we didn't hear something soon, volleyball analysis would be next.

New York called again. They hadn't run a commercial all day, and unless we had more than guesses about what had happened at the airport, they were pulling the plug at two-thirty A.M., Munich time.

That was seventeen minutes away.

"Lean on Bader," I told Geoff Mason. "Tell him he's gotta find out *now*."

The console phone rang five minutes later; it was Marvin. He'd just seen his friend Otto Kentsch, assistant to the chief Olympics spokesman, coming out of a meeting, eyes watery. Kentsch wouldn't go on the record, but he told him: The hostages were dead. All of them.

I found myself suddenly faced with the oldest dilemma of the news producer. If I put the story on right now, we'd have a worldwide scoop. But what if, by some long chance, Kentsch was wrong and the whole world heard ABC blow it?

I decided to wait for confirmation. Better right than first. I had what I needed to hold the network, though, and I wanted Jim to prepare our listeners.

"Looks very dark for hostages," I whispered into his earpiece. "Announcement soon. Don't get their hopes up."

We kept waiting for word. Fifteen minutes . . . thirty . . . forty-five. At Olympic headquarters, they were reviewing the day for the media in half-hour increments, halting between each one for French, then English translation. German thoroughness, God Almighty!

Finally, at 3:17 A.M., twenty-three hours since I'd stood in the parking lot marveling at the wonder of an Olympic night, Reuters removed all our doubts.

"FLASH! ALL ISRAELI HOSTAGES SEIZED BY ARAB GUERRILLAS KILLED."

We could go with it.

"Official," I whispered to Jim. "All hostages dead."

He turned to look straight into the camera. For the first time that day, he appeared truly tired.

"I've just gotten the final word," he said. "When I was a kid, my father used to say our greatest hopes and worst fears are seldom realized. Our worst fears were realized tonight . . ." He paused. Then, "They're all gone."

It was said that a billion people around the world watched the telecast of the memorial service the next morning. Flags flew at half staff (except those of the Arab countries), the Munich Philharmonic played funereal Beethoven, and after Avery Brundage disgraced himself by talking about everything except the murdered athletes, men in yarmulkes thanked Germans for trying to save Jewish lives.

I kept one eye on the service, the other on a documentary segment Don Ohlmeyer was putting together on the events at 31 Connollystrasse. ABC News hadn't wanted it ("From *Sports*?" they said, further corroborating exactly what I thought of them), so that night, on our own time, we would jam all the commercials together in front and in back and run the segment ourselves without interruption.

The Games went on for another four days, melodrama in every one. In the basketball finals, the U.S. team—which had never lost a game, much less a gold medal in basketball's thirty-six years as an Olympic sport—was defeated by the Soviet Union, with the aid of a ref who put three extra seconds on the clock after time ran out. In the quarter-finals of the 1,500, Jim Ryun, world-record holder in the mile and America's middle-distance sweetheart, became entangled with a Ghanaian runner, sprawled to the track, and cried foul; officials said it wasn't. In the 400, Wayne Collett and Vince Matthews of the U.S. squad, and both black, placed first and third; joked and back-scratched during "The Star-Spangled Banner," and were banned from the Olympics for life. "The 'land of the free'? I can't believe in those words," Matthews told Howard.

Closing ceremonies are a highlight of any Games, and after operating two and a half weeks on three hours of sleep a night, I was looking forward to those of XX Olympiad with special relish. Apart from the lighted tribute to Avery "Brandage," they went off with German precision, and as the Olympic torch was extinguished, Jim McKay read A. E. Housman's "To an Athlete Dying Young." One verse caused his voice to crack:

Smart lad, to slip betimes away
From fields where glory does not stay,
And early though the laurel grows
It withers quicker than the rose.

The network called to say that the broadcasts had done well. I learned how well after I came home. Each week we'd been on, forty-nine of fifty top-rated segments on television were the Olympics—a dominance never attained by any series of programs on any network. More than half of all the households in America had watched at least some of the coverage. ABC, which had sold every commercial second at a premium price, would post the first profit in its history. And the televising of fourteen hours of tragedy—not by News, mind you, but by Sports—would bring a total of twenty-nine Emmys. "The achievement," the *New York Times* wrote, "carries a special significance in the world of American television, as another milestone in the emergence of a full-fledged third network force."

But maybe best of all was a telegram that had come in shortly after we signed off, that unforgettable marathon night. Jim McKay had shown it to me.

"You made us all proud," it read.

And it was signed "Walter Cronkite."

Flood Tide

Television networks, not being charities, judge success in dollars and cents.

By that measure, I was doing swell by the end of 1972. Revenues for ABC Sports—$3 million when I signed on with Scherick—were now $120 million (more than CBS and NBC Sports combined), and before too many years, *Wide World of Sports* alone would be bringing in nearly $200 million. That would fund a raft of additional programming to go with the events we were continuing to add to the schedule, most recently the Sugar Bowl (filched from NBC) and a series of heavyweight championship fights with the likes of Joe Frazier and Muhammad Ali (dreamed up on our own). Last, but hardly least in the ratings, we were doing more memorable "one-shots," such as the Billy Jean King versus Bobby Riggs "Battle of the Sexes" tennis match, televised in live prime time from a packed Houston Astrodome.

My personal life was also taking a substantial turn for the better with Ann Fowler, a sports-savvy former Miss Alabama, who'd been my secretary. We were living together now, and with Bear Bryant and Joe Namath's blessings, would marry soon.

Everything, in short, was roses. Then I met up with Jack Kent Cooke.

Cooke was one of those billionaires who collects sports franchises as others do stamps. He owned, or would, the Toronto Maple Leafs, the Washington Redskins, the Los Angeles Kings, a minor league baseball team, and a professional soccer team. When we first crossed paths, he was in his Los Angeles Lakers phase, and insisted that I come out to tour their garish new arena, the faux Greco-Roman "Fabulous Forum." After the inspection, Cooke conducted me and his PR staff to a purple-and-gold luxury suite, ordered drinks, and before leaving to check on his television and real estate interests, invited us to enjoy as many rounds as we wished. When I returned to New York, an envelope from the Fabulous Forum was waiting; it contained a $75 bar bill.

I'd heard that Jack had once been a whiz selling encyclopedias door to door; now I knew why.

My next encounter with Cooke was more expensive. In 1973, the NBA contract came up, and sniffing cable and pay-per-view riches, Cooke demanded we cease televising league home games as a prerequisite for renewal. I demurred, noting that ABC had spent millions acquiring exclusive television rights, and that our contract option included a first-refusal clause and a requirement that the NBA negotiate "in good faith."

One man's legal agreement is another's temporary inconvenience, however, and after rallying the owners of the New York Knicks and San Francisco Warriors to his cause, Cooke quietly obtained from CBS the promise of a deal giving him everything he wanted. Then he and his cohorts set about devising contract conditions, including announcer, schedule, and format approval, designed to produce an ABC Sports rejection. Their brainstorming was guided by my old assistant Barry Frank, who was now working for Mark McCormack's International Management Group, the largest and most prestigious of the sports agencies. Among IMG's clients was the NBA, and it was as the league's representative that Barry met one afternoon with Cooke and his friends in the bar of New York's Plaza Hotel. The purpose of the get-together, Barry would later state on a witness stand, was to "find as many ways as we can . . . [to] fuck ABC." Barry came up with the best: requiring whoever held the NBA contract to begin airing that week's game every Saturday afternoon between two and three o'clock, New York time, from October to December. That, no coincidence, was when ABC televised NCAA football.

CBS did take over the NBA contract, but I was not through with Jack Kent Cooke just yet, however. When CBS began televising the NBA, it found itself confronted by a brand-new second edition of *Wide World,* plus *The Superstars,* an unapologetic ratings grabber suggested by—wouldn't you know—Barry Frank, and featuring pro athletes competing in sports other than their own. "Roone's Revenge," as the combo was dubbed, kicked hell out of the NBA.

Again, all was well with the world.

The trick was keeping it that way, as the larger ABC Sports loomed, the more determined was the effort to cut it down to size. Nowhere was that more true than the Olympics, where William S. Paley was out for my skin.

Having his network all but blacked out by ABC's coverage of Munich had not amused CBS's chairman, who'd made securing the 1976 Summer Games in Montreal a top corporate priority. NBC, coming off the debacle that was the 1972 Winter Games in Sapporo ("Roone Arledge's finest moment," a critic called it), was also in the fray, and had sent Carl Lindemann and Chet Simmons to Munich to negotiate a rights agreement with the visiting Montreal organizers. By then, though, I'd had my fruitful tête-à-tête with the Montreal organizers. I hadn't come away with a deal, but I hadn't sought one. Instead, I'd used the occasion to establish a personal relationship, just as I had—and CBS and NBC thankfully hadn't—with the Innsbruck, Mexico City, Grenoble, and Munich organizers. We'd been a close match in relishing good food and drink, and as a result, Chet and Carl received a *québecois* "Don't call us, we'll call you."

Chumminess, however, has its limits, and I knew that Montreal—which was on its way to losing $1 *billion* on the Games—would soon be cutting a deal with someone. My worry was that it would be CBS, as the organizers were about to hire Marvin Josephson, founder of the world's largest talent agency, International Creative Management, and a very, very good friend of Bill Paley.

It was against this backdrop that, in mid-November 1972, Jim Spence and I presented ourselves at the Quebec trade mission in Rockefeller Center for a noon appointment with Paul Deroschers, head of the Montreal negotiating committee. Outside, rain was coming down in buckets, and Deroschers, who'd had a meeting that morning in New Jersey, was late. My anxiety kept pace with the passing minutes. At twenty after twelve, I grabbed Jim's arm.

"Let's get out of here," I said. *"Now."*

I jotted a quick *à bientôt* to Desrochers, then propelled Jim to a taxi for Toots Shor's, where I phoned my office and left instructions that my whereabouts were unknown.

"You want to tell me what this is about?" Jim said when I came to the table.

"Calculated avoidance," I answered.

"Why are you avoiding him?"

"Because," I said, "if we'd met with Deroschers, we would have lost the Games."

Now Jim really was perplexed.

"Look," I explained, "Deroschers can't make a deal on his own. Only the full committee can, and they're in Montreal. If we'd stuck around, Deroschers would have walked our offer over to Josephson, who'd have been right on the phone to Paley, and that would have been that. The rain, Jim, is our salvation."

"So now what are we going to do?" he asked.

I took a sip of an arriving Bloody Mary and smiled. "Fly to Montreal as soon it stops pouring."

The plan, as I laid it out, was simple. We'd blow into town unannounced, make one irresistible offer, and tell the organizers it was take it or leave it, then and there. If it worked out, Josephson and Paley literally wouldn't know what hit them. It was guts ball, but I thought it was our only shot.

"What are you going to bid?" Jim asked.

"Leonard's given me the authority to go to twenty-four million," I said. "But twenty-five is such a nice, round number, don't you think?"

Everything in Montreal proceeded according to the script, and a few minutes before one A.M., November 18, in a cigar smoke–filled room of the Queen Elizabeth Hotel, there was a shaking of hands. Then came the catch. If a formal contract wasn't ready for signing by eleven that morning, the organizers said, pushing me as I'd pushed them, Marvin Josephson's phone would ring. Contract drafting ordinarily consumes weeks; we now had ten hours. We also didn't have a lawyer, those employed by ABC being snuggled in their Manhattan beds. I found a number and woke a grouchy one, while Jim went down to the front desk for a typewriter and a supply of carbon paper and hotel stationery. With me relaying clause constructions from the attorney, he then began pounding away, page after laborious page—forty-one in all. When he began to flag around four A.M., I refueled him with scrambled eggs and coffee bought at an all-night eatery, and he tapped out the last sentence just after nine.

When the news broke, CBS and NBC accused me of all manner of malefactions, including slipping $5 million to the leader of Quebec's ruling Liberal Party. I signed a Canadian affidavit swearing that it wasn't so, placing my hand on a Bible that turned out to be in French.

"How do I know this is a *real* Bible?" I asked.

There was less hassle winning the 1976 Winter Games three months later, as I seemed to be the only one who really wanted them. Avery Brundage, railing against depredations on amateurism by ski manufacturers, tried to abolish them altogether before leaving office, but though his successor, Lord Killanin, of Ireland, saved them for Denver, Colorado, environmentalists pushed through a referendum forbidding the spending of a taxpayer dime on facilities. Innsbruck had recently been tapped to fill in, mostly because the runs and rinks from the 1964 Games were still in place. But neither the Tyrol nor the time difference appealed to CBS, which decided to pass on bidding for the rights. NBC did make a half-hearted offer, but I bested it with $10 million—fifty times the price of the first Innsbruck rights.

The industry thought me addled, and I wondered myself after finding almost no recognizable names on the competitors' list. But one U.S. figure skater caught my attention, a perky, ducktail-bobbed eighteen-year-old from Greenwich, Connecticut, whom we'd featured on *Wide World*. Her name was Dorothy Hamill.

Before beginning to figure how to build seventeen days of coverage around an ice skater few gave any chance to win the gold, there was a more immediate matter. Don Meredith was once again threatening to bolt—and this time he seemed serious.

Monday Night's 1973 season had been even more fractious than the three that preceeded it, Howard, as usual, front and center as the cause. He was merciless in picking on Gifford, and Don, fed up with the bullying of "my brother," bit back. For long stretches, they wouldn't speak to each other between games; the atmosphere in the booth, Frank said, was "like Omaha Beach."

But Don's unease went beyond Howard. He was going through a welter of changes and reassessments, from a new marriage to the smart and protective Susan Dullea, ex of actor Keir; to a growing fascination with painting, poetry writing, and Kurt Vonnegut; to falling under the spell of a sports guru who preached that anything connected with professional athletics was, ipso facto, corrupting.

How all this was impacting became clear during a preproduction meeting in Detroit, week six of *Monday Night*.

"I shouldn't have started this season," Don said, announcing that he was quitting. "I'm all talked out. I haven't got anything to say about football anymore."

I talked him into staying, but the next week, in Denver, he said on the air, "Welcome to the Mile High City, and I really am." Then he giggled.

A week later, he referred on the air to the president of the United States as "Tricky Dick."

I read the three of them the riot act afterward.

"You guys are really blowing it," I said. "This show has made you all rich and who you are, and you're pissing it away."

That simmered the nastiness, and seemed especially to sober Don. He returned to being Dandy for the rest of the season, and during a 34 to 0 blowout in Houston by the Raiders, delivered a crack that would endure in *Monday Night* history. As the camera swept the emptying hometown stands, it settled on a sleeping fan, who—somehow knowing he was on national television—snapped awake and flipped the country the middle-finger salute.

"Howard," said Don, "he's telling us we're Number One."

From the good humor, I assumed that the upcoming negotiations to renew his contract would go on without unusual struggle. I continued to think so, even after Howard reported in late December that Don was retaining Ed Hookstratten, a lawyer/agent who was tight with NBC Television president Herb Schlosser. To Howard, who had recently turned down an NBC offer to host a weekly variety show, this could only mean that "Hooks" would soon be trying to cut Meredith an acting/sportscasting deal at 30 Rock. I was aware of Don's acting ambitions (he'd already appeared on a well-received episode of NBC's *Police Story*), but told Howard to relax. I'd talked to Meredith after the last game of the season, and been assured that he wanted to re-up. Just to be on the safe side, I later checked with Don after the Super Bowl in Houston, and again at the Bing Crosby Golf Tournament in Pebble Beach. Both times he repeated that he'd be back.

In late February, however, Howard called from the annual NFL meeting in Miami to say he'd run into Carl Lindemann, who'd crowed that NBC was on the verge of snatching Meredith. Once more, I thought Howard an alarmist. Lindemann was always blowing smoke, and less than twelve hours before, I'd spoken to Don, who'd been rapturous about the draft contract I'd recently sent him. But to calm Howard down, I said I'd call Don again, and dialed his number in California, where he was shooting another *Police Story*. When he came on the line, I asked him point-blank whether there was anything to the Lindemann story. Don sheepishly hemmed and hawed, then said, "I don't know what to tell you, Roone."

I felt as if I'd been kicked in the head.

"I'm flying right out," I said. "Don't sign or do anything until we talk. I'll call you when I get to the Beverly Wiltshire."

When I got to the hotel, Don and Susan were waiting. We had dinner, stayed up all night drinking margaritas and talking, then shortly after dawn, Don and I played squash. We didn't talk about the contract; I'd already offered everything I could think of.

"Roone," he said, as we lay like zombies against the court wall, "I'm not 'Dandy Don.' There's this character I send out named that and people like him because he makes them laugh. But he's not me. I'm Don Meredith."

He didn't have to say more; I knew he was gone.

The replacement hunt began the next day. I considered Joe Namath and O. J. Simpson, Burt Reynolds and Bill Cosby, then a wing full of the NFL Hall of Fame: Paul Hornung, Willie Davis, Sam Huff, Bart Starr, Jimmy Brown, Dick Butkus, and Bill George. Those who were available weren't right; those who were right weren't available. Then, with the preseason two weeks off, and the talent search four months old, Howard proposed "the ideal candidate": Fred "The Hammer" Williamson, former defensive back for the Oakland Raiders and Kansas City Chiefs, and star of such "blaxploitation" films as *Hell in Harlem* and *The Legend of Nigger Charlie*.

Howard had met him during an appearance on the *Merv Griffin Show*, been impressed by his obvious smarts and antiestablishment views, and invited him on his radio program, where, or so Howard said, Williamson had been a hilarious smash. All I knew of Williamson was that he was a good-looking trash talker who'd taunted the Green Bay Packers before

Super Bowl III, and for his troubles had been carried from the field, unconscious. I listened to the tape of Howard's radio show, however, and agreed: There was something here. A viewing of Williamson's latest epic, *Three the Hard Way,* confirmed the impression, and I invited him to meet me at dinner with Howard and Frank.

He flat-out charmed us, and after a couple of two-on-two pool games back at my apartment, I said to Howard and Frank, "Meet your new partner."

When I introduced him to the press, The Hammer was The Mouth.

"I don't see how I can miss," he opened. "I am a star and will continue to be a star." In Fred's ongoing account, he'd also be "the sex symbol," "the 'color' commentator," and a boon to Howard by being "another target to throw rocks at." Frank wasn't going to prosper, though, since, according to Williamson, he'd be so magnetic, "they won't even know that Gifford is there."

Finally, a reporter got a word in edgewise.

"How do you intend to prepare for your new assignment?"

Said Fred, who was wearing a gold chain hung with miniature penis and balls for the occasion: "I'll go home and swim a lot in my pool, go to the latest discotheque in Los Angeles and brush up on my dancing, dress real pretty, and show up."

I thought he was kidding.

Five minutes into the first exhibition game, I realized that the joke was on me. By halftime, after Fred had called Howard "an old cripple" and worse, I also knew he wasn't our guy. I paid off his contract two weeks later.

Now who? Well, I thought, there *is* Alex Karras.

Alex, who'd attained glory as Terminator-in-Chief for the Detroit Lions' defensive line, had been among my original batch of candidates, and there'd been a lot to like. He was funny, had presence, and knew how to handle himself in front of a camera, as demonstrated—vividly—in *Cat Ballou* when he knocked out a horse. Frank, who in his playing days had had an experience similar to the horse's, vouched for his hardiness ("He's the only guy I know who held his sweat socks up with thumbtacks"); and Howard, recognizing Karras as infinitely slower on the comeback draw, vouched for his all-round sterlingness. What worried me was his gambling. It had gotten Alex a one-year suspension from the NFL, like Paul Hornung, who'd been simultaneously sidelined for the same offense. Pete Rozelle, who'd been the object of most of the bile, had cleared me to hire him, but warned me to expect trouble from the owners. I might have taken the risk if I hadn't discovered that Karras was a columnist on the side. His field of expertise: how to bet *Monday Night Football.*

With the season days away, one $600,000 mistake behind me, and no one better around, I could no longer afford to be so fussy. Karras agreed to forgo the scribbling and I put him on.

He had a great line his first game. When the camera caught a tight shot of a behemoth Raider lineman, steam rising from his shaved skull, Alex said, "That's Otis Sistrunk. He's from the University of Mars."

Sad to say, Alex never uttered another. But the ratings not only held, they increased. Howard's fame grew in lockstep with them, and he began talking of running for the U.S. Senate, in order, as he put it, "to solve the problems of the world." In 1975, however, he put those plans aside when ABC gave him his very own variety show, *Saturday Night Live with Howard Cosell.* In a detour from rationality, I agreed to produce.

My experience in the entertainment biz until then consisted of one program: *The Main Event,* a Frank Sinatra comeback concert in Madison Square Garden that ABC aired live in 1974. Frank wanted a boxing format, complete with ring, got Howard to emcee, and asked if I'd produce. Sinatra's coming out of retirement was historic, and at my Garden City, Long Island, grammar school in the 1940s, Bing fans wore copper pennies in their loafers, Sinatra's silver. I'd been a silver kid, and the show was one for my scrapbook.

Saturday Night Live with Howard Cosell did not work out so well. It might have been Jimmy Connors singing with Paul Anka, or Howard introducing everyone as "brilliant," or the eight P.M. time slot. As I told a reporter, "You could have Elizabeth Taylor doing a striptease and it wouldn't get a fifteen share." The only certainty was that *Saturday Night* was put out of its misery after twenty-two weeks, and that wounds to my ego were balmed by relief.

Innsbruck, however, was beginning to create intramural anxieties. It was to be the first Winter Olympics to take over prime time, to the undisguised irritation of ABC's entertainment chief, Fred Silverman.

As he'd already proved at NBC, and would later at CBS, Freddie was the man with the golden gut. He'd brought the network *Happy Days,*

Laverne and Shirley, and ratings respectability for the two years he'd been on the job, and didn't want his run disrupted by two weeks of skating and schussing. Words were exchanged, higher ups entreated, and though my real estate remained intact, I got the message: Better produce.

Dorothy Hamill came through, winning gold and putting her haircut on tonsorial wish lists. But it was a twenty-one-year-old Austrian skier, and a $250,000 decision to line the entire mile-long downhill run with cameras, that made history. Franz Klammer was not supposed to mount the top step of the victory stand. He was skiing fifteenth, the snow was iced and rutted, and Bernhard Russi of Switzerland, the defending Olympic champ, had an insurmountable lead. But down the mountain a superman in gold Lycra hurtled himself, not skiing the course but flying it at eighty miles per hour. Half a dozen times he seemed on the edge of killing himself, but as the cameras caught every suicide swerve, he somehow stayed upright. And when he reached the bottom, 33/100 of a second faster than any man ever had, Austria had gold, and television a moment like none seen before.

TV Guide judged Klammer's run the most exciting televised sports event in a quarter century, and when I came home with ratings that would help make ABC number one for the first time in its history, Freddie Silverman was my friend.

Montreal—the Olympics of Nadia Comaneci and her perfect tens—was almost an anticlimax after Innsbruck, but not for Howard, who was all too pumped up describing a Yugoslav pummeling a Romanian in a middleweight match. I'd taped the fight, doubting there'd be a use for it, but a glitch in New York opened up a hole that needed filling. Cueing up the tape, however, I noticed something amiss: The Romanian was wearing Polish colors. Bigger problem: According to the event schedule, he *was* Polish. The entire bout, Howard had been identifying the wrong fighter from the wrong country. Oh, the chops licking if someone actually put this on the air. My better angels resisted, however, and I ordered the laying in of a new announce track. Not long after, America's most famous sportscaster was sitting in an empty boxing arena yelling his lungs out into a microphone.

It was not the only thing Howard owed me for that summer. A few months before, ABC Sports moved closer to *über alles* status with the pilfering of Major League Baseball from NBC in a four-year, $92-million deal that gave us the regular season, plus the All-Star Game, the playoffs, and the World Series. After the contract was signed and safely locked away, I informed baseball commissioner Bowie Kuhn that Howard would be doing the pregame commentary, an announcement that sent normally sweet-tempered Bowie into paroxysms. Over his dead body, he vowed. Never in a million years. Wasn't going to happen—and if I tried to make it happen, he'd give baseball back to NBC that afternoon.

In view of Howard's publicly calling baseball "a medieval pastime," I could appreciate the commissioner's upset. But I was not about to knuckle under. No Howard, no ABC money, I told Bowie, who knew as well as I did that NBC wouldn't come close to our rights fee. Once Bowie had an opportunity to reflect, I was confident, he'd also realize that not only was ABC's contract airtight, but that any attempt at tampering would produce no end of headaches from Cosell.

"Go out to lunch with Howard," I cheerfully urged. "Underneath it all, you'll see he's really a fan."

Bowie didn't believe a word of it, but what I said was true. Offer Howard national television time, he'd have good words for Pick Up sticks.

It came to pass as predicted. Howard emerged from lunch proclaiming Bowie his new best friend, and saying of baseball, "It's a game that I have loved since childhood."

We added the Preakness to the schedule a year later, and by every reckoning, in and outside 1330 Sixth Avenue, the dominance of ABC Sports was now complete—in programming, announcers, production techniques, technical innovations, and staff. "The Network of the Olympics"—the new station-break tag—was the 800-pound gorilla, the outfit that paid the most, moved the quickest, performed the best. We'd become what I'd wanted us to be since the morning I'd walked into Ed Scherick's two-room office. And it was making me restless.

I enjoyed the perks that went with being number one: hopping the Concorde to Paris, being chauffeured by Jag to work, bon-mot dropping with Rainier and Grace, getting good tables at Lutèce and Le Cirque and—maybe most of all—being able to pick up the phone and say, "Let's go to St. Andrews and play golf."

But I needed more: to be pushed again; to do something larger.

I'd already had offers. Just after Montreal, NBC approached with a multimillion package to consult on sports and produce entertainment programming. Word that my contract was soon to expire showed up in the television columns shortly thereafter, eliciting lucrative feelers from Hollywood, and a lunch invitation from Marvin Josephson.

Despite—or because of—being outmaneuvered for Montreal, he wanted to be my agent, and said that I'd be one of two clients he'd personally handle, the other being Steve McQueen. That turned my head (I'd always wanted to drive like Steve did in *Bullitt*), which swiveled when Marvin added that he could extract millions for me from ABC, along with virtually anything I desired professionally.

"Leonard Goldenson will kick and scream, but he'll pay," Marvin said. "He can't afford to lose you."

I was not sure, but still, the prospect of a million or more a year was enticing. I'd been investing heavily in divorce since the split from Joan (she'd married her attorney), and a recent ABC contract awarded bringing in the Olympics with five years of $2,000 raises. No one put a gun to my head to sign it; the money simply never seemed as important as the work.

Nonetheless, I put Marvin off, as well as NBC and the others. Delaying decision making was my well-worn practice, and the nesting instinct was still strong. More than any of the houses I'd lived in, ABC was home.

Fred Pierce, president of ABC television, and my sturdiest backer in the executive suite, had been given the job of keeping me from straying, but not the tools to accomplish it. ABC couldn't match the figure NBC was dangling, and even if I were interested in running the Entertainment division (which I wasn't), Silverman was rightly and securely ensconced. Since I also lacked the appetite for climbing the corporate ladder, our discussions through the fall went nowhere, and in December, we called a time-out so I could chase the rights for the 1980 Moscow Olympics.

The intrigue surrounding these Olympics would have suited John le Carré. For me, it had started with a call several months before from Lothar Bock, a West German facilitator who generated an aura of mystery about himself. Whatever the source of his income, Bock had legendary ins with the Soviets, and for a finder's fee in excess of what I'd paid for Mexico City, volunteered to put them at ABC Sports's service. Bock and I didn't hit it off, however, and instead, I asked R. Sargent Shriver, former ambassador to France, founding director of the Peace Corps, and brother-in-law of the late John F. Kennedy to do the door opening. Sarge, in turn, enlisted the assistance of David Carr, an ex-legman for Drew Pearson who'd gone on to be chairman of Colt Industries and a senior power at Lazard Frères. David clearly had done well at both, as he maintained a yacht on the French Riviera and sumptuous apartments in Moscow, Paris, and New York. It wouldn't have surprised us if he had connections with the highest levels of the CIA, KGB, and Mossad.

CBS and NBC were also out for Russian bear, CBS especially. Paley had made a personal visitation to Moscow; his subalterns were being ferried between Teeterboro and Shermetevov aboard the company jet as if it were the Washington shuttle; and, in a low moment for the house that Edward R. Murrow built, the network had aired a documentary on Soviet delights that could easily have been mistaken for a Politburo production.

On arrival in Moscow—where rare was the phone line that wasn't tapped—I discussed countermeasures with New York via a prearranged code based on famous athletes' numbers.

"I think NBC will offer Red Grange," I'd say. "But there's talk they could drop Ted Williams from the deal."

Translation: I suspected NBC would bid $77 million, though it might be $9 million less.

Increasingly, though, I became convinced that the Soviets were playing us Amerikanskis like three scorpions in a bottle. Accordingly, I drew up plans for a first strike: Rather than bid against each other, we'd pool a single offer, then divvy up the coverage. Elton Rule leaped at the notion, and remembering the Montreal sure thing that wasn't, so did Bob Wood at CBS. Chet and Carl also wanted to sign on, but asked for time in order for NBC's lawyers to mull over antitrust objections. One way or another, NBC had to decide soon; bids were to be submitted the next day.

I was in my hotel room, waiting for the answer, when David Carr called saying to meet him in the lobby. He put a finger to his lips when I came down, then led me out to a smoke-belching limousine that looked like an old Packard. Fifteen minutes later, it deposited us behind the red walls of the Kremlin. I looked inquiringly at David as a brace of guards walked us to a third-floor office, but he shook his head.

Only when we were ushered into an ornate chamber hung with crystal chandeliers did he speak. "Ignati Sergeivich," he said to a burly, silver-haired man standing beneath a giant portrait of an especially resolute Lenin, "I believe you know Roone Arledge."

I certainly knew him. Ignati Sergeivich Novikov was deputy premier of the Soviet Union and head of the Moscow Olympic Organizing Committee. We'd met during a *Wide World* trip several years before, and I'd come away with no doubts: In Soviet sports, his word was law.

Novikov beamed, heartily pumped my hand, and motioned me to one of the velvet chairs lined up against the brocade walls. "I think we can make a deal with ABC," he said.

Later, I got a call from Elton. We'd been playing phone tag all night, and he didn't know about my intimacy with Comrade Novikov.

"I got NBC to go for it," Elton said pridefully. "They're in the pool."

"They're *what?*" I exclaimed.

"We have an agreement," he said. "I'm going down to Washington to get a waiver from Justice. It's all set."

"You don't understand," I shouted, ignoring whoever was listening in. "I think we can get it for ourselves!"

Elton said it was too late, an agreement was an agreement.

I yelled a final time, then called Novikov to tell him he would be part of a pool. But Chet and Carl, obviously, hadn't bothered with codes when talking to 30 Rock; Novikov knew that.

I returned to Moscow around Christmastime, but it was no use; through the good offices of Lothar Bock, NBC had just been handed the 1980 Summer Games for $87 million.

They'd never see air. Shortly before the Games were to begin, the Soviets invaded Afghanistan, Jimmy Carter organized a boycott, and when the dust settled on the insurance claims, NBC posted a loss of $35 million. I hadn't liked losing, but if there had ever been a good time to, this was it.

Back in New York, negotiations with ABC were no further along than before I'd left for Moscow. Money wasn't the issue; I'd already indicated that I would accept considerably less than the NBC offer for the right job. But Fred and I couldn't come up with the job.

In February, with the likelihood growing that I'd end up at NBC by default, we had a long, sorrowful dinner at Jimmy Weston's, then adjourned to P. J. Clarke's for nightcaps.

As we swizzled scotches, we gossiped about ABC, which, with the exception of one division, was finally running on all cylinders. The exception was News, where for decades ABC had been known as "the last with the least."

"It's just killing us," Fred said, explaining how the dismalness of the News division was preventing the network from attracting more and better affiliates.

"Station owners love Entertainment, love Sports, hell, they even love Daytime," Fred said, "but when you get to News, that's when their eyes roll."

I was on the side of the station owners. It was hard not to be; the stories about ABC News were legend. Until 1963, it hadn't even had its own camera crews, and trailed the other networks going to an evening half hour by five years. At one point, the affiliates wanted to junk the whole division, which in one ten-year stretch went through seventeen different anchormen, including a duo of Harry Reasoner and Howard K. Smith from CBS. They were the best of the lot, but not good enough to budge the *Evening News* from the ratings cellar. So four months before, ABC News had teamed Harry with Barbara Walters, who'd been lured away from the *Today* show for $1 million—a move that made the network and Barbara laughingstocks. "This isn't journalism," CBS News president Dick Salant said, "this is a minstrel show." Worse, it didn't work. The program had half Walter Cronkite's audience, less than two-thirds that of NBC's David Brinkley and John Chancellor. It was the same across the ABC News board: third in every category—and then only because there were three networks. If there were five, I thought, it would have been fifth; ten, tenth.

"Fucking place is cursed," Fred said, finishing the story of WSB in Atlanta, the latest CBS station that would have switched to us, except for News. "Trade Walter for Barbara? *Sure.*"

He shook his head, then, as if struck by something, and shot me a look.

"I don't suppose you'd like to run it, would you?"

"*News?*" I laughed. "I didn't know you wanted to get rid of me that badly."

We both laughed at that, and a few minutes later said good night.

I got in unusually early the next morning, in order to catch Fred alone.

"Remember asking me last night if I wanted to run News?" I asked.

"Yeah," Fred chortled. "Crazy idea."

"Wanna hear something even crazier?"

"What?" Fred said.

"I do."

Coming to News

Sports broadcasting was—and is—a fabulous experience. I used to think I was the luckiest guy in the world because I was doing work I loved. Imagine living in the midst of *Monday Night Football,* or the homestretch of the Kentucky Derby, or the eighteenth hole at Pebble Beach, and actually getting paid to be there! Plus, I was awfully proud of everything we'd accomplished. We'd started with less than nothing. In a decade, we'd become the kings of sports programming, numero uno, and we'd done it my way, producing events not by plunking cameras on the fifty-yard lines and droning out the facts that were right before the viewers' eyes, but the way reporters write stories—good guys and bad guys, drama, color, background, beginning, middle, and end. One hallmark of ABC Sports was being skeptical, sassy, and tough. Our success, as Howard Cosell had said maybe a million and one times, was telling it like it is.

But News.

At least in my imagination, News was what separated the men from the boys. Certainly, as far back as I could remember, it was what made people in the trade call CBS the Tiffany network. The same network, mind you, could produce night after night of the lowest-common-denominator prime-time sitcoms—*The Beverly Hillbillies, Petticoat Junction,* and *Hee Haw* were all aired on the Tiffany network—but it didn't matter. The aura of Ed Murrow and his group of journalists still lent class to CBS, even after many of them, Murrow included, had died. Walter Cronkite was now the standard, and the depth of fine reporters who manned the bureaus, abroad and at home, was unparalleled.

This didn't mean that CBS always topped the news ratings. Chet Huntley and David Brinkley had combined in the late fifties on NBC's nightly *Huntley-Brinkley Report*, which held on to number one into the early sixties. *Huntley-Brinkley* dominated the political conventions, which were the pièce de résistance of television news. CBS had also consistently failed in the morning, whereas Pat Weaver, NBC's legendary programming guru, had launched the *Today* show in 1952 with a pleasingly low-key but unknown Chicagoan as its host, Dave Garroway, and his pet chimpanzee, J. Fred Muggs. *Today* ruled the morning for years with the likes of Hugh Downs, Barbara Walters, and Jane Pauley as hosts, and though we would later give it a run for its money, and top it for several years with *Good Morning America*, CBS News, to its immense frustration, would swap one formula for another, one host for another, from Walter Cronkite himself for several years in the fifties to Bryant Gumbel most recently—only to fail and stumble and relaunch and fail again.

But it was still CBS one turned to for the big, breaking stories that marked television—and American—history. CBS was the authority, the standard. And it was CBS, long the leading producer of news specials, that in 1968 launched what would become the most popular, and longest-running, news program in television history, *60 Minutes,* with Mike Wallace and Harry Reasoner as charter reporters and Don Hewitt, already a veteran of *See It Now,* producing.

I confess that I'd always been a little bit in awe, and more than a little envious, of News, and I'd always been conscious of bringing journalism into producing. The closest I'd ever come to doing it myself was the Munich Olympics, where, for two days, by the force of circumstance, I'd become the "executive producer" of a great unfolding news story, and I'd never forgotten the excitement of it. All during the Watergate crisis, like so many Americans, I'd been glued to television. The day Nixon resigned— I remember it as a rainy day in August—I watched every second. That night I went to the ballet—Baryshnikov, a gala night, a top-ticket throng at Lincoln Center—and there, sitting directly behind me, was Harry Reasoner, having just arrived from Washington. Talk about jealousy!

Once upon a time, back in the late forties and deep into the fifties, much of television had been live, with all the vividness, the immediacy, and, above all, the unpredictability that the medium brought into our living rooms. But reduced costs, the need for efficiency, and the desire to control had brought an increasing reliance on taped footage, and the last bastions of live TV, the only places, really, where spontaneity and unpredictability still prevailed, if you could capture them, were Sports and News. I think that was why, more than anything, I'd always loved broadcasting sports. But news, in comparison, was reality; news was important; news was the world we lived in. News, to mix metaphors, was the big leagues.

I was also aware that some of the truly great American journalists had served an apprenticeship in sports reporting before finding their way into news. (I'm thinking first and foremost, obviously, of Scotty Reston of the *New York Times*.) If it could happen to writers, why not producers?

The morning after our night at P.J.'s, I walked into Fred Pierce's office.

When I told him I wanted to do News, he stared at me a moment, thinking. He didn't say, *Gee, I thought that was just booze talk.* On the other hand, he didn't say, *Wow, that's the greatest idea I've heard since the invention of the cathode tube.*

"There's one problem," he said at length. "It's not my job to give. News reports to Elton, not to me."

I knew that.

"Why don't you at least tell Elton I'm interested?" I suggested. "Maybe the three of us ought to have dinner together. The sooner the better, as far as I'm concerned."

We left it at that, but Fred called me before the morning was out. Dinner was on for that same night.

Some of the speed, I'm sure, had to do with the plight of News, but some of it probably had to do with me too, the rumors circulating in the trade that I might leave. Fred would certainly have bent over backward to keep that from happening. With Elton, I was less sure.

We knew each other, we were friendly, but we used to joke back and forth at the annual affiliates' meetings that it took meetings like this for us to run into each other, and at one such, when Elton introduced me at a dinner using our standard repartee, I stood and with a totally straight face said, "Thank you very much . . . *Elvis*." Which brought down the house. But Elton was a sleek and well-groomed West Coaster, conservative in manner and dress, a seasoned corporate executive, while I was an East Coaster who had nothing against either working or carousing into the wee hours and typically steered clear of corporate politics. Elton worked the inner circle of the ABC hierarchy; I didn't. Elton had done World War II and Korea, emerging as an infantry captain, and I'd done the battle of Maryland, emerging as a GI. His focus was Entertainment, mine was Sports. And, I hoped, News.

It was an interesting dinner. Elton, to some extent, adopted the party line. He wasn't sure, he said, that ABC News required that much changing. For one thing, it already had a president, Bill Sheehan, a former chief of the London bureau and a well-liked veteran of the company. Yes, the *Evening News* ratings continued to be dismal, but Harry and Barbara had only been on together a few months. Given time, they'd be a smash. Why should we rock the boat now?

Leonard thought so too, Elton said. In fact, he let on, when he'd told Leonard about my proposition that very afternoon, Leonard had said that making me president of News would be "like throwing the deed to the family farm on the casino table."

Besides, Elton said, if I went to News, who'd run Sports?

"I will," I said. "I want to be president of News *and* Sports together. I can do both at the same time, and neither one will suffer."

Elton looked at me as if I truly was nuts, but I meant what I said. The truth was, the clout I had, inside and outside ABC, came from Sports. If I gave it up, there was no chance of bringing about the wave-making changes I knew were necessary to fix News.

I didn't put it that way, though. What I said was, "I've thought it through very carefully, Elton. I'm throwing the deed to the family farm on the casino table, too."

We left it that way for the moment. I was pretty sure Elton knew as well as I did that News was a basket case, but he couldn't admit it. For my part, Marvin Josephson was still waltzing me around from time to time with visions of a glorious future. When I told him about News, he said, "I can get you millions of dollars, Roone. M-I-L-L-I-O-N-S. Come with me first, make your millions, then you can go to PBS and get your rocks off doing the news."

I heard his siren's song all right, but I couldn't bring myself to follow it. Meanwhile, although I'd never said "Give Me News or Else" to Fred and Elton, the gossip columns that traffic in such rumors were filled with speculation about my leaving.

All in all, I had the feeling that Elton was intrigued by the idea, that he thought I had it in me to make News a winner. But he wasn't one to risk the family farm.

Finally, in late February, he found a solution.

Fred Pierce called me into his office.

"Congratulations, Roone," he told me in his office. "We're going to give you the presidency of News. But Elton has changed the reporting structure. He's turned News over to me. You'll report to me, and I'll be the one to announce the appointment."

If and when the shit hit the fan, in other words, no one was going to be able to blame good ole Elton for it. But I could have cared less. From my point of view, it was like a dream come true.

I asked Fred if I could have a few months before it became official. I had people to talk to, plans to prepare, particularly at Sports, where I was to continue as president, too. Fred suggested early May for the announce-ment—fine with me—and that I move over to News physically the begin-ning of June. I also told Fred I wanted Bill Sheehan to stay on as my number two. He knew too many things I didn't, and his continuing pres-ence, I hoped, would make the transition smoother. That was fine with Fred and, more important, Bill agreed to it, too.

My next call was to Jim Spence. It was evident that News would soon be claiming the bulk of my attention and that Sports needed day-to-day oversight. Jim knew the division's nuts and bolts best, had a flair for administration, and, as he'd demonstrated the night we'd wrapped the Montreal deal, was not only a crackerjack typist but tireless and dependable.

Not long afterward, Ann and I hosted a small dinner party at our weekend house in Sagaponack, on eastern Long Island. One of the guests was Peter Jennings, who was visiting from London. We'd been friends since before Munich—to the extent that the prickly Peter would allow any-one to be close to him—and, when the dessert plates were cleared away, we walked out onto the beach and down toward the ocean. Peter lit up a Dunhill as I fiddled with my pipe.

"I want to tell you something in confidence that I haven't told anyone else," I said to him. "I've been having discussions with management, and it looks like I'm going to be taking over News."

"Well, well. So that's what it's all about," Peter said. "I heard you'd been talking with our masters about something, but I never imagined it was News."

I waited for good wishes and Godspeed.

It didn't come. What I got instead was another "Well, well."

I went to get Walter Cronkite's reaction a few days later at lunch at the smorgasbord place he favored on West Fifty-eighth. Walter was unabashedly my television news hero, as he was everyone else's, and securing his neutrality, if not his approbation, counted for a great deal. He and I had a friendly relationship, if not a close one, and I knew him to be a more complicated individual than the sometimes stern, sometimes reassuring avuncular figure we all knew from television. I'll never forget a dinner we had one time—Art Buchwald, I know, was with us—when the subject of *Deep Throat* came up. I'm not talking about Woodward and Bernstein's mysterious source for *All the President's Men,* but the porn movie—the first porn movie, in fact, to be promoted to the general public as one that crossed over out of its category. Whether it did or not was a subject of quite some debate.

Someone at dinner asked if anyone had seen it, and Walter, to my amazement, said, "I have."

That seemed odd and amusing to all of us. Someone else asked Walter if they'd sent him a cassette.

"Not at all," he said. "I was curious about it. So we went to see it in a regular theater."

At that, I remember, I burst out laughing.

"Why is that so funny?" asked Walter.

"Well," I said, "I was just imagining a couple of schoolteachers in New York on vacation, deciding they were going to do something naughty. Like sneaking off to see *Deep Throat*. And there, standing in line in front of them at the ticket window, is America's most trusted man!"

But Walter had a dimension a lot of people never saw. He'd been known to dress in drag for his CBS staff's Christmas party and lead them sonorously in carol singing. More seriously, he had any number of friends and admirers in the business, and God knows, I wanted his advice. To show what an amenable fellow I could be, I held forth at our smorgasbord lunch on a favorite cause of his—extending the evening newscasts to an hour. I said I was all for it, and that I thought that I could bring ABC along if CBS took the lead. Walter brightened with pleasure, and we fell to talking about the new elements we'd add with an extra half hour. I plumped for interviews, cultural features, in-depth reports—what we called the "back of the book." The idea wrinkled Walter's mustache. He wanted more hard news and only hard news—particularly that emanating from the nation's capital.

"Washington," he said, "is magical."

Magical?

I was stepping, clearly, into a different world.

The more soundings I took, the more conflicting advice I got, and nobody was jumping up and down, saying, *Gosh, Roone, that's the best news I've heard in years.* Opinions varied particularly over how long it would take to make us competitive. Jack Chancellor of NBC, another lunch confidant, ventured that, with luck, I could bring ABC News into the game in ten years, maybe seven. Morley Safer of *60 Minutes* was more optimistic; he put it at five. Elton Rule told me not to feel pressured. "We're not looking for miracle workers," he said. "It might even take a year." Dick Beesemyer, ABC's head of affiliate relations, was as sympathetic as could be. "Look," he said, "the station owners understand this is going to be a tough job. But, boy, if you could turn News around in a few weeks, these guys would really, really love it."

A few weeks to do what might take a decade. Be careful what you wish for, Arledge.

Opinions were equally divided over what direction we should follow. My own instincts were the Walter way—more hard news—but Dick O'Leary, who supervised the network's owned and operated stations, wanted us to follow the *Eyewitness News* model. *Eyewitness News,* which was what the O & Os called the local news, was much less formal and less portentous. People walked casually about the set, chatting, teasing each other, and the banter, or "happy talk," as we called it, had made the local newscasts of four of the five O & Os number one in their markets. There was no reason, Dick said, that it couldn't do the same for *ABC Evening News.*

The tabloid style had its defenders, too. Many local channels had gone that way, focusing in their newscasts on crime, scandals, and entertainment—a kind of watered-down *National Enquirer* approach. I was also made privy to any number of surveys that warned against making the news too intellectual. They counseled avoiding televising anything that smacked of being "foreign" and eschewing such terms as "racially imbalanced," "strategic arms," "pork-barrel legislation," and "Republican conference leader"—all yawners, we were told, which would encourage our viewers to reach for the remote.

But I wanted to make ABC News smarter, not dumber. I wanted us tougher, not softer. Most important of all, on the big, breaking stories that made a network's reputation, I wanted us always first and best. If we couldn't match Walter Cronkite—who could? (not even CBS could, now that Walter's retirement was drawing near)—we would find our own way of competing, and we would beat our rivals. As I took to saying later, "The day the world ends, I want people to tune in to ABC to watch it happen."

Easy to say. But making it happen?

In Sports, half the battle was getting the rights. Once you got the Sugar Bowl and the Kentucky Derby, they were yours exclusively. No other network could put them on, and if a viewer wanted to watch them, he had no choice but ABC. But when it came to news, the audience had a choice. We all fished in the same pond. You became number one only by competing for every story, every hour, every day.

And ABC News was starting at rock bottom.

New people I could hire, new equipment I could buy, new production values I could impose. But more important, and more urgent, I had to change the prevailing mentality of an organization that expected to lose and didn't mind losing. Bill Sheehan was a respected journalist and admirable human being, but, like his predecessors, he'd run ABC News like a club, a friendly hangout where you played poker, had drinks with the boys, went home early, and the next morning looked at yesterday's tape. It was like the newspaper Charles Foster Kane bought in *Citizen Kane:* Little was urgent, less was rushed. There was a grayness about the culture, including the hair color of those who created it. Or, as my irreverent assistant Jeff Ruhe put it after his first ABC News staff meeting, "I'd love to have the Grecian Formula franchise for this organization."

That was the interior problem. But there was an outside one, too.

My appointment as president was announced May 1, 1977. Rose petals were not strewn.

"Arledge Will Head ABC News," the *New York Times* headlined, identifying me as "one of television's leading showmen," "Disclaims Theatrical

Flourishes." And the sports columnist Robert Lipsyte opined that no one should be surprised to see an anchor team composed of John Denver, Mason Reese, and Farrah Fawcett take over.

Time magazine, for its part, warned that the movie *Network* was about to spring to life. (This prompted a phone call from Paddy Chayevsky, author of *Network,* to assure me that I was the last person he'd had in mind as a model for his attack on the industry.)

ABC News personnel were widely reported reaching for smelling salts. "Now the new ABC symbol is going to be a jockstrap," an unnamed news editor was quoted as "grumbling" to unnamed colleagues. At the Washington bureau, a joke was said to be circulating that I was undecided about what to do with the middle of the *ABC Evening News:* Call it "halftime" or put on a band. And that was just the beginning. I was going to replace Harry Reasoner with Howard Cosell (so "rumor" went); News personnel had backed an attempt by Bill Sheehan to continue reporting to Fred Pierce (untrue); ABC was about to become *Wide World of News* (a line repeated in twenty-three stories).

The criticism, even though I thought it unjustified, bothered me less than its personal vehemence. There was a nasty and positively gloating edge to the media coverage, and what I had done to deserve it, I had no idea. To some extent, I suppose, there was carryover (of a here-they-go-again kind) from the slamming ABC had taken over Barbara Walters's salary. But one thing became clear to me: Television news was looked on, at least in the media, as some kind of sacred, almost virginal precinct whose purity was constantly under threat of violation by us crass types from other domains. Entertainment, for instance. And now, Sports.

It got to me finally, and I hit back. If television news was so good, I said, where had it been during Watergate? Waiting for all the president's men to hold a press conference to say, yup, we done it? How come every American knew seemingly everything there was to know about Olga Korbut, yet, until the Senate hearings, 90 percent didn't know what Bob Haldemann looked like, let alone what he did or thought? How had the most powerful information medium in history let the second most powerful man in the country stay anonymous? Why was it that newspapers were always wrestling with their formats to enhance reader interest, while television news believed that being credible was being dull? Wasn't there something to worry about from the polls that found that one in four who watched television never looked at the evening news? Could it be that the most important program a network aired had no relevance to people's lives?

ABC News was going to change the face of television, I concluded, and I had no apologies for it.

Maybe it didn't change any minds out there, but it made me feel better. Now all I had to do was convince ABC News.

That, Fred Pierce told me, would involve some doing, reporting that he'd just had a visit from Peter Jennings and diplomatic correspondent Ted Koppel.

"What did they want?" I asked.

"For me to bring back Sheehan," Fred said.

"And what did you tell them?" I asked, trying to cover my shock.

"To have a nice flight home."

Fred advised me to relax. No one liked change, but once the News guys got to know me, everything would settle down. He added that he and Bill Sheehan had come up with a means to speed the process along: a division-wide get-together the last weekend in May at the Montauk Inn, way out at the end of Long Island. Senior correspondents and producers would come in for either a Saturday or a Sunday session, we'd exchange views, and all would go away one big, happy family.

"The sun, the surf, your charm," Fred said, "How can it miss?"

The idea took me by surprise, and I didn't like it, the more so since Fred himself was going to be there, and Tony Thomopolous, who'd taken over Entertainment after Fred Silverman completed his network troika by jumping from us to NBC. But there was nothing to do but go ahead with it.

On the appointed weekend, I gathered with my new charges around a giant U-shaped table. I sat at its head like a vacationing executor about to read his own will. But, apart from announcing investments in upgrading equipment and facilities (something I hoped would win me points), I mostly listened. Which was just as well. It was later reported that my utterances were accompanied by a vice president doodling "bull," the person next to him adding "shit." Moreover, every time I tried to promise that better days lay ahead for us, someone was ready to leap down my throat. Like Frank Reynolds, our lead Washington correspondent, who snapped, "You really think we're a bunch of losers, don't you?"

I avoided a direct answer, but Frank's reporting instincts were keen. The haughtiness in the room, among the Washington hands especially, reminded me of student days at Columbia, where we assured ourselves that the dreadfulness of the football team was proof of how much better we were academically than Harvard and Yale. It was the same here. ABC was dead last, and those on hand were proud of it. Didn't it show that they were purer than NBC and CBS? That they didn't pander or stoop to a level that might attract viewers?

In this temple of the unwatched, caring whether anyone was watching was sacrilege.

Sunday morning picked up where Saturday afternoon left off. Fred asked that there be no leaks to the press. Well, but these people saw themselves as the press, and sure enough, Ann Compton, our Capitol Hill correspondent, got up and accused Fred of "McCarthyism." And that was the high point. From then on, the meeting degenerated into "us" and "them," until a young, mod-looking guy I didn't recognize stood up.

"I promised my wife I'd come home employed," he said, "but with all deference to my colleagues, I gotta tell you that what you've been hearing is garbage. You're becoming president of a third-rate organization. Third-rate people, third-rate management, third-rate equipment, third-rate mentality, third-rate desire. If you're ready to fix those things, you can have a news division. If you're not, we might as well all go home right now."

Dead silence.

I whispered to Bill Sheehan, "Who the hell is *that?*"

"Jeff Gralnick," he answered. "Produces pieces for Barbara. He's good. But you'll have to forgive him. He just got in from Tel Aviv and he's jet-lagged."

"Nothing to forgive," I said. "At the break, tell him he still has a job."

After the session ended, I spotted Gralnick at the bar—alone—and walked over.

"You got any questions?" I said.

"Just one," he said. "Why should I work for you?"

Tough kid. He reminded me a little of a redhead Ed Scherick had once hired, a guy by the name of Arledge.

"Because you're going to work harder than you ever have," I said, "and you'll be better than you ever thought you could be."

Gralnick regarded me evenly, weighing what I said.

"Okay," he said. "You've got me."

One of the biggest hoo-has of that hostile weekend at Montauk was when someone asked what I thought of Geraldo Rivera. Geraldo, at the time, was dividing his efforts between doing celebrity interviews for the Entertainment division's *A.M. America* and hosting *Good Night America,* which was a sort of cross between *60 Minutes* and *Don Kirshner's Rock Concert.* As always with Geraldo, both activities were causing a hell of a stir.

"He may go over the top sometimes," I said honestly, "but with the right handling, he's the kind of reporter who could be terrific for us."

The groans could be heard halfway to Manhattan: Geraldo Rivera was everything the ABC News establishment despised.

I didn't know him personally, but what I'd seen of his work—which had won him Emmys and enemies—had impressed me. He was self-involved and shameless, sure, and I wished his hair weren't so long, and that he hadn't taken a dope test on camera and I wished that he hadn't gotten into a fistfight with Roger Grimsby, the WABC anchorman.. But he'd run through a brick wall to get a story, and when he was on the air reporting one, he reminded me of Howard: You had to watch.

Bill Sheehan had refused to hire him, which is how he'd become the property of Entertainment, apparently removing himself from my prospective clutches. But one morning, two weeks after Montauk, *Good Night America* was pink-slipped into oblivion. Oaths spewed from Geraldo to bosses, and by noon, he'd been fired from *A.M. America* as well.

He came to see me that afternoon, and I was impressed. Among other things, he turned out to have done over 300 news pieces for *A.M. America*—which I think few people realized, myself included. Reputation or not, he struck me as just the kind of investigative reporter we had to have—forthright, tough, and, okay, egocentric—and I hired him virtually on the spot.

As it turned out, 1977 was a big year for hot stories. Terrorists seeking independence for South Molucca, part of the old Dutch East Indies and the new Indonesia, seized and held a train with fifty-five passengers in Holland. In July, James Earl Ray, the assassin of Martin Luther King Jr., escaped from a Tennessee prison. A week later, the North Koreans shot down a U.S. helicopter.

Then, on July thirteenth, at nine P.M., New York City went dark. Unlike the previous blackout in the city, in 1965, known for its peacefulness and the generosity of New Yorkers to each other, this one brought out rioters and looters, and we were first on the air with a prime-time special. At the same time, we had our share of misfires. When, on September twelfth, Steve Biko, the antiapartheid activist, died of head wounds in a South African jail (twenty years later, five former policemen admitted to having killed him), our Johannesburg correspondent got fired because he was last to cover the story. I was sending a message in the process: Last was for losers. I wanted a new aggressiveness. I wanted us to be first.

All along, though, I'd been on the lookout for the Big Story to show just how good we could be—and when it hit, on August 10, 1977, I guess I went a little overboard.

I was in an editing room late that evening, recutting a documentary, when I learned that David Berkowitz, the notorious "Son of Sam" serial killer who had terrorized the women of the city of New York for a full year, had just been arrested. Here was what I'd been waiting for, and right in our own backyard, too. I got the crews cranked up, gave the troops their marching orders, grabbed a walkie-talkie, and headed to One Police Plaza—for all the world like George F. Patton racing to be first at the Rhine, although part of me wanted to see how well our people operated on such a high-profile case.

According to the account that appeared later in the *Los Angeles Times,* Roone Arledge arrived at three A.M., "dressed as if for a touch football game, a glass of scotch in one hand, a portable radio in the other, directing his network's 'feeds to the coast.'" The *Times* was right about the time and radio, wrong about the attire and the scotch. This last, I confess, still irritates me. I mean, can you imagine *anyone* walking into police headquarters, just after they'd caught one of the most wanted men in New York City history, waving a glass of scotch in the air? But I was up the rest of that night, managing wall-to-wall coverage, including a Barbara Walters one-on-one with the police commissioner and commentary from Jimmy Breslin and a shrink. Typically, though, only two things would be remembered about the "Son of Sam" segments the next evening: their combined length (nineteen and a half minutes of the twenty-two available for delivering the day's news) and Geraldo—togged out in jeans and T-shirt—calling Berkowitz a "fiend."

I didn't smell trouble until Barbara threw the broadcast to Howard K. Smith and I heard Howard say, "There *were* other things that happened today."

Uh-oh.

Did I say "overboard"? That was hardly the word, according to a letter signed by our Washington bureau, expressing "concern" over the "tone" of the broadcast and Geraldo's having proclaimed Berkowitz guilty before an indictment, much less a trial. No matter that what Geraldo had actually said was, "This is the man who the NYPD says is the fiend who killed all those women." Soon after I received the missive, marked "Personal and Confidential," its contents were reprinted in the television column of the *Chicago Daily News*.

Everyone had been waiting for the first sign of Arledge tabloidism, and a couple of months into the job, I'd served it right up.

A week later, August 16, 1977, there was another flap when we opened the *Evening News* with the mysterious death, just before airtime, of Elvis Presley at the age of forty-two. CBS and NBC had gone with Ronald Reagan's nineteenth denunciation of the Panama Canal Treaty. Sorry, as far as I was concerned, there was no contest as to which story should lead, but my opposite number at CBS had a different view.

"Elvis Presley was dead—so he was dead," Dick Salant told the press. "Our job is not to respond to public taste. Our job is to give people not what they want but what they need to have."

Oh really, I thought. And who decides what people "need"? A former corporate lawyer like Dick Salant? Journalists who believe themselves wiser than everyone? Who dares to say, "We know what's good for you"?

Later, on this and other occasions, Salant would tell me privately that I'd done the right thing. But at the time, I bristled, the more so when, even as I was fighting on all fronts, I was, so to speak, blindsided from the rear, in the form of an invitation to appear before a Congressional subcommittee that was investigating "Network Sports Practices"—most notably, mine.

What the lawmakers were after was ABC's involvement in the scandal surrounding a recently canceled boxing tournament organized by the flamboyant, controversial fight promoter with the stand-up hairdo, Don King. With Howard Cosell and the new president of ABC News (yours truly) among the witnesses, and federal grand juries in two states intent on hanging somebody, the media pounced on the story like vultures, talons drawn. I confess that, in different circumstances, I'd have jumped on it, too.

In the fall of 1976, Jim Spence, my number two in Sports, had gotten a call from King, pitching a ten-week elimination tournament in a number of boxing weight classes, to be called *U.S. Boxing Tournament of Champions.* This "momentous, historic moment," as King described it, would feature top-contending fighters certified by *Ring Magazine,* the so-called Bible of boxing, and lest there be any suspicion about the outcomes, referees and judges were to be selected by James A. Farley Jr., head of the New York State Athletic Commission and son of FDR's postmaster general.

Spence, who'd been the architect of a series of ABC prime-time fights, had done business with King before (Ali versus Ron Lyle in 1975, the first-ever network million-dollar fight), and was hot for the tournament proposal. So was Howard Cosell, who saw boxing as his personal preserve, and would be calling the fights along with Foreman. King's tournament, the irrepressible Cosell said, was "A dream come true for many faceless, hardworking fighters who toiled in backwater arenas for a couple of hundred bucks and the use of a locker."

We'd announced the $1.5-million deal in September 1976, set an initial air date of January 16, 1977, and by December, King had signed most of the fighters. That was where the trouble began.

Looking over the roster, Alex Wallau, a young ABC Sports promo maker and boxing aficionado (who is now president of the ABC-TV network), noticed that none of King's fighters was ranked by *Ring* as a top-ten contender. Malcolm "Flash" Gordon, publisher of a mimeographed boxing sheet, noted the same thing, as well as the fact that some of the would-be "champs" hadn't fought in as long as four years. Then a manager of a fighter who hadn't been selected wrote ABC that his man had a much better record than most signed by King. (Indeed he did: Undefeated Marvin Hagler was to become the light-heavyweight champion of the world.)

Jim Spence instructed Wallau to check things out and write up a report.

This Wallau did, turning in a detailed dossier on December 11, 1976. But Jim—who insisted, against my better judgment, on coming to

Moscow to participate in the Olympic negotiations—barely gave it a glance. Instead, he told Wallau to poke around some more and boil his conclusions down to far fewer pages. When Jim got back to New York, he found Wallau's latest effort waiting for him. Still too lengthy, he decided, and he had an aide digest the highlights in a memo. It was this document that brought me my first word of what had been going on, and I went through the proverbial roof.

According to Wallau, half of the six fighters on the debut program were palookas, and twenty of the remaining forty were by no stretch sterling. Jim dismissed the findings as the opinion of a new, untested temp, but with the first show only days off, I needed more assurance. I told Jim to secure sworn affidavits from King and the other principals involved (including *Ring Magazine*) that there'd been no funny business in picking fighters. I also asked Howard to get a reading from Angelo Dundee, a fight-game legend who'd trained Muhammad Ali.

Great idea, Howard thought. "Angelo," he said, "wouldn't dare lie to me."

One and all, including Dundee, affirmed that everything was on the up and up, and we opened as planned in Pensacola, Florida, before 3,000 screaming sailors on the deck of the U.S.S. *Lexington*. But as the show prepared to move to the U.S. Naval Academy for week two, Wallau discovered that a light heavyweight King's office claimed possessed a 13 and 0 record had in fact lost a fight in Rhode Island. The error, however, was caught before air and seemed minor

The scales began falling from my eyes by week three. Literally just back from Moscow, I was watching from home as a fighter named Scott LeDoux pummeled the bejeezus out of an unfortunate named Johnny Bourdeaux. But to my astonishment, and that of Howard and George Foreman, and seemingly everyone in the arena, the unanimous verdict of the judges went to Bourdeaux.

LeDoux thereupon cried "Fix!" and drop-kicked Bourdeaux as he was being interviewed by Howard. In the process, Howard's toupee was knocked sideways. Moments later, *The American Sportsman* went on normally—that's when it was scheduled to start—and I grabbed for the Roone phone.

"Goddamn, you can't just go off the air on something like that!" I shouted at Chet Forte, who was producing. "The name of ABC Sports is on this thing. Get the kid back, and let Howard interview him!"

Oh boy. The things you do when you play God.

Boxer LeDoux was calmer when he reappeared on screen, but his charges were absolutely explosive.

"I was told before the fight that I couldn't win," he said. "Don King control[s] . . . all the fighters in this tournament. We're the only outsiders."

If the accusation was true, ABC Sports was in for a world of trouble and Don King faced possible criminal charges. Just to name one possible charge, in a number of states it's illegal for the matchmaker of a boxing event to manage either of the fighters he's brought together in the ring.

Time, I decided, to get better acquainted with Alex Wallau. After reviewing the details of his warnings to Jim, and realizing the potential damage to ABC's reputation, I ordered Jim to get affidavits from all the fighters, swearing that their listed managers really were their managers, and I issued a statement that any boxer who felt unfairly excluded should contact me.

These moves failed to put the fire out. Within days, the *Chicago Daily News* was confirming Wallau's discovery of the phony fight records and hinting that King was using the tournament to pressure boxers into signing with him. This was followed by the *Chicago Tribune*'s television critic, Gary Deeb, charging that *Ring* had falsified records and that ABC Sports seemed "oblivious to the cruel charade."

Trying to control the damage, I threatened the *Tribune* with a libel suit. Then I accepted their offer of an op-ed page rebuttal, in which I wrote, "The tournament [is] beyond reproach because of the controls instigated by ABC."

Then a Texas fight manager called my assistant, Jeff Ruhe. The manager claimed that his ranked fighter had been excluded from the tournament while two unranked Houston boxers had been selected. Perhaps, the manager opined, the reason was that one of the unranked fighters had turned over a third of his $7,500 purse to a manager Don King called "my foreign representative."

I sent Jeff on a plane to Houston. He came back with confirming affidavits. Another call from another Texas fight manager produced another affidavit—this from yet another Houston boxer who swore that a Maryland manager offered to get him into the tournament by having *Ring* doctor his record to include victories in two 1976 Mexico City matches that had never taken place.

The day *Ring* released its 1977 *Record Book,* I had Alex Wallau get a copy bright and early. Comparing what it said against the 1976 edition, it became clear that eleven tournament fighters had "competed" in a total of thirty nonexistent bouts. The next morning, hours before the tournament's semifinal was scheduled to begin, I announced that ABC Sports was suspending televising the U.S. Boxing Championships, "pending the outcome of a full-scale investigation," and that I had engaged Michael Armstrong to conduct it. A former DA, Mike Armstrong had been chief counsel to the Knapp Crime Commission that had exposed wholesale corruption in the NYPD.

Armed with information we provided, federal and state prosecutors began separate investigations. They yielded no indictments, but plenty of embarrassment. Angelo Dundee, it turned out, had not told Howard that four of his fighters were participating in the tournament; James A. Farley Jr., the tournament's incorruptible "unpaid consultant," resigned after charges of multiple conflicts of interest; and for providing "rankings," *Ring* had been paid a fee of $70,000.

In late August, Mike Armstrong released a 300-page report. He'd uncovered no wrongdoing by either ABC Sports or Don King. But the Armstrong finding that received the most publicity was faulting the management of ABC Sports for not having taken better precautions before the start of the tournament.

No, I didn't fire Jim Spence. I didn't fire Roone Arledge either. But shortly thereafter I was summoned to Capitol Hill.

That the heads of NBC and CBS Sports were also being grilled (the former over how exactly NBC had landed the Moscow Olympics and how come they'd run a Russian-produced "Life of Brezhnev" as part of the bargain; the latter about a "winner-take-all" tennis tournament that wasn't) didn't make sitting at the witness table any more comfortable. Simply appearing added to rumors that I was on the verge of being removed as president of ABC News. I said I had no intention of quitting, and ABC said it had no thought of making me quit.

Instead I became a figure of fun, not only in the outside world but among the old guard at ABC News, too. In the words of *Newsweek,* I'd been "duped by a bunch of cigar-chomping, wisecracking sharpies casually pulling tricks that are as old as boxing itself."

It was a rough baptism, everywhere I turned in 1977. Finally I got sick of reading about what a lousy job I was doing, and I told my secretary, Carol Grisanti, to withhold further bad news from the daily pile.

The next day, my office copy of the *New York Post* had a large hole cut from the middle of page three.

"What's missing?" I asked Carol.

She answered: "You don't really want to know."

And that was even without Harry and Barbara!

Harry and Barbara

One of the first things I needed to do, when I became president of ABC News, was take Harry Reasoner to lunch. Instead I procrastinated, dreading it, the more so because I admired and liked the man: his dry Iowa wit, his sardonic take on life and the news business, his self-deprecating way of spinning stories, his love of sports and the outdoors. In fact, I liked everything about Harry Reasoner, and when we finally did go off to Alfredo's together, I came back to the office certain that, under other circumstances, we would have become good friends.

But I knew something else, too: I was going to take his job away, and I felt terrible about it.

It wasn't fair to Harry, but his pairing with Barbara Walters on the *ABC Evening News* was catastrophic, and the only way to end the disaster was to get rid of one of them. All you had to do was tune in. There was avuncular Harry, as steady and trusty as he'd been all through the CBS years, and there next to him was Barbara, the best interviewer in the business but visibly awkward and uncomfortable in these surroundings. On his own, Harry was excellent, maybe not quite Cronkite or Brinkley but one of the four or five best and clearly a star at ABC. On her own, Barbara was fabulous—so long as she wasn't anchoring. But put the two of them together and what you had was like arriving for a dinner party at the house of a couple trying to maintain a truce in front of the world while waiting to claw each other's eyes out.

The verbal cuts were mostly Harry's doing.

"I was with her on Nixon's China trip," he'd said at the press conference announcing Barbara's hiring, "but I never actually saw her work. All I know is that she rides the bus well."

There'd been similar digs since.

"You know, Harry," Barbara had said, finishing a report on Henry Kissinger. "Henry didn't do too badly as a sex symbol in Washington."

To which Harry had replied: "Well, you'd know more about that than I would."

But it wasn't all Harry's fault either. He hadn't wanted to share anchoring with Barbara in the first place, and he'd agreed only after an additional $200,000 and a pledge that his new, decorator-designed office would be the exact same dimensions as Barbara's. (His was done up in tans and rusts; hers—typewriter included—in Provençal pinks.) But the clincher had been a promise Sheehan had made him: that he could leave after eighteen months if the marriage didn't take.

In addition to the notorious $1 million in salary (half of which was being paid by Entertainment for prime-time interview specials), Barbara had been the beneficiary of multiple other inducements, the most notable being a hand-over-heart assurance that network evening newscasts would soon be stretching to an hour—ample time for the interviews that were the source of her fame. The plan collapsed when CBS backed out, and so did any real chance that Harry and Barbara in tandem would ever work.

One of them had to go. Deciding which was coldly simple. Barbara was the future of ABC News, Harry wasn't. Because while there were other Harry Reasoners in television, there was only one Barbara Walters.

If anyone had paid her dues to get there in television, it was Barbara. She'd started out as a writer on the *Today* show, had been a "Today Girl," had finally gotten to do some interviewing on the show—but only "soft" interviews, nothing close to newsworthy. Hard news remained a carefully guarded male protectorate. When Barbara finally breached it, she could only conduct serious interviews in tandem with a male announcer, and even then she was only permitted to ask the fourth question in. (The first three belonged to the man!)

She and I had been casual friends before she came to ABC. I remember one dinner out, Barbara with her then-boyfriend Alan Greenspan, me with Ann. Alan, of course, was a star in his field, I was a prominent sports producer, you'd have thought Barbara's focus would have been on the boys. Not so. While I was asking Alan about things like petrodollars and next year's gross national product, Barbara was riveted on Ann, listening to her describe growing up in Birmingham, Alabama. Ann was neither sophisticated nor powerful; there was nothing "in it" for Barbara. But she was simply interested—interested in people—and, in addition, sensitive to what Ann might have felt like had she been bypassed in the shoptalk. I saw that night a very human side of Barbara that I would never forget.

While still at Sports, I'd kept in quiet touch with her. Either she'd call me, or I her, to get my reactions to this or that program, and I'd listen to her tales of woe—"I'm drowning," she'd say—about Harry, about the razzing she was getting—headlines like "Million Dollar Baby Handling Five and Ten Cent News," which, to my mind, wasn't far from the truth. Even before that, ABC had made an absurd decision that, among other things, showed how badly screwed up News was. Having presented Barbara at the announcement of her hiring as the penicillin that would cure all News division ills, they then saw fit to keep her off the *Evening News* for six months. Why? Simply because Bob Siegenthaler, the only producer deemed capable of producing the program, was unavailable.

By the time I officially became News president, I'd already made up my mind that abruptly moving Barbara off the *Evening News* would wreck not only her self-confidence but, in the process, ABC News. But arranging the mechanisms that would save her and the *Evening News* was going to take time, and the affiliates were screaming for a quick fix. Fingers had to be stuck in the dike, and right away.

I began with rhetoric. Revolution, I proclaimed, was in the wings. Mini-cams and satellites would put us on top of any story in the world. Coverage would be better, more interesting and lively. I was going to change the face of News.

Thankfully, no one asked too many questions as to how.

One thing I did decide—call it the Cronkite influence—was to fly in the face of what every viewership survey had counseled. Sheehan had taken their advice, memoing correspondents and producers to come up with "more stories dealing with the 'pop people,' the fashionable people, the new fads." What needed constant remembering, he'd said, was that viewers were "interested in many things that are not intrinsically important."

Well, I didn't think the audience was stupid, just ill served. Yes, Roger Caras's reports on pets were heartwarming; and, yes, a psychologist giving tips on relationships might have saved a marriage or two. But was that what the *ABC Evening News* was for? I had no evidence apart from my gut, but I believed that the purpose of network television news was to provide information on key stories so that you could go to dinner that night or work the next morning with a level of intelligent involvement you didn't have before. People tuned in for content, so they could go away saying, "I never realized that, I know more today than I did yesterday." That's why viewers watched. To be informed. And the *ABC Evening News* wasn't informing them.

Changes in production would help. When I arrived at ABC News, Bill Sheehan had given Bob Siegenthaler, the executive producer in charge, the summer off and he refused to descend to New York from his Maine hideaway. In fact, he wasn't coming back until September. That wasn't good enough for me. I had my first go-round with Sheehan because, after searching high and low, I found no one better than Av Westin.

Av Westin had once called himself "the guru of television," and his résumé gave him cause. He'd been executive producer of the Cronkite news and guiding light for PBS's acclaimed *Great American Dream Machine*. He had also been executive producer of the *ABC Evening News* until 1975, when he'd got involved in a turf war with Bill Sheehan that ended with Av leaving.

Bill was positively stricken about the possibility of Av coming back. Did I want a shiv in my back? he wanted to know. He got lots of others to warn me too and, if I didn't want "Siggy"—as Siegenthaler was known—there were other candidates. But either the candidates he proposed weren't available or I didn't want them.

Av Westin, to my mind, was a formula producer but a good one, and I thought I could work with him. I asked him to come in and we met in my old Sports office so that no one uptown at News would know about it. He was a well-dressed, gray-haired, fast-talking Easterner, loved by most correspondents but given to abusing producers who worked under him and management types he had to deal with.

I laid it on the line with him. I told him I knew all about his reputation as a troublemaker. He said it was unfounded, and I told him I didn't care what he said. I wanted him to come to work for us, even though it meant going against the advice I'd gotten. But if I ever caught him playing politics, he'd be out the door before he even realized someone had him by the collar and the seat of the pants.

Was that clear?

Yes, sir.

So we set to work. We got rid of all the phony "chitchat" that Barbara and Harry struggled with, and with it the "two-shots" of them together. When either spoke now, they were pictured alone, and they were speaking less and less, courtesy of the "whiparound," which had correspondents handing off directly to one another. When a story needed studio setting up, increasingly Frank Reynolds in Washington or Peter Jennings in London did the setting. We also featured a thrice-weekly commentary by Howard K. Smith. Smith's days as one of Edward R. Murrow's boys lent him gravitas, and his decades at CBS and ABC made him one of the best-known news personalities on television. I also wanted production elements that would "say" ABC News over and over again, on radio as well as television, creating over time a kind of Pavlovian brand recognition. This led to the opening fanfare of drums and trumpets that is used to this day to introduce every News program, and to the signing—ABC Moscow, ABC London, and so on—in uniform graphics.

The tinkering wasn't perfect—one critic counted forty-three times that correspondent names were displayed or mentioned in a single program!—but the overall effect was a much more immediate, where-it's-happening newscast. If the ratings didn't budge, the changes showed that ABC News was starting to stir. Critics wrote that the Harry-Barbara friction had begun to diminish—as well it should have, because we had cut their combined airtime to three minutes a night.

All I'd done though was buy us some time. I needed help—lots of it—and new blood, and sinew too, and I found both in a Boston cop's son named David Burke.

It was Steve Smith, the guru of family finance for the Kennedys, who first put me on to Burke. Now in his early forties, David had been the sturdy right arm of the Kennedys whenever there was big trouble afoot—as in the case of Chappaquiddick. He'd served a similar purpose for Howard Stein when the Dreyfus Fund was desperate for a merger, and, most recently and stunningly, for Governor Hugh Carey when the New York City fiscal crisis threatened to unhinge the entire American economy. He was a man who'd been around power all his working life, and he wasn't afraid to use it. "If David Burke's going to stab you," it was said, "he'll stab you in the front."

Steve Smith's recommendation was seconded by Bill Moyers and Felix Rohatyn, who'd worked with David during the New York fiscal crisis. Steve brought us together for lunch at "21" and I became a believer too at that very first meeting. David told me straight out that he wanted to get into television. He also told me straight out that there were only two people he'd work for in the business.

"Bill Paley and you," he said.

Who was I to question such coruscating judgment?

We made a deal soon after, and I asked him what he wanted for a title. He chose V.P. and "Assistant to the President," opining that the latter gave him all the clout he needed, and I began to lay out all that we were up against, beginning with the Washington bureau.

As David would shortly find out (the denizens of the bureau soon took to calling him *consigliere* behind his back), they were dug in and hostile not only to outsiders but to any new initiative. Like the new building. For some years, the bureau had been housed in a downtown office building, but in one of my first moves as president, I insisted we start over, from the ground up, on De Sales Street, behind the Mayflower Hotel and close to the White House.

No credit to management for that. In fact, the Washington people were soon fighting over what kind of building we should have.

Shortly after David arrived, we went down to Washington for a dinner we'd organized with the bureau, at the Madison Hotel, one which quickly turned into a shootout. The first course hadn't even been served when the skirmishing started.

Question: What was my excuse for leading off the *Evening News* with Elvis?

Answer (Arledge): "For Christ's sake, am I going to have to wear a hair shirt the rest of my life over one show? Why's this such a big deal to you guys?"

Because they made it a big deal. It didn't stop there either. Every new proposal I gave voice to was shot down, and every idea they came up with reduced to keeping things the way they were. At one point, I went to the john, to cool off as much as out of necessity, and that's when David opened up.

"I've never heard such a bunch of uninspired crap in my life," he said. "And I don't hear any enthusiasm here for what we are trying to do. You better understand that Roone is committed to shaking up the News division. And let me tell you, we're going to shake the hell out of it. If you're smart, you'll get with the program."

At this, Frank Reynolds could contain himself no longer. He leaped out of his seat.

"I don't know what your friend here thinks he is doing," he said, referring to me, "but we've been working hard all of our lives in this business. We've been doing good work, and we don't even know you, and we don't have any need to be saved. Who do you think you are to come down here and talk to us this way?"

"A viewer," David replied.

David's chilly reception in Washington was matched when I brought in Dick Wald as senior vice president. I'd known Dick since Columbia. He'd been editor of the *Herald-Tribune* and president of NBC News. When Herb Schlosser became head of NBC, he fired Dick, who was on the verge of selling his house and going to L.A. to work for the Times-Mirror Company when I caught up with him. I thought he would lend us an air of legitimacy among our snooty Washington brethren. Wrong. Dick had an acerbic tongue, to be sure, but the Washington bureau, it came back to me, thought itself "purer" than NBC.

This was typical of what went on—the us-and-themness that seemed to take over no matter what we did. There was only one answer to it, really, and that was new people. I made only one correspondent hire early, Sandy Vanocur, formerly of NBC and the *Washington Post,* whom I put in charge of organizing an investigative unit. I'd realized from the beginning, though, that fresh bodies were a priority—at the top as well as in the ranks. And following the principle I'd developed at ABC Sports—that ambassadors counted, and image, and connections—I made a run at Bill Moyers.

Lyndon Johnson's one-time press secretary had been doing a series of documentaries for PBS. They were distinguished, and so was Bill. He had an almost palpable soberness, an intellectual heft, a genuine social conscience. Having him on our air, I thought, either as a documentary host or an *Evening News* commentator, or both, would say loud and clear that ABC News was a new force in television.

"If you come with us," I said to him over one of our many dinners, "you'll be in the forefront of broadcasting. If you stay where you are, you'll be a footnote in television history, and everybody will say, 'Remember Bill Moyers? He did such good work on PBS. But think of the impact he might have had, had he been on ABC!' "

He didn't quite buy it. The courtship dragged on endlessly, but every time Moyers was on the verge of succumbing, he'd find a new excuse not to: his loyalty to PBS; the $1 million CBS was dangling in front of him; my still being listed as executive producer on *The Superstars*. I'd soothe him, and we'd begin the cycle all over again. Lucky Bill wasn't a girl, I thought: You can't be both hooker *and* virgin. Eventually, though, he went with CBS, which put him somewhere between the two.

Wooing Moyers, though, confirmed two things: 1) the journalist who wrote that accepting an offer from ABC News was akin to "voluntarily joining a leper colony" hadn't been wholly wrong; and 2) that to land the truly big names, I had to have a stellar supporting cast in place. So David and I went shopping. First stop, NBC and its dirt-tough, drop-dead-good-looking Congressional correspondent, Cassie Mackin. She'd been making sixty; NBC was about to raise her to ninety, and we grabbed her for a hundred. That signing made trade headlines, but it brought me a letter from $62,500-a-year Sam Donaldson.

"If your White House correspondent isn't also worth that much," wrote the eminent Sam, "you ought to replace him with someone who is."

"I agree with you, Sam," I wrote back, letting him sweat a day before I bumped him to $100,000, too. All at once, correspondents from other networks began returning our calls.

As Willie Sutton once said, he robbed banks because that's where the money was. I concentrated on CBS because that's where the talent and the legitimacy were. For a time, we had a revolving door, people leaving, people entering. We had some turndowns too—like Moyers and like Charles Osgood, whose $120,000 salary CBS nearly tripled to shield him from us—but acceptances vastly outnumbered them: Sylvia Chase, Barry Serafin, Judd Rose, Hughes Rudd, Ray Gandolf, Hal Walker, Jeff Greenfield, Richard Thelkeld. There were raids elsewhere, too: Lynn Scherr from PBS, Chris Wallace from NBC, George Strait and John Quinones from local TV. I didn't overlook print either. Jim Wooten came over from the *New York Times*, and twenty-nine-year-old John McWethy of *U.S. News*

& World Report became ABC News Pentagon correspondent after I saw him on TV giving Jimmy Carter a hard time at a press conference. I'd also lure away front-line producers and directors in the months to come. By the time we were done, more than twenty-five of other networks' best worked for ABC and the prevailing "fraternal" culture of News had been broken.

In late October 1977, I received a call from an Israeli "consultant" and widely presumed Mossad agent, who was a sometime fixer with the International Olympic Committee. I'd never met him, but he greeted me as if we were schoolmates, extolling the Munich coverage, and saying that my name was venerated from the Golan Heights to the Red Sea. Whatever he wanted out of me, I figured, had to be equally grandiose.

As it turned out, he wanted to give me something grandiose. He'd heard we were working on a story—as indeed we had been—involving Anwar Sadat, president of Egypt, who was looking for a breakthrough in the Middle Eastern situation. Menachem Begin, prime minister of Israel, he said, would welcome a visit to Jerusalem by Sadat. Sadat, however, had to make the first move, which was where ABC News came in. If we could get Sadat to come, the "consultant" told me, he could deliver Begin. Therefore, I was to dispatch a correspondent to Cairo to ask the Egyptian leader whether he'd come to Israel if invited. The answer, my interlocutor assured me, would be yes. It had all been arranged.

He wouldn't disclose how he'd come by this information, other than that it issued from the "highest, unimpeachable sources" with reputations beyond reproach. "We get a chance for peace, you get a scoop that changes history," he concluded. "How can you beat a deal like that?"

I put down the receiver undecided as to whether this was the craziest call I'd ever gotten, or the most momentous. Was my visitor telling the truth? Or setting me up for a con? Either way, why me? I didn't want to look a gift horse in the mouth, but I didn't want to be swallowed by it either. Somehow, I needed to check his story.

Was it pure chance? To this day, I can't decide, but who should drop by the office that night but Mr. International Intrigue himself, David Carr. During my abortive efforts to land the Moscow Olympics, Carr, whom Sargent Shriver had put me on to, had been my key intermediary. He'd seemed to know everyone on both sides of the Cold War. Among other things, he'd gotten me behind the Kremlin walls, and it was in no way his fault that we'd blown the deal.

Leave it to Carr to show up just when I needed him. I poured him a drink and related my conversation with my "consultant," saying I had no idea whether or not he was on the level.

David heard me out. Then he asked innocently, "Mind if I use your phone?"

"Be my guest," I said.

He pulled out an address book, said he was calling Israel. Whoever he was calling, it was the middle of the night over there, but someone picked up the phone and, whoever it was, they chatted briskly back and forth, David relating my story, then listening.

When he hung up, he turned to me.

"You can take what you've been told to the bank," he said.

"How can you be so sure?" I asked him.

"Because of whom I just talked to."

"Oh? And who was that?"

"Head of the Mossad. I caught him at home."

Even I knew that Mossad was Israeli intelligence.

Anyone else but David Carr and I might have suspected I was the victim of some complicated charade. As it was, my every instinct told me to put Barbara on a Cairo-bound plane immediately. She'd interviewed Sadat on the *Evening News* ("Bar-Bar-Ra," he'd flirtingly called her), and prying the unlikeliest stories from the most unwilling interviewees was her trade. But the shootouts with the ABC News old guard had rendered me cautious, and I decided first to seek the advice of John Scali, our United Nations correspondent, a former ambassador to the UN, and a crucial intermediary between the Kennedy White House and the Soviet embassy during the Cuban missile crisis.

Scali scoffed that Barbara "doesn't know diddly-squat about the Middle East." The man to send, he said, was Peter Jennings, who knew his way around the region and had done a biography of Sadat for an ABC show called *Action Biography.*

Peter, ever the contrarian, proved difficult to convince. The idea that I was the one calling him, telling him what to do, may not have helped, although I can't imagine who could tell Peter Jennings what to do and not have him instinctively rebel. In any case, when I reached him in Johannesburg, where he had gone to cover the antiapartheid struggles, he met my story of prospective events in Jerusalem with the same enthusiasm he had shown on my becoming his boss.

Peter said he'd check with Bill Seamons. Seamons was an old-line correspondent who'd been made head of the Jerusalem bureau. If Seamons thought there was anything to what I'd told him, Peter would consider going.

I'm not one to pull rank easily. But when Peter checked, and Seamons was disbelieving, I hollered at him, "I don't care if you consulted with the burning bush, I want you in Cairo! *Yesterday!*"

Bitching as he went on about a seventeen-hour flight for nothing, Peter nevertheless did as ordered, and seventy-two hours later, he was in the Egyptian presidential palace, popping the question he'd come for. To his stupefaction, President Sadat said yes, he was ready to go to Jerusalem.

Unfortunately, Sadat's response was not recorded for television. Peter—either out of spite or because he was sure I'd dispatched him on a fool's errand—had neglected to bring along a camera crew. Peter, since, has claimed it was my fault, that I should have dispatched the crew—sorry, that's not how it worked!—but the result was like the proverbial tree falling in a forest with no one around. Meanwhile, Menachem Begin was making a speech at the King David Hotel, in Jerusalem. Bill Seamons managed to get to him there, popped the question, and the Israeli prime minister confirmed that, yes, he would be extending an invitation. We did run a radio bulletin, but Av Westin—concluding that no pictures signified no importance—buried the scoop on the *Evening News*. Which left the door open to others, notably Walter.

By this time, the canny Mr. Cronkite had tumbled to the story. No sooner done than he rounded up Sadat and Begin for a split-screen satellite interview, fast footwork that would have Walter remembered ever after as "the broker of peace" and leave me fuming in the dust.

Peter was assigned to be aboard Sadat's plane when he flew from Cairo to Jerusalem. I'd had it in mind that Barbara should be waiting in Jerusalem in the slim hope of snagging an interview with one or the other of the leaders. Then, the day before Sadat's departure, it dawned on me that I had Peter and Barbara in exactly the wrong place. *She* should be on the plane, the better to charm Sadat, *he*—great at extemporizing—should be in Jerusalem, describing Sadat's arrival and address to the Knesset. But how to get them there? The two capitals were technically still at war, and there hadn't been direct flights between them since 1948. I managed to find and get through to the Egyptian ambassador in Washington. Given the pressure of time and the historic importance of the event, not just to his country and mine but to the world, he simply had to get us clearance to land and take off.

His excellency agreed.

Barbara was less sanguine.

But I had no time for stroking or coaxing.

"Get your ass on that plane," I shouted at her over the phone, "and come back with Sadat!"

While Peter, at Lod Airport, outside Tel Aviv, was doing a masterful job of setting the scene for our audience, Barbara, on the flight with Sadat, found herself squeezed in with the journalistic heavies of the world, including Cronkite and John Chancellor. Like all of them, she was panting for an interview. But how to get one without tipping everybody off?

Barbara's answer was to slip the president a note. She made it simple: "Will you allow me to interview you in Jerusalem?" And listed two choices: "Yes," "No," followed by two more below: "Alone," "With the prime minister."

As they were deplaning, an aide returned the note to her.

Sadat had circled "yes" and "alone."

But Barbara had built a career on always wanting more. So while attention was concentrated on Sadat shaking hands as he went along the red carpet, she pulled Begin aside and whispered some words that had him say to his visitor, "Let's do a favor for our good friend Barbara."

So it was that the three of them—the two leaders and our own Barbara Walters—gathered in a Knesset conference room before Sadat's speech.

"Don't you think she's the prettiest reporter you've ever seen?" asked the Israeli prime minister.

"Oh, I can't say that," Sadat suavely replied. "I have to go back to my country where we also have pretty reporters." Then he gave Barbara a kiss.

The twenty-nine-minute interview that followed was remarkable not so much for what was said as for who was saying it—and, of course, on whose air. ABC News, everybody! "The last with the least" network had pulled off an unprecedented coup and on Broadcast Row in New York, the talk mirrored *Butch Cassidy and the Sundance Kid:* "Who *are* these guys?"

Some of the gloss was lost when Cronkite, learning of Barbara's coup, secured his own sit-down. Even though this was after Sadat's speech, not before, Walter, being Walter, received far more attention than we did. CBS could and did put it on *60 Minutes* whereas the best ABC could do, with no news programming on Sundays in those days, was break into the regular programming with a special-bulletin excerpt of Barbara's interview and give the full twenty-nine minutes in a special a couple of hours later.

There was justice, however, small perhaps but nonetheless satisfying. Watching the conclusion of the raw CBS satellite feed, I heard Walter say to his interviewees when he thought he was off mike, "Did Barbara get anything that I didn't get?"

That quote was in all the next-day columns.

Walter blamed it all on me—somehow, in his words, I'd broken "the sanctity of the satellite," although who had ever sanctified said sanctity (other than Walter) I have no idea. But the accolades were showered on Barbara, and I even had support from—of all people—Frank Reynolds! Frank, on his own, had gone to Rome to be close by in case we needed his services. We didn't, but I had a note from him afterward saying how proud the troops in Washington were of us.

The only negative in our midst was Harry Reasoner. He continued to sulk. True, I hadn't used him in the coverage—there was no real place for him—but now I wanted him to introduce Barbara and her interview, and when he balked, I had to go negotiate with him myself in his dressing room. "All right, I'll *do* it," he said begrudgingly.

I'd been putting off coming to final grips with maybe my knottiest problem, the *Evening News.* Now I thought to myself, *The time has come, Arledge.*

To do what? had always been my question. I'd had conversations with possible replacements for Harry, but even the right candidate wouldn't make Barbara any better at anchoring. The viewership surveys Fred Pierce kept sending told me what I already knew: that she simply wasn't comfortable delivering the news and that it showed.

No amount of production cosmetics was going to fix that either. Nor would a new coanchor. Drastic steps were called for, and I wasn't sure whether Barbara's contract allowed even a tiptoe.

Perusing its 100-plus pages, I noted that among the perks her William Morris agents had extracted were a second secretary, a personal research assistant, a makeup consultant, a wardrobe mistress, and a hairstylist. All were paid for by ABC, which also footed the bill for the hairstylist and researcher to accompany her on out-of-town assignments— or as the contract rendered it, "at such times as Artist performs any of the agreed-upon services at any location other than at Artist's base of operations."

But the clauses that interested me most were those spelling out editorial guarantees. While ABC had refused Barbara's demands for a nightly "What the News Means to Me" segment, and for guest approval on the once a month she hosted the Sunday panel show, *Issues and Answers,* she hadn't come away empty-handed. The contract stipulated that airtime and assignments were to be split down the middle with Harry, dead even, and that she'd be given equal prominence—down to the type size of her name—in all promotional campaigns. The contract, whose like I'd never seen, also went into what happened if Harry, under any circumstances, should disappear. The contract came within an eyelash of giving her outright approval of any new coanchor. Certainly it gave her full right of consultation, every step of the way.

I pondered how to get around that. The answer came not only from semantics but from another idea I'd been mulling over. Barbara's contract only used the word "anchor"; it didn't say boo about "desk." Or even "desks," because the more I thought about it, the more I realized that I had no one I could pair with her and no one to put on solo.

Someday, I thought, we would get there. Our own solo anchor, able to compete with the best. But I didn't expect I'd get there until ABC News showed itself a contender.

So, desks.

But how many? And where? And occupied by whom?

New York would have been the obvious first choice and Dave Burke had a nomination: Robin MacNeil, ex of NBC, now of PBS's *MacNeil/ Lehrer Report.* I thought there was good reason for why *MacNeil/Lehrer* was the only national evening news program with ratings lower than ours, and judged Robin a bit of a stiff. But he was classy too (profiles noted that he spoke French and baked his own bread) and he had the public television seal of approval. We had many meetings. Robin was intrigued to the point where he said, "I'll be a piece of meat if the price is right."

In the end, though, geography, not price, was the stumbling block.

Robin was New York based, and I couldn't have him in New York because of the Barbara factor. To put it bluntly, if my object was to ease Barbara out of the anchor's chair without seeming to, then I couldn't bring in an outsider to occupy a New York "desk." So Robin would have to move. But his wife wouldn't let him leave the city, and that was that, although Robin told the press the cause was "philosophical," not geographical, differences.

By now, it was February 1978, and Harry, whose *Evening News* future I'd long and publicly been saying was uncertain, was noisily demanding to be let out of his contract so he could return to CBS. But I wasn't going to let him go without a tussle. He was a valuable piece of manpower in the right situation, and ideal, I thought, to host a magazine show we were planning to call *20/20*.

Something had to be done, though, as Harry's press interviews were becoming more barbed, and his "fivesies"—the name he gave just-before-air visits to the Café des Artistes bar—more purposeful.

Of course there was always Howard Cosell's solution: himself.

He even quoted Walter Winchell in his pitch. " 'Other people report the news,' Winchell said. 'I make it public.' Well, I do the same thing."

"Precisely, Howard," I said, imagining the lurid headlines. "And that makes you a columnist. You dispense opinions, not facts. And having you dispense them on the *Evening News* wouldn't be good for you, wouldn't be good for ABC, and sure as hell wouldn't be good for me. So no . . . no, *no*."

Howard, as was his wont, refused to be deflected. To plead his case, he dragooned Fred Silverman, who'd recently left ABC to become president of NBC. "Put me and 'The Midget' on together," said Howard when he came back to the charge. He was referring to average-height Jim McKay. Apparently that had been the ever helpful Fred Silverman's suggestion, the evening news with Cosell and McKay. I remained unmovable, which Fred doubtless counted on: A Cosell pissed at me might be lured to NBC! Of course he wasn't proposing that Howard and The Midget anchor their news either. Howard finally figured out the game and dropped his campaign, but I'd won another black mark in his secret book of grievances.

That left me still looking for anchors, er, deskmen. At the end of the day, Washington was easiest. It was inevitable that it be Frank Reynolds.

Frank had been down the anchor path before, and the 1968 to 1970 experience was not a fond memory. "If you're on the FBI's 'Ten Most Wanted List,' " he'd said at the time, "the best place to hide is the anchor chair on the *ABC Evening News.*" He'd also become a target. Viewers deluged ABC with mail attacking this good friend of Ron and Nancy Reagan as a left-winger, and in going after the "nattering nabobs of negativism" who allegedly infested the Fourth Estate, Nixon's soon-to-be-indicted vice president, Spiro Agnew, singled Frank out for special mention, apparently because he was not requisitely enthusiastic about the Vietnam War. Frank's cause wasn't aided by his anchoring partner, Howard K. Smith, whose son (and later ABC News correspondent) Jack had undergone horrific trials in Vietnam, transforming his famously left-wing father into a famously right-wing backer of Agnew's press bashing.

In the end, Frank had gone back to political reporting, at which he excelled. I'd always thought he came off as a bit grim and pompous on television—"The Monsignor," David Burke dubbed him—but for sheer dedication and grit, we had none better. I needed him sitting at the national affairs desk—live from Washington, which would put him literally on the doorstep of great events.

Another thing I'd decided to put a premium on, against everybody's advice, was overseas news, an area to which neither CBS nor NBC was paying much attention. That meant a desk in Europe, and Peter Jennings, already in London, was the acknowledged class act of overseas television correspondents. Back in the mid-sixties, Peter, then as green as a twenty-six-year-old could be, had also had an anchoring stint, one even unhappier than Frank's. But he'd quit before self-inflicting serious damage and had built a superb reputation since, reporting from Africa, the Middle East, Europe, and Southeast Asia.

Okay, so he'd tried to get me canned. Who was it who said nobody's perfect?

That made two desks (three, counting Barbara, whom I'd slotted as "chief correspondent for special events"). I wanted one more. L.A. was my first thought, but not much happens there that's nationally newsworthy besides Hollywood, and the logistics—the time difference, the costs—made it problematic. My second idea was Chicago, capital of the Heartland, which until now network anchors had seen only from an altitude of 30,000 feet.

The longer I thought about it the better I liked it, the more so once I found my deskman. No one had ever seen a black network anchor, period. But that was about to change, as soon as I named Max Robinson, the adored anchor at WTOP in Washington, chief domestic correspondent.

Robinson had come to my attention via a *People* magazine article about his role in concluding without bloodshed a radical hostage taking at B'Nai B'rith's Washington headquarters in 1977. He sounded interesting, so I looked at his tapes, which wowed me. He was a big, handsome, deep-voiced man, whose delivery reeked authority. His background was also impressive: strong, middle-class parents; a younger brother, Randall, who was head of Pan Africa, the most prominent antiapartheid organization in the United States; a hitch in the air force and some college at Oberlin; then television. His first job had been reading the news behind a slide at a cracker Virginia station, which fired him the first time he showed his face. Washington was next, where he'd won a national Emmy.

A ticket, it seemed to me, with every hole punched.

Had I probed, I might have found some other things. Such as that the script that had helped Max win the Emmy had been written for him and read from a TelePrompTer. Or that after one of his frequent benders, he came into work hours late and sometimes not at all. Or that in a drunken, depressed moment in 1973 he'd walked onto his apartment balcony, pulled out a pistol, and popped off twenty rounds against an unsuspecting world.

But all I knew was that the camera loved Max Robinson and that if I was going to sell our new *Evening News* as groundbreaking, I needed him.

Barbara was ecstatic when I told her what was in the works. "This is what I've been wanting to do from the day I was hired," she told me. "Right from the start, I asked them *not* to put me on the air just to read."

I talked to Harry through his agent. The time had come. I no longer needed his high-profile dissidence, on or off the air, and I freed him from his contract.

With a new name, *World News Tonight*, we debuted on July 10, 1978.

We'd taken our dog-and-pony show around before and gotten our share of negatives. Research and Sales hated the name. ("World" and anything that smacked of "foreign" were no-nos from their point of view.) At a meeting with the Washington bureau, someone said the new *News* had no pizzazz. Others complained that it wasn't "new" at all. The affiliates pointed out, through their executive committee, that Frank and Peter were both failed anchormen. Then the media critics took turns swiping at us. "What do you have that's new?" asked Kay Gardella at a press preview at "21." "I don't see anything new here." At the same time, what was "new" was hostilely received. It was written that the program was here, there, and everywhere—seven shifts of location, the *Washington Post* noted, in the first ten minutes. We were also laced for "layering"—Reynolds introduces a story and pitches to Jennings; Jennings explains more and pitches to correspondent, who by then has only half the story to tell—even though we tried to avoid the problem by having one desk introduce a whole segment.

But no one could say that our first program didn't inform. The lead story of the day—Anatoly Scharansky's trial—was the subject of reports from Moscow, Washington, Tel Aviv, and Paris; the others were a Barbara interview with Alan Dershowitz, and a commentary by Howard K. Smith. Which of the networks, I asked myself, had done it better?

And Walter Cronkite agreed!

"ABC News," he said, "is showing pizzazz."

The pizzazz question aside, there were problems that quickly surfaced—technical at first, and then personal. I'd planned to have the day's big story covered by Frank or Peter or Max, in the field. But the logistics were nightmarish, the costs outrageous. It also proved difficult to find space for a Barbara interview more than once or twice a week. The critics were right in one respect: We frequently tripped over ourselves trying to figure out who should introduce what, and when. And Max Robinson was smoldering.

Jeff Ruhe told me he'd been complaining about airtime, but I didn't know the depths of his upset until I called a senior hands' dinner in New York, some three months after *World News Tonight* went on the air.

It would become known at ABC News as "The Last Supper."

The evening started off well, with toasts and mutual congratulations. We'd been first with a number of stories, and, according to several national surveys, viewers believed that ABC now led all networks for hard news. But, in the midst of the backslapping, Max appeared principally focused on the waiter expeditiously bringing his next drink. Finally, as we were leaning back with cigars, Av Westin raised the airtime issue. He and I concurred, he told the group, that, as senior man, located at the hot center of the important news, Frank should formally be primus inter pares. He should open and close each program and do most of the correspondent introductions.

Peter endorsed the notion. And Max exploded.

Putting him behind Reynolds, he said, was like forcing him to the back of the bus. Why didn't we just come out and say it? He was second class; the white boy was always number one.

Frank stood up and told him he was full of it, whereupon the meeting degenerated into a free-for-all of name-calling and accusations.

Peter tried to play peacemaker afterward. He walked Max around the neighborhood for an hour, urging him to give his job a chance. There were stories to be told. Get out and see the country, Peter counseled, report from Denver and Kansas City and Minneapolis and Omaha as if they were Paris, Budapest, Moscow, and Berlin. But Max would have none of it. He was an anchor, and we were making him a boy.

I would have to deal with the Max problem, but meanwhile Howard K. Smith was put out, too.

For reasons I could only guess at, Howard K. had gotten it into his head that when Harry and Barbara came to an end, he'd be appointed sole anchor, a position he'd held before the arrival of Reasoner. I'd never suggested this to him. In fact, Howard had been one of my heroes when I first took on News (and before and since), the one person we had who could deliver commentaries, or editorials, in a class with Sevareid and Chancellor. But now, apparently miffed that he'd been put aside, he'd greeted the format change by telling a reporter the day it was announced, "Sounds like a Punch and Judy show to me."

The quote had been given wide media play. I checked on its accuracy, then tracked Smith down in the Midwest where he'd been giving a speech at the time of his assessment.

"What the hell were you thinking about?" I said. "A crack like that just kills us."

Smith denied making the remark. When I told him I'd had the reporter read me his notes, he owned up but still offered no apologies.

"It's my opinion, and I'm entitled to it," he said. "Or is muzzling one of the most respected newsmen in the country part of your new format, too?"

"That's so much bullshit," I replied.

A few days later, Smith showed up in my office, his wife in tow. As if instructing the village idiot in universally known truths, she attested to her husband's importance and the deference I ought to be giving him. Howard did the same, though at greater length, concluding his peroration by cataloging the alleged deficiencies, personal and professional, of

Av Westin, our executive producer and, ironically, one of Smith's biggest supporters.

By then I'd had enough, and I adjourned the meeting.

That afternoon, Leonard Goldenson sent me a copy of a letter that had just been delivered to him by messenger. It was from Howard K. Smith, saying that our division was in rudderless turmoil and could only be saved by naming him to the board of directors with special oversight for ABC News.

Leonard ignored the missive; so did I. Some months later, when the five-year contract extension and salary increase I proffered wasn't to Howard's liking (or presumably his wife's), he simply quit. It was a sad ending—Howard had been so good, for so many years, that he deserved to go out in style amid the praise and admiration of his colleagues—and it was one I regretted even after reading Howard's parting shot. It was a "classic conflict," he told the AP, "between a boss who took over the news department not knowing very much about news and an employee who'd been in news forever, since it started, and who knew everything."

Maybe he was right about the first part. I hadn't known everything about the news business when I took over. But I was learning. Oh, how I was learning.

20/20

World *News Tonight* was the beginning of the beginning, and no more. To be competitive, we had a long way to go.

It had been an article of faith with me from the day I arrived to create a weekly magazine show. CBS had one; NBC did, too. My colleagues and the affiliates had given me a go-to-it the moment I started talking about it, and why not? Hadn't *60 Minutes* been one of the most profitable hours in television history?

Yes. But memories in our business are short.

60 Minutes had debuted on September 24, 1968, at ten o'clock, opposite the top-rated ABC series *Marcus Welby,* which had creamed it then and continued to cream it for the next four years. Ratings improved only marginally when CBS moved the show to six P.M. Sunday in 1972, an hour frequently preempted by the stations, and it wasn't until 1975—*eight years* after the first broadcast—that *60 Minutes* began attracting a significant audience. What changed everything then was a shift of one hour. The industry in the early seventies had been under frequent criticism for its programming, and one answer, proposed by CBS itself and then adopted by the FCC, was the so-called family hour, Sundays from seven to eight P.M., set aside for family or public affairs programming. Whether *60 Minutes* filled that bill may have been questionable, but that's where CBS put it, and, with virtually no competition, it had become an everlasting triumph.

And here I was, preparing to take on Goliath via a prime-time slot. From the beginning, I resolved to do all I could not to copy *60 Minutes* and to set the new program apart. In format, look, story selection, cast, tone, and approach, we'd be the yin to their yang, the brash new kid on the block. Just as it had been at Sports, our feistiness would be our success. But little did I know what I was getting into.

My first move was making feistiness personified, Geraldo Rivera, our chief reporter. I thought it a twofer: The new program would profit from his unique storytelling ability, and I'd score points with my old guard by getting him off *World News Tonight*. Sylvia Chase, a standout among our recent hires from CBS, was assigned to it too, along with Dave Marash, a burly, bearded ex-sportscaster with an investigative bent. Add the class and Washington experience of Sandy Vanocur, and occasional essays by a roster of outsiders, and we'd have an A-list reporting team.

What we didn't have was an executive producer, host, or production staff, and the months were ticking by. Finding the exec producer was key. But hiring Av Westin for *World News Tonight* appeared to have drained the pool of qualified candidates willing to come to ABC, and I had no one I could promote from the ranks. Furthermore, the Entertainment division had been unhappy about giving us the prime-time hour, and I couldn't afford to give them an excuse to reclaim it. Into the breach stepped Tony Thomopolous, who'd succeeded Fred Silverman as head of Entertainment. He had the perfect man for me, he said—ABC's executive in charge of late-night and early-morning programming, Bob Shanks.

I'd known Bob for several years, and thought him bright, creative, and a person who inspired loyalty from his troops—all crucial qualities for getting a show off the ground. He'd come from entertainment, first at the syndicated *Mike Douglas Show,* then at our own *Good Morning America,* which he'd taken from nowhere to vanquishing the *Today* show. This latter was no mean achievement. In morning-television terms, it was tantamount to scaling Everest without oxygen *or* Sherpas.

Even before Bob and I started talking, I sensed that the powers that be at ABC had begun to fidget. Having announced the new program, why was I now dragging my feet? And then, almost immediately after my first meeting with Bob, my phone began to ring. How did it go? What do you think?

Well, what I really thought was that I could do a lot worse. Sure, I might have preferred someone with a real background in television news, but I knew someone else who hadn't had that either when he came to News, fellow by the name of Arledge, and I could—and did—argue (with myself) that Bob's very lack of news background might give us a better shot at a fresh and different program.

Bob, for his part, insisted on having a free hand. He didn't want anyone—meaning me—looking over his shoulder. I thought that legitimate, and it was also, I admitted to myself, something of a relief. The truth was that I was too darned busy right then to be obliged to look over Bob's, or anyone's, shoulder. Besides, I believed you had to let producers have their way, once the ground rules were agreed to. Otherwise, you ran a very real risk of stifling their talent.

Noble sentiments, I'm sure, but in hindsight, how monumentally naive they seem, at least with regard to this particular occasion, and what trouble they would get us into!

Nevertheless, the day I hired Bob, I could hear the corporate sigh of relief all through the building. My only serious admonition to him could be summed up in four words: Don't be *60 Minutes*. But how he went about that, I agreed, would be strictly up to him. I'd be available to him when he needed me, but the people he used, the format, the host—all these decisions would be his.

His first major move was to hire as senior producer Harold Hayes, a Rhodes scholar, North Carolina Baptist preacher's son, and longtime editor of *Esquire*. It was an odd choice, I thought, as Hayes had no television production experience and his new job would require him to devise and assign television stories. But Bob told me not to worry. Who better to run a magazine than someone who actually had? I wasn't fully convinced, and my anxieties weren't eased when Hayes began filling the staff with print people who had no television experience either. But that was part of the plan, Bob said: Fresh eyes would see what our jaundiced ones missed.

Meanwhile, he'd come up with a terrific name for the new program—*20/20*—and he was doing exactly what I'd asked: being different.

His first candidates for host were certainly different: Julian Bond, the civil rights leader; Ben Bradlee, editor of the *Washington Post;* Pete Hamill, the author and columnist; Carl Bernstein, of Watergate fame; Sam Dash, the Senate's chief Watergate investigator. Fine men all, but not a minute's anchoring time among them. Well, another of Shanks's candidates at least *watched* a lot of television: Marvin Kitman, the TV critic for *Newsday*. (Regrettably, I lost Kitman's audition tape. I'd planned to air it the next time he compared my judgment to an orangutan's.)

Bob tested all these and others, but not a one was remotely right. Once again, time was a-wasting, and Bob had run out of ideas—until, sitting twenty feet from him, he found his man.

I may have met Harold Hayes before, but it wasn't till after he had been handed the host's job that Bob Shanks brought us together. Three things became immediately evident: He favored three-piece suits and two-tone shoes; his Carolina cum Oxford accent was off-putting; and his contempt for television was nearly as profound as his distaste for me.

A few days later, I was asked to another lunch to meet another instant television celebrity, Hayes's cohost-to-be, Bob Hughes, the Australian-born art critic of *Time*.

Hughes, on first impression, was a treat: a hard-drinking, all-outdoors man's man, more Down Under than Crocodile Dundee. He was also, I learned, an immensely talented writer. But there was just one problem, and I laid it on Shanks on the way back to the office afterward.

"I hate to say it, Bob," I told him, "but I can't understand a word the son of a bitch says. He's got an accent that would kill a koala."

It was too late, Bob said. He'd already hired Hughes—a done deal. Besides, the chemistry between the two men was terrific.

"Hayes and Hughes," he said, "Hayes and Hughes. I'm going to make that a catch phrase all across the United States. And as for the accent, well, I can't help it if our culture just doesn't produce men like this. I think people will get used to it."

"Maybe so," I said, "but I think it's a big mistake."

"Hayes and Hughes" sounded a little too much like a vaudeville act to me.

In hindsight, I should have trusted my misgivings and stepped in right then. But there were several reasons for why I didn't. First and foremost, I had pledged that I wouldn't unless I had to. I'd told Bob Shanks the magazine was his, and Bob was a seasoned pro. I was also, as I mentioned, up to my eyeballs extricating Barbara from Harry, plotting the changes that would result in *World News Tonight,* and supervising the production of *A Crack in Time,* a technically groundbreaking documentary on that epic of a year, 1968, that Jeff Gralnick was mounting, which involved "walking" Frank Reynolds through the events of the year, much in the manner of what the films *Zelig* and *Forrest Gump* would later do.

Compounding the problem was location. ABC had no room for the *20/20* unit on Sixty-sixth Street, so we housed them in the closest space we could find—on Sixtieth, west of the old Coliseum. This left them much more to themselves than was healthy for them. Whereas I was normally an inveterate snooper, walking down the halls to see what people were up to and stopping to chat and encourage along the way, I made only one visit to *20/20* headquarters in the weeks leading up to the first program. One detail of that visit, I confess, troubled me greatly: Nowhere in sight was there a television set.

Still, I crossed my fingers and trusted in Shanks's weekly assurances that his staff was "on a mission," determined to produce a program that would point the way to television's future

"Think of a cocktail party with the brightest minds in Manhattan all in one room," he said. "That's what you're going to see."

The plan was that *20/20* would debut June 6, 1978; air weekly the remainder of the summer; switch to a once-a-month schedule in the fall and early winter; then take up a permanent weekly time slot after the first of the year. It was no way to build an audience, but it was the best Fred Pierce could do for us, and we took it.

As premiere night approached, reports drifted back from the front. Geraldo was collecting gruesome footage depicting the grisly fate of jackrabbits used in training greyhounds for racing. Hayes and Hughes, meanwhile, had been working secretly on something known only as "The X Project." Now it came out. "The X Project" was a new investigation of Chappaquiddick. Or had been. At the end of the day, after all the cloak-and-dagger stuff, not to mention the time, effort, and money, Chappaquiddick turned out to have been a tragic accident! (The segment was dropped, the footage never shown.) But there was encouraging news as well. To cover the arts, Shanks had hired Tom Hoving, the former director of the Metropolitan Museum of Art; to report on science, Carl Sagan, the famed astronomer. These I took as very good signs. Both men brought an intellectual and creative dimension to the program, and both turned out to be remarkably adept at using visuals to explain complicated material.

I saw a few segments in the day or two before airtime. The Flip Wilson one appalled me, but I kept my own counsel when everyone else found it wonderful. Sander Vanocur's piece on an ultrasecret U.S. military group, the first of a two-parter, was first-rate. I made a couple of suggestions here and there, certainly not major ones, but Peggy Brim, whom I'd brought over from Sports to be *20/20*'s coordinating producer, begged me to back off. Shanks and his people, she said, were "very fragile," and serious tinkering would be bad for their nerves and the program. A little later, Dave Marash seconded the diagnosis, reporting that even my minor fiddling was being called "King Kong swinging down from the trees, mashing bananas in people's faces," and had moved Hughes to repair to the Café des Artistes bar to plot unspecified "rebellion."

With one stipulation, I agreed to cease and desist from further kibitzing. I wanted to be sure we had at least one live segment, and to this end I urged that the program closer be a live Sam Donaldson interview with Senator Ted Kennedy, who'd be visiting Arlington Cemetery on the tenth anniversary of his brother Robert's assassination. *60 Minutes* never went live. We would, and I wanted us to right out of the box.

Otherwise, I kept my pledge, busying myself with other matters until, just as the first *20/20* began airing, I suddenly focused on where we stood. Television is a transparent medium and a cruel one. You make your mistakes in full view of the world, and the downside, when you're wrong, is precipitous indeed.

My resolve to stay away crumbled. I could no longer help myself, and I went to the control room.

To my astonishment, though, there was no sign of either Shanks or his director. How could that be? I located them finally in the bowels of the broadcast center, trying to figure out how to take in the live feed from Arlington. They resolved that problem in time for Sam and the senator to go on, and the show closed as planned—horribly, I thought—with a Claymation caricature of Walter Cronkite saying, "That's the way it was."

Congratulations all around in the control room. At the risk of being a killjoy, I told Shanks, "Don't confuse getting off the air on time with a successful show."

But spirits continued ebullient at the postproduction party—in and of itself a rarity in News, if not in Entertainment. As for me, I couldn't join in the festive atmosphere. Even though I knew full well that no new venture in television rates a ten the first time around, I felt a mounting sense of foreboding. "Let's see what the returns are," I said, hoping against hope that I was wrong.

The returns were unanimous.

"Dizzyingly absurd," the next morning's *New York Times* judged. "Like being trapped for an hour at the supermarket checkout counter, and having to read the front pages of the blabby tabloids over and over again," said the *Washington Post*. And that was just the beginning. "Information packaged like a Krazy Kat cartoon" . . . "a Monty Python parody of a TV news show" . . . "a smudge on the great lens of television". . . "the trashiest stab at candy-cane journalism yet made by a TV network."

All in all, they constituted the worst notices I'd read since the start of *Sunday Schedule*, all those years ago at NBC. If, in my heart of hearts, I knew the show was bad, I still didn't want to believe it was that bad. At least not till I'd sat quietly, by myself, and screened the tape from start to finish.

By coincidence, I was obliged to spend much of that next day going over my new contract with Fred Pierce and the lawyers, something I'd promised Fred I'd do. Because Fred Silverman had pitched ABC a contractual curveball when he skipped to NBC—a clause intended to prohibit him from taking a job with a rival network didn't apply, he claimed, because he was becoming president of all NBC, not just the network—management was now antsy about me. They wanted a signed agreement. I'd been ducking the ordeal for weeks—okay, months—but now the moment had come. I had meetings on top of that, and the early evening was also shot, for Ethel Kennedy was hosting a Special Olympics benefit at Bloomingdale's, and it was a must-attend for me. So it was night when I got home and, all alone, popped the show tape into my VCR.

It was that bad.

Hard to assess what was worst. Geraldo's endless shots of greyhounds eviscerating jackrabbits deserved consideration, but so did the Claymation puppet figures that did lip-synching: a Claymation Jimmy Carter doing Ray Charles singing "Georgia on My Mind" and the aforementioned Claymatian show closer. To me, though, the strongest candidate was the comedian Flip Wilson, surrounded by his children, bursting into tears after he described, in bloody detail, how he'd beaten his daughter with his belt. And then there were the hosts, referring to themselves and each other as "Hayes" and "Hughes." At any rate, that's the one thing they said that I could make out.

The critics, I realized that night, had wildly understated the case: This was one of the great television fiascos of all time and a tremendous embarrassment to ABC News. I could point the accusing finger till I was blue in the face, but *I* was the one responsible, no one else. I'd taken News to the brink of disaster.

The thought made me crazy. How could I have stood by? How could I have let it happen? And what the hell was I going to do about it now?

I knew three things for sure.

One, rather than allow it to be repeated, I'd kill the show outright.

Two, Hayes and Hughes had made their last appearance on ABC air.

But finally, and most important, having dug the hole, I was going to get us out of it. I may not have been entirely sure how, but I was going to fix *20/20.*

Personally.

Daylight brought a terrific migraine with it. But then, almost as soon as I opened my eyes, I got lucky. There, on my television screen, was Hugh Downs, guest-hosting for David Hartman on *Good Morning America.* Good old Hugh, I thought. Times changed, but Barbara's former *Today* show coanchor was eternal, a Gibraltar of bland congeniality in a fad-tossed television sea. He'd done it all: pitched Alpo and Brylcreem, sidekicked for Jack Paar, hosted a game show, offered learned dollops on everything from gardening to astrophysics to the piano playing of Oscar Levant. He'd been at it so long, he held the *Guinness* record for most appearance hours on television—10,000 and climbing.

In fact, wasn't I the one who'd insisted that Shanks include Hugh earlier in his host search? But on the audition tape, Hugh, who'd been in semiretirement, had seemed stiff and artificial. His hair appeared to have been dyed a peculiar shade of red, and there was a positively funereal air about him.

This morning, though, he looked positively perky. Host *20/20?* I thought. Nobody could be less "different" than Hugh Downs, but look where "being different" had gotten us, and who better was I going to get on such short notice?

I called Hugh's agent at William Morris. Yes, Hugh was available. Yes, he was interested. Before the day was out, we had a deal.

Meanwhile, Shanks was waiting for me when I got to the office, at my request.

"You know," he began bravely, "it didn't measure up to my expectations either. But I'll fix it."

I shook my head. I told him to sit down, and he shrank in his seat as I delivered the bad news.

"In a way, Bob," I said, "this is more my fault than it is yours. I wanted a program that would break every mold, and, by God, that's what you did. You fulfilled your end of the bargain—you made something different—and I admire you for that. I only regret I didn't get involved earlier. But I can't let ABC News be embarrassed any further. So, until we get back on track, *if* we can get back on track, I'm taking charge."

It wasn't much consolation that I told him I wanted him to stay on and keep his title. He looked like I'd just kidnapped his child, and I guess I had. I then asked him to warn Hughes and Hayes that their services would no longer be required, and to gather them and the whole *20/20* production staff. I wanted to speak to them.

Even I wasn't ready for the waves of anger that greeted me. It was almost palpable. Hayes and Hughes didn't show up—Hayes would eventually try to sue us (unsuccessfully)—but some of those who attended were crying, most were furious, all were stunned. For one thing, they didn't know me, and they'd been stepchildren at ABC—partly, but not entirely, by their own choice. More important, they genuinely believed they had set television on its ear, and now here came the Counter-Reformation, out to undo all their good works. If I'd been in their shoes, God knows, I'd have felt the same way. But I wasn't, and I intended to be at ABC the next day, week, month, year; most of them, I knew, wouldn't be.

I plunged into the daily stress and strain of producing an hour-long show, determined more than ever that we were going to succeed, and our second *20/20*, on June thirteenth, at least stanched the bleeding. Hugh was trademark fatherly, reports on cesarean births and nuclear terrorists were solid, and my junking the cutesy production gimmicks made the program less frenetic. What aired wouldn't disturb Don Hewitt's sleep, but it was a step toward survival, and the critics were more kindly. "Roone Arledge," *Newsweek* said, "didn't become the Toscanini of TV sports technology without learning when to hit the stop-action button."

I took no joy in having to push it. Ironically, many of the elements Bob Shanks had used in that dreadful first show would become production commonplaces in later years. But programs aren't viewed for their little innovative bits; they're seen as a whole, and *20/20*'s debut had been a disconnected mess.

In addition, ABC News needed credibility. Once we proved we could reliably produce as well as the competition, we could do the envelope stretching that would beat it. Until then, one question had to be our production guide, and I drummed it into the brainstorming sessions we held: "Why would anybody watch this?"

We built on what we had—the lively and provocative commentaries of Hoving and Sagan, Vanocur's investigations, reports by Sylvia Chase (on fuel-tank safety in the Ford Pinto, for one), and Dave Marash (on low-level radiation among others)—and began to add profiles of celebrities from the entertainment and sports worlds to the mix. Jackie Gleason, as I recall, was one of our earliest subjects—a controversial, larger-than-life figure on the way to being enshrined as a national treasure. We did Jim Bouton, the baseball pitcher turned author, and Mick Jagger and the Rolling Stones. We did Bobby Orr of the Boston Bruins and Lauren Bacall. All along, though, one of our hardly secret weapons was Geraldo Rivera.

Not that he was ever easy, on screen or off. When we'd first negotiated with him that February—we being principally myself and Irwin Weiner, our VP for Financial and Talent Affairs and a very close collaborator—Geraldo was represented by the agent Jerry Weintraub, and we'd worked out a three-year deal that would pay him $225,000 for years one and two and $275,000 for year three. (At the time, this was very much in the range of what we paid our top reporters—the Jenningses, the Reynoldses. Barbara Walters's million was a total anomaly.) We shook hands—done is done—and went about our business.

The next thing we knew—I think it was Irwin Weiner who got the first call—Jon Peters was on the phone. Peters, it will be remembered, was the former hairdresser who'd married Barbra Streisand and was on his way to becoming a Hollywood producer. He and Geraldo, it turned out, were neighbors in Malibu, and Peters, or so he claimed, was Geraldo's representative.

Well, we said, we were sorry, but we'd already made a deal with Geraldo and there was nothing to negotiate. Not so, said Peters. Not so, said Geraldo.

If we were sorry, Jerry Weintraub squealed like a stuck pig. His language—which I heard at the very top of the decibel range—is hardly reprintable. But Geraldo stood by Peters, and in the end, eating proverbial crow at a lunch at Alfredo's with the two of them, I'd settled on a three-year deal for $275,000 per annum plus a $25,000 annual contribution to pay for Geraldo's staff.

But he was worth it.

One week he was in Berlin, uncovering heroin use and trafficking by elite U.S. troops. Another week, a veteran terminally sick from exposure to Agent Orange was telling him, "I died in Vietnam and I didn't even know it." In a third, he was on a Missouri farm filming an abandoned tank containing enough dioxin to kill every person in nearby St. Louis—concluding that adventure by breaking the jaw of a hulking cowboy who tried to stop him from taking pictures.

Our original plan had been for *20/20* to start its regular weekly schedule in January 1979. That didn't actually happen till the spring, but Geraldo played a key role in our May thirty-first relaunch with the first of a two-part account of playing Rambo in Laos, searching for American POWs. In September, he scored again—big time—with a startling and dramatic exposé of the cover-up in the drug death of Elvis Presley. Until that hour-long reportage, I doubt that at the time most Americans knew how important a role drugs had played in Elvis's last years or among his Graceland entourage. The subject may have been pop—the tabloids, to this day, make Elvis a staple—but Geraldo's detailed, careful, and revelatory reportage of a ruined life and lifestyle was work to be proud of, a landmark in his career, and it pulled in a 25.7 rating in the Nielsens, translating into 16.9 million viewers.

Meanwhile, though, my energy was beginning to wane. Shanks by this time was long gone, and Jeff Gralnick, who'd been invaluable in helping with the early cleanup, had returned to *World News Tonight*. I'd hoped I could fill the executive producer gap with Al Ittleson, a well-regarded former WABC *Eyewitness News* chief, but after a short period, it became apparent that that wasn't going to work out either.

I found myself spending most of my nights and all my weekends on *20/20*, overseeing all the scripts and the segment footage myself and chairing during the day the zillion and one meetings that go into a weekly prime-time hour. I'd become the de facto executive producer. As much as I relished the work, and as gratifying as it was to turn the program not only into a ratings hit but into an award winner too, I couldn't begin to do justice to my other responsibilities and stay breathing. I had to make another change, and so I turned once again to Av Westin.

Thank the good Lord I had Gralnick and Rick Kaplan, a twenty-nine-year-old six-foot, seven-inch force of television nature I'd snatched in a raid on CBS News, to take over at *World News Tonight*. I knew they'd be great at it, and they were. Av himself had been doing competent work with *World News Tonight*, but the long form was his métier, and he would prove it on *20/20*, introducing, among other innovations, beautifully crafted "process" pieces tracking composers, dancers, and musicians while they were creating their art. After an hour-long, critically hailed look at depression, mental and physical health reports also became a *20/20* staple, and with the addition of John Stossel, an Emmy-winning pickup from the CBS station in New York, so did the consumer investigations that changed laws and produced indictments. Of course, the ABC Sales department was crazed about my hiring Stossel lest we alienate our advertisers, but whatever advertisers might have thought of leaving were captivated by our mounting ratings.

Without the constraints of the rigid *60 Minutes*'s three-stories-and-out format, *20/20* could take on any topic at any length. "Policy gaming," for instance, or war games played at the highest level, was central to national security planning. Yet no one had ever seen it in action who didn't have a top-secret security clearance. Twenty-two million did, after we commissioned *20/20*'s "If You Were President." Culled from a two-day crisis-management exercise supervised by the Georgetown Center for Strategic and International Studies, and featuring the likes of former undersecretary of state Joseph Cisco and former chairman of the joint chiefs of staff, Admiral Thomas Moorer, the one-hour, unrehearsed special portrayed the decision-making process when—I'm not kidding—Arab terrorists threatened to blow up the World Trade Center with a dynamite-packed oil tanker. Round and round the arguments and counterarguments swirled, leaving the final decision to the unseen "President"—who was none other than the viewer at home.

Such programming brought *20/20* four Emmys in its first two years on the air. Nearly a third of all the sets in use between ten and eleven P.M. Thursday nights were now tuned to ABC. And the audience was growing:

For the week ending June 1, 1980, less than halfway through its second season, *20/20* was the most watched program on television—a distinction it had taken *60 Minutes* a decade to attain. That particular show featured segments on Mount Saint Helens, gifted children, and sexual fantasies.

But something, I continued to believe, was still missing. It was an old idea of mine, and maybe old ideas are the ones that die the hardest. I thought the program needed Barbara Walters. I also thought Barbara needed the program.

I'd first broached being host to Barbara while *20/20* was still in the planning stages, but I'd gone out of my way not to be encouraging. This was a new program facing great odds, I'd warned, and the media fringe that earned its living Barbara baiting would pounce on the slightest slip. I did everything but write in big letters that accepting my pro forma offer would be career suicide. Barbara needed no hint. "I can't take the chance of a failure," she'd said.

Her involvement with the program since had been episodic. Nonetheless, there'd been some moments only Barbara alone could have generated—such as sixties radical Abbie Hoffman surrendering to her on camera after six years on the lam from drug charges. "Barbara Walters' Secret Date with Abbie," bannered the *New York Post*.

Barbara had also wangled the first television interview with Nixon since his famous sit-down with David Frost. Frost, however, had paid $1 million to the ex-president. *20/20* paid not a sou. Like a gored matador, Don Hewitt howled, as he always howled when anyone challenged the supremacy of his *60 Minutes,* that he'd turned Nixon down because of all the conditions and restrictions Nixon's entourage had insisted on, and further, that one hour live on *20/20* wouldn't compare with fourteen and a half minutes taped on *60 Minutes*. I've no doubt that he'd have produced an excellent segment if he'd had Nixon, but in the first place, he didn't, and in the second, there was no comparison in my mind between a live show and an edited one. The issue was all about control. *60 Minutes* put control squarely in the hands of Mr. Hewitt and his splicing editors who could carve up and slant a tape as they saw fit. When *20/20* went live, control remained totally with the participants, in this case Barbara and the former president, and what came across on the screen had the unvarnished, unpredictable drama of a heavyweight championship fight. For my money, no taped show could match it.

The public seemed to agree.

"Go ahead," Nixon said, inviting Barbara to take her best shot. "Ask whatever you want. It's your show."

"It's *our* show," she jabbed back. "You give the answers."

After a number of nearly even rounds, came the knockout blows.

What about the Oval Office tapes?

"I shouldn't even have installed them."

"Are you sorry you didn't burn them?"

"Probably I should have."

"But Watergate was you, Mr. Nixon. Don't you feel responsible?"

"I can understand . . . the anger," he said, wobbling.

"That's it?" she asked. "That's all?"

"Yes," he said, going down for the count. "That's the answer."

I came out of the control room when the program was over and we posed for still pictures. In one of them, I put my arms around the "combatants" and touched the back of Nixon's suit with my palm.

It was drenched with sweat.

20/20, though, was now Hugh Downs's show, and Barbara was Hugh's friend, they went way back together, and so, while she was an occasional contributor, doing interviews in between specials, she was no regular. As the months wore on, however, there was less and less for her to do on *World News Tonight*, where the press of events was making Barbara's newsmaker interviews almost an afterthought. Her prime-time specials were a source of huge revenues for the network, as well as for Barbara, whose "Barwall" company produced the programs, but the specials appeared only four times a year and Barbara increasingly complained that her friends didn't know where to see her. What she wanted, she said, was a regular home.

Then matters came to a head. On March 31, 1981, when John Hinckley tried to assassinate President Reagan, *World News Tonight*, leading with Sam Donaldson and Frank Reynolds, threw everyone into the breach—*except* Barbara. The producers simply didn't think of her. When she phoned in late that afternoon, she was deputized to interview Gerald Ford, a third-level assignment that received third-level play.

The next morning, I got a call from Lee Stevens, president of the William Morris Agency. His client, he announced, wanted her contract terminated.

Much as I sympathized with Barbara's anger, I also knew that her ABC deal was coming up for renewal, and, though I didn't know all the ins and outs of it at the time, I recognized that this was but the opening ploy in what would be a most complicated choreography.

Looking back, I could write a book about negotiating with Barbara. The contract itself, when we got there, was like negotiating the Treaty of Ghent, but long before, there would be the carefully planted stories of her unhappiness (in this case, how restless she was on *World News Tonight*). Interspersed would be the gossip-column items (the columnists were all her buddies) of being wooed by other network suitors. Then the predictions in print of how devastating her departure would be for ABC. All of which were accompanied by Barbara saying that, in her heart of hearts, she wanted to remain where all her friends were, but . . .

This, however, was only the overture. I came to understand, in time, how the opera itself would be sung, but I also knew it to be opera buffa and not tragedy. Meaning that there was no way I was going to lose Barbara Walters, who was not only an extraordinarily valuable asset to ABC but a personal friend. And Barbara knew it, too. Not that this kept her for a minute from exacting the courtship, the wooing, the jumping through hoops that characterized every negotiation I ever had with her.

Irwin Weiner would spend a few agonizing months sparring with Barbara's agents. Then, at the eleventh hour, when all seemed lost, she and I would meet for dinner—not, of course, to discuss terms (even though some of the conditions might actually be discussed) but really to convince each other, like mating birds, that we still belonged together. Sometimes, Barbara would even stop talking to me, not taking my calls, refusing dinners. Sometimes she would tell people she was afraid to see me lest I seduce her into accepting less than she was worth. But then, again through intermediaries, it would be time to make up. Promises would be made, accommodations, understandings, and then suddenly there would be a road map for me to follow with her representatives.

In this particular instance, after considerable skirmishing, I got a call from Lee Stevens inviting me to a meeting at Barbara's Park Avenue apartment "to discuss his client's future." When I arrived on the appointed afternoon, I found him with Lou Weiss, his fellow *capobanda* at the William Morris agency. Clearly the moment of truth was at hand, which became the more apparent when Barbara, having served us coffee in bone china cups, circumspectly disappeared.

"It seems to us," Stevens said, "that what Barbara really needs in the future is to be host of *20/20*."

"I'm sorry," I said. "You mean *co*host, don't you?"

"I meant what I said."

"Wait a minute, Lee," I said. I was dumbfounded. "Please say that again."

"We think Barbara should be the host of *20/20*."

I knew a lot of agent stories, but this one topped them all.

"Are you sure of that?" I asked.

"Yes," said Stevens, shooting an uncomfortable look at Weiss.

"Well," I said, "the last time I looked, number one, we already had a host, and, number two, he was your client. Are you telling me you're trying to push Hugh out of this?"

Lee himself wasn't Hugh's agent, Ron Yatter was. But Ron Yatter worked for William Morris and Lee Stevens was William Morris's president.

"Well," Lee said, "we'll have to deal with that."

We talked on, but this was the gist of the conversation. And the gist of my reaction, if unspoken right then, was that Barbara or no Barbara, I wasn't going to let them do it. While I myself envisaged her as coanchor, I also recognized that Hugh Downs, perhaps strangely, was the heart and soul of the program. He might have just sat there every week, smiling at the camera, but that's what the public wanted and expected, and I wasn't about to change it. Nor, for that matter, was Hugh. In the negotiations that followed, when it came to defending his professional prerogatives, he was hardly the gentlemanly Milquetoast. The issue, for him, wasn't money. We had made a deal which was still in force, for $200,000 in year one, $300,000 in year two. Nor, if I wanted Barbara to appear regularly, would he have any problem with that. Making her coanchor, though, was simply "not acceptable." That would be seen as a demotion for him, and, he added, politely but pointedly, it would violate his contract.

In addition, Hugh had some ego needs of his own. Even if Barbara was to become a regular, he wanted to make the opening introduction and the close of each show and be the only one who would look directly into the camera. Barbara could introduce her own pieces and debrief correspondents, and he was agreeable to on-air chitchat toward the end of the program. But only if Barbara were shot in half- or three-quarter profile, and symbolically seated well to his left.

I seemed to have taken up residence between the proverbial rock and a hard place. But there is always an out if you look hard enough, and in this case, it was Barbara.

If Barbara would agree to forego formal designation as *20/20* coanchor, I told Stevens, and meet Hugh's finally not-so-unreasonable demands, I would make her the highest-paid personality in television news.

Stevens conferred with his client.

What exactly did that mean?

With Irwin Weiner back in the fray at my side, we began to haggle. A five-year deal, going from the much-publicized original million dollars she started with at ABC.

Good, but not quite. What about a signing bonus?

Done.

And what about her rights in her Barwal company?

Done.

But that was just the money part. If Hugh ever left *20/20,* Barbara wanted top billing and to be sole anchor.

I balked. Again, this was an issue of control I was unwilling to give up. We haggled. I agreed that, if Hugh ever left, we would give Barbara a reasonable run as sole anchor to see if it worked. But if it didn't work, ABC News reserved the right to go back to two anchors.

Stevens took this back to his client. It was okay. But oh, there was one more thing she wanted: a cutback in the number of specials she was required to do for Entertainment, from four to three—with no drop in salary.

Done (with a sigh).

And the right to refuse "unplanned" specials, i.e., those that came up at the last minute—like Begin/Sadat—because of a major event in the world.

Done, done, done, and done.

I'm telescoping the time span, I know. But why should I have to suffer it all over again, in every excruciating, stomach-churning detail? And the tangos I did with Barbara along the way?

But finally came the magic words.

"We have a deal," Lee Stevens said

Having been roasted in the media over her original pact with ABC,

Barbara had no desire for a repeat, and her formal addition to the *20/20* cast in September 1981, was not so much announced as whispered. Her exclusive interviews in the coming weeks, though, took care of the splash: Jean Harris sobbing as she admitted her love for the "Scarsdale Diet Doctor" she'd shot to death; Patty Hearst saying, "I'd really forgotten how much I hated those people," as she viewed the tape of the bank stickup with her Symbionese Liberation Army kidnappers; Claus von Bulow, a month after his conviction for attempted murder, keeping a straight face while professing hope that his wife, Sunny, emerged from her coma to prove his innocence.

In other words, it all worked out in the end. Even for Hugh. He got a fat raise in his next contract, negotiated, it should be said, by a new agent (another William Morris one). And *20/20* took up residence in the prime-time elite slot, a position it still occupies two decades later.

So we all lived happily ever after.

At least until 1985, that is, when Lee Stevens died, and it was contract time again with Barbara.

But that, indeed, is another story.

Nightline

Maybe this will sound too crass, too parochial, too egocentric. But if it does? Well, the hell with it!

I was itching for the world to have a crisis.

Not a calamity on the scale of nuclear war or global pestilence, mind you (even the ambition of a television news producer knows some limits), but one of those international *Perils of Pauline* sequences like Sadat/Begin, when all attention was focused on a single, overwhelming event, with—hopefully—a happy end.

"Sometime, somewhere," I'd been saying, "a story will break, and we will be in a position to cover it better than anybody else, and then people will say, 'How did they get to be as good as they are?' "

Then, on Sunday, November 4, 1979, a mob of Iranian "students" invaded the United States embassy in Tehran and took fifty-two Americans hostage. The moment I'd been waiting for had arrived.

(Were they really "students"? We had our doubts, and in due course we dropped the word in exchange for "militants.")

But a bit of background first. I've mentioned before the ongoing debate, led by Walter Cronkite, over taking the evening news to one hour. I'd never thought it would get very far—our affiliates would kick like steers before they'd give up their lucrative seven P.M. game shows—although I was ready to take ABC wherever CBS led. But I had my eye on a different time slot. Why couldn't we do the same thing at night that we'd done with the hour between six and seven, that is, extend our local *Eyewit-*

ness News, which ran from eleven to eleven-thirty P.M., with another half hour of national, or international, news?

From Steve Allen to Jack Paar to Johnny Carson, *The Tonight Show* on NBC had dominated the time period for as long as I could remember. CBS had long since given up the ghost. As far as ABC Entertainment was concerned, having had Joey Bishop, Dick Cavett, and Don Kirshner's rock concerts sent back on their shields, they were now countering with reruns of *Charlie's Angels* and *The Love Boat.* There was a door open, and for some time, subjects permitting, we'd been quietly usurping the eleven-thirty time slot with assorted instant specials. These ranged from the death of Elvis, shortly after I took over at News, to Skylab reentering the atmosphere and the fifty-five mile-per-hour speed limit. Celebrity passings (Groucho, Bing Crosby, John Wayne) were also staples, as well as disasters, natural and Congressionally made. Give us an excuse—even one so slight as "Soviet ballerina temporarily detained at JFK"—and we would produce a special.

The time period, in fact, gave us a unique opportunity to show that ABC News was a serious player. Whenever there was an important breaking event at night, or an ongoing hot story, I wanted people to turn automatically to ABC, because the more we strutted our reporting stuff, the better the odds that those same viewers would check out what we were offering at six-thirty P.M. It was guerrilla war, fought on a second front, and my biggest worry was that CBS might wake up and take notice of what we were up to.

We were also doing it on the relative cheap and attracting an audience that beat anything Entertainment put up, facts I did not fail to impress on the allocators of ABC airtime. Our most recent outing—four back-to-back specials on John Paul II's visit to the United States in late October—had even given Carson a run in the ratings. But His Holiness wasn't going to be dropping by every weeknight. To nail down the eleven-thirty slot permanently, I needed an unbroken string of attention getters only a bona fide crisis would provide.

I didn't even recognize it at first. Some ten months had elapsed since the dramatic overthrow of the shah of Iran the previous January by Islamic fundamentalists led by the redoubtable Ayatollah Khomeini. It had been a huge story then, and we'd had Peter Jennings in the plane seat next to the ayatollah on his triumphant return from exile in France. But the U.S. news crews, ours included, had long since departed, the cries of "*Marg am Amrika*" ("Death to America") had died down in the streets of Tehran, and Iran had dropped off our collective radar screens. I expected the latest controversy—over our allowing the shah to enter the United States for cancer treatment—to end quickly, and this latest hostage taking it had engendered, I thought, would be over in a day or two.

When I first heard the news, I called the ABC News assignment desk to make sure we were covering it. Stan Opotowsky, who was in charge of the desk, told me that Bob Dyk, a London-based ABC Radio reporter, lately returned from Tehran, was on his way to Heathrow Airport with a cameraman even as we spoke.

"Nobody else had a valid visa," Opotowsky said. "Anyway, it'll probably be over by the time he gets there."

"My guess too," I said, "but all it'll cost us is a couple of plane tickets. You did the right thing. Thanks."

Two more days went by, however, with the embassy personnel still locked up. Moreover, Dyk was satelliting back pictures of enormous crowds outside, burning the U.S. flag. He was doing a superb job, which later made him a full-time television reporter with us, while CBS's and NBC's late-arriving crews had been turned back at the airport. For the price of a couple of plane tickets, we had a week-long exclusive on the biggest story in the world, and 1.5 million extra households were watching *World News Tonight*.

Day four brought images of a handcuffed and blindfolded American diplomat being paraded before a howling mob in front of the embassy. We went with an hour-long, prime-time special that night.

"We need a name for it," I said in a meeting that day. "Anybody got any ideas?"

And it was Jeff Gralnick who came up with it: "*The Iran Crisis: America Held Hostage*."

Frank Reynolds anchored. We had reports from Tehran, where Khomeini was still calling us "the Great Satan"; Washington, where the Carter administration didn't know what to do; and New York, where union men were refusing to service Iranian planes and ships. But it was the man-on-the-street interviews that stood out. "I'd like to see us go in there and get our hostages," an unidentified Manhattanite told Ann Garrels. "If it means a quarter more a gallon for gasoline, I'm willing to pay it, and I think all the rest of the people are, too."

The next morning, I had occasion to measure the impact of *America Held Hostage*. I had to fly up to Lake Placid, New York, for a press conference on our Olympic preparations. But the sportswriters weren't interested in the fifty miles of television cable we had strung on White Face Mountain. They wanted to know about Iran: Would we send more correspondents? Would there be more specials? Where would the coverage go from here?

It was the same when I got back to New York. From the baggage handler, the taxi driver, the doorman, the elevator operator—Iran, Iran, Iran was all you heard.

Except at ABC.

Not only had planning not begun on a new special, but no one even saw the need. The hostages were still hostages, I was told. What more was there to add?

Foot-dragging from the network, I could understand: Satellite time was expensive, public affairs commercials hard to sell. But the resistance wasn't coming from Elton or Fred; it was my own division. If CBS and NBC weren't rushing to cover the story in a major way, why should we?

It was the old News ethic, rising once more from the coffin. At Sports, the staff was like the marines. When a beachhead was spotted, it was seized, without buts or by-your-leaves. Doing television better, smarter, and quicker was all that mattered. It was why ABC Sports was number one, and ABC News wasn't.

Yet.

"I'm going to make this very simple," I said to one of the old guard, who was counseling caution. "Fifty-two Americans having guns held to their heads in Iran is news, okay? And reporting the news is what we do here. So I want you to put a special together *now*. And I want you to keep getting specials ready until I tell you to stop. Clear?"

Apparently, it was. Forty-eight hours later, with a new, hard-line regime in Tehran threatening to put the hostages on trial as spies, we were on the air with a second special. Just as we went on the air, because of the time difference, dawn was breaking in Iran. The impact was terrific. We drew an audience half again as big that night as the first, and two more words were tacked onto the title: "*Day 11.*"

On Day 12, I called Fred Pierce.

"I want to make an announcement tonight," I said, "that we'll continue our coverage nightly, as long as it lasts."

"Define how 'long,' " Fred said.

"Three, four weeks tops," I replied.

Fred agreed and Frank Reynolds signed off that night, saying that *America Held Hostage* would be back again tomorrow. "In fact," he added, almost offhandedly, "we'll be on the air every night at this time with a broadcast about the crisis in Iran as long as there is a crisis."

I found the announcement tepid, uninspired. This was unprecedented news coverage, and I wanted drums drumming, trumpets blaring. So, the next day we took out full-page ads in all the major papers proclaiming ABC's commitment to stay with the story, come what may, to the very end. Industry reaction divided along psychiatric lines, some thinking me totally nuts, others only mostly. From David Burke's soundings, ABC's Washington bureau was in the first camp.

"Screw 'em," David said. "We gotta go for it. We'll never have a better shot at getting the half hour."

"Besides," I laughed, "what do these guys know? They've only spent their whole lives in television news."

David laughed too, but we both knew the gamble. We were embarking on something no one had dared do before, attaching our hopes to an open-ended story half a world away whose outcome depended on the whims of a fanatical cleric. The unlikeliness of the enterprise was half the reason I'd bought the ads: Drawing a line in the sand in sixty-four-point type made it impossible for corporate ABC to back out now.

November twenty-ninth was Frank Reynolds's fifty-sixth birthday, and after burning the candle at both ends with *World News Tonight* and *America Held Hostage* for almost three weeks, he took the night off. As a substitute, I elected our diplomatic correspondent, Ted Koppel.

Initially, I hadn't thought much about Ted one way or the other. Nor he of me, I suppose. He'd done his best, in fact, to terminate my employment, joining Peter Jennings in telling Fred Pierce that naming me president of News was not far removed from anointing P. T. Barnum archbishop of Canterbury. We hadn't met at the time of this assessment, as Ted was on child care leave while his wife, Grace Anne, attended first-year law school. His main work for ABC was anchoring the *Saturday Evening News*. He had seemed reasonably competent at it, but I was as struck by how his chipmunk cheeks and odd-parted auburn hair lent him an uncanny resemblance to Alfred E. Newman. The *Saturday Evening News*, I should say, was something of a graveyard for us, as for our competitors, but even anonymity has its uses, and while Koppel was off on vacation, I replaced his executive producer with Jeff Gralnick, whom I was grooming for better things and who I wanted to have a free hand at on-air experiments in a slot where mistakes and failures would be little noticed.

At Sports, mind you, I commonly switched producers and made assignments without consultation or fuss. I thus thought nothing of the move until a letter arrived from the aforementioned Koppel, saying I'd trespassed grossly on News division sensibilities, and that he was hereby quitting!

I thought little of it, for I had Tom Jarriel and Sylvia Chase to try out on *Saturday Evening News*. As for the Koppel resignation, well, I thought, I'd deal with it when I had time.

Apparently unaccustomed to being ignored, Ted left a flurry of messages with my secretary, Carol Grisanti, requesting a face-to-face meeting. These, I treated likewise. Undaunted, Ted kept calling—with, however, a switch in tactics. If he charmed Carol, he must have figured, he'd get to me. What's more, the switch worked. When I could no longer stand having my ear bent about "cute, sweet Ted," I succumbed and let her schedule a lunch.

So it was, over pasta and red wine, that I heard the life story of this charming and interesting man, from his upbringing in England, where his parents—prosperous German Jews—had taken refuge from Hitler in 1938; to the family's move to the United States in 1953 and the schooling at Syracuse and Stanford that followed; to his becoming, at twenty-three, the youngest correspondent in ABC News history. He'd run bureaus in Miami and Hong Kong; had covered the war in Vietnam; had traipsed the world with Henry Kissinger, who'd offered him an appointment as an assistant secretary of state.

That was where I had him pigeonholed—as a State Department reporter. But, as Ted was quick to demonstrate, he had other talents, one of which was an uncanny ability to impersonate the famous. He ran through a number of them for me—Nixon, William F. Buckley—to my mirth and admiration, all the while reminding me that he could do other things on the news besides anchoring.

"Have you seen my work on the conventions?" he asked.

When I acknowledged that I hadn't, he said he'd send me tapes.

"I promise I'll look at them," I said, "if you'll do Nixon one more time."

Which he was glad to do.

The convention tape was terrific, but after the lunch, nothing would have surprised me about him. Anyone who could discourse expertly about Kremlin arcana *and* balance a dog biscuit on his nose (Ted later demonstrated the skill on the *Letterman* show) had to possess unusual gifts, including, the tape revealed, skill at interviewing. He had the ability to cut through obfuscation without being obnoxious; he was sharp but polite, opinionated but not doctrinaire. He was also spooky smart and wasn't bashful about saying so, but he wore his cockiness well. He also knew how to ingratiate himself with others—I was the only person he'd ever known, he would say more than once, who was smarter than he was—and the fun he poked at himself was part of the same trick. You found yourself not only admiring Ted Koppel, he made you *like* him, too. And that perhaps was his most formidable ability.

I soon had him back on the diplomatic beat full time, but I also looked for new ways to stretch him and use his talents. This led to a ten-part series on national security that he did for *World News Tonight* in April 1979. Network newscasts, at the time, didn't air ten-part reports on anything, which was precisely one of the reasons I commissioned it. But I also, much more simplistically, wanted to know more about the odds of the United States blowing up. If I were interested, my programming calculus went, viewers would be, too.

And so they were. Three months in the making, *Second to None* opened with Ted out-Murrowing Edward R. Murrow's ominousness ticking down of the steps to doomsday and proceeded to the utter absurdity of nuclear-age civil defense. (What would happen to New York City in the event of a nuclear attack? Not to worry. According to the master plan then in force, Manhattan was to be evacuated one tidy block at a time—all in the twenty minutes' warning we would have once Soviet missiles were in the air!) After eight more nights of bone-chilling reports, the series went on to win major awards and was the catalyst in getting *World News Tonight* out of its last-place ratings ghetto. From then on, for the next two decades, *World News Tonight* would be either in first or second place and, once Walter Cronkite retired, most often in first.

Ironically, Ted didn't marry easily to the Iran story, which commenced for him while he was passing a familial Sunday afternoon in suburban Maryland. He bitched about having to come in to do a State Department stand-up on his day off, and he continued to bitch each time a new installment of *America Held Hostage* disrupted his schedule. But the complaints ceased as soon as he began sitting in for Frank, who departed to cover the presidential campaign in mid-December.

Now Ted couldn't get enough of the show that, at my direction, had moved from the "Will they be killed?" question to a national teach-in on Iran, Islam, and U.S. foreign policy—prime-cut Koppel meat. One night, *America Held Hostage* would delve into SAVAK, the shah's notorious secret police; another, the differences between Sunni and Shiite Islam; still another, the consequences of the CIA's overthrow of the shah's left-leaning prime minister, Mohammad Mossadegh, back in 1953. There were programs on Persian history and geography; the hostages and hostage families; the shah's policies, strengths, foibles, and liabilities, and those of Khomeini, down to the meaning of his black turban. An entire show addressed "What is a Mullah?" Members of the ruling "revolutionary council" became household names, and foreign minister Sadegh Ghotbzadeh—a Georgetown flunk-out, I had Ted note—a regular living room guest.

We were the only network, I noted with pleasure, that pronounced Ghotbzadeh correctly. Walter flubbed it night after night. But that was only symptomatic. No demonstration went uncovered, no diplomatic stone unturned, no military option unexamined. Live and in color, the Iran crisis was the property of ABC.

There were times when the White House wished it weren't so. It had welcomed *America Held Hostage* early on, believing that nightly crisis coverage would be President Jimmy Carter's ally in fending off Ted Kennedy's challenge and winning renomination. But as time wore on and the commander in chief looked and acted more hapless than presidential in the crisis, Leonard began getting calls saying that a program whose very title bespoke haplessness wasn't helping the country. Or, for that matter, ABC's broadcast licenses.

"What do you think?" Leonard asked me one day, recounting the patriotic pressure.

"I think it proves we have a helluva show," I said.

Leonard smiled. "So do I," he said. "And as for that Koppel fellow, I think he could be the next Cronkite."

We continued on through Christmas and the New Year without further interruption, but I was straining resources. We now had five crews in Iran, one or another of which had the embassy staked out around the clock. In New York and Washington, the staff I'd borrowed from other programs for "temporary duty" was now in its second month of eighteen-hour days, seven days a week. One producer had had T-shirts made up saying, "ABC News Held Hostage," and even Koppel was beginning to wonder how much longer we would press on.

But I had no intention of stopping. The Iran crisis had come gift-wrapped by the gods. Had it occurred much earlier, the instant, open-ended satellite transmission that made the program doable wouldn't have existed. And I could only count it as a sign that, of all the Third World spots in which the United States could be embroiled, Iran had the best television facilities. Even the eight-hour time difference between New York and Tehran seemed arranged by fate: When the hostages's new day was just dawning, so was our night's program hitting the airwaves. Every star was aligned, including the Ayatollah Khomeini. Thanks to him, "three or four weeks" had become an open-ended run and ayatollah or no ayatollah, I had no intention of ending it.

The late-night audience we were not supposed to attract was now nearly the size of Carson's—and bigger on certain major news nights. We were also sharpening the way we conveyed information. One night, the Iranian chargé d'affaires Ted was to interview refused to come to the studio, claiming he'd be arrested by the FBI. So we sent a crew to his embassy and "brought" him to the set in a green-screen chroma key. This is the now familiar technique that allows an announcer—a weatherman, for instance—to appear to be standing in front of a panorama when in fact there is nothing behind him but a blank green wall. The image of the panorama is electronically inserted to create the illusion. In this instance, it appeared that the chargé d'affaires and Ted—who was actually addressing a blank frame—were talking through a window. But keeping the Iranian at electronic remove shrank his image and enlarged Ted's, shifting the psychological balance between subject and interviewer. Koppel was now in command.

The moment I saw the difference, we made it permanent. No guest sat face-to-face with Ted anymore. Instead, guests were conducted to a windowless room off the set where the only company was a staring camera, the only means of communicating a microphone *we* shut on and off. I myself have been a guest on the show a few times over the years, and it's amazing how the procedure makes you lose control, to Ted, of the moment. It isn't genteel, it may not even be fair. But it makes for great television.

Live television too, with no exceptions. I laid down the "live-only" rule at the very beginning of *America Held Hostage,* and its enforcement cost us some guests. Nonetheless, we wouldn't budge. There was an edge and an immediacy to live television that tape couldn't match. Moreover, going live gave us an extra two, three, or four hours for late-breaking news to come in. Finally, the risks that went with being live—a technical breakdown midstream, a guest stalking off mid-show—kept the whole staff on the balls of their feet. I knew we'd lose that the first time we permitted taping; accommodate one guest, a hundred others would demand the same. In time, I calculated, the attraction of speaking unedited would outweigh the desire for a good night's sleep. If we lost a few guests in the interval, so what? Being live, when no one else was, gave us cachet.

Week by week, my plans for a permanent program were coming together. I wasn't yet ready to take them to Fred, though, as one element was missing. I was still trying to define what it was, when on January 23, 1980—*Day 80* for the hostages—Jimmy Carter delivered what turned out to be his last state of the union address.

We had lined up a superb covey of guests: Sadegh Ghotbzadeh in Tehran; Soviet radio commentator Vladimir Pozner in Moscow; and, in America, Secretary of Defense Harold Brown and Senators Joe Biden of Delaware and Richard Lugar of Indiana. As an experiment, we decided at the last minute to tinker with the format: Rather than the usual television practice of interviewing the first talking head, then moving to the next and the next until all had said their pieces, we wanted Ted to engage them in group conversation and see where the back and forth led.

I'd thought it might be interesting. Instead, it was magic. They talked, they argued, they debated, they did everything real-life people do when thrashing through a topic, except these people were on three different continents! It was like watching a symphony, with Ted as the conductor, knowing just when to bring up the horns and fade out the strings. He made music that night, and I found my program.

Selling it as is was the hard part. Leonard now liked the notion of late-night news, but he had his own ideas about how to pull it off. Look at the millions CBS was making from *60 Minutes,* he said. Why couldn't we do the same? An investigation every week, spread out over five, cliff-hanging nights. Find the story, gather the evidence, build the case, and on Friday, confront the bad guy with the goods.

How about a little entertainment in the mix? someone said. A Hollywood report, say?

To which Elton added, Maybe sports and weather? Like the local news, in other words. Only national.

I gently swatted down those ideas, and when no one came up with anything better, I finally got the nightly half hour I wanted. We'd continue to track the Iran crisis until its conclusion, but our focus from then on would be broader: We'd look ahead as well as behind, examine issues as well as events. It would be *America Held Hostage* without the hostages.

I set Monday, March twenty-fourth, as premiere date and told Bill Lord, a nineteen-year ABC veteran who was going to be executive producing, to start hiring a permanent staff.

Then, at the eleventh hour, Fred got a call from Larry Pollack, station manager of WFIL, in Philadelphia, ABC's most powerful affiliate and the station with the most highly rated local news coverage. When Larry talked, Fred listened, and Larry was unhappy. If, after watching his eleven o'clock news, fans were going to have to sit through an additional half hour of Ted and his pointy heads before they got to their favorite entertainment reruns, then they'd stop watching his eleven o'clock news altogether. And that would cost him ratings and revenue. Accordingly, he said, he might well decide to run old movies instead of Ted.

Fred inevitably passed Larry on to me. I couldn't begin to follow his logic, but there was no mistaking the implications of his threat: A blackout at WFIL would send clearance dominoes toppling throughout the network, dooming the program before it got off the ground.

I shouted at him, he shouted at me, but in the end, as absurd as it was, I had no choice but to compromise with him. Monday through

Thursday, our as-yet-untitled program would run for twenty minutes rather than the thirty I wanted, allowing Farrah Fawcett fans an earlier fix. Fridays, when the start of the weekend drastically reduced the size of the news audience, we wouldn't air at all.

In other words, better half a loaf than no loaf at all.

This wasn't the last time our programming would run afoul of the redoubtable Larry Pollack and WFIL. A few years later, when we launched *This Week with David Brinkley,* our scheduling ran into Larry Pollack's Sunday-morning movie. The compromise, in that instance, was to give the affiliates an additional feed on the show, an hour earlier than we planned. Such was the power of a powerful affiliate.

I went off to produce the 1980 Winter Games, which would be the only Olympics Americans would see that year. Two days before the previous Christmas, the Soviets had invaded Afghanistan, and Jimmy Carter was in the midst of organizing a boycott of the Moscow Summer Games. But that was NBC's problem. Mine was Lake Placid, where U.S. chances for gold were decidedly slim. Certainly, the hockey team was given no chance whatsoever. For one thing, it was composed entirely of amateurs—college players, in large part—because the pros of the National Hockey League were then banned from Olympic competition. For another, it was drawn into the same bracket as the Soviets, who'd whipped the NHL All-Stars 6-0 and the Olympians themselves 10-3 in a Madison Square Garden exhibition just before the Games. Too bad, I remember thinking; the country could have used a boost, even though hockey was hardly our national sport.

But as it turned out, we got two boosts. The first was one of the truly great performances in U.S. sports history, and indeed of all the Olympic Games since the beginning of the century. The speed skater Eric Heiden, excelling in a sport that was scarcely a traditional American domain either, was on his way to winning an astonishing five gold medals. ABC Sports, meanwhile, was getting the network's biggest audiences since *Roots II,* and on four of the first seven nights of the competitions, our programs beat all comers.

We had, though, paid little attention to the ice-hockey schedule. It called for two games per night, only the second of which would be in prime time. When the United States team started to win, we asked the schedulers to switch the impending U.S. versus USSR game to prime time. The head man of Russian radio and television at the time, though, was a hockey nut and he refused the change. Because of the time difference, he wanted the earlier start so that he, himself, could watch the Cold-War clobbering he assumed was in store for us. The opening face-off remained at five-thirty P.M. It never even occurred to me—till later—to go live anyway, because that would have meant preempting that untouchable icon, the affiliates' local news. So we stayed with prime time, even though it meant going with tape delay and, I've always believed, a concurrent falling off in the size of our audience.

I was still muttering to myself, just before the game began, when Ted Koppel popped his head through the control room door. I couldn't imagine why he was here, and I was too busy to ask. I gave him a wave, and went back to my monitors. A few moments later, they filled with one of the most memorable upsets ever recorded in television sports.

Producing a game, it goes without saying, is not at all like watching one. Your eye isn't on a rink of ice or a sweep of green turf but on a dozen flickering screens in a dark control room. You are removed from the action more than any fan in the stands, yet more intimately aware of it than even the players on the field. You're seeing everything, the whole time. You don't cheer for a team, you root for an event.

But it was different this night. Somehow the incredible story and the din and the color penetrated my head, and I'll never forget the final countdown when it became clear that the unthinkable, the utterly unimaginable, was happening before the eyes of the world. "Do you believe in miracles?" I heard Al Michaels saying into my earphones as the entire American squad stormed and swarmed from their bench and mobbed their victorious goalie, Jim Craig, who wrapped himself in an American flag. And I heard myself answering him above the roar, "*Yes!*"

Few people today remember, but that victory only assured us of a silver medal. The finals were held that Sunday against a fine Finnish team, before a television audience that rocked with patriotic fervor as the now unstoppable Americans stormed their way to the gold medal.

I flew down to Miami afterward for a look at the Florida primary; mulled over what it would mean to have the Republican winner, Ronald Reagan, as my president; then, almost a month since I'd left, returned to New York, where embarrassment was waiting. Ted, I'd learned by now, was not a hockey fan. He'd come to Lake Placid hoping I'd lay hands on him as the new program's host. In the blur of producing the Olympics, I'd neglected to tell him what I assumed he knew. Of course the program was his! Who else could it have been? He accepted my rueful apology now, and we turned to another item that had slipped through the cracks: deciding on the program's name.

Part of the name, I thought, had to be "night," the rest of it generic enough not to lock us in on subject matter. I also wanted something that would call up the late-night, semi-insomniac grittiness of cigarettes being smoked, of black coffee being drunk. As always, whatever we came up with would have to trip memorably from the tongue.

I gathered Ted, Bill Lord, Dick Wald, Dave Burke, and a few other senior hands in my office, and we brainstormed.

And brainstormed.

And brainstormed.

News Night, Night Time, Night Brief.

Awful.

Night Journal, Night Diary, Night Chronicle.

Worse.

An hour slipped by. Ted said it was like trying to dream up a joke. Finally, someone proposed *Nightline,* a play on horse racing's "the morning line."

It sounded like "phone line" or "clothesline."

"Crappy," Ted called it.

"Not even an English word," Bill Lord agreed.

"You know something?" I opined. "It all depends on the show. If it's great, the title will get remembered as a great title, too. But if it's lousy, the name won't matter, because we'll be off the air and not a soul will give a damn what we called it."

We settled, tentatively, on *Nightline.* The next day, Dave Burke became a naysayer. His wife hated it! So we argued some more, and finally, I said, "If we stick *ABC News* in front of it, it won't be so bad. *ABC News' Nightline,* that's what we're going with."

In other words, sometimes great titles come about through inspiration. But sometimes they're generated by sheer exhaustion!

I kept the rest of the show planning purposefully minimal. Going live afforded us the luxury of being able to put off story decisions until the day of air (or, I hoped, till the *night* of air), and I left the format deliberately loose. I wanted the program to be a moveable feast of interviews, taped reports, town meetings—anything compelling that presented itself. How *Nightline* told a story would depend on the story.

From whence the telling would occur was more contentious. Ted, who had four children in Washington-area schools, had no desire to relocate to New York, and I had no desire to lose control by having production move to D.C. Even more than *Wide World of Sports,* I looked on *Nightline* as my special baby, and I wanted to be close at hand as it grew up, participating in choosing guests, subjects, critiquing the processes in a person-to-person, face-to-face way. I settled the conflict by splitting the baby: Ted would stay put in Washington; *Nightline* would continue to be produced by a creative team based in New York.

I came into the office the morning of March 24 not knowing what we were going to do on debut night. The AP wire decided it for us. Hours before an Iranian extradition request was to arrive, the shah, who'd lately taken up exile on a Panamanian island, fled to Cairo, and the Iranians were planning a massive demonstration outside the U.S. embassy in Tehran just as the first edition of *Nightline* would be signing on. Bill Lord told me the news, and he began gearing up a four-element show: first, a satellite report from Bill Blakemore at the demonstration, then separate live interviews with a hostage relative and a Khomeini representative, followed by a closing taped piece on Ted Kennedy's New York primary campaign. By early afternoon, the interviews were set. Dorothea Moorefield, whose husband, Richard, was U.S. consul general and now a prisoner in Tehran, would speak from a studio in San Diego; Ali Agah, the Iranian chargé d'affaires who'd feared arrest by the FBI, would appear from his embassy in Washington, which he now feared leaving because of protesters.

But Lord wasn't satisfied; the premiere, he thought, needed more than the standard interviews. The answer hit him a few hours before air: Ted would interview Mrs. Moorefield and Agah *together.*

Ted low-keyed the introduction: "This is a new broadcast in the sense that it is permanent and will continue after the Iran crisis is over. There will also be nights when Iran is not the major story, when we will bring you briefly up to date on Iran, but will focus on some other story. That's not the case tonight. For the first time on television, we'll provide the opportunity for the wife of an American hostage to speak live with an Iranian official."

Agah, who hadn't been aware of what was in store until that moment, registered shock. In the control room, I held my breath, expecting him to rip off the mike and stalk out. Then I heard Mrs. Moorefield saying, "How can you continue to hold these innocent people?"

Agah's nostrils flared, his eyes narrowed. If looks could kill, ABC News would have been ready for interment.

"How could you remain silent in the past twenty-seven years," he retorted, "when your government was involved in torturing, killing, and doing all kinds of corrupt actions against our people?"

Mrs. Moorefield was rattled, but only for a moment. "Why are we not allowed to hear from the hostages?" she asked. "Why are we not corresponding with them? . . . Why isn't there mail coming out of that embassy in Tehran?"

Ali blamed it on the CIA, but Mrs. Moorefield wasn't buying that. "I don't see how a letter from my husband to me . . . could be a threat to your security in any way."

I saw magic on the screen. "Forget the Kennedy piece," I said to Bill Lord. "Let it go, let it go."

And so he did.

It was a remarkable first program, even though Tom Shales's review in the *Washington Post*, always true to form, determined otherwise:

"The program, supposedly a breakthrough . . . represents at best a great leap sideways and at worst a pratfall backwards for television news. The premiere did not provide viewers with anything worth knowing, and the broadcast looks to be merely another unpleasant side effect of the Iranian mess, since it would never exist if the nightly hostage reports hadn't earned boffo ratings for ABC.

"The first program was weighed down with a contrived confrontation . . . When anchor Ted Koppel announced that 'for the first time' such a clash would occur, he sounded like the host of one of those old bleeding-heart and humiliation TV shows of the 50s—*Strike It Rich* and *This Is Your Life*, and that sort of thing. The gambit was cheaply theatrical, mawkish and self-promotional. . . . Of course, it really wasn't news at all. It was new news, neo-news, non-news, pseudo-news, a sugary news substitute. Newsohol."

Shales concluded with a bow in my direction: "Past performances by the likes of Geraldo Rivera and shows like *20/20* suggest ABC News is unembarrassable, but shows like *Nightline* must be producing a few red faces around the shop, at least among the old-timers who remember what news used to be."

I'd gotten the same and worse from Shales before, and been advised by students of his ego that if I wished it stopped, I had but to make a cooing call. Not this red-headed Scot. My phone stayed in its cradle and I pretended not to read the columns.

Nightline had a more positive impact elsewhere. Shortly after the premiere, we later learned, the door of Richard Moorefield's blacked-out cell at the U.S. Chancery building in Tehran swung open, and a guard growled, "Your wife appeared on American television. She talked about your conditions here." It was the first word any of the hostages had gotten from the outside world in 143 days. "If my wife was appearing on national television, that meant that the hostages were still in the public eye," Moorefield later said. "The American people had not put us on the back pages." A few days later, Moorefield's cell door opened again. This time, the guard had mail.

The hostages remained an unbroken part of *Nightline* until their release a few minutes after Ronald Reagan was sworn in as president, January 20, 1981. We'd held an office pool on the subject—I can't tell you who won—but I do know that it was the 444th day from their seizure in November 1979 and that 444 happened to be *Nightline*'s extension when you dialed ABC News in Washington.

By that time, we had already held debates on the Equal Rights Amendment, the death penalty, homosexuals in the military, and the advisability of allowing tots to play organized football. Programming by gut rather than audience surveys, we'd done shows on toxic-shock syndrome, the Mariel boat lift, the eruption of Mount Saint Helens, Chicago organized crime, the thirtieth anniversary of the Korean War, the *Voyager* space probe, the reemergence of the Ku Klux Klan, the Miami riots, the baseball strike, and the rise of Islamic fundamentalism, which, I still remember, opened with a live shot of the sun coming up over Khartoum. Weeks of frostbitten labor and the repair of a microwave relay run over by a yak also produced the first-ever live shot from the summit of Mt. Everest, which looked gorgeous when it came in—five minutes after *Nightline* went off the air!

The more successful we became, the more we played fast and loose with time strictures. When conversation was gripping—as it was during a postelection thrashing of the religious right a critic called "the best of the genre ever aired on any network"—I called in to let it run. In that instance, we were on till nearly two A.M.

We also went on the road—to the Middle East, to a memorable and historic series in South Africa (as I'll describe in due course), to Korea, to China right after Tiananmen Square. Airing late and being live paid off in programs the competition couldn't match. Half an hour after the news broke of John Lennon's shooting in December 1980, a scheduled show on the Polish Solidarity movement had been junked and *Nightline* was on the air with live reports from the hospital where Lennon died and the candlelight vigil of weeping fans outside the Dakota, the apartment building he and Yoko lived in on Central Park West and Seventy-second Street. On NBC and CBS, Carson and old movies continued playing. It happened again with the disastrous failure of the "Delta Force" hostage rescue attempt. Word from the White House came just after Ted had signed off for the night. Within five minutes, we were back on the air with reactions and analyses from ABC correspondents around the world that lasted until dawn.

I was on the "Roone Phone" that night with Ted, as I was almost every night during *Nightline*'s first year and a half. Sometimes, I'd call during the program to suggest a question or when to extend or drop a line of inquiry. I'd hound him about the seemingly small things that, added up, make the difference, like reidentifying a guest for viewers tuning in late. Explain, contextualize, make clear, I hectored. Never assume. Tell the audience what they are about to see, what they are seeing, what they have seen. Viewers were smart. Make them smarter. They had curiosity. Satisfy it. Don't take them for granted, don't think them dumb. Be different. *Always,* be different.

There were more calls when a program was done. To plan, to pull apart what had gone wrong and how to make it better, or, simply, just to talk to Ted. I'd been in many empty studios after midnight. I knew how lonely they could be.

The report card, as always, was the weekly Nielsen numbers, and what they said was startling. Nearly 10 million people were watching. Virtually every night we were ahead of CBS and within striking distance of Johnny. A steadily increasing number of nights, we were beating him. Johnny himself was talking about "Ted Floppel" in his monologue; there wouldn't be those jabs if he wasn't noticing.

Singly at first, then in a stampede, the critics took notice, too. "A quiet revolution in late-night news television has erupted while most of the nation slept . . . or watched Johnny Carson," the *Christian Science Monitor* proclaimed. "Global in perspective, intimate in presentation, and always rivetingly spontaneous . . . *Nightline* has become the thinking man's alternative."

Most of the kudos focused on Ted—"a hardworking, dependable, straight-as-an-arrow, ultimately triumphant tortoise of a newsman" in the words of one journal—and his mastery of seeming politeness—"May I put it to you, sir"—as he lowered the boom: "I honestly don't know what you are talking about."

Tom Snyder, no slouch himself at interrogation, was quoted as saying that Koppel's show ought to be called "Knifeline," while a pundit described Ted's interviewing style as "a verbal and rhetorical combination of Sugar Ray Leonard and Mikhail Baryshnikov—a succession of jabs, rejoinders and judicious-to-delicious interruptions."

To *Time*, Ted was "the best serious interviewer on American TV"; to *Newsweek*, "the fastest rising star in television news"; to *New York*, which put him on its cover, "the smartest man on television." An apotheosis of sorts was reached with a newspaper profile that began: "Ted Koppel is modest. Ted Koppel is smart. Ted Koppel is fair and nice and warm. Ted Koppel is, it seems, perfect."

But for me the greatest relish was in reading an appraisal that appeared after *Nightline* had been on the air just short of ten months. "Smart, classy" *Nightline*, the author wrote, "represents the most successful programming initiative in the history of ABC News."

Nicely put. But then I always did think Tom Shales of the *Washington Post* had a way with words.

Even Larry Pollack, the Philadelphia station manager, ate a modest portion of crow. He ditched Farrah the same week the *Post* changed heart, and ABC announced that, henceforth, *Nightline* would be running a full half hour, five nights a week.

Nonetheless, I continued to hover like an anxious father who can't quite believe that his favorite child is not only walking, but winning the 100-yard dash. *Nightline*'s birth had been so improbable, its success so counter to every late-night television maxim, I couldn't fully take it in. There wasn't an audience for serious programs, I'd always been told. They never worked. Ever. No one was saying that about *Nightline* anymore, but I wasn't ready to put down the "Roone Phone." Not until I was absolutely sure.

Then, one day in the spring of 1981—"Morning in America," the new Reagan administration was calling it—my own phone rang. It was Bill Lord, saying he'd booked General Alexander Haig, the new secretary of state, for a program that night on an E-Seven economic summit that was winding up in Ottawa. Haig's appearance, Bill said, would be another jewel in *Nightline*'s crown. However, a problem had developed. President Reagan would be flying back to Washington aboard Air Force One when *Nightline* aired, and Haig, who wanted to accompany him, was requesting to be interviewed on tape.

"I know the policy," Bill said, "but he *is* the secretary of state, and the guy he wants to fly with *is* the president of the United States."

"Please give the general our regrets," I said.

"Roone..."

"I mean it, Bill. Tell Haig that if he won't appear live, he can't be on *Nightline*."

Bill swore and hung up.

A few minutes later, though, he called again; he'd passed on what I'd said to the secretary of state.

"And?"

"He says he'll be glad to catch a later ride."

I'd won. And so had *Nightline*.

Brinkley

In September 1980, ABC News was the recipient of a piece of extraordinary good fortune: William A. Small was named president of NBC News.

I knew Bill Small primarily by his reputation, which was excellent. At CBS, where he'd toiled for seventeen years before his NBC hiring, he'd been counted first class as a journalist and news executive, particularly in running the network's Washington bureau during Watergate. When the knives were out for Dan Rather, Small had been his most steadfast defender, turning aside all attempts inside and outside the network to muzzle him. For standing by his guy and the First Amendment, he'd won the admiration of the entire press corps, and a ticket to New York to become number two to CBS News president Dick Salant. The only significant rap against Small was his lack of so-called people skills. He was thought to be cold and abrasive, and not inclined to suffer fools, which appeared to mean anyone who disagreed with him. This was said to have cost him the CBS News division presidency in 1979, when Salant hit retirement age. Salant, though, soon turned up at NBC as vice chairman in charge of news, where his first move was to bring in Small as division president.

My tutor in these matters had been Dick Wald. Dick and I had been classmates at Columbia, where he'd been an editor of *The Spectator,* and I'd followed his career with interest. He'd been editor of the *Herald-Tribune* and later president of NBC News, at least until he'd said no once too often to his boss's desire to install talk-show host Tom Snyder as *Evening News* anchor. When Bill Sheehan departed for a public-relations job at

Ford, I'd recruited Dick as ABC News's senior vice president, knowing that his credentials in the journalistic community would stand us in good stead.

Initially, he'd had trouble finding himself at home with us, most particularly with the Washington bureau. "If you think we need some guy from NBC to help us," Frank Reynolds had huffed at Dick's hiring, "you're mistaken." Some of it was Dick's doing too—he had a prickly side—but in time he'd become a key collaborator, particularly when it came to the innards of our business—the News desk, the News bureaus overseas. Now, his knowledge of NBC and Small came in handy as we plotted our next undertaking.

I'd long had my eye on a forgotten, and even neglected, corner of network news, where I thought ABC could make a stand and topple the competition.

I'm talking about Sunday morning. Ever since God invented television, NBC's *Meet the Press* had been the dominant Sunday panel show. Like its virtually identical competitors, *Face the Nation* on CBS, and our own last-ranked entry, *Issues and Answers,* it had a lock-step format: one host (currently Bill Monroe, an NBC journeyman with an unfortunate resemblance to Ichabod Crane); a revolving panel composed of two print reporters and a correspondent from the network; the week's worthy (typically, a visiting foreign minister or a congressman pushing a bill); and thirty minutes of velvet-glove questions eliciting pear-shaped answers. Without detectable change, that's how *Meet the Press* had been operating since beginning life as a radio program in the 1940s.

The system worked well enough, I guess, for *Meet the Press* and its guests, whose pronouncements were invariably quoted in the next day's papers. I didn't find the experience terribly enriching, though, and I saw no compelling reason for why the Sunday-morning news ghetto had to be one great yawn. Among other things, *Meet the Press* and its brethren never explained why what you were watching was important. Instead, it was assumed that you knew all about people like the prime minister of Tanzania, and why what they had to say was significant, and if you didn't, tough. There he was in a bland studio, with no background on who he was, fielding dry questions of little relevance to you, and there was no compulsion for you to do anything other than switch off the television, reach for your golf clubs or fishing rods or lawn mowers, and, breathing a great sigh of relief, head off to the Sunday activities of your choice.

It was no accident that the Sunday-morning news audience diminished each succeeding mile beyond the Beltway.

At least CBS had its *Sunday Morning,* Charles Kuralt's program (now Charles Osgood's), and NBC, even though it failed, kept trying with its weekend version of *Today.* ABC had nothing. I mean, literally! ABC, for lack of anything better, gave its early Sunday air to the local stations for a variety of independent religious and other programs—until, that is, it was time for *Animals, Animals, Animals,* an independently produced network show that was about . . . well, animals. Then followed the equally forgettable *Issues and Answers.*

I thought viewers deserved better, and I'd been saying so publicly since the early 1970s, when news programming was none of my business. Now that it was, I began laying plans for a Sunday program that people would watch not only because they would have to be informed but because it was interesting, alive, and unpredictable, and which, in time, could become as significant to the intellectually curious audience as their major Sunday newspapers. I wanted panelists people would tune in to simply to hear what they had to say, much as people waited for and read the offerings of their favorite newspaper columnists, and I wanted the most important guests, from all over the world, who would come to see us as the best vehicle for their views.

The way I planned it, we would open with an update on the news of the day; move to a reported "set-up" piece which would personalize the guests as well as present the issues surrounding their appearance; then head into extended, tough-minded questioning before concluding the program with an analytical "reporters' round table" and a wrap-up from the host. The host was key. I wanted someone of sufficient intellectual weight and charisma to direct the "orchestra" of elements I was putting together, someone who could control the intellectual prickliness I hoped to foster. People like that simply don't grow for the plucking, but even as we searched, I began to work on the rest.

One major problem for me was the thirty-minute limitation. There was no law—at least none that I knew of—that said the Sunday news shows could be no longer than half an hour. It was tradition, nothing more, nothing less. Well, too bad about tradition. I wanted double the time, period, and that meant that the existing lead-in, *Animals, Animals, Animals,* had to go. No one could seem to recall how it had come under the aegis of the News division, nor did anyone ever appear to have worried that a number of affiliates weren't carrying it. But that made it perfect for our purposes: The weakest of the herd is the easiest prey.

I had, then, the time slot and the concept. Another concern was that one of our competitors would wake up just as we had and set out to fix Sunday morning. Dick Wald said I had nothing to fear from NBC. *Meet the Press* had gone for so long unchallenged that the powers at 30 Rock, himself included, had never given its renovation an instant's thought. He was confident that the same would be true of Bill Small, who, meanwhile, was busily irritating almost everyone who worked for him by trying to remake NBC News into CBS News. This was good for us: Disenchanted NBC personnel would soon be coming to market. In the meantime, we could expect growing turmoil at CBS, which Small had marked for whole-sale poaching.

Small first enticed the Kalb brothers, Marvin and Bernie, to NBC and then made Marvin host of *Meet the Press,* a challenge to us in that his long service as CBS State Department correspondent made him a major Washington draw, whereas we still had no one to host the new entry I envisioned. But the shake-up at NBC News continued, and we began to hear—much to my amazement—that one of the people Small had managed to alienate was the division's most famous asset, one David Brinkley.

I couldn't believe it at first. If there was a single figure in television news who equaled Walter in stature, it was David McClure Brinkley, who'd grown up in Wilmington, North Carolina, had first earned his spurs in print journalism, then had joined NBC in 1943 as the network's twenty-two-year-old White House correspondent. As he wrote of those early days in his memoirs, "to say so much as one word on the grand and glorious NBC network was to ascend to what NBC people thought was heaven, with RCA microphones replacing the harps." David's distinctive, clipped, Southern-accented style made his voice instantly recognizable. His writing was the most literate and his wry wit the most memorable on the airwaves. He'd played poker with Harry Truman, covered Winston Churchill's famous Iron Curtain speech as well as innumerable political conventions. He first attracted national attention as Washington correspondent of the now forgotten but then highly popular *Camel News Caravan with John Cameron Swayze,* and, in 1956, together with Chet Huntley on the *Huntley-Brinkley Report,* he'd literally invented the position of the modern news anchor. At their peak, one poll found, Huntley and Brinkley were more famous than the Beatles, Cary Grant, and John Wayne.

But, after fourteen years, the five-times-a-week bidding of "Good night, Chet . . . Good night, David" ended when Huntley retired to his native Montana. Brinkley paired with John Chancellor for a time, then cut back to nightly commentaries, and, when ratings sagged, coanchored with Chancellor again. When Small joined NBC, they'd been back together for three years. Small ended the arrangement his first month on the job, yanking Brinkley off the *Evening News* and pressuring him into hosting NBC's latest attempt at a weekly magazine. NBC, it should be said, had already set some kind of world's record for televised magazine failures, and Brinkley's reward for being the good soldier was having the *NBC News Magazine with David Brinkley* slotted at ten P.M. Friday—directly opposite the CBS megahit *Dallas.* The result, week after humiliating week, was an icon of television news presiding over the lowest ranked of the networks' fifty prime-time programs.

Dick, who'd known Brinkley for going on twenty years, was a regular ear for his old friend's torments, and offered ABC as the solution. But Brinkley hung back. NBC, he said, was his "womb"; leaving it would be "a tragedy"—expressions of loyalty that might sound odd, even disingenuous, in today's world, when stars and their corporate employers part company at the drop of a hat, but which were very real for people of an older generation who had helped found and form our industry.

I ran into Brinkley socially a couple of times during this period, and the toll Small was exacting was evident. David seemed world weary, and what had been wit and good humor now came off as snide and sour. To an extent, I think his disenchantment was brought on more by what Small didn't do than by what he did, even though he had attempted to eliminate the modest bonus payments Brinkley received for traveling to New York to host his program.

In the meantime, by spring 1981, plans for our new Sunday program were nearly complete. I had solidified the format, put *Animals, Animals, Animals* on the road to extinction, told the people at *Issues and Answers* that their program would soon be canceled, and announced a fall launch to the affiliates. I'd booked the full hour and begun recruiting some prospective panelists. I'd done this all, mind you, without having found the host. We'd sounded out Bill Moyers and Ben Bradlee, the editor of the *Washington Post*, among others. Moyers said no, and Ben Bradlee did too, although he later agreed to be a panelist. Meanwhile, as I realized full well in my insomniac hours, the orchestra was taking its seats, the instruments were beginning to tune up, and I was taking a hell of a gamble. But there are times when, if you don't plunge ahead, you end up doing nothing.

Among the panelists—in fact my first choice—was the conservative columnist George Will. Pundits of Will's ideological stripe—William F. Buckley and Bill Safire among them—were hot just then, and George, who enjoyed especially good relations with Ron and Nancy Reagan, was among the most sizzling. I also liked him personally, admired his way of speaking in complete sentences and paragraphs, and enjoyed how he mixed quotations from John Locke with references to Mrs. O'Leary's cow. But what locked him in on my host radarscope was the totality of his un-television-ness. A bespectacled Princeton Ph.D. who dressed like an undertaker, wore bow ties, and quoted the classics—who couldn't notice such a classically anti-charismatic figure?

When I first asked George if he were interested, he said that attending church was more important to his Sunday mornings. So, I suspected, was getting to Jack Kent Cooke's box at RFK Stadium, for the owner of the Redskins liked to invite Washington pundits and personalities to the team's home games. But then Bill Small went the proverbial bridge too far: In July 1981, while David Brinkley was on vacation, he reassigned Paul Friedman, Brinkley's producer.

I'd nearly lost Ted Koppel by doing the same thing. But I'd been new in television news at the time and hadn't known better. Bill Small did. Brinkley announced that he was through with the magazine, expecting—as did everyone in the industry—that his employer of thirty-eight years would respond with a new assignment.

None was forthcoming.

"What do you think our chances are?" I asked Dick Wald.

"I think he'd leave tomorrow if he could afford to do it," Dick replied.

"You're kidding, aren't you?"

"No. And he'd come here, too. He hates CBS even more than he does Bill Small."

I thought I'd lost my capacity for shock after all that had occurred at ABC News during the last two and a half years, but when Dick suggested that David Brinkley's door might be open a crack—*David Brinkley*, for God's sake!—it took a couple of seconds for the idea to register. Here not only was the new Sunday program's host, the anchor for all our convention and election coverage and whatever else I could dream up, but bottled-in-bond certification that ABC News was now and irrevocably major league.

Could it possibly be true?

"Ah," I said to Dick, "do you think you could arrange a lunch? Like before I wake up?"

At Nanni's the next day, I laid out our new Sunday-morning entry for David. I waxed eloquent about the wasteland of Sunday morning and how we were going to breathe life into the desert. I went into the format in glowing detail. He said to my delighted ears that this was exactly the kind of program he'd always wanted to do. More important, he had two significant suggestions. One, if *he* were doing the show, *he'd* want to report the opening news segment himself (rather than leave it to another reporter) and second, *he'd* turn the closing statement into a more extended commentary on the passing moment (which, in time, came to be called "David Brinkley's homily").

I've italicized *he* above for the obvious reason. He was already talking about *This Week* as his!

We even, as I recall, talked about money—if not at the luncheon table, then shortly thereafter. I already knew from Dick Wald that David would have to forego a rich benefit package at NBC if he asked them to let him out of the remaining four years of his contract. We had to cover him, and we did, to the tune of $850,000 a year for the four years. But that was it, and in every other respect, landing David was the easiest negotiation with a bona fide star that I've ever engaged in.

I expected hosannas when I told Leonard Goldenson that I'd landed one of the seminal figures in television news. Instead, there were ho-hums. Was Brinkley really the image I wanted for ABC News? he asked. Wasn't the elder statesman, well, *too* elder?

Leonard wasn't asking; in his politely nudging way, he was suggesting that sixty-one-year-old David Brinkley didn't quite mesh with the *Happy Days* image ABC was trying so hard to cultivate and would I please forget

I'd ever heard of him? Others in the company were equally dubious. Not only was Brinkley over the hill, but why was I making such a big fuss about Sunday morning?

As far as I was concerned, the only risk was that fatigue and sourness I'd detected on his NBC programs, but my recent conversations with David had been characterized by the enthusiasm, wit, and graciousness of the old Brinkley. I was ready to blame the lapses on Bill Small. Otherwise, I didn't care if David Brinkley was 101, he represented the class and clout I'd been after. I argued back that getting even one-tenth of the Brinkley of yore would give the new Sunday program character and definition neither of its competitors possessed, and bring the network enormous prestige in the bargain. I could tell Leonard wasn't entirely persuaded, but I also knew he wasn't going to order me *not* to hire Brinkley.

"All right," he said finally. "If nothing else, the old coot will make election night classier."

Everything moved quickly after that. In exchange for giving up the benefits package, NBC released Brinkley from the four years remaining on his contract, and on September 4, 1981, he announced that he was leaving the network. Fifteen days later, I introduced the newest addition to ABC News at a press conference at Tavern on the Green, before a major media contingent and many of David's friends. "There is greatness in this room," I intoned.

George Will was equally convinced. He told me that if a spot were available on the new program, he wanted it. Ben Bradlee of the *Washington Post* took one too, but only temporarily. He thought it a bad idea to do business with pals—meaning David and me—and besides, that editors and journalists should report the news, not voice off-the-cuff opinions. I rounded out the initial cast with Karen Elliott House, the Pulitzer Prize–winning diplomatic correspondent of the *Wall Street Journal* and a reporter not at all shy about voicing her views, and Hodding Carter III, who'd recently returned to journalism after a stint as Jimmy Carter's State Department spokesman.

This Week with David Brinkley was now ready to go.

The guest for our first scheduled program, November 15, 1981—or so I thought—I fell into rather than picked. At a dinner Barbara Walters was hosting, I found myself chatting with David Stockman, the Reagan administration's budget director, and point man on the new administration's "supply-side" economic theory. Democrats were howling that "Reaganomics" would bankrupt the government, but until now, Stockman had been making an unbudging case to the contrary. Something about his manner, though, told me that the young ex-congressman from Michigan was fudging.

"I understand the deficit is going to be a lot larger than anybody realized," I said conversationally.

"You're right," Stockman said, staring into his drink. "It's going to be a real killer. Hundred twenty-five million in the red at least."

I wanted to bolt straight to the broadcast center with my scoop. Instead, I casually asked Stockman if he'd like to be the first guest on *This Week with David Brinkley*. He said sure, equally casually.

I could hardly contain myself. A brand-new show, and right off the bat, we'd have the hottest "get" imaginable inside the Beltway ("get" being talk-show slang for "getting" the most desirable guest of the moment). And the most explosive too, if Stockman would only hold off on his thunderbolt till the day of the program.

Sad to say, Stockman had been even more unguarded with William Grieder of the *Atlantic Monthly*. When his comments about Reaganomics being window dressing for making the rich richer hit the stands two days before our airtime, there was an enforced end to his loquaciousness. The White House peremptorily canceled his appearance. Embarrassed, they offered Vice President George Bush as a replacement, but I, good citizen that I normally am, was in full-fledged rebellion. I certainly wasn't going to have the White House telling us who our guest would be, even if it was the vice president of the United States. I held no brief against George Bush, mind you, but my message back that day (to borrow from Patrick Henry) was: Give us Stockman or give us nobody.

Nobody.

I've often thought that a great trivia question would be: Who was the featured guest on the first *This Week with David Brinkley*?

Well, you're absolutely right! It *was* Senator Fritz Hollings of South Carolina!

Hollings at the time was hardly a nobody, and we had Felix Rohatyn on too and the Republican senator from Colorado, William Armstrong, but the guest list was still something of a letdown after my near miss with Stockman. Still, the reviews were okay, except for my then least favorite critic, the aforementioned Mr. Shales of the *Washington Post,* who insisted on calling Karen House "granite-faced."

Nor could the next two weeks be described as dazzling. But a few days before the third show, my wife, Ann, had an epiphany. We'd been lying in bed watching *Nightline* as Ted Koppel deconstructed the idea that Mu'ammar Qaddafi of Libya had dispatched hit squads to assassinate President Reagan.

"You know," she said when the program ended, "I wonder what he'd say."

"Who?"

"Qaddafi. What do you think?"

Sometimes the greatest ideas come at the least probable moments.

I picked up the phone and dialed the home number of our executive producer, Dorrance Smith.

"What would we have to do to get Qaddafi?" I asked him when he answered, sleepy voiced.

"What do you mean, Roone?"

"Just what I said. Qaddafi. Why don't we get Qaddafi for this Sunday?"

Not only did he think it was the dumbest idea he'd ever heard, but did I really have to wake him up to lay it on him?

"For Christ's fucking sake," he blasted, "you don't just pick up the phone and say, 'Hey, Colonel, how'd you like to be on TV next Sunday?' What's gotten into you?"

The more he objected, of course, the better I liked the idea.

"Well, call whoever you've got to," I ordered him, "and get somebody over there."

"But, Roone—"

"Give it your best shot. Do everything humanly possible to make it happen."

I knew how unlikely it was, but to get the impossible, I'd learned in the past, you sometimes have to demand it. With a lot of middle-of-the-night phone calls, and the chartering of a jet to get a correspondent to Tripoli, Dorrance actually delivered, and there we were, that Sunday morning, still uncertain of getting a decent TV picture the way the preshow satellite monitors were stuttering and flashing, but suddenly—as clear as a bell!—there was the colonel primping in his tent.

"This is the goddamnedest thing I've ever seen," Ben Bradlee said as we watched Mu'ammar fluffing up his hair in front of a mirror.

"Next, he'll check his lipstick," David added.

Well, it was strange all right, and the interview that followed—Qaddafi calling Reagan "silly," "ignorant," and a "liar," and urging the American people to rise up and overthrow him—was stranger still. But just putting Qaddafi on blew the show off like a rocket. It had much the same shock impact as when we'd broadcast the U.S.-USSR track meet on *Wide World of Sports* from Moscow at the height of the Cold War. The next day, *This Week with David Brinkley* was all over the newspapers, and on the television map forever.

I still wasn't altogether satisfied. I knew from experience that any new television program goes through a shakeout period, almost like a theatrical play doing previews in the hinterlands before it comes to Broadway. Now Ben Bradlee dropped out, and Karen was gently pushed, and George Will and David himself were far too gentlemanly. We needed some sass, some prosecutorial bite—someone, if you will, to play Cosell to their Frank and Dandy.

Of course, that someone was sitting right under our noses, on our own staff.

His name? Sam Donaldson.

Until taking over News, I hadn't quite realized the swath Sam cut in Washington. After all, he'd only been on the White House beat since the inauguration of Jimmy Carter. I did know, as it was impossible not to know, that Sam was outsize in personality, outrageousness, and decibels employed to shout his questions at presidents. A free spirit from the Southwest, he had playfully suggested that he was going to gnaw on a female correspondent's arm. If this was part act—with Sam, you could never quite be sure (which was, in itself, part of his "act")—it had also gotten attention from outside the Beltway as well as in. Despite his brazenness and his tenacity when it came to getting the story—I'm sure people liked to watch him because they were never quite sure what he was going to do or say next—he commanded absolute respect from the Old Guard of the Washington press corps. During an after-dinner speech at the Washington correspondents' banquet, the "Doonesbury" cartoonist Gary Trudeau once said, "If television hadn't been invented, Sam would go door-to-door"—a great line, but also one that Donaldson's colleagues said was true. He wasn't the buffoon of the corps, he was the envy of it.

The more I thought about it, the more I realized that Sam on *This Week with David Brinkley* would change the chemistry in an instant.

And so it did.

David and George at first didn't know what to make of a Doberman pinscher suddenly let loose on the set. Nor, for that matter, did Leonard and his fellow executives. "He's too loud," Leonard said. "Can't you shut him up?"

Of course I couldn't—who in the world could shut Sam up?—but the sometimes abrasive shouting matches between him and George worked because of David's overall gentility. And *This Week* took off. Within three months, it had buried *Meet the Press,* which would not recover in the ratings for another quarter century. Within six months, anyone who was anyone in Washington and wanted Sunday exposure called *This Week* first. Within twelve, CBS was getting rid of the anchor who'd hosted *Face the Nation* for the last fifteen years. What's more—much to the astonishment of the men with the abacuses who surrounded Leonard—*This Week* even became a modest profit center for ABC News.

There was something else, too. I wanted to create an "in" place for Sunday mornings in the nation's capital, a place important people on the interview circuit would want to linger. So, in our new building on De Sales Street, we invested much more in our greenroom than our competitors, the greenroom being the area adjacent to the studio where guests go before and after their appearances. We even had a bartender turning out Bloody Marys and mimosas, and a buffet sufficiently stocked to keep people at brunch even after we'd gone off the air.

It all worked.

Over the years, the round-table panel would have various members in addition to George and Sam. Jim Wooten and Tom Wicker come to mind from the early days, as does Jody Powell, former press secretary to Jimmy Carter. Later on, Cokie Roberts joined the fray, adding her charm, perspicacity, and insider's knowledge to the mix. From time to time, *This Week* ventured from its home base—the most memorable of these sorties, to me, being the Gorbachev-Reagan get-together at Reykjavík, Iceland, and the fiftieth anniversary of the D-day landings on Omaha Beach in 1994—and our guest list constituted a veritable *Who's Who* of the political scene of our times. But the man who held it all together was David Brinkley, and even after he retired and *This Week* transmogrified into *This Week with Sam and Cokie,* it was still David's urbanity, his sense of irony, his bemused observations about the passing human comedy that informed the program and gave it its tone and intellectual liveliness.

To celebrate *This Week*'s primacy, I hosted a dinner at my apartment in David's honor just after the program's first anniversary. All the ABC News and Sports heavies came around to pay their respects, as did many from the competition, including Walter Cronkite himself. At the end, I rose to offer a toast.

"We are honored," I said, "to have here in our midst two of the greatest figures in television history, two personalities the entire country tunes in to every week to hear their views, two media heroes who tower over the rest of us . . ."

Etc., etc.

I paused at last.

"*Two?*" Walter erupted in mock horror.

There were hoots and laughs, but none louder than David Brinkley's. When the room quieted, I raised my glass again.

"I speak, of course, of Frank Gifford and Howard Cosell."

The line was greeted by roars of delighted laughter. When it died down, I launched into the serious toast, ending in congratulations and a heartfelt thank-you. But even before I got to that punchline—"David Brinkley"—our guests were on their feet for a much deserved standing O.

ABC News, I realized that night, had come a long, long way.

WNT

I was beginning to think that Providence was taking a special interest in the fortunes of ABC News.

Bill Small alienating David Brinkley . . . the Iranians seizing the U.S. embassy . . . happening to catch Hugh Downs guest-hosting on that blackest of mornings after the *20/20* debut—at the very least, the Nielsen guardian angel had sure been sitting on my shoulder. But what I was working at in the spring of 1979 was something the Almighty Himself rarely did. And that was change the standings in the network evening news.

This had occurred exactly twice in television history: the first time, in the late 1950s, when NBC's *Huntley-Brinkley Report* knocked the *CBS Evening News with Douglas Edwards* out of first place; the second, a full decade later, when Walter Cronkite reclaimed the top spot for CBS. ABC's evening news was distinguished for consistency; it had maintained an iron grip on last place for thirty years.

No one knew quite why the evening news programs were so entrenched, but I used to say it was like your favorite drink. If you were a confirmed scotch drinker, you didn't one afternoon decide, "Gee, I've been drinking scotch all my life, so I'll have a bourbon today." Same with watching the news. The raw material was nearly identical on every channel. Once you got hooked on 2, 4, or 7, you stayed hooked, unless one of two things happened: either a new planet suddenly appeared in the heavens (as with *Huntley-Brinkley*), or the known universe shifted (Chet Huntley retiring from NBC to do American Airlines commercials, allowing

Walter his opening on CBS). There was a third possible way for things to get stood on their heads, which was for a program to so turn off its audience as to commit ratings suicide. But that had never happened, and I wasn't counting on Cronkite or Chancellor to break the streak. If there was going to be a change, I had to force it.

Normally, the first step would have been enlisting a world-class anchor. Unlike sports, where who announced the World Series mattered considerably less than who owned the television rights, in news, the face on the tube usually determined the thrill of victory or the agony of defeat. Many qualities were required to be a winning anchor, including a proven record of success, which ruled out everyone at ABC News. I knew and liked John Chancellor, but there was no reason for him to leave NBC. The same went for Walter. About to begin his ninth year at the top of the ratings heap, he was contentedly imprisoned by a hefty, long-term contract that gave him the whole summer off on his sailboat.

Necessity thus mothered the three-headed blur of production razzmatazz that was *World News Tonight*. Harry Reasoner described the program's bang-bang pace as "the Arledge shell game," and he was right. The faster the troika moved on and off stage, the harder it was to detect the absence of a real anchor. Furthermore, it was the only way I could deal with the Barbara problem. The graphics I'd installed as assistance in explaining the who, what, when, where, and why of events (journalism's purpose, I was under the impression) also generated heat. Then-NBC's Dick Wald, unaware that he'd soon be senior vice president of ABC News, called them "cartoons for adults."

None of these so-called revolutionary production techniques was new. In fact, we'd been using them at ABC Sports for twenty years. But what was new was our determination to build on content. I was convinced that the only way to win was to generate the best journalism, over time, and that's what we set out to do. We didn't always get there first, but we got our share, and then, increasingly, more than our share. When the United States decided to establish full diplomatic relations with China, it was *World News Tonight* that broke the story. And not even the *New York Times* ever revealed the vote on a U.S. Supreme Court case two weeks before the decision was announced. *World News Tonight* did it—twice!

That was the plan, and it was working. Survey after survey found that the content of *World News Tonight* was the hardest, most aggressively collected news on television. In February 1979, after less than six months on the air, we scored the highest ratings ever attained by an ABC evening newscast. Eight weeks later, while Ted Koppel's *Second to None*, his ten-part series on military preparedness, was airing, *World News Tonight* moved past NBC and into second place for the first time in the network's history.

Into second place, mind you. Maybe that doesn't sound like much—who was satisfied with being second?—but we'd been last for so long, and had *accepted* it for so long, that the psychological jolt to us all was positively intoxicating. I had champagne delivered to the newsroom, and gave a speech so charged with emotion that, for once in my life, I had trouble getting the words out.

By July, when *World News Tonight* marked its first anniversary, 2 million new viewing households had been added to the audience, Cronkite's lead had been slashed 40 percent, and Walter's people were beginning to look in the rearview mirror. "They're off the mark faster and their reporting is better," CBS News president Bill Leonard told an interviewer. "They're now fully competitive."

A lot of the credit had to go to the producers. Jeff Gralnick and Rick Kaplan had a get-the-story-at-all-costs style, Darwinian by design, that drove out the less hardy. If it hadn't been for ABC dropouts, how would Ted Turner ever have staffed his new CNN? They also damn near killed Peter Jennings. In Beirut for the annual Lebanon war, Peter was ordered by Gralnick and Kaplan to pitch camp in the city's most lethal neighborhood. Peter protested; they insisted; he went. Just as he was signing the hotel register, a truck bomb blew out the front of the building. When Peter called to scream that he'd been bloodied, Jeff asked, "Did you get good film?"

The boys told me about the incident at our nightly postmortem, when we picked apart the broadcast in my office. I made a note to send Peter a kidding cable, and we got down to the usual: What hadn't worked? Why hadn't it? What would make it better? These sessions frequently stretched past midnight, and if something occurred to me afterward—tell Peter that his four-in-hand was too foppish . . . remind Max that politicians never "admit," they "acknowledge" (only criminals "admit")—my middle-of-the-night phone call brought no complaints from them. Somehow we always ended up in sync—maybe because the three of us were working as if life depended on it.

The obsession with every broadcast second paid off. *World News Tonight* was on a trajectory to lead NBC for the next two and a half years, and a *TV Guide* survey of politicians and officials found ours "the most aggressive news operation" in Washington. With the price of *World News Tonight* commercials up 40 percent in the latest quarter, we could not only justify the purchase of state-of-the-art equipment a generation beyond the competition's but could also finance a second wave of talent poaching. At CBS, a sign was posted in their Washington bureau: "Will the last person leaving for ABC please turn out the lights?"

The only naysayer on the staff was Frank Reynolds. He was unhappy with the broadcast, its content and his role on it, and especially unhappy with what he called "my masters," meaning me. I, he thought, was a carnival barker.

This represented a 180-degree turn from his note following the Sadat/Begin coup, and as best as I could parse it out, I'd done a number of things to offend him. The first, and apparently worst, was making him *primus inter pares* of *World News Tonight*. The primus part, he didn't mind; having to share with the pares he did, publicly calling it a "put-down" of his abilities.

"I don't want to be blowing my own horn," he told writer Barbara Matusow, "but I didn't come into this thing simply because of the way I part my hair or wear my suits. I spent years reporting, out on the campaign trail and around the world. I have some knowledge of the news business. Nobody likes to be downgraded."

The "suits" Frank mentioned were another vexation. "The Gray Ghost," as he was nicknamed in Washington, was devoted to light colors, which, combined with his pallor and silver-white hair, tended to wash him into camera nothingness. Darker clothes seemed a reasonable solution to me, but Frank responded as if I'd commanded conversion to Shintoism. The sartorial stalemate went on for months, and at one point, I was on the verge of settling it by dressing everyone in blue blazers, as though they were the new crew for *Monday Night Football*. Sanity intervened at the last moment, and I instead dispatched a tailor to the bureau to outfit Frank in midnight blue and dark gray.

But everything was always a negotiation, none more prickly than getting Frank to read stories not deemed Reynolds-worthy, a category that included all aspects of popular culture, the entertainment world and rock stars, and anything else that smacked of disrespect for the seriousness of pursuing the nation's business. Nor did Frank like ending the program on an upbeat note; a starving Ethiopian—preferably, a mother of six—was more his style.

Peter Jennings, I must say, had the same tendency and, particularly on Fridays, typically getting the weakest ratings of the week for all the network news programs, viewers wanted a closing "up" before the weekend. I went looking for a repeatable idea, something that would bring people to ABC News every Friday and keep them watching. It took some time to find it, but we eventually did. It was called "Person of the Week"—a regular Friday feature that may have been modeled on *Time* magazine's person of the year but that often chose obscure, but admirable, people as its subjects. And sure enough, our Friday ratings rebounded.

In our disputes and negotiations with Frank, voices were never raised, and in the end, it was usually Frank who gave way. Well, sort of. For, once the objectionable piece had run, there he would be, irritably drumming his fingers on the anchor desk, his face the very image of disapproval. For my part, I'd have normally been much more hands-on, ordaining what was going to be and who was going to decide it, but Frank was the alpha wolf of the Washington bureau; as he went, so did the pack. So I continued to tiptoe around his sensibilities rather than confront them. I was reluctant even to appear in the bureau, for being seen as trying to mark his turf. I was wearying, though, of being looked on as the enemy by someone I had helped make a household figure. I wanted an on-air talent I could collaborate with, as I did with Ted. I needed one, if we were ever to catch Cronkite. And there was one who fit that description to a tee.

I'd first taken notice of Dan Rather during Watergate, when, as CBS White House correspondent, he seemed to television what Woodward and Bernstein were to print: the lonely crusader, determined to get at the truth. Sometimes, I thought, he was too determined for his own good. When he received an ovation rising to ask a question at the National Association of Broadcasters Convention in Houston, Nixon teased, "Are you running for something?" To which Rather stonily replied, "No, sir, Mr. President, are you?"

He was pilloried that time for sassing back, but the remark was show-stopping and gutsy, and as my readers can now attest, I had a weakness for showstoppers with guts.

It wasn't until Rather joined *60 Minutes* in 1975, though, that I began to fully appreciate the breadth and depth of his talent. His stories were terrific, his image seized the screen. It was like watching a panther pacing in a cage: coiled, restless, ready to pounce. I thought he was the hottest comer in all of television. Viewers seemed to think so, too. When Rather joined Mike and Morley and Harry, *60 Minutes* became a full sixty minutes of first-rate news broadcasting.

Surveys put Rather's popularity second only to Cronkite's. But he was also second in the betting of who'd succeed Walter when he hit the retirement age of sixty-five in late 1981. The odds-on favorite was Roger Mudd, the network's chief congressional correspondent and Cronkite's regular substitute for nearly a decade. Roger was perfectly cast in the CBS mold: steady, sober, smooth, polished, superbly competent, just a little dull. There was no risk of the unexpected from Roger; it wasn't in his DNA. Dan, on the other hand, was aggressive, pushy, unpredictable, a little dangerous—the very model of ABC genes.

The problem was availability. Rather's contract still had more than a year to run, and his loyalty to CBS was—to use one of the down-home-isms of which Dan was so fond—"tight as a rusted lug nut on a fifty-three Chevy pickup."

But goldarn if David Burke's wife, Trixie, didn't decide that she and the kids would spend the summer of 1980 in the country. Left on his own, David filled up the nights dining with agents, among them one Richard N. Leibner, whose long list of clients included Mike Wallace, Ed Bradley . . . and Dan Rather. David told him of my disappointment in Dan's being locked up, and Richie—who, if you mentioned the weather, would tell you about a weathergirl he represented—said I was premature to despair. Not two weeks before, he'd had a long visit with Dan and his wife, Jean, and they agreed that with Mudd blocking further advancement, it might be time to explore other opportunities.

I began searching for snagging clues in Dan's two best-selling books: *The Palace Guard,* an account of Nixon's henchmen, and *The Camera Never Blinks,* an autobiography. Money didn't look to be the primary lure, to judge from what he had to say about Barbara's ABC contract—"a heist," Dan called it.

"Is anyone worth $1 million per year?" he wrote. "In my own view, no one in this business is, no matter what or how many shows they do, unless they can find a cure for cancer on the side."

Of course, Dan, at the time, was writing about *someone else's* million. He might think differently if I said it could be his.

Reading on, I was struck by a passage in Rather's autobiography relating a first encounter with a journalism professor at his alma mater, Sam Houston State:

" 'Why are you here?' he demanded. 'Do you know why you want to major in journalism?'

"I said, 'It's the only thing I ever wanted to do.'

"He said, 'What makes you think you can do it?'

"I kind of bristled. 'Well, I *know* I can.' "

There was the same tone of excited certainty every time Dan recounted a story he'd chased. Here was a guy who, more than anything else, wanted to be super-reporter. Well, I thought, I could give him his wish.

We met for lunch at Nanni Il Valetto, on Sixty-first between Park and Lexington, a neighborhood favorite that drew John Gotti for the pasta and me for its location off the media dining trail. If there is such a thing as instant like, it occurred at Nanni's front table. At the end of a three-hour schmooze about Dan's hopes and my dreams, I was ready to sign him up, writing out an agreement on the tablecloth. But there was that nettlesome matter of the contract that already existed.

"Roone," Dan said, "I don't know whether to look at my watch or bark at the moon, I'm so tempted. But in Texas, a deal's a deal, and I'm a Texan."

Why couldn't he be from Jersey? I thought.

We continued to meet the rest of the summer and into the fall, talking about everything except the obvious. It was like playing defense in basketball: You always wanted to keep your hand on your man.

We were still chitchatting to no apparent point in late October when a blind item appeared in Liz Smith's column in the New York *Daily News*, disclosing our tête-à-têtes and saying that Dan was ABC bound. The story wasn't true, of course, but it served Richie Leibner, who, I guessed, was the source—although to this day Richie denies it. No sooner did Rather get into work that day than Bill Leonard summoned him to his office demanding to know why he at least hadn't given his employer of so many years the opportunity to negotiate. Dan's protests of innocence didn't lessen Leonard's panic, which allowed Richie Leibner to assume the guise of Mr. Reasonable. His client would love nothing more than a deal that would keep him at his network home forevermore, he said; all CBS had to do to get the ball rolling was start talking about a new contract.

This CBS did. At the same time, Richie Leibner continued talking to us. All of a sudden, the unavailable Dan Rather wasn't quite so un-.

I wasn't popping the champagne corks just yet either. Bill Leonard had formidable resources, first and foremost the CBS News mystique of which Rather was plainly in awe. To wean Dan away from the House That Murrow Built was going to require concerted, imaginative effort, a blunder or two by CBS, and more than a little luck.

I enlisted Dave Burke in our two-pronged attack, schmoozing Leibner and hand-holding Dan. We agreed that he could promise most anything so long as we kept it in the conditional, what-if mood. If there was one thing we did not want to do, it was pledge what we couldn't deliver. We also needed deniability with the Washington bureau in case we didn't land him.

I assumed that CBS would dangle taking over for Cronkite one unspecified day in the future in their negotiations with Dan, almost certainly in combination with Mudd, who had a large and influential constituency. And if it came down to being the deal maker, I'd offer Rather sole anchorship of *World News Tonight,* but I wanted to avoid doing so if I possibly could. Forcing Frank out, especially for a CBS import, would be likely to alienate the entire Washington bureau. Even more disastrous would be offering Dan the job and having him turn it down. Then I'd have no Rather and a pissed-off bureau—a grisly foreshadowing of what would happen to the company twenty years later when they not only failed to land David Letterman but antagonized Ted Koppel in the process. Consequently, Dave and I left ourselves wiggle room in our conversations with Dan, to wit:

"I think you'd be fabulous on *World News Tonight,*" said Arledge.

"You do?" Rather replied. "Gee, that's a nice compliment. I know Frank from the White House. It'd be great working with him."

With him, I noted. With that as a base, I easily sketched out everything I had in mind. Anything Dan wanted to do, he could: report the big stories on *World News Tonight;* host documentaries; contribute to *20/20;* be a regular on *Nightline* and *This Week.* I'd give him his own prime-time magazine, get producers he chose, give him a say in how we programmed and whom we hired. He would be involved in the highest echelons of our decision making. I wanted him, I said, to be "the logo" of ABC News.

"I wouldn't want to put anybody out," said Rather.

"You wouldn't be," replied Arledge. "Remember what you wrote in *The Palace Guard?* 'Proximity is power.' "

Rather's mouth dropped open. I confess, shamelessly, that I thought it would.

In the anonymity of the back booths of Chinese restaurants, David Burke was following up. We even put some numbers on the table. What would Dan think of, say, $2 million a year . . . *if* everything worked out.

From thereon, when Dan spoke of ABC News, the word he used was "we."

I pulled out all the stops, bringing ABC's top brass into the socializing meetings, all the way up to and including Leonard Goldenson. By mid-December, all the portents were good. The talk of $2 million—double CBS's offer—had made Richie Leibner an ABC cheerleader, and Jean Rather seemed to be on board as well. NBC, which had been halfheartedly in the derby, had dropped out, and CBS seemed to be wheel spinning. As I'd expected, it wanted Dan in anchor tandem with Mudd, which was okay with Dan but not with Mudd, who'd allegedly been harboring a not-very-secret dislike of Rather for years. That put CBS squarely on the dilemma's horns, with no convenient way of getting off.

Nonetheless, I had forebodings. CBS had yet to move up its big gun, founder/chairman William Paley, and when it did, ABC's money edge would lose its sheen. Every ratings point Rather gave to the *CBS Evening News* brought roughly $5 million to the network's bottom line. Bill Paley would spend whatever it took, say whatever was required, not to lose that. I could almost hear his invocations of CBS News traditions as he walked Dan around to the bust of Edward R. Murrow that adorned the premises. Dan would have to be granite to resist.

As we inched toward Christmas, though, waiting every day for the other shoe to drop, it dawned on me that, either way, we weren't going to lose. If Rather signed with CBS, Roger Mudd was even more likely to leave. If Mudd stayed, it meant we'd have gotten Dan. Either way, the pressure would be on CBS to confront the biggest loss of all, the one they'd been dreading and ducking—understandably!—lo these many years. And that was the retirement of Walter Cronkite. This was far from my goal in wooing Dan—competitive as I may be, my middle name, after all, wasn't Machiavelli, and Walter was an icon of our whole industry, not just CBS. But the future was suddenly very close indeed.

Ann and I had planned a skiing vacation over Christmas, but she came down with a bad flu, which shut us in the apartment and gave me the opportunity to reread Dan's books, the pages of which were soon scribbled with notes. I examined them as if preparing for one of Mark Van Doren's exams at Columbia. Everything was riding on what would take place in the next two or three weeks, and I was determined to leave nothing to chance.

Four days into the New Year, I hosted a dinner party at our apartment for Dan and Jean. All the ABC senior staff were on hand with their spouses, a way of showing the Rathers we were one big, tight, happy family. Naturally, the about-to-be-ex of one of the ABC folks chose the occasion to air some marital laundry, but it was an otherwise successful evening, and from the warmth of Jean Rather's good-bye hug, I couldn't help thinking her husband was in the bag.

But a week went by, without hearing from Dan, and I began having second thoughts. When another week did as well, my worry turned to alarm. Richie, who'd been equally elusive, finally revealed the cause: CBS had made a counteroffer—a very major counteroffer. He wouldn't tell me the terms, only that Dan was agonizing.

I decided to play the Mudd card. It was time to talk to Roger about his plans. He had to be boiling that CBS was offering Dan the job he'd always assumed would be his. If I could provoke him just a little more, he'd threaten to quit if they gave Dan the full anchor, and that, in turn, could upset the Rather applecart. In the best of all possible worlds, I'd then have a clear shot at Dan, and CBS would be left with a wounded Mudd.

David arranged a Nanni's lunch for the three of us, but Roger, alas, didn't follow the script. He said he wouldn't even consider working for a news organization that employed Geraldo Rivera. This was a conversation stopper in and of itself, but it was just the beginning of Roger's "critique" of ABC News. Besides, he predicted, he'd be sitting in Cronkite's chair soon enough.

"You haven't *heard?*" I asked innocently.

"Heard what?" Mudd said.

"It's all over town. Rather's been offered that job."

"Preposterous," Mudd snorted.

I found it hard to believe, first off, that the rumors had passed him by, but even more, that the idea had seemingly never occurred to him.

All he said, when he left, was a huffy: "I'm going to get to the bottom of this one."

Once he was gone, I turned to David.

"Are you thinking what I am?"

"Yeah," he said. "Blockhead."

"Amen," I said.

Time got wind of the mating dances in early February, and told Richie Leibner it was doing a cover, whoever walked off with the bride. For Dan's picture to be on it, they informed Richie, he had to make up his mind by the middle of the month. Richie promised that he would.

A few days later, when I went to Lake Placid to produce the Olympics, I still hadn't heard from Dan, but his silence told me all I needed to know. The ghost of the great Murrow had won.

Dan called to confirm it himself on Valentine's Day morning, a few hours before he was to be introduced at a press conference with Walter.

"I think you made the right choice for yourself," I lied. "In your shoes, I'd have done the same thing."

We talked a few minutes more, Dan describing CBS's full-court press which, just as I'd imagined, had included personal stroking from Paley. "Roone Arledge," he said finally, "know this now and know it always: Dan Rather will walk through fire in a gasoline suit for you."

"Yippie-i-o-kai-ay," I wanted to reply.

Time's cover headlined Dan as "The $8 million man," which was somewhat short of the truth. When all the this's and that's of his ten-year contract were toted up, the actual cost of keeping him from us was $30 million—plus the award of Cronkite's "managing editor" title and an array of editorial powers it had taken the most trusted man in America a whole career to accumulate. What startled me most, though, was that in scrambling to get Rather, CBS had pressured Cronkite into stepping aside six months in advance of his scheduled retirement.

It would have been great to have Dan, who, I thought, would have been a much better fit at ABC, but I hadn't walked away empty-handed. I'd removed "Everest" from the landscape by forcing CBS's hand, and there was a two-fer when Roger Mudd stormed out of the CBS Washington bureau Valentine's Day afternoon, never to return. In fact, I had him to another lunch, but Roger was so busy listing the things he wouldn't do (move to New York, work overseas, for starters), we never got around to what I might like him to. NBC hired him as chief Washington correspondent five months later.

Despite all the benefits, despite my underlying premonition, all along, that the pull of CBS might prove too great for Dan to leave, I suffered a major letdown. To have come that close! If nothing else, it showed me that ABC News still had a way to go in the clout department.

But it also convinced me, and my colleagues, that we were going to have to do it on our own. And so we did. *World News Tonight* did fine without Roger or Dan, holding on to an undisputed second place for the next two years. That may not have been good enough for me, but it proved that we were on our way. Meanwhile, though, I had trouble of a different and unexpected sort.

It all started in the summer of 1980 when a front-page series in the *New York Times* set out to examine the relationship between ABC and Aaron Spelling, who was the producer of such fare as *The Mod Squad, Fantasy Island, The Love Boat, Hart to Hart, Charlie's Angels,* and *Dynasty*. What had aroused the *Times*—as well as the Los Angeles district attorney and the Securities and Exchange Commission—were weekly $30,000 payments the network had been making to Spelling and his producing partner, former ABC programming chief Leonard Goldberg. The funds were listed on the *Charlie's Angels* books as "producer exclusivity" fees. In fact, the accounting appeared to be a way of allowing Spelling and Goldberg to avoid splitting some of the profits with the show's cocreators, actor Robert Wagner and his wife, Natalie Wood. Alter a lengthy investigation, the Los Angeles district attorney concluded that there was insufficient evidence to bring charges.

Though no criminal charges were filed (Wagner and Wood settled out of court), the articles were an embarrassment, particularly to Elton Rule, who personally oversaw the network's arrangements with Spelling, which were unique in the industry. Even more eyebrow raising was the *Times*'s disclosure that Spelling and Rule were longtime friends and that ABC had raised questions about the close business ties among Rule, Spelling, and Goldberg, and a lawyer who represented them in a joint business deal outside of ABC.

I'd had my professional ups and downs with Elton, but personally we got on well. More to the point, as number two to Leonard Goldenson, he was my boss. Now I had to confront the decision as to whether he was a story, too.

The only time I'd even considered such a question was nearly two years before, when it had come up hypothetically during a lunch with Fred Pierce and Dave Burke.

"I just want to understand who's in charge of what," Fred had said. "I'm the president of the network, right?"

"Right," we replied.

"Which means I'm your boss, right?"

"Right."

"So I could tell you not to run a story that would hurt the company, and you wouldn't run it, right?"

"Wrong."

Even Fred laughed at the time, but the point was as simple as it was fundamental: If you were doing news, you covered the news. If you self-censored because a given story made the company look bad, then what you were doing was something else, not news.

There was nothing funny or hypothetical about the *Times*'s articles, however, and I couldn't run a credible news organization and ignore them. When I heard that *World News Tonight* was launching an investigation, it didn't even occur to me to stand in their way.

Journalists being journalists, few things energize them more than the chance to zing the person who signs their checks. With unusual gusto, a four-and-a-half-minute piece—*Moby-Dick* in television terms—was put together. I was out in Sagaponack that day and all I had was the script. The script itself was tough minded, but there's a world of difference between reading and seeing. If I'd been in town, I'd undoubtedly have gone in and watched, and conceivably I'd have told the producer to hold off for a day, hoping that the story would blow over. On the other hand, I didn't want us to be lambasted in the press for being the only network news *not* to cover the story that evening. So, based on the script, I let it roll, and it wasn't until I turned on my home television set and saw the images that went with the words that I realized how truly devastating it was.

One shot, taken from a helicopter, showed a sprawling warehouse and shopping-center complex in which Elton Rule and Aaron Spelling were coinvestors. Another caught an ABC Entertainment vice president trying to slink away, that very day, from our own ABC News investigator. Then came the coup de grâce: Elton's progeny in the beaming company of Uncle Aaron.

I could imagine Elton at this moment, steam pouring out of his ears. I wanted to leave it at imagining, as I didn't relish talking to the boss we had just trashed, the more so when I had no intention of apologizing for the trashing. But if I were going live again with Elton in the same company, I knew I had to make the call.

I reached him in L.A., where he'd been fielding condolences from industry friends.

"I'm sure you're very unhappy," I opened.

"*Unhappy?*" Elton said. "You know what everyone is saying out here? '*Your own company*—sandbagging you!' You haven't made me 'unhappy,' Roone. You've made me feel the village idiot!"

It was more than a while before Elton would speak to me again, and I could hardly fault him. But the experience also solidified my conviction that a news division was no place for palace politicking and that running a news division was no job for someone with his eyes on the corporate ladder. For there were instances when you were simply going to have to do things the people upstairs wouldn't like.

I wasn't always so sage. A couple of months later, for example, I made Carl Bernstein Washington bureau chief.

I should preface the story by saying that I thought Carl Bernstein and Bob Woodward the most effective investigative journalists of my era (by the way, I still think so) and an inspiration for a whole new generation of reporters. Furthermore, I hadn't started out with the bureau chief's job in mind. What I'd really wanted Carl to do was a two-hour documentary about how Henry Kissinger managed to emerge from Watergate unscathed, when high crimes and misdemeanors were occurring all around him. What a combo it would be: co-god of investigative reporting takes on sole god of the Nixon White House, and Carl, who was at loose ends at the moment, having departed the *Washington Post,* saw the genius of the notion. But after thinking it over, he apparently got cold feet.

We had a crash meeting on the subject, David Burke, Dick Wald, and I, just before Carl was scheduled to come by the office. He was too good a recruit for us to let him just walk away, and it was Dick Wald who said, "What about Washington bureau chief?"

We had a vacancy coming up—the incumbent was close to leaving— and we'd been kicking around various possibilities, but the idea of Carl hadn't so much as occurred to me.

And suddenly, there he was. The Kissinger idea, as I've said, hadn't clicked. Other possible projects had been vaguely introduced, and Carl had responded just as vaguely. Although he hadn't said no to anything, he didn't seem all that hell-bent on coming to ABC.

So that was the state of affairs when I heard myself say, "What would you think about being Washington bureau chief?"

From the way Carl's eyes lighted up, you'd have thought that he'd just discovered the transcript of the missing eighteen minutes of Oval Office tape.

"That'd be great!" he said.

As this book should make abundantly clear, acting on impulse can sometimes bring about wondrous results and other times it's an invitation to total disaster. Now that I'd all but given Carl the job, the casting seemed inspired. He'd be the seal of approval on the worthiness of ABC News. Doors that had been closed would now swing open. Scoops would magically tumble through them.

The Reynolds claque, no doubt, would howl that I was "star fucking," and do you know something? They'd be right! But stars are stars for a reason, and I thought ABC News could use all the stars it could get. People who wouldn't talk to anyone else talked to a Barbara Walters. They took David Brinkley's call because it was David Brinkley. And the celebrated, at the risk of repeating myself, have celebrated connections. In fact, it was because of Henry Kissinger himself that I first got on the trail of Carl Bernstein, because Henry had invited me to a dinner party for Richard Nixon, which is where the prospective documentary first took wing.

(David Brinkley, I must add, remembered the evening ever after, for Nixon kept addressing him as "Chet.")

In other words, I wanted Carl Bernstein because he *was* Carl Bernstein. I talked to Bob Woodward and Ben Bradlee about it. Both seconded the motion. Carl, they said, was unique, and Bob confided that Carl had been mostly responsible for the Watergate reporting that led to *All the President's Men*.

I should have asked, unique . . . for what?

Instead, I entrusted the management of ABC's 345-person Washington bureau to someone who everyone but me seemed to know couldn't have organized a one-car funeral.

The howls I'd expected were more like shrieks. With both the outgoing bureau chief and his deputy leaving the premises, there was no hope of breaking Carl in gently. Appalled by the new leader's nightclubbing with Bianca Jagger while his wife, Nora Ephron, sat at home (something else I'd missed), Frank barely acknowledged Carl's existence. In other bureau precincts and cliques, reaction split between horror and hilarity. But the joke was on me, because I was the one who'd hired him.

Time does not always heal wounds. As it turned out, the thing that interested Carl most about being ABC News Washington bureau chief was being able to say he was ABC News Washington bureau chief. This produced the predictable with Frank and his colleagues, and Carl asked that I come to Washington to bestow a public vote of confidence. I did, and did so a second time a month later. The third followed a few months after that.

At the fourth such request, though, I drew the line.

"Carl," I said, "I can't make these people respect you. You have to earn it from them."

Estimable words.

In April 1981, I gave up. I turned the bureau over to an old-guard favorite and assigned Carl new duties as a special reporter for *Nightline*. He lasted there for three largely invisible years.

Meanwhile, if I'd been wondering what else could go wrong . . . well, I was on a roll. A UPI story, datelined Northhampton, Massachusetts, Monday, February 9, 1981, read as follows:

> Max Robinson, a black anchorman on ABC's "World News Tonight," blames the television network for racial discrimination during coverage of the presidential inauguration and the return of the 52 American hostages.
>
> Robinson told a Smith College audience Sunday that he and

all other black journalists were excluded from covering the stories and said the omissions were representative of his treatment at ABC.

Robinson said he submitted his resignation because of the omissions, but he said it was refused for "obvious reasons."

Robinson called the media a "crooked mirror" through which "white America" views itself and said it is time for black America to make itself known.

He said ABC wants him to speak like "any old white boy" and not incorporate his history, culture or views "and certainly not speak out of experience."

I'd become accustomed to Max's gripes ever since he called Frank "a bigot" at the "Last Supper" meeting. Frank and Barbara had limos, and he didn't. The producers kept ignoring his Midwest story suggestions, and he wasn't getting the third of the airtime that belonged to him by right. On and on, and in between, bouts of not showing up for work. But this—his comments at Smith College—was beyond even Max's pale. I called Chicago and left word that he was to be in New York Wednesday morning, no excuses. Then I went back to scanning the wires, which were pouring on the details.

According to the AP, Max had also taken shots at black politicians for being Uncle Toms and at Nancy Reagan for wearing designer gowns while her husband was cutting social programs. But we'd gotten most of the venom.

"When Ronald Reagan was crowned and our hostages came home, there was an orgy of patriotism the likes of which I have never seen in my young life, and I'm forty-one," Max was quoted as saying in his speech. "And I must tell you that I watched from the sidelines because ABC elected not to include me in the coverage of either event, even though I'm the national desk anchor responsible for a good deal of the ratings at ABC. They have admitted it publicly, and they have admitted it to me. So I had to ask the question: Why am I being excluded?"

Max's answer came immediately: "In this patriotic fervor, black people would interfere with the process. . . . I think that was an unconscious racism operating where suddenly black people were wiped off the tube."

Baloney.

Max hadn't been assigned to these events for reasons of geography.

The hostages were welcomed at West Point, the inauguration took place in Washington. Neither was on his beat. Keeping black correspondents off the air wasn't true either. George Strait covered the inauguration, Hal Walker, the arrival of the hostages in Frankfurt, while Royal Kennedy was with one of the hostage families.

I also hadn't turned down Max's resignation for a very simple reason: He hadn't submitted it.

I'd known it would be tough on him, being dropped into a strange city to do a big job for which he'd had no preparation. In the studio, though, he was terrific. But it was like pulling teeth to get him out into the country to report, which was the whole point in putting him in Chicago. I'd given him Betsy West and Phyllis McGrady because I'd thought it would help if I equipped him with the best writers and producers. I'd had David Burke shuttling to Chicago to be his special ear; the last trip, Max had challenged him to an arm wrestle, then had passed out drunk.

It was hard for me to understand how someone so gifted could be so troubled. He had it all, and it still wasn't enough.

I arranged for him to meet me at my sports office, at 1330 Sixth, to throw off any reporters who might have the building up at Sixty-sixth and Broadway staked out. Max came in spouting denials. He hadn't said any of the things that were in the papers. He'd been victimized, done in by deliberately distorted quotes.

"Guess the nigger was getting too uppity," he said, "and they had to cut me down."

"Look, Max," I said, "I don't want to humiliate you, and I don't want to get into a fight with you, and I don't want to have to publicly call you a liar. But when you go out of here, you have to have something better to say than 'It didn't happen.' Because, chances are, someone had a tape recorder at that speech."

Max glared at me. "I'm telling you, I didn't say it."

"I'm not going to fire you because you voiced your opinions," I said. "But if you have complaints from now on, bring them to me and we'll deal with them. I can't have you running around giving speeches on college campuses saying the entire News division is racist. I want this thing fixed. And the first thing we have to do is come up with a statement."

We spent the next two hours negotiating the wording. I wasn't happy with the end product, which had Max denying he'd accused ABC of racism and admitting only that his remarks "were not sufficiently precise." But I'd pushed him as far as he was going to go.

The draft was typed up, and Max said he had to catch his plane.

"Take a later one," I said.

"Why? What are you talking about?"

"I need you to teach me something."

"About what?"

"About racism and about you," I said. "I want to learn from this. I want to know how you look at things. Yes, I'm a white man, that's how I was born. But when you use terms like 'unconscious racism,' I don't understand what you're talking about. For all I know, I may be guilty of it. I don't think I am, but I need you to explain it to me."

Max looked at me suspiciously, as if trying to decide if I was conning him.

"You sure you really want to know?" he said.

"I told you I do. You've got to at least trust me about that."

"Okay," Max said. "I'll satisfy your curiosity. You *are* an unconscious racist. All white people are. Only difference is, some of you hide it better than others."

He went on like that, getting more and more bitter, for over an hour. When he finished, the only thing that had been added to my understanding was how angry he was—as much at himself, it seemed, as at me.

I thanked him, and wished him a good flight back, and reminded him to call whenever he wanted to talk. He gave my hand a limp shake and half-waved good-bye.

The exchange did our personal relationship no good, but it galvanized me. Not long afterward, I called together all the black people on our staff. I told them I wanted us to do an hour-long documentary, but one using only black staff. There was to be no input from anyone else, either in the writing or the research or at the production end. And that was how *Growing Up Black in White America,* narrated by Carol Simpson and George Strait, came into being as an ABC News special.

Meanwhile, though, a package had arrived from Northampton, Massachusetts, the home of Smith College. Inside it was a tape. Listening to Max Robinson speaking all the words he'd sworn to me he'd never uttered, I marveled, once again, at how damned good he was at the mike.

Going Solo

It may be an old cliché in business, but sometimes the best deals really do turn out to be those you don't make.

Odd occurrences kept dogging Dan Rather, all the months he waited for Walter to vacate his chair. He claimed he'd been kidnapped by a Chicago cabdriver over a $12.50 fare. He told the *Ladies' Home Journal* he'd sampled heroin as a cub reporter in Houston. He played "Gunga Dan" by dressing up in native garb for a *60 Minutes* expedition into Afghanistan. Worst of all, he mightily offended Walter Cronkite by making it clear that his advice was no longer welcome.

This last struck me as not only weird but lacking in smarts.

I couldn't figure out what had gotten hold of Dan, but there was worse to come. On March 9, 1981, *The CBS Evening News with Dan Rather* made its debut. The new anchor was tense, jumpy, grim, abrupt, as visibly itchy in his skin as Walter Cronkite had been at ease in his. It was as though everything that made me like Dan so much—the charm, the good humor, the utter genuineness—had been sucked away, and it was almost painful to watch.

I kept checking in every night, looking for improvement. Three weeks elapsed with none. Then, the afternoon of March thirtieth, as I was speculating with Dave Burke about how much longer Rather's jitters would last and how we could most capitalize on it, the news desk called. Sam Donaldson was at the Washington Hilton hotel, we learned, and someone had just tried to assassinate the president of the United States.

CBS News had *become* CBS News covering such events; this time, it was our turn. Four minutes after the shots rang out, Sam, who'd been standing fifteen feet from Reagan when John Hinkley Jr. began firing his .38-caliber revolver, was on the air with the first bulletin. And ABC News remained first the rest of the day: first with pictures of the shooting; first with word that the president had been gravely wounded; first with reports of every important development.

"CBS and NBC would have been well-served keeping an eye on the ABC monitor," the Associated Press wrote. "CBS was late on the story, late on many details, and behind on breaking events much of the day. . . . At NBC, ABC's dust was swallowed in big gulps. If there is such a thing as a loyalty pact between viewers and network, it was sealed with ABC News being first and best when it really counted."

The critics' only cavil was Frank Reynolds's reaction to the news that presidential press secretary James Brady had in fact survived, when all the networks had quoted White House and Capitol Hill sources as saying that he was dead. "Let's get it straight!" Frank snapped over the air, slamming down his palm on the anchor desk. "Let's get it nailed down, somebody!"

Had Walter Cronkite spoken the words, they'd have been inscribed over the entryway of every journalism school in the country. Coming from Frank, they were portrayed as losing one's cool. Apparently, viewers didn't think so, for they watched ABC News that day in unprecedented numbers, and I can't believe a single one turned to another channel because Frank Reynolds reacted emotionally to the high and tense drama of the moment.

Rather, meanwhile, continued to fumble at CBS. By early June, he'd lost nearly half the lead bequeathed by Walter, and rumbles were getting louder that he would soon be replaced, either by a rehired Mudd, or by the folksy host of the *CBS Morning News,* Charles Kuralt. With the pot nicely bubbling, I decided to give it another stir by going after *Today* show host and former NBC White House correspondent Tom Brokaw.

It was not my first flirtation. I'd tried to hire Tom shortly after Gralnick and Kaplan—"Starsky and Hutch," as Brokaw called them—began producing *World News Tonight.* He'd slipped away then, flatteringly explaining that nobody else could become a star at ABC News as long as I was there because I was the star. Both of us knew that was malarkey. (Producers and managers are never the stars. Not even the illustrious Don Hewitt is the star of *60 Minutes.*) The truth was that Tom was quite pleased to be at NBC, which at the time was making noises about pairing him with Tom Snyder on the *Evening News.* Much had happened since, however, including Bill Small removing Tom's friend Bob Abernethy from the *Today* show the same week Abernethy's wife died. Having spent five years reestablishing *Today*'s primacy, Tom himself had wearied of rising at four-thirty A.M. Also, his contract was about to expire, and there seemed no place for him to go at NBC, which had guaranteed Roger Mudd that he'd be Chancellor's successor.

I wanted Tom—but as what, was the question. His boyish looks and easygoing manner fooled me into thinking he didn't have the heft to anchor *World News Tonight* on his own—(Boy, was I ever wrong!)—and if there was one thing we didn't need, it was yet another "desk" on the program. But Tom as a kind of super-reporter was something else.

An exploratory lunch established Tom's interest, and we commenced clandestine get-togethers. Hoping to dazzle the pride of Yankton, South Dakota, I set up one rendezvous at the triplex ABC maintained at the Plaza Hotel. During the Ali fights, which were blacked out all over town but which we had because they were going to be aired on delay on *Wide World of Sports,* I'd used its sixty-foot living room for closed-circuit broadcasts, inviting the likes of Sinatra, Kissinger, and Woody Allen to partake of our hospitality. The only trouble was, arriving first at this particular lunch, I discovered that the person who was supposed to be there to let us in was nowhere to be found. I waited in vain for someone to show up. Instead, Tom arrived. I couldn't have us standing there like a pair of fugitives from the Keystone Cops. We had to find someplace else. We rode down in the elevator, only to bump into all sorts of people in the lobby who recognized us, and taxied over to a restaurant I knew where we could talk discreetly and unobserved. There was only one hitch: The restaurant in question was closed! Tom started laughing at me, and I joined in, and unable to conjure up an eatery where we wouldn't be spotted, we wound up, two high-powered television big shots, in the Brokaw living room, eating sandwiches while we plotted the future.

Tom was great fun to be with, and we'd always hit it off. A few meetings later, I had the feeling we were on the verge of making a deal. Before handshakes could be exchanged, though, Thornton Bradshaw, RCA's new chairman, intervened. Bradshaw was familiar with Tom from Los Angeles, where he'd run Atlantic-Richfield when Tom was anchoring at NBC's owned and operated Channel 4. Bradshaw told Tom that he was about to appoint another of his L.A. pals—producer Grant Tinker of MTM—chairman of NBC, and that a new day, minus Bill Small, was dawning at the News division.

After Mudd offered to share the *Evening News* anchoring with Tom when John Chancellor switched to a commentator's role in 1982, it was all over but the contract details, which were whoppers: seven years at a reported $18 million, and editorial powers beyond even Rather's, including say-sos and broad consultation rights that virtually applied to any pin dropping at NBC News.

Meanwhile, there were unintended consequences to having Chancellor out of the picture. As I'd calculated—correctly, it turned out—Mudd's appeal to viewers would approximate what it was to me. Given the turmoil and changes at both rival networks, the unthinkable happened. For the week ending July 17, 1981, *World News Tonight* became number one—yes, *number one!*—the first time since the network's founding that we had reached the top. Though our tenancy proved temporary, we stayed within a statistical eyelash of Rather until the last week of October, when *World News Tonight* edged into first place again. We were there the next week as well, and for the first time in CBS history, the *CBS Evening News* was dead last.

Unthinkable. Like the Yankees.

I didn't believe that Bill Paley would tolerate the humiliation, and he didn't. Two weeks after Rather touched bottom, the news division was handed over to Van Gordon Sauter, an ex-newspaperman who in a dozen high-profile years at CBS had been Paris bureau chief, general manager of the Chicago and Los Angeles O & O's, and the network's chief censor. Not bad for a former writer for the *National Enquirer.*

It soon became evident that Sauter had been studying us. Within weeks of his arrival, the *CBS Evening News with Dan Rather* began to look very much like *World News Tonight,* everything from introductory music to commercial "bumpers" promoting upcoming stories, from live Q and A's with correspondents in the field to splashy, identifying graphics.

Sauter's ideas about content were entirely his own, however. News from Washington and overseas lost ground to lost-puppy-dog stories that tugged at the heartstrings—"Moments," Sauter called them, ordering that every broadcast contain two or three. Then, one night, Dan happened to appear wearing a sweater under his jacket. As far as I know, it was an accident and not the result of some focus-group study, but the ratings went up. The next night, no sweater. But the next time Dan wore a sweater, up went the ratings again. Presumably, Sauter turned the heat down in the studio after that because the sweater, from then on, became a sartorial feature of the *CBS Evening News.* A further clue to what lay ahead came in the form of Sauter's instructions to producers: "Watch *Entertainment Tonight,*" he said. "It has a lot to teach us."

Veterans of the Murrow-Cronkite era were appalled, including Cronkite himself. But the informal, down-market, downright cuddly approach worked, complete with the participants walking around the set: By January 1982, the *CBS Evening News with Dan Rather* was back in first place.

What Sauter did was hardly new. The same changes had been urged on me when I took over ABC News, and I knew it was the shortest route to Nielsen Nirvana. But I hadn't been tempted to follow it then, and I wasn't now. I also wasn't overly troubled by Rather's return to the top. *World News Tonight* still had a lock on second place, and the distance to first was a fifth of what it had been when Cronkite was at his peak. Moreover, I was counting on Sauter to shrink it further. Already, his tinkering had senior hands heading for the exits and made our wooing lunches shorter. For one thing, no time had to be wasted gabbing about "CBS News traditions."

But then, for the saddest and least foreseen of reasons, we ourselves began to self-destruct.

Frank Reynolds had inevitably found out that I'd been romancing Rather, and he refused to believe I hadn't used his job as bait. He also was deeply annoyed that I'd made Brinkley coanchor of national election-night coverage. My pointing out the eighty share David had won doing the elections for NBC hadn't endeared me either. I'd had a brief hope for better relations when *World News Tonight* surpassed NBC in the ratings, but Frank hadn't been moved, nor had he been the few weeks we'd been number one. I was still the barbarian in the temple.

I could conjure up other reasons for his resentment too, from his treatment by my predecessors during the Agnew era to my making Carl Bernstein Washington bureau chief. But however guilty I tried to feel, I was never able to persuade myself that I was Lucifer incarnate. Frank, obviously, couldn't be shaken from the opposite conviction, and lately I'd concluded that the best means of keeping peace was keeping distance. As often as I was in Washington, and despite all the hours I spent with our producers and Ted and David, I seldom called Frank just to chitchat. Our relationship was correct but formal. More important, it had no effect, either way, on *World News Tonight,* which continued to prosper. I believed that, as long as we tended to our hard-news knitting instead of trying to imitate our imitators, sooner or later we'd catch Rather again.

Then, in mid-January 1983, Frank hurt his leg while vacationing in Key Biscayne, Florida. At the time, the only notable aspect of the injury was how it was incurred: At the age of fifty-nine, Frank had been flipped from a surfboard. A month later, however, he hurt the leg again, slipping on a patch of ice during a Washington snowstorm. The pain left him hobbling on a cane, and he thought he'd aggravated a wound he'd suffered as a World War II infantryman. By March ninth, though, he was feeling well enough to attend a black-tie extravaganza at the Waldorf-Astoria in New York, where I was awarded the Gold Medal, the International Radio and Television Society's highest honor.

The evening was television-industry modest: The West Point Glee Club, Menudo, Arsenio Hall, and Ann Jillian performed; Walter Cronkite, Tom Brokaw, and Dan Rather attested to what a fine fellow I was, as did my colleagues Barbara, Peter, Jim McKay, Howard Cosell, and the two Franks, Gifford and Reynolds. Frank Reynolds spoke standing on his gimpy leg from below the raised stage, and ex-presidents Nixon, Ford, and Carter conveyed flattering sentiments via videotape. So did the current occupant of the White House in presenting the IRTS gold medal. "Roone," said Ronald Reagan, "your contributions have been significant enough. I want you to know that I consider Sam Donaldson a small price to pay."

A week later, the Washington bureau sent word that Frank's doctors had reexamined his throbbing leg and discovered a hairline fracture of the femur. Surgery was required, and he'd be laid up for three weeks.

He seemed unusually tired when he returned to the air on April third, but I assumed he'd soon be back to normal. Instead, he appeared more drawn every day and visibly struggled getting through the April twentieth newscast. The next morning, Frank's wife, Henrietta, known to one and all as "Hank," called the bureau to say that he'd taken to his bed with a bad case of the flu.

Three weeks went by with no further news. This was worse than any flu I'd ever heard of. Everyone in the bureau, though, professed ignorance, and the messages I left with Frank's secretary asking him to call went unanswered. Then, on May twelfth, Hank Reynolds phoned the bureau. Frank's "flu" had just been diagnosed as a severe case of viral hepatitis, apparently contracted from a tainted blood transfusion during his leg operation. He'd be recuperating for another four to six weeks.

A few days later, Hank called again. Make that twelve weeks.

Now, I was truly worried, and not just for Frank. Already, our ratings had begun to unravel. David Brinkley had been doing most of the filling in, and through no fault of his, the distinctive, deliberate, reflexive cadences that had made him a legend were all wrong for the rush and rhythm of *World News Tonight*. I was reluctant to start tinkering with the latter, assuming that Frank would be back, and I wouldn't in a million years have tried to change David Brinkley.

David himself was due to leave for a vacation, but when, the Friday before his scheduled departure, I called him to say bon voyage, I got the following response:

"I'm not going anywhere," he said.

"What do you mean?" I asked.

"I signed on to be a team member, and the team's in trouble. The beaches will just have to get along without me."

That, I thought, is what icons are all about. But week by week, the audience for *World News Tonight* hemorrhaged away. By July first, when I brought Peter Jennings to Washington to spell Brinkley, more than a fifth of the viewers were gone, and NBC had been back in second place for five straight weeks.

My own composure had known better times. The state of Frank's health remained a mystery, and there seemed to be no way to get to the bottom of it. I'd wanted to call him a dozen times—as, for instance, when someone reported back to the Washington bureau that they'd spotted Frank at a well-known Washington hospital—but whenever I reached for the phone, one of the tenders of the Washington flame invariably warned that any inquiry would be taken as an assault on the Reynolds dignity. Less intimidated by such considerations, Dave Burke had a go at fact-finding by showing up at Frank's suburban Maryland house bearing flowers and get-well wishes. He got no farther than the door. Her husband, Henrietta Reynolds said, wasn't up to receiving callers.

ABC News was now at risk for fear of offending its leading internal critic. When I told the bureau that if I didn't hear something definitive about Frank's condition soon, I'd have to start making plans for a permanent replacement, producer Bob Frye, an old Reynolds friend lately returned from London, offered an out: If Frank approved, he'd accompany me to his bedside, where I could converse with my lead anchor through a hospital-style screen.

Imagine it! This was too much even for me.

Looking back on it, what's truly amazing is that not a single person I worked with, or for, spoke out in all those days, encouraging me to make a change. It was as though we were all waiting. But I couldn't promote the appearances of David or Peter, as that would wound Frank, and I couldn't promote the return of Frank, as I didn't know when—if ever—that would occur. I was stuck with the worst of both worlds: old viewers turned off by not seeing Frank, new viewers who, while they might have been lured by Jennings or Brinkley, I had no means of attracting.

I knew the situation couldn't go on much longer. But I didn't know how to end it.

Then, on July twelfth, Peter got a phone call from Frank, inviting him to lunch.

"And bring a tape recorder with you," Frank said. "I want to practice."

Peter's report was encouraging. Though Frank had lost considerable weight, tired easily, and seemed years older, he'd joked and traded bits of ABC gossip and wolfed down a full meal. Best of all, Frank was chomping at the bit to get back to work.

He was dead within the week.

It wasn't clear which had killed him: the viral hepatitis he'd acknowledged or the multiple myeloma bone cancer he'd concealed for the last five years.

He'd been diagnosed, I learned later, in the summer of 1978, shortly after the start of *World News Tonight*. His doctors told him that the illness was terminal, but that he might live another three or four years, possibly even longer. Frank shared the news with his family and two old friends at ABC: David Newman, his producer, and George Watson, the longtime Washington bureau chief. Frank had been weighing telling me, but Watson—whom I'd recently hired back as vice president in charge of standards and practices—advised that coming clean might cost him his job.

That Frank could believe it boggled me. But that I'd let months go by without demanding the truth boggled me more. I can't imagine doing the same thing today.

Meanwhile, we had our strange and gifted colleague to mourn. I was in Los Angeles when I heard the sad news, late that Tuesday evening. The next morning, at four A.M. local time, I appeared on a *Good Morning America* special about Frank, along with Rather, Brokaw, Koppel, Jennings, and host David Hartman. I flew back to New York for the first of innumerable meetings with David Burke, Dick Wald, Irwin Weiner, and the producers about *World News Tonight*. On Friday, we all went to Washington along with ABC's top brass, first for a wake with the grieving Hank, then on Saturday for Frank's funeral, where I was to be a pallbearer.

It was the most moving of events, televised live from an overflowing St. Matthew's Cathedral, with President Reagan and the first lady in attendance. Personal condolences from the pope were read. Then we all went over to Arlington cemetery where, thanks to Ronald Reagan's personal intervention, Frank was buried in style—with the honor guard, the folded flag, the playing of "Taps," the twenty-one-gun salute. And all of us, stirred by the poignancy and patriotism of the ceremony, and by the sense of a momentous passing, sat by the grave site along with the first family. The only significant absentee was Max Robinson, for whom there was a vacant seat next to Nancy Reagan.

It was Frank Reynolds, however, who had the last word; he went into his grave wearing a light-colored suit.

When it came to putting our shattered program back together, I'd already made the first decision: We were going with the single anchor I'd wanted from the beginning. Combing the list of candidates didn't take long, either. There were only two: Ted Koppel and Peter Jennings.

Ted, I thought, would blow Rather right out of the water. Viewers and critics adored him; he possessed all the reporting and interviewing requisites; and his on-air mien conveyed steadiness and self-assurance—qualities surveys found conspicuously lacking in Dan. But if I went with Ted, I'd lose him for *Nightline,* a unique program for which he was uniquely suited. *Nightline* was my baby and I refused to put it at risk. Ted seemed to have the same opinion. Whenever there had been speculation about his taking over *World News Tonight*, he'd publicly disclaimed interest, saying that he thought it would be "boring."

But those denials were in the context of forcing Frank out, whom Ted revered. Peter was a different story. They weren't close, their age made them natural rivals, and a time or two, I heard Peter making cracks about Ted's "deification."

Ted hadn't said anything negative about Peter; he hadn't said anything lavishly complimentary either. I also sensed in Ted, the born Brit, an amusement bordering on disdain for Canadian Peter's English pretensions. Whatever his feelings, I knew I had to sound him out on a job I hoped he didn't want.

"Do you still feel what you've always said about anchoring *World News Tonight?*" I began.

"Roone," Ted cut in, "let me make this easy for you. I think that Peter will be a terrific anchor for us. Go sign him up."

Easier said than done.

Right after the funeral, Peter and I flew back together to a birthday party being given for him that night at Gil Kaplan's. Simply getting him to sit in for Frank, in the days before his death, had required a trans-Atlantic trip on my part and a personal plea, and even then he'd agreed only grudgingly. Part of his reluctance, I knew, had been the appearance of being seen as back-stabbing Reynolds. But he was also an instinctive contrarian whenever I wanted something from him, no matter how innocent. If I told him that jumping off a cliff was a bad idea, he'd walk to the edge for a confirming look. His suspicions went beyond the usual skepticism of journalists. With me, it was entirely personal.

The irony was that I'd known and liked Peter longer and better than I had anyone else at ABC News. When I was offered the presidency of the division, he was the first person from News I'd confided in—and he'd been the first to try to block it. Things hadn't changed since. When I called to compliment his performance, as I frequently did after a broadcast, knowing that it was the middle of the night in London, and that no one else would be there to say a good word, the reply was always on the order of, "Oh, so you didn't think I screwed up too badly this time."

Professionally, I couldn't win for losing with Peter. Yet when something was amiss in my personal life, no one was more extravagant in his concern. I'd heard of Peter's relationship with his father, the broadcaster whom Peter himself had once called the Edward R. Murrow of Canada. Peter, born Peter Charles Archibald Ewart Jennings, had routinely been defiant, had left school in the tenth grade and, according to him, the school was not sorry to see him go. Unfortunately, it appeared that I'd become like dad to his rebellious inner soul.

There were other drawbacks with Peter. He didn't have Ted's gut competitiveness, disdained stories that so much as hinted of audience getting, and in those days—odd for someone in Peter's profession—despised being prominent, which, among other things, made it impossible to get him to do promotion.

Then there were his Englishisms, such as pronouncing "schedule" "shedual," "been" "bean," and lieutenant "leftenant," and his insistence on referring to, say, "the American senator Strom Thurmond," as if, as Av Westin pointed out, there were a Pakistani senator Strom Thurmond.

Against all that, Peter was a terrific news man; a handsome, authoritative presence; the best-read autodidact I've ever known; a demon doing his homework; and the ablest ad-libber in the business. Never was this more apparent than on September 11, 2001, when he literally took charge of ABC News in our coverage of the national crisis. He was on that day an anchor in the truest sense of the word, outshining all our competitors in one of the most important news stories of our times, and his performance led to our winning the coveted Peabody Award for distinguished journalism.

I began my campaign to convince him on that Sunday flight and continued the next week through a long dinner at Alfredo's. It was an uphill struggle. Peter came up with every reason under the sun for why he couldn't do it, shouldn't do it, didn't want to do it. He loved living in Europe and didn't want to leave it. He and Kati, his wife, and their two young children had a great life in London, a wonderful circle of friends, and the only negative was that he went to work either at eleven-thirty or twelve-thirty at night, depending on what the time difference was. He was happy with the way things were. Why should he give it all up?

And for what?

Right then, the whole world was his beat. He could roam the planet on the trail of great stories. He didn't think he knew America well enough—American politics, American stories and people—to flourish as an anchor on this side of the Atlantic. Besides, if he left London, what would happen to our European coverage? How committed were we to Europe? If anyone in American television was committed to covering the world, it was I, and Peter knew it. Wasn't *World News Tonight* our name?

But that wasn't the point either.

There was one thing that kept occurring to me, but I didn't want to bring it up. Years before, Elmer Lower, then president of ABC News, had hired Peter from Canada and brought him in to be the *Evening News* anchor. At the time, ABC News was a total disaster—a very distant and deserved last to the other networks—and Peter had been too young, possibly too pretty, and probably too Canadian to make the proverbial silk purse out of our sow's ear.

What affect was that earlier failure having on him now?

"Let me tell you a story about Stirling Moss," I said, after he'd hemmed and hawed and said no a good half dozen times. "As you know, he was the greatest Grand Prix driver of his time, maybe the greatest who's ever been, but he never won a world championship. Do you know why that was? It was because he refused to drive anything but English cars, when they weren't competitive with the Italian Ferraris. Ferrari pleaded with him to drive for them, and it would just about have guaranteed him a world championship. But Stirling wouldn't. Instead, he prided himself on finishing third, driving cars that, in other hands, wouldn't have lasted till the finish line. And do you know what I think was the reason?"

"Sounds like he was a very patriotic man," Peter said.

"Yes, he was," I said. "But that isn't why."

"What then?"

I leaned across the table. "Because, in his eyes, it was better being number two, always striving for the top, than to be the front-runner."

"Do you mean he was afraid of failing?"

"No. Stirling would run risks on the circuit with the best of them. But he wanted the comfort zone of not always having to win. He wanted to be the underdog."

Peter looked at me long and hard, but his position didn't change.

Somehow, I didn't take it as final. I took it as reluctance, certainly, and contrariness too, but I wasn't about to give up. This didn't keep me, the next day, from putting a call in to Roger Mudd. I'd learned from Dick Walk that Mudd was out as an NBC anchor, and I thought I'd better touch all the bases in case it didn't work out with Jennings or Koppel. But my heart wasn't in it. I wanted Peter.

Then, that weekend, I found help.

Peter and Kati were spending the weekend in the Hamptons, not far from my place in Sagaponack, and I invited them to dinner Saturday night at 1770 House, an ancient Hamptons establishment I knew would appeal to Anglophile tastes.

There we got into it again, I at my most persuasive, Peter at his most evasive—the same litany of reasons for why he couldn't, until Kati finally got in a word.

Kati Marton, I should say, was European through and through. She was also a career journalist. Hungarian by birth, she was the daughter of the one-time Associated Press bureau chief in Budapest in the years before World War II. She herself had served as ABC's Bonn correspondent. Now, in the most positive of ways, she got on Peter's case.

"You know," she said to him, "you've wanted to anchor the evening news all your life. You know you'd be great at it, too. You'd be spectacular. It would be good for all of us. And now—just when Roone's offering it to you, *World News Tonight,* what you've always wanted—you're being difficult. You're balking when you should be accepting. You *have* to take it, Peter. You'd never forgive yourself otherwise."

Thank you, I said in my mind. I may even have said it aloud, may even have shouted it. Because even as the conversation went on—the pros, the cons, the what-ifs—I realized that the deal was done.

And so it came to pass.

Not without conditions, of course.

Peter's biggest what-if was what would happen if anchoring didn't work out, and/or if he and Kati and the children couldn't take the change in lifestyle, and/or if he didn't find the new job "journalistically satisfying." He was worried, professionally, about giving up reporting altogether. Some anchors did, some didn't. There was no law that Peter had to; it would be up to him.

"If I'm here a year and it doesn't work out," he said, "I want the right to go back to being chief foreign correspondent in London."

I didn't like the idea for two reasons. The first was that I didn't want Peter to have an out. I wanted him to plunge into the job wholeheartedly,

without looking back. But he also wanted the position—chief foreign correspondent—left open in the interim and the title not given to anyone
else.

Reluctantly, I agreed to the first part. But on the second, I fudged a
little. I said we weren't going to fill the job now—and in fact for quite a
while we didn't—but I did have someone else in mind and I knew Peter
wouldn't be happy about it.

The someone was Pierre Salinger. The former press secretary to President Kennedy had been working for us in Paris and had proved himself to
be a highly valuable asset. For one thing, Pierre could pick up the phone,
and the next day you'd be in the Elysée Palace, chatting with Valerie Gis-
card d'Estaing. (I knew because he'd already done that for me.) Beyond
that, he was also a hell of a journalist. Through his innumerable contacts
and a group of Middle Eastern lawyers who'd sought him out, he managed to get a line on the secret negotiations to obtain the release of the
Tehran hostages long before anyone else, Woodward and Bernstein
included. We set up a special unit for him outside our regular news operations so as to maintain secrecy. As a result, when the hostages were finally
released the very day of President Reagan's inauguration, we were on the
air in prime time the next night with the terrific three-hour documentary,
America Held Hostage: The Secret Negotiations, that had won every award television could bestow and had even prompted that congratulatory phone
call from Walter Cronkite.

Nothing, in the long run, was going to prevent me from giving Pierre
the job, which in due course we did.

There was one last person I had to deal with in regard to *World News
Tonight.* I'd been putting it off, in part to give myself a chance to cool
down. I'd been mightily irate with Max Robinson after he'd failed to show
up for Frank's funeral, where I'd arranged for him to sit next to the first
lady. He claimed after the fact that he'd been laid low by cold medicine. I
didn't believe it for an instant, and had I been braver, I'd have fired him
then and there.

At the same time, his career at *World News Tonight* was over and done
with. I offered him instead a transfer back to his beloved Washington, and
a job reading the "News Brief" once each weeknight. The news brief was a
sixty-, or sometimes a ninety-, second news update that we inserted into

the prime-time program breaks. Max accepted when I added anchoring a weekend newscast, but he quit after less than a year to coanchor a ten P.M. news program on the NBC station in Chicago. A few months into that $500,000-a-year job, he went to Cleveland to attend an awards ceremony, and never came back. Eventually, he turned up at a substance-abuse clinic in California. But the demons continued to haunt, and following a second stint at another rehab facility, he went home to Virginia, broke, despondent, and suffering from AIDS.

"I think one of my basic flaws has been lack of esteem, not really feeling great about myself, always feeling I had to do more," Max said in his last public interview. "I never could do enough or be good enough. That was the real problem."

Five days before Christmas 1988, he died in a Washington hospital at the age of forty-nine. A group of us went to the funeral, which, in its own way, was as impressive as Frank's. It was held in a Washington church packed to the rafters, with a truly memorable choir. Jesse Jackson was there, as were any number of African-American leaders, including Max's brother Randall. All of us bore witness to the sad ending of a great but wasted talent.

So we started over again.

I set Peter's debut for Monday, September fifth, which featured another first-night appearance. The day after Frank's death, Reuven Frank, who'd succeeded Small as NBC News president, had informed Roger Mudd that he was through as coanchor, and that come the first Monday in September, Tom Brokaw would be flying solo. I'd sent Tom congratulations, then begun battening down. For the first time in two decades, all three networks had only one horse in the race.

Jennings, Rather, and Brokaw. And so it has remained ever since.

Peter was starting off exactly as the troika had—in last place, an ocean away from CBS. *World News Tonight* had lost 3.5 million viewing households and getting them back was going to be a struggle. It was a new world, and Ted Turner's upstart CNN—the "Chicken Noodle Network" it had been called not many months before—was now a part of it. Local news, which was expanding to two, even three hours in major cities, was a growing threat as well, and the powerhouse entertainment schedule that had helped us meet it had become a memory.

The press was likening *World News Tonight* to a comet that had streaked across the sky, incandescent, then gone. Sauter, who'd recently been promoted for turning Rather around, had the exceedingly bad taste to tell a reporter we were "dead in the water."

I clipped out the quote quietly and taped it to my nearest monitor.

Sports Redux

By 1983, my second marriage was falling apart. That's the only way I know how to put it. Two people who'd been very close simply weren't there for each other anymore, and didn't recognize it, and then, when one or the other did recognize it, rushed together again in tender, highly emotional reconciliations, or attempts at reconciliations.

Only to separate again.

The first hint that something might be wrong was early in the year, around the time Frank Reynolds was cracking his leg on an icy sidewalk. Ann began taking long trips. For a while, I was too busy to pay attention. Either that or I was simply denying what was as plain as day. Then we tried marriage counseling. The psychologist called me "an accommodationist." Maybe I was, but if so, Ann was a "confusionist," sending me mixed signals at every turn. For example, at that aforementioned International Radio and Television Society award dinner, she toasted me and I still have a picture from that evening: Ann and me, arm in arm, beaming. (Right next to us in that photo, smiling just as wide, happened to be O. J. Simpson and his new wife, a blond stunner named Nicole Brown.) But a few hours before, I found out afterward, she'd called her lawyer.

In our different and separate, yet strangely clinging, ways, we were both suffering from midlife crises. Ann's took her off, finally. Mine took me down, into depression.

"Are you having fun?" I asked Secretary of State George Schultz at a dinner one night, during the breaking up with Ann.

"I didn't take this job to have fun," he said.

"I know, but do you go home at night feeling enjoyment from what you are doing? Do you feel that it's unique and important?"

"Yeah," he said, "I guess I do."

Well, I had too, once upon a time, when I was out in the field, producing. I was in good physical shape in those days. I went hunting and fishing, I had fun. Now I was in lousy shape, and if I went into the bush now, on safari, there'd be four hundred calls and cassettes sent in on elephants.

Some days, I found it hard even to get out of the empty bed in the morning, even to go through the motions at the office. It was as though I was in deep mourning. I went to see Fred Pierce, telling him that he ought to find someone else to run Sports, and if my mood didn't change soon, News, too. Fred wouldn't hear of it, but I wasn't kidding. The prospect of continuing to do what I was doing, grinding it out for the rest of my days and doing a half-assed job of it, was too bleak for me to bear. I went from a psychologist to a psychiatrist, and little by little, I began to climb my way out of the hole. Friends helped—male friends in particular, many of whom had been through similar experiences—and so did work, the challenges that called like so many sirens. One day, when I realized that I was spending the hours before my sessions with the psychiatrist thinking up subjects to entertain him with, I knew I was on my way. I ended the psychiatry and . . . well, hey, life goes on, doesn't it?

News, I realized, had become my passion. I wasn't giving Sports nearly the attention it required. My hope had been that Jim Spence would cover for me, and he had, measured by hours invested. But Jim's grinding input wasn't showing up in output. It also had become evident that people skills were not high on his CV. He preferred ordering to leading, and in a business where relationships are 90 percent of the battle, he came off as pugnacious and pompous. As a result, we'd lost several key events, most recently, NASCAR, a supposedly done deal that slipped away to CBS just as the popularity of stock-car racing was starting to spread beyond Dixie.

At a minimum, I should have moved Sports from its old Sixth Avenue offices up to Sixty-sixth Street, where News was and where I could keep closer tabs on it. Instead, I'd been handling the problem with Arledge indirection, going around Jim to deal with John Martin, a suave ex–submarine officer I'd recruited whom I could send without worry to deal with the Juan Antonio Samaranches of this world (Samaranch being the head of the International Olympic Committee). With a little help from me—I'd deliberately feigned indifference to the Olympics by staying home from the proceedings and sending John, a supposed underling, in my place—he'd managed to secure the 1984 Winter Games in Sarajevo for us, and we would be back in the Summer Olympics business that summer with the Los Angeles Games.

I was convinced that John would be a splendid leader for ABC Sports. Unfortunately, Don Ohlmeyer, who'd left us to go to NBC, and then left NBC to run television for Ross Johnson at RJR Nabisco, thought just as highly of him and offered him a whopping salary. I spent hours reasoning with John, trying to persuade him to stay and take over Sports—and failed. I saw his going as a terrible loss, and I believe, to this day, that had he stayed, much of the trouble that awaited Sports down the road could have been avoided. In any case, six months later, in our small world, the three of us met up again when RJR Nabisco bought a 20 percent stake in a money-losing cable channel ABC had just acquired. Most everyone at the network thought the purchase crazy at the time, but the operation happened to be called ESPN.

I was now determined to unload the Sports job, and my next serious candidate was Peter Ueberroth, a travel-company operator then heading up the Olympic Organizing Committee for the 1984 Summer Games. I'd first met the jut-jawed Peter while vying for the television rights, back in 1979, and I'd become increasingly impressed by him, for one thing by the way he had smoothly avoided all the mishaps that had bankrupted Montreal in 1976. But, as with John Martin, I was not alone in my admiration. When I offered Peter the presidency of ABC Sports in late 1983, he was already in the midst of negotiations to succeed Bowie Kuhn as commissioner of Major League Baseball.

I was so desperate I even turned to David Burke, whose interest in sports began and ended with playing touch football with the Kennedy clan. David wisely turned me down. Meanwhile, despite my inner misgivings, I thought Jim Spence deserved to be considered for the job, but when I brought it up with Fred Pierce and Leonard Goldenson, they were negative. Their nomination—with which I heartily agreed—had been Herb Granath, who'd gotten advertisers to pay $150,000 a minute for *Monday*

Night Football before taking over Video Enterprises, ABC's cable and new technologies division. But Herb had decided that his heart lay with cable.

With no other obvious candidates on the near horizon, I put the successor search on hold, and turned my attention to 1984. It looked to be a killer. Maybe it was a sure remedy for a failed marriage, but over the next twelve months, I was to produce two Olympic Games, a pair of political conventions, a national election, assorted major golf tournaments, a presidential inauguration, and ABC's first-ever Super Bowl—in between seeing to *World News Tonight, Nightline, 20/20,* and *Wide World of Sports.* Something was going to give in all of this, and I had a feeling it might be me. My old friend Howard Cosell was doing his best to ensure that it was.

I thought I'd put the Howard problems to bed when Don Meredith returned to *Monday Night Football* in 1977. NBC hadn't been the promised land after all, and Don had come home saying, "Why play in Greenwich, Connecticut, when you can play Broadway?" Howard had been happy to have him back, and, initially, things were, well, dandy. No more than the usual vituperation reigned in the booth, and record audiences tuned in. But, in 1982—the year after Pete Rozelle knocked the rights' price up to $7 million a game—the NFL Players Association went out on strike, and the next year 5 million viewing households disappeared. With the economy wheezing, the signs were that the 1984 season would mark the first time *Monday Night Football* lost money in the fourteen years it had been on the air.

That, I thought, could be fixed. Howard I wasn't so sure about.

He'd turned from being provocative, outrageous, and entertaining to being bitter, vindictive, and paranoid—mostly, I thought, because he was bored. Bored with football and fans, bored with sports ("silly little contests," he said), bored with an occupation he felt—maybe rightly—was beneath him.

After all those years being the best at what he did, Howard wanted a life change, a transformation that would have others regarding him as seriously as he did himself. At one point, he even considered making a run for the U.S. Senate. At the least, he wanted to anchor *World News Tonight.* He didn't seem to believe my first dozen turndowns, but when I failed to respond to his open appeal for the job in a Tom Shales column, the message at last sank in.

Retribution followed.

His first shot, taken in the aftermath of the bloody Larry Holmes-Randall "Tex" Cobb mismatch in November 1982, was announcing that he would no longer cover the "parasites in professional boxing"—principal blame for whose spawning he placed on ABC Sports. So no one would miss his point, Howard made it while testifying before Congress, calling for boxing's abolition. He next went after the "lying, fraudulent NCAA," and the "sick hypocrisy of football mercenaries posing as students on the nation's campuses." Shortly thereafter, Walter Byers decided to award part of what had been an exclusive ABC franchise to CBS.

Baseball, which I sweated bullets arranging for Howard to announce, got it too, in particular St. Louis Cardinals owner Gussie Busch, whose Anheuser-Busch brewery was one of ABC's biggest advertisers. When a Budweiser executive called to straighten out—politely—a couple of facts Howard had mangled during a *Nightline* appearance, Howard screamed at him, "You little pipsqueak! I don't give a shit about your company's advertising!" But these were but darts next to the weekly napalm Howard laid down on Pete Rozelle, who went from being a friend to "arrogant" and "manipulative," not to mention "a liar"—for trying to block Al Davis from moving his Oakland Raiders to L.A.

Frank and Don, doubly guilty for actually having played football, Howard described as "men without intellect, without training, without my background in law, without the spontaneity of articulation that I possess. In other words, the jockocracy." O. J. Simpson, whom I'd added to the show and who revered Cosell almost as a father figure, joined the ranks of the scorned after kidding about Howard's football expertise at a fan luncheon. Juice, with his "deplorable diction," was thereupon cast into the outer darkness as one of the jocks conspiring to destroy the career and reputation of Howard Cosell.

According to the executives Howard buttonholed every morning in the lobby of the ABC building, the leader of this cabal was me. As flattered as I might be at being lumped with the jocks, I was worried about the effect Howard was having on *Monday Night Football*. Frank said he left the booth some nights "feeling like a survivor of Omaha Beach," and many of Howard's exchanges with Don were now just plain mean. The recent ratings falloff, I thought, was not coincidental.

I was also concerned for Howard personally. His incessant chatter about "people out to get him" had assumed clinical dimensions, his drinking was worse than ever, and he'd driven off many of his old friends, including his producer and old gin-rummy partner, Chet Forte.

I told him he was blowing it, that he had to stop dumping on the shows that provided his livelihood. It had no impact. Pete Rozelle was now calling weekly, pressing for his removal, but I refused. For all his flaws, Howard was still a giant. He'd invented sports journalism, fought all the good fights, and even now could win over a hostile crowd. But Pete was right: I had to get Howard under control.

The first game of the 1983 season, Dallas at Washington, offered what I thought was the opportunity. As the second quarter drew to a close, Alvin Garrett, a diminutive receiver who'd been cut by two teams before Redskins coach Joe Gibbs picked him up, grabbed a Joe Theismann pass and ran for a good gain.

Howard said excitedly, "Gibbs wanted to get this kid and that little monkey gets loose, doesn't he?"

Watching at home, I groaned: "Monkey" was not a word to be used about black athletes.

I called producer Bobby Goodrich in Washington on the Roone Phone.

"What's the reaction?" I asked, not needing to say what I was referring to.

"The press guys are all going apeshit," Bobby said.

I groaned again. "Okay, have Howard address it as soon as the second half starts. Tell him I said he can't duck this one."

Howard followed orders, sort of. "According to the reporters, I called Alvin Garrett a 'little monkey,' " he said, when he came back on the air. "Nothing of the sort, and you fellows know it. No man respects Alvin Garrett more than I do. I talked about the man's ability to be so elusive despite the smallness of his size."

His half denial changed nothing. Reverend Joseph Lowery, head of Martin Luther King Jr.'s Southern Christian Leadership Conference, had already dashed off telegrams to the media denouncing Howard as a racist and promising demonstrations at every Monday night broadcast until he apologized. Tuesday the print media joined in the hammering, and I issued a press release, lauding Howard for his "superlative and continuing record of promoting harmonious race relations." I kept loudly defending him the rest of the week and through the next, partly because he'd been grotesquely defamed, partly because I thought that if I stood up for Howard, he might remember who his friends were.

Endorsements from Jesse Jackson, Arthur Ashe, Bill Cosby, and Jackie Robinson's widow, Rachel, faded the controversy. Even Alvin Garrett said Howard was great. However, in October, Howard told me he wanted off *Monday Night Football,* and that this time he really meant it.

I urged him to relax, take a few weeks off; he'd feel (and, I hoped, act) differently.

"You're sixty-five, Howard," I said. "You don't need to push so hard. You're the champ and everyone knows it."

Howard skipped three games. But when he came back, nothing had changed, nor did it the rest of the season. I saw no utility in further attempts at appeasement, and, avoiding Howard, departed for Lausanne, Switzerland, in January 1984, to bid on the Calgary Games of 1988.

I wasn't happy to be making the trip. The headquarters city of the International Olympic Committee was pretty enough, and I'd been a frequent visitor. Traditionally, host organizing committees handled television rights, but the IOC, intent on getting more of the pie, had flipped the roles, and this made me uneasy. What's more, they were going to auction off the rights—"putting three scorpions in a bottle," I'd once called it—a bite-to-the-death situation between the networks that we'd always managed to avoid in the past. To top it off, if we *didn't* get Calgary, I feared it would cast a negative shadow on our televising of Sarajevo, which was just a few weeks off, and there is nothing more anxiety provoking than going into a bidding war feeling you somehow *have* to win.

On the plus side, Jim Spence thought he had a deal with Barry. Barry was my old assistant Barry Frank, someone we both knew well, now a senior vice president for Mark McCormack's International Management Group. The IOC had hired IMG's subsidiary Trans World International to deal with the U.S. networks, and TWI had sent Barry to Lausanne, to advise and consult.

During the course of a number of meetings, Jim had let on to Barry that the network had set a bid limit of $275 million. Barry assured him that the figure was a winner.

The way the logistics of the day worked, I was upstairs in a hotel room, with an open phone to New York. I wanted Fred Pierce and Leonard Goldenson in on the negotiations. We all wanted to keep the

Olympics—they had become an ABC tradition, and a highly profitable one—but we all shared the same misgivings. Jim, meanwhile, kept going down to the meeting room on the floor below where the committee was in session. At the end of the first round, ABC, at $208 million, and NBC, at $200, were fairly close. CBS brought up the rear at $180. CBS dropped out after round two, which left us at $261 million, NBC $250. In consultation with Fred and Leonard in New York, I went to $280 million in round three, $5 million more than our original limit, and $12.5 million more than NBC.

Another round. We went to $300 million—$19.5 million higher than NBC.

In between, Jim got hold of Barry and started shouting at him. "This is crazy. It has to stop!"

"I know," Barry said. "I'm trying."

Another round went by with NBC and ABC now deadlocked at $300 million. I huddled transatlantically with Fred and Leonard. Leonard said we would still make a profit up to $315 million. But that was the absolute top.

ABC won it in the next round with a bid of $309 million—$217.5 million more than we'd paid for Sarajevo. Samaranch wanted me to come down and pose for pictures. I wouldn't. Barry came to the room and wanted to shake hands. I wouldn't do that either. More important than my anger over the proceedings, however, was another warning that began sounding inside me. With so much money now riding on the Games, and more each bidding season, sooner or later the games themselves were bound to be changed. I'm no prophet, but that's exactly what's happened since, first with the addition of professional athletes in competitions such as ice hockey, more recently with the introduction of the new so-called sports. The latter may be needed to fill up a vastly expanded prime-time schedule, and the vastly expanded prime-time schedule may be needed to "justify" spiraling costs, but in the process, our wonderful Winter Olympics have been cheapened into something closer to the X-Games than to an international celebration of high achievement in sports.

I confess that in some measure I bear responsibility for the above. I was the one who helped make ice dancing a prime-time event (see below), and I convinced the powers that be to bring all the medalists back for the stars-on-ice exhibition that is now a very popular feature of the last night of the Games. But still . . .

Anyone for wrestling on ice?

Calgary, though, was four years away. In the meantime, we had Sarajevo, just weeks away. I hadn't wanted to produce these Games personally—I'd expected John Martin to do it—but I ended up being the only one I could trust, and when things started to go wrong, it was just as well. We'd built an elaborate opening—and most of our pre-Olympics promotion—around the U.S. hockey team repeating the "miracle" of Lake Placid, but twenty-seven seconds into the first period of an opening-round game with Canada, the Canadians took the lead and never lost it. The Yugoslavian weather wouldn't cooperate either. There was no snow for a week, then twelve inches in twenty-four hours, accompanied by fog and mountain winds reaching 120 miles per hour. That put an end to skiing for five days and forced us to fill an hour's worth of prime time with compulsory figures in ice dancing, a feat that taxed our production ingenuity to the utmost. Nevertheless, we were well behind where we were supposed to be in terms of audience—or in terms of what we'd told our advertisers.

"Beset by Troubles, Arledge Era Over," *Variety* headlined at the time.

But then—this is the beauty of the games—like a lightning bolt rending the gloom, the excitement started. First an American, Phil Mahre, won the slalom gold—a rarity for our ski team—and his twin brother, Steve, took the silver. To top it off, Phil also became a father for the first time, news our Donna De Varona was able to break to him on the air on his way to the victory stand. Overwhelmed, Mahre began to weep. Viewers were apparently moved as well, for their growing numbers suddenly began to exceed all expectations.

And they stayed tuned. They stayed for Torvill and Dean, the magical skating pair from England who wowed an international audience with a performance that seemed to transcend everyone's who had ever taken to the ice. They stayed for Katerina Witt, the gorgeous East German skating champ, and for five-foot, three-inch Scotty Hamilton, victim of a near fatal, growth-stunting childhood disease, who won figure-skating gold for the United States. They stayed, in sum, for the magic, and we ended up with a Winter Olympics that was a major financial and critical success.

On April eighth, however, even as I was being congratulated on Sarajevo at an ABC affiliates meeting, the Soviets squared accounts for Jimmy

Carter's Moscow boycott in 1980 by withdrawing from the Los Angeles Games. Teams from thirteen satellite countries immediately followed suit.

Leonard rounded up the lawyers and consulted the insurers. He called the pullout "an Olympic catastrophe." But I didn't think it was.

So the Communists were staying away. All it would mean was more medals for the home team. Whether the purists liked it or not, the vast majority of our television audience looked on the Olympics as a competition between nations. This is one reason why the Summer Games, where we had long dominated in track and field, had historically been a bigger draw than the Winter, where the Alpine and Nordic countries tended to outperform our athletes. In the case of Los Angeles, the more Americans we could count on to win gold, the greater our success. We wouldn't lose viewers, I said to Leonard; if anything, we'd *gain* them. The Soviets, I believed, had done us a favor.

Mine was a minority view. The only person I knew who shared it was Peter Ueberroth, who was not exactly disinterested. ABC still had $70 million in rights payments left to pony up, and our contract stipulated that if any of ten designated teams withdrew from the Games, we were to be reimbursed for all loss. Since the now departed Soviet Union, Cuba, and East Germany were among the ten, Peter, who was projecting a $12-million profit only if ABC paid in full, saw his whole venture toppling before it even began.

But I stayed cool—until, that is, I went to the doctor with a sore throat one June day and was told I might have thyroid cancer.

I checked into the hospital that afternoon, and was operated on the next morning. I awoke to good news/bad news and an anxious-looking Leonard Goldenson at my bedside. The good news was that the operation had been a success. The bad news was that I couldn't speak a word. I managed to convey to Leonard that I'd be fine, and so would the half billion riding on me two and a half weeks later when the games opened.

Ten days later, against the doctor's orders, I served as executive producer on the Democratic National Convention in San Francisco. Eight days after that, I was in a Los Angeles control room, looking at a bank of seventy vacant monitors. I knew full well what it would take to bring them to life for 187 half-hour broadcast hours: 3,500 employees at 23 separate Olympic venues strung out from Santa Barbara to San Diego; 900

vehicles; 30 commissaries stocked with 25,000 steaks, 20,000 melons, 12,000 cartons of milk, and 50,000 soft drinks; 2,725 hotel rooms; two custom-built 60-foot boats (to cover canoeing and rowing); six cranes; 208 cameras; 96 videotape recorders; 660 miles of television cable. And one executive producer, who at the moment was feeling lousy.

I'd ignored the doctor's orders not to use my throat in San Francisco, and that morning—opening ceremonies day—I'd risen from a night of no sleep in an air-conditioned room set at Arctic, to find my voice a croak. Puzzling how I'd get through the next seventeen days, I went to my broadcast-center office, which I found occupied by network lawyers in open warfare with the Los Angeles Olympic Committee over how much we should be reimbursed for the massive defection of the Soviet bloc.

The eminent television producer David Wolper had been appointed impresario of the opening ceremonies, and no one would ever accuse him of thinking small. Later that day, 84 pianists in white tie and tails would bang out *Rhapsody in Blue* on 84 concert grands; a 750-member all-star college band would march across the coliseum green while an 11,000-voice chorus sang Woody Guthrie and Michael Jackson tunes; and a spaceman wearing a jet pack would land on the 50-yard line, after which 92,500 spectators would perform card stunts. And that was just the first twenty minutes. Ronald Reagan would then declare the Games open and teams from 140 countries would troop in, with the indefatigable Jim McKay and Peter Jennings prepared to say something about each and every one of them. After that, a mystery honoree—in this instance, Rafer Johnson, the 1960 decathlon champion—would light the Olympic flame, and we'd be off.

Then my hot-line phone rang in the control room. We'd had one installed linking Ueberroth and me, in the event of a terrorist attack—the nightmare of every Olympics producer since Munich. Instead of a terrorist attack, this time I got a blast of Ueberroth. ABC, he raged, had just reneged on an understanding about what was to be withheld because of the Soviet withdrawal.

"I hear you've lost your voice," Peter stormed at me, "but not before you fucked me royally!"

"Peter," I managed to get out in a whispering rasp, "you've got it wrong. I'm the one who's on your side."

It didn't matter whether he could hear me or not. The phone had already been slammed down at the other end.

On that cheerful note, I went on to produce the XXIII Summer Olympiad.

For the record:

Total U.S. audience: 180 million (a record).

Ratings: Highest ever for an Olympic Games.

Advertising revenues: $435 million (another record).

Profits to ABC: $75 million (and another record).

Television-created stars: Mary Lou Retton, first American woman ever to win an individual gold medal in gymnastics, sixteen years old, four feet, nine inches tall, with a smile as wide as the Santa Monica freeway. Greg Louganis, who dominated both diving competitions with a skill and ease that put him light years ahead of the rest of the world. Carl Lewis, who did the same in track, with three sprinting gold medals and one in the long jump.

It also didn't rain once; there were far fewer traffic jams than predicted; 6 million people attended; ABC didn't sue anyone; Peter Ueberroth turned in a profit of $150 million and was named *Time*'s "Man of the Year."

I did him a friendly turn at the closing ceremonies. I called him just before they began and told him that, once he was introduced, he should wait a full two minutes before going out onto the field, because we would be running commercials. This he did, and instead of missing his entrance, we showed him walking out to a cheering standing ovation. In return, some months later, when he and I had lunch in New York at Le Cirque, he brought along as a souvenir for me an Olympic torch.

All ended well. Most important of all, though, I recovered not only my voice at the L.A. Olympics but my secret self. I found it in the dark of a control room, whispering phrases like "Go, Jim," "Roll tape," "Up music," "Thirty-second break"; "On my count: five, four, three, two . . ."

Life had joy in it after all, and mine was here—doing what, in my heart of hearts, I knew no one else could do as well.

I flew to Dallas after the closing ceremonies for the Republican Convention, and when I got home, I learned that Howard had quit *Monday Night Football*.

Again.

For the umpteenth time. And the last.

I remember sitting in my office, wondering whether to call, but as I debated with myself, a story about Toscanini came to mind. He'd been a genius as a conductor, and other than General Sarnoff himself, no one had contributed more to the stature and presence of the Radio Corporation of America than the maestro of the NBC Symphony. But Toscanini was also an emotional Vesuvius, a tyrant abusive to all those around him, and every year, the same scenario would play out. Toscanini would quit in a rage. It took the General himself to stroke and coax and cajole to get him back, after which the orchestra played on, to the delight of millions of listeners. Until the craziness started all over again.

Then one year, the story ended differently. This time, when Toscanini quit, the General didn't call. He had had enough. The law of diminishing returns had set in, and it was over.

Howard and I met for lunch at "21." He had just come out with a new book of memoirs, his third, entitled *I Never Played the Game*. I hadn't read it, but Ted Koppel had. Apparently Howard had ripped me all through the book, tagging me with all the grievances he'd harbored—that I'd never given him a shot at *World News Tonight,* that I'd belittled him at the Olympic Games, that I'd kept him from the full flowering of his genius by sticking him in the announcers' booth with a bunch of illiterate jocks, and so on.

But this was the most complicated of men. Guess who one of the people this 300-page hardcover shredding of Roone Arledge was dedicated to?

Yes. Roone Arledge.

I'd decided that the time had come to stop talking Howard out of his resignation, and I knew it was going to be a tough lunch. But I hadn't bargained with the book factor.

"Well?" said Howard, with his lopsided smile. "What do you think of it?"

"Think of what?"

"Think of my book! What else?"

I admitted that I hadn't read it yet.

"I don't believe you, Arledge," Howard said. "Come on, you're pulling my leg, aren't you? You've read it."

"No, really," I said.

"You really haven't read my book?"

"I just haven't gotten to it yet," I said lamely.

He expected me, as usual, to talk him out of resigning from *Monday Night Football*. I didn't. When he waxed eloquent on why he never could go back into that booth again, I agreed with him. The more I agreed with him, the more he carried on. Of course, I said, he would continue for ABC, announcing horse racing and baseball as well as his weekly reportage-and-opinion show, *Sports Beat*. But as much of a blow all this must have been to his ego, it was nothing compared with the fact that I hadn't read his book. The first, he could argue with himself, was business and, after all, didn't it befit the villain of *I Never Played the Game*? But the second was personal, a personal betrayal.

I see us standing outside "21" at the end of that meal as we had so many times before, the two of us side by side on Fifty-second Street, Howard, who was a tall man, in his characteristic slump, head down, shoulders down, cigar in his mouth.

"I can't believe it," he is still saying, shaking his head. "You'd have been too curious. You couldn't have resisted reading it."

The obsessive words, as well as the image, fill me with an irrepressible sadness.

The end of an era.

On the other hand, impossible friend, my comparing you to Toscanini would have pleased you no end!

There was *Nightline* trouble in the spring of 1984 when I made Rick Kaplan executive producer. As usual, I made the move for multiple reasons, but the main one was that I thought Rick's talents and imagination would be a definite plus for Ted Koppel. I had endless discussions with Ted about this, but he still balked. In part it was the old story of the stars of news programs not wanting anyone imposing change from above, but Ted, perhaps out of some inner insecurity, had resisted every producer change we ever made. But part of it was a clash of personalities. Ted was urbane, deliberate, reserved. Rick, a towering six-seven, was impulsive, gregarious, restless, an incorrigible enthusiast always searching for the next big idea. In fact, it wasn't until Rick came up with the South African venture, early in 1985, that he and Ted managed to put their differences aside.

Talk about big ideas. As Rick spun it to Ted, *Nightline* should go to

South Africa, then in the deep and painful throes of transforming itself from an apartheid state, and do a week of programs, the crown jewel of which would be a confrontation between Nobel Peace Prize winner Archbishop Desmond Tutu, and whoever the apartheid regime of Pieter Willem Botha appointed to debate him. Such interactions between South African whites and blacks had never happened before, on screen or off. *Nightline* would make history, and perhaps help change it as well.

Ted Koppel loved the idea. Then Rick laid siege to David Burke and me. I knew it was going to be almost impossible to pull off, that in addition it would be very expensive, and, finally, that it might not be a standing-room-only event for an American audience. With all these things going for it, I of course told Rick to go for it! In truth, I found the idea irresistible. It was exactly what News should be doing in general and *Nightline* in particular—reaching out, trying the impossible, wanting to change the world. How often did any of us have a chance to affect history?

Betsy West, senior *Nightline* producer, and Tara Sonenshine, a booker who was a favorite of Ted's, were dispatched to Capetown to try to set it up. They reported the results of their efforts in a conference call with Ted in Washington and Rick in New York. After protracted negotiations, the South Africans had bent—a little. They'd said okay to the week, but not the debate. Government officials never had—and never would—appear with a black opponent of apartheid. No one, black or white, was permitted to challenge apartheid on South African air.

"Cancel whatever meetings you have and just come home," Ted said, cleverly assuming that the South Africans would be listening in. "Tell the South African government there will be no apartheid on our broadcast. Your visit there is over. We want you to come home."

That did it. Early the next morning, an anxious government press aide called Tara Sonenshine. Yes, there could be a debate after all, and no less than foreign minister F. P. "Pik" Botha would participate on the government side. Furthermore, the South Africa Broadcasting Company now wanted to air the debate itself, although they refused our set-up pieces (that is, the historical and biographical background segments that we would use as an introduction in America).

It looked like it was going to be on after all!

Accompanied by Ted, my assistant, Nanci Dobi, Joanna Bistany, and other members of the *Nightline* staff, I flew to Johannesburg in mid-March.

Rick was already way over budget, but I didn't care. Ted and I agreed that a week from South Africa might be too much for an American audience, but I didn't care about that either. I was going along as a backstop to Rick—whenever we had something this important and potentially tricky, I believed in being in the trenches with our producers—but also to participate in what I saw as a great moment for ABC News.

The deep divisions that afflicted the country made their presence known in sometimes subtle ways. Harry Oppenheimer, the head of DeBeers, the diamond cartel, had Ted and me to dinner at his estate outside Capetown, and as he guided us at dusk to the pavilion overlooking the veldt, he complained about the new highway that was obstructing his view.

"What highway?" I asked.

"It's right in front of your eyes," Oppenheimer said.

I looked again, and ever so dimly in the gathering dark made out tiny dots of moving light. Right in front of my eyes? Yes, but they must have been at least twenty miles away! Not for the first time, since landing on South African soil, I was reminded uncannily of the landed white rich of the old American South or the oil rich of our Southwest and their vast ranches, and the cushy *grand seigneur* lives they led at the expense of others. Similarly, as we wandered through Capetown, a beautiful city at a glance, backed by mountains and set by the sea, I thought of my visits to my Southern relatives as a boy, and how beautiful those cities and towns were too—if you managed to ignore the separate drinking fountains, and the tumbledown shacks on the back streets, and the servants always of one color.

South Africa was like that. And it too was in the often agonizing process of change. As the *Rand Daily Mail* editorialized, after the fact: "It is an indictment of our rulers and the TV service they have created that a programme of such vital importance should have been created by an American team."

The evening of Monday, March eighteenth, fifteen minutes before air, Ted and Rick stood nervously in the stairwell of a Capetown television studio while I waited in the control room. Ted, who'd quit smoking before the trip, was puffing away again, and furiously. We'd decided the smart thing would be to schedule the debate as the first program rather than the last. That way, as someone pointed out, if we got kicked out of the country, at least we'd have made one great show. But we were still apprehensive that, at the last minute, the South African government might cancel the whole deal.

Rick looked positively green.

"You feel like barfing?" Ted asked him.

"You got it," Rick answered.

"Me, too," Ted said.

They came inside for mike checks. I leaned forward in my control room chair and laid a hand on Rick's shoulder to wish him good luck. He jumped at the touch.

On the set at last, Ted looked at a pair of monitors, one showing "Pik" Botha in his office, the other Tutu at his church. It was an unprecedented moment. Black men simply didn't appear on South African television except in taped news-coverage segments. In addition, the apartheid government had previously refused to deal with Bishop Tutu or to recognize him as a legitimate leader of his people.

"Good evening, Bishop," Ted began.

"Good evening," Tutu replied.

"Good evening, Mr. Foreign Minister," Ted said.

"Good evening."

"Mr. Minister, would you like to say hello to Bishop Tutu?"

Five awful seconds passed, each one seeming to last a year.

"Good evening, Bishop," Botha finally said.

I saw a small smile flicker across Ted's lips, and heard Rick heave a sigh. The impossible was coming true.

Later, both blacks and whites would say that the next thirty minutes started change in South Africa. In the midst of it came Tutu's statement, all the more passionate because of the simple, short sentences he used:

"I am a bishop in the church of God. I am fifty-three years of age. You would, I suppose, say that I am reasonably responsible. In my own country, I do not vote. According to this government, I am not a South African. My travel document says of my nationality that it is undeterminable at present. So blacks have been turned into aliens in the land of the oppressed."

As he spoke, Tutu held up his identity card.

Joanna Bistany told me later that the director from South African television who'd been sitting next to her started to weep. I knew only that, as America listened and bore witness, things would never be the same again for these people. I felt almost a chill, and looking down, saw that my grip had snapped my pipe in two.

I walked out to the set, where Rick was helping Ted untangle himself from his IFB.

"You know," Ted said to Kaplan, "you're a great producer."

Rick smiled. "I do know, and I want you to know, I think you're a great anchor."

I put my arms around the two of them.

"Let me make it unanimous," I said.

My euphoria was short-lived. When I got back to the hotel, a message was waiting for me from Fred Pierce: "Call ASAP. Urgent."

"What's up? I asked when he came on the line.

"I can't discuss it on the phone," Fred said, "but you've got to get back here on the first plane."

"I can't do that, Fred. I've got a meeting scheduled with the president of the country! He's going to be Ted's final interview, and to cancel the appointment would not only be rude, but it could jeopardize the rest of our programming." Furthermore, I explained, we had a scheduled interview the next day with Nelson Mandela's wife, Winnie. She was a "banned person," and she'd be breaking the law by talking to us.

"Then you'll have to fly back there," Fred said. "But right now we need you in New York. There's no getting out of this one, Roone."

He would tell me no more, said he couldn't.

I was determined to make it back to South Africa (and I did) for the interview with the president, but on the plane to London, where I'd catch the final leg to New York, I had plenty of time to puzzle over what could be going on. Leonard had been making noises about retiring since turning seventy-nine, but if and when that came about, it wouldn't be on a hush-hush basis. There had been talk too of late about the parts of ABC being more valuable than the whole. Spinning off something like the publishing division, however, wouldn't warrant my presence. The only thing left was a takeover, but that didn't seem likely either. Both Howard Hughes and Harold Geneen of ITT had tried to buy ABC in the sixties, and neither had gotten anywhere. Television networks were more than corporate commodities; they were "public trusts," in the FCC definition, and the only time one had changed hands was in 1953 when Leonard Goldenson's United Paramount Theaters bought ABC.

Well, I'd know what was so important soon enough; I flicked off the overhead light and went to sleep.

The car that met me when I finally arrived at Kennedy the next morning paused at my apartment just long enough for me to take a shower and grab a fresh shirt, then took me over to ABC's big conference room just in time for Leonard's speech.

All the top brass of the company were there, including Fred, looking like the emcee at his own wake.

"I have an historic announcement," Leonard began.

I was too out of it to absorb everything said during the next hour and a half, but I took in the high points: ABC was being sold to Capital Cities Broadcasting, the largest of our affiliate groups. Leonard had successfully held out for $118 a share (18 being his wife, Isabelle's, favorite number), which translated into $3.5 billion, four times what the company had been worth in 1981. Cap Cities, which owned stations in Philadelphia, Houston, Buffalo, Fresno, Raleigh-Durham, Hartford-New Haven, and Tampa-St. Petersburg, were broadcasters, not quick-buck artists; with chairman Tom Murphy and president Dan Burke, Leonard said, we'd be in good hands.

I took in some of the financial nitty-gritty details, such as the opportunity that awaited us holders of selected stock options, and felt pretty good about the whole deal. I was about to get modestly rich, and my new immediate superior was the younger brother of Johnson & Johnson chairman Jim Burke, who just happened to be my good friend and Sagaponack neighbor.

The *Times*, the next morning, would headline the deal across the top of page one. As it turned out, we had Ronald Reagan to thank for the prospective fattening of our bank accounts. He'd appointed Mark Fowler chairman of the Federal Communications Commission, and Fowler, in turn, had lifted the FCC's limit on station ownership from seven to twelve, clearing the way for Cap Cities to buy out Leonard. Wall Street was judging the transaction a masterstroke by Leonard Goldenson and a coup for billionaire investment guru Warren Buffett, whose $500-million stake in Cap Cities would be worth $100 million more in less than a week. As for Cap Cities, they turned out to have fingers in a number of media pies. These included Fairchild Publishing, owner of *Women's Wear Daily;* a chain of a dozen radio stations; fifty-four cable systems; miscellaneous periodicals by the score; and ten daily newspapers, among them, the *Kansas City Star* and the *Ft. Worth Star-Telegram.*

As impressive as the collection was, Cap Cities was still only about a fourth the size of ABC. However, their profit margins—50 percent in the case of its TV stations—were quintuple ours, thanks to relentlessly squeezing every cent out of every dollar. Tom Murphy himself proudly told the story that, when Cap Cities had painted its Albany headquarters some years before, the two sides that couldn't be seen from the street were left undone. In New York now, where the offices of Messrs. Murphy and Burke were located appropriately across the street from St. Patrick's Cathedral, the entire corporate staff—including secretaries—came to twenty-nine people; at ABC, the vice presidents alone numbered more than a hundred.

Meanwhile, I called South Africa to give Ted the news and ask how the Winnie Mandela interview had gone (without incarceration, he said), then, having confirmed my flight back to Johannesburg, headed into a joint meeting with my own senior people from News and Sports. There were jokes about ABC's chief financial officer, Mike Mallardi, changing his name to Mike Moriarty, but the mood was mostly glum. They'd read about Cap Cities' tightfistedness too, and reports were circulating about the relish with which it went about union busting. I repeated Leonard's line about the new owners being broadcasters just like us and tried to reassure them that any changes would be minor, but the expressions on their faces said no sale.

I had little time for any misgivings of my own. I saw Fred Pierce before I skipped town again.

"Where do you stand with these guys?" I asked him.

"I'll be vice chairman," he answered, as if announcing that he'd just been appointed head janitor. Fred had been in line to succeed Leonard—until this deal.

"And you'll be reporting to?"

"Dan Burke," Fred said. "Just like you."

Fred was my most steadfast booster. All I knew about Dan, aside from his brother, was that he'd once worked in the Jell-O division of General Foods. In the back of my brain, I watched a small, dark cloud just beginning to form.

But Goldenson and Murphy, as befit the architects of the deal, were all smiles to the world. Leonard said that joining Cap Cities and ABC was "two and two equals five," while Murphy proclaimed that he viewed the acquisition as "a public trust" and that the company never interfered with its editorial people.

As for me, I got back on an airplane and completed the third lap of my aerial marathon to the bottom of the globe—New York to Johannesburg to New York to Johannesburg—and then on to Capetown again where we interviewed the president of South Africa. Along the way, the media caught up with me about the Cap Cities acquisition.

"These are people we've dealt with for years," I was quoted as saying. "We know them and we like them. Nobody knows better than Tom Murphy how to reach success and circulation in broadcasting."

I managed to bob and weave my way through their questions, talking about "assets" and the "improving profit picture," and by and large I got away with it. But the line that was attributed to me, even though I think it was Leonard who said it first, was:

"The canary has just eaten the cat."

Cap Cities

Whoever said it, Cap Cities was not amused by the "canary" crack.
Well, they weren't amused by a lot of things, particularly when they
discovered that the network's projections of advertising revenues were too
rosy, and that our 1985 projected profit of $70 million (the highest of any
of the networks) was likely to disappear in 1986. In truth, they came into
ownership at a particularly difficult moment in network history. The
costs of competition continued to escalate, while the proliferation of
cable had begun to have an affect on certain kinds of advertisers, who left
the networks for cheaper rates elsewhere.

Television sports advertising was contracting for the first time in two
decades. Every network was going to lose money, even on the formerly
can't-miss NFL. *Monday Night Football*'s hit for the 1985 season would be
$25 million, the overall loss for ABC Sports $40 million—with bad or
worse to come in 1986.

There were a number of reasons: competition from pay-per-view and
cable (including our own ESPN, which we'd bought from Getty Oil); network sports programming glutting the airwaves twenty-eight hours per
week; the lunatic spiral of rights fees, which now accounted for eighty-two
cents of every ABC Sports dollar. But the biggest culprit, ironically, had
been our own L.A. Olympics. More than half the advertising available for
all sports on *all* networks—*for the entire year!*—had been spent on those seventeen days. We'd not only captured the market, we'd sucked it dry.

As for me, I'd never worried before about profit-and-loss statements.
My mandate had always been to grow my divisions, first Sports, then

News, and I was aware that every year up to this point had been 15 to 20 percent better for ABC Sports than the previous one and that, in addition to our having won more awards than CBS and NBC Sports together, we were annually bringing in more than their combined revenue.

But times, I knew, were changing. Even before Cap Cities arrived, I'd been going at our Sports budget on my own. Production costs had been trimmed on every event. Hiring was frozen. A new college football deal was wangled at a third of the price of the old. And for the first time in the eighteen years I'd been running the division, I'd let the competition snatch jewels I judged too expensive to keep, such as World Cup soccer.

I'd also decided to hold the line on the upcoming bidding for the 1988 Summer Games in Seoul. Barry Frank was again fronting for IOC, and using the standard calculus—rights for each Olympics are three times more valuable than the last—had the Koreans dreaming of a $1-billion-dollar payday.

Well, they wouldn't be getting it from us. I was making one bid only: $225 million, exactly what we'd paid for L.A. NBC and CBS, we'd heard, would both be topping ABC by at least $75 million, so I passed on the pilgrimage to Lausanne.

News was a different story. In fact, when Capital Cities took us over, News was a bright spot in ABC's difficult 1985.

By custom and tradition, mind you, network news divisions weren't supposed to make money. News, in the old view, was a public service imposed by the FCC, and the millions lost in its broadcast was evidence of high-mindedness, as well as a justification for airing *The Beverly Hillbillies.*

So, at least, went the thinking at CBS, the so-called Tiffany network.

I'd always had a different view. I thought that news could—and, without jettisoning principle, *should*—make money. Even more, I believed that News could and should be at the heart of a broadcasting empire, not a weak-sister adjunct to Entertainment and Sports. This was the philosophy behind the way we built ABC News and, in the process, helped enrich the stockholders of ABC Inc.

We'd been profitable for the better part of a decade, and in 1985, while CBS News and NBC News were dripping red ink, ABC News would be making a profit of $55 million.

To produce cash, though, takes cash, and as at the other networks, the ABC News budget—$55 million in 1977, $275 million now—had exploded, though not with the same bang as CBS and NBC. We were also turning out more programming than the competition—better than a fifth of everything ABC put on the air, triple the amount it had been when I took over. And we were doing it with the smallest news division in the industry. I was as proud as could be of what we'd accomplished. But I was also uncomfortably aware of some facts:

Such as that the networks' prime-time audience, which had been 95 percent of all televisions in use in the seventies, was now 77 percent, down 10 points in the last four years and continuing to fall. The same went for network news viewership: 72 percent of American households tuned in in 1981, 62 percent today. In San Francisco—liberal, educated, well-informed San Francisco—Vanna White turning alphabet letters on *Wheel of Fortune* at seven P.M. was a bigger draw than Peter, Dan, and Tom combined! Then there was the data on cable: virtually nonexistent in 1970, currently in 38 million American homes, 600,000 of whose occupants were watching CNN every day. The advertising money being taken from the nets? $1 billion per year, $2 billion four years down the road. And that didn't include the network Rupert Murdoch was busily putting together, which would emerge as Fox.

As depressing as this may sound, though, I saw it differently than most of my peers and certainly than the critics who seemed to get particular delight from denouncing network news. To this day, and all through the "down" years (which would continue into the 1990s), if you put all the evening news programs together from the three networks (allowing for differences, mind you, they are still basically the same program, covering the same material and vying for the same huge audience), you would still have an over 50 percent share of the viewing public, with roughly 18 percent shares at ABC and NBC, and 15 or 16 percent at CBS. Over 50 percent, mind you. In any given television year, there are only one or two television programs that reach that level. (The Super Bowl and the Academy Awards come to mind. What else?) In other words, while the audience for network news has indeed eroded, the news division is still a big, and very powerful, and potentially very profitable part of any major broadcasting company.

And so it was in 1985.

Nonetheless, the world I'd flourished in was changing. The era of the founders ended abruptly in the mid-eighties, when Bill Paley finally relinquished CBS to Lawrence Tisch and the Loew's Corporation, when General Electric bought General Sarnoff's NBC, and when we were sold to Capital Cities. The new owners brought with them a totally new culture. They were bottom line focused, cost cutting conscious, margin happy, forecast obsessed. They talked about "product" rather than "programs," "assets" rather than "people." They tended to think short-term, and the fluctuations of their companies' stock was vastly more important to them than building long-term enterprises in which they and their colleagues and employees could take pride. (When, some years later, Madison Square Garden, the legendary home to so many sports stars and unforgettable events, was sold to Cablevision, the new owners proudly announced that they would "put good product on the floor.")

Nevertheless, this new breed brought something important to television in what inevitably would be a period of consolidation after years of growth and expansion, and that was financial discipline. The entire industry was in need of it, ABC included, and hearing my mother's voice loud and clear from out of the past—"Control your own destiny!"—I set out to anticipate the changes I knew would be in store for us once Cap Cities took formal control of the company at the beginning of 1986.

Quietly, I gathered a small circle of trusted senior hands and told them I wanted them to examine every ABC News cranny and nook around the world for waste. We called it the Siegenthaler Commission because they were to bring their findings back to Bob Siegenthaler, the onetime executive producer whom I was in the process of moving into a management role and who would shortly be co-opted by the network. By July, Sieg had pulled together the list of recommended changes, and some thirty of us repaired to a hotel in White Plains, off the beaten track, for a no-holds-barred review.

Some of the suggestions, such as cutting back satellite time, I accepted immediately. Others, like combining the staffs of *World News Tonight, 20/20, This Week,* and *Nightline* into an undifferentiated lump, I rejected. The big savings came from slicing 200 positions, all but a handful through early retirements and not filling empty slots.

What I was doing, I thought, was merely prudent and rational. But it didn't fully prepare me, or my people, for the onslaught that was soon upon us. Not that we didn't have early warnings in the months before Cap

Cities took over formally. I had a strong indication of it from journalist Marc Gunther, who described to me a chat he'd had with Dan Burke, our new president-to-be, about financial waste at ABC. Amazingly—at least to me—Dan raised the subject of the three limos that allegedly had been necessary to ferry Fred Pierce, me, and Jim Spence to David Wolper's house in Los Angeles when we were acquiring the rights to the Olympics.

"If they made $75 million on the L.A. Olympics," Dan said, according to Marc Gunther, "and the limos cost three hundred each, more, probably, but say three hundred, I would argue that one car was okay and they could have squeezed in, and then they would have made $75,000,600, instead of $75,000,000. There's no defense for waste."

I thought Marc was pulling my leg, but he swore he wasn't. Absurd as it was—and is—for me to have to defend our "profligacy," the truth is that when you're in L.A. on business, you have to have a car, and a driver too if you don't know your way around. As I recall, that day the three of us had totally different schedules and whereabouts before the meeting with Wolper.

Of course, Dan Burke would have defended himself by saying he was simply making a point. Yes. And the point of not liking waste was shared. (Who in business, I'd like to know, actually *likes* waste?) But this kind of finger-pointing, with the focus on alleged expense-account excesses, reflected a kind of drill-sergeant muscle flexing that pointed up profound differences in attitude. The Cap Cities people were used to the tight ships and big margins of running stations, and well they should have been, because local stations are far more profitable than the networks to which they are affiliated. The reasons for this are several. From the very beginning of the industry, the networks have paid the stations to air their programming. After all, it is the individual stations who are licensed to broadcast, not the networks, and just as in the case of newspaper and magazine publishers who pay their distributors, "compensation," as it's always been called, paid to the stations has been the only way to reach the public. At the same time, it is the networks that bear the high costs of programming, including all the prime-time shows, which are by far the most costly, risky, and "wasteful" part of the television business. When it comes to what goes out over their airwaves, the risks involved to local stations are small indeed.

In the Cap Cities mentality, therefore, costs rigorously controlled equaled greater profits and cost controls included curtailment of our supposed lifestyle, with accompanying wrist-slapping admonitions. We could live with them, too. In a way, they took me back to our old NCAA days, when ABC was small and struggling and I used to put the hotel bills of our whole crew on my single credit card so that I could monitor what each and every member was spending. Well, we were no longer small and struggling, but we'd gotten fat in the process.

Just so long as they didn't tinker with my work, or the "product" we put out on the air.

Meanwhile, I had Sports and News to run and that fall, with or without Cap Cities looking over our shoulders, that meant the usual run of crises.

Howard, as I've already related, was one of them.

Donald Trump, strangely, was another. For three years, we'd been broadcasting the springtime schedule of the United States Football League, with beneficial results for all. But The Donald, owner of a New York franchise, wanted more. Remembering how the AFL, once upon a time, had forced its way into a merger, and wanting a franchise in the NFL for himself, he convinced his fellow owners to switch the USFL's games to the fall season. No way, I told him. The last thing anyone needed was more fall football. During a round of golf, I informed the big but erratic hitter that he was begging for bankruptcy, and that I had no wish to accompany him off the cliff. Besides, I had a little fall event of my own called *Monday Night Football*. The response was a multimillion-dollar lawsuit, charging that ABC Sports and the NFL were "involuntarily conspiring" to drive the USFL out of business.

(To this day, I have no idea how one can "conspire involuntarily," but never mind.)

As a result, and in what was a colossal waste of time, I found myself laboriously trying to explain to a jury how it was that ABC had made more money—in the one given year the USFL lawyers focused on—on the USFL than it had on *Monday Night Football*—which happened to be true—but why this did not, by any means, make the USFL a more valuable property! The jury, however, seemed to understand. They awarded The Donald and his league—which, sure enough, folded—damages in the amount of . . . one dollar!

And then, to make a trifecta, there was Geraldo Rivera. I'd put up with him for so long, as I hope I've made clear, for the same reason I had Howard. Increasingly, though, the bad was outweighing the very, very good. *Viewpoint,* a program I'd created as a forum for viewers to come forward with their criticisms and complaints about ABC News, might as well have been renamed *The Rivera Hour.* I'd conveyed my displeasure during recent negotiations by declining to offer even a token raise. Geraldo expressed his by letting the old agreement lapse without signing the new one we'd offered him.

Neither of us was budging by late September when Av Westin showed me a Sylvia Chase report, based in part on an about-to-be-published book alleging that the Kennedys and organized crime had been involved in the 1962 suicide of Marilyn Monroe.

Three months and thousands of dollars in the making, the twenty-six-and-a-half-minute piece claimed that both the president and his brother had had affairs with Marilyn; that the Mob possessed blackmail material in tapes gathered by wiretappers hired by Jimmy Hoffa; that Bobby visited Marilyn hours before she ingested a fatal dose of barbiturates; and that one of the Kennedys' brothers-in-law, Peter Lawford, had rid Monroe's home of incriminating evidence before the cops and the media arrived.

Av called the story "solid journalism," and was ready to run it.

I needed convincing. I simply didn't believe that his "facts" were accurate. The damning tapes the Mob allegedly possessed were nowhere to be found, and the only evidence that they'd ever existed was the word of underlings who had been employed by the Kennedys' Enemy Number One, Jimmy Hoffa, who was conveniently dead. From my point of view, the story about Peter Lawford playing Mr. Fix-it rested mostly on the recollections of actress Deborah Gould, whose information came from the few weeks she spent as the third of Lawford's four wives—*fourteen years* after Marilyn's demise! As was the case with all the other principals in the piece, Bobby Kennedy was dead too, but there were numerous credible eyewitnesses who placed him five hundred miles away the day he supposedly drove Marilyn over the edge by saying he wouldn't be leaving Ethel and the eleven kids for her after all.

"Av," I said, when the screening was over, "if you're going to devote half of *20/20* to a premise this explosive, you'd damn well better be able to prove it. This isn't close."

"Does that mean you're killing it?" he asked.

"Not yet," I said. "Call it 'saving you from embarrassment.' If you can come up with the goods, I'll take another look. In the meantime, you should cut this thing in half."

"But what am I to tell my people?" he protested.

"Tell everyone it needs more editing, that's all."

I assumed weeks would pass before I heard anything more of Kennedys and Marilyn Monroe, and perhaps I never would again. But ten days later, Av was back. The piece had been recut, and he announced that he wanted to run it that night.

"Want to watch with me?" I asked Dave Burke.

David looked as if I'd just invited him for a tipsy spin on that Chappaquiddick bridge. Not only had he worked for the Kennedy inner circle, he was still very close to members of the family.

"I'm recusing myself on this one," he said.

I stuck my head into Joanna Bistany's office. As mentioned, she'd been deputy to communications director David Gergen in the Reagan White House, and she was now my director of news information.

"How about you?" I asked.

"I'm no Kennedy lover," Joanna said.

"All the better," I replied.

We watched. No question: The piece *was* shorter, but if there was any other difference, I couldn't detect it.

"That's *it?*" I asked at the end.

Av nodded.

"What do you think?" I asked Joanna.

"I'd love to believe it, but, excuse me, Av, to me it's just so much bullshit."

I turned back to Av. "When it comes to attacking the president of the United States, *any* president of the United States, I'm from Missouri. Show me. As for tonight, you'd better run something else."

That, I assumed, would be that, but Av, being Av, couldn't leave well enough alone. He stirred up Geraldo. Geraldo had neither seen the Monroe piece nor had any connection to it, but that didn't deter him from enlisting Hugh and Barbara to link arms on the set after the show was over to pledge loyalty to Av Westin.

"Arledge," Geraldo vowed, "is not going to get away with this."

"We were appalled," he said, "that Roone would override a respected, honorable, great newsman like Av. We were appalled that the head of this network would suddenly show such an interest in this particular story when he hasn't shown personal interest in so many others we've done."

Next day, gossip columnist Liz Smith, an old friend, called me. She didn't say anything about Geraldo, only that she'd heard that I'd "censored" *20/20* for fear of offending the Kennedys, Ethel in particular.

"Nonsense," I said. "The piece in question just wasn't good enough for us."

One of us, Liz or I, called it "sleazy." She printed that I said it, which, to the best of my recollection, wasn't so. But as I was getting myself in trouble with Barbara and Hugh Downs, Geraldo was headed for a weekend in California and interviews with *Time, People, Newsweek, Variety,* the *Hollywood Reporter,* and the AP, poolside at the Bel Air Hotel.

"If a politician did this, we'd all do an exposé," he said. "I am shocked and appalled. Such a decision has never happened before. The circumstances suggest that cronyism is involved."

The charge that I was buddy-buddy with the Kennedys had no relevance. In fact, I had been friendly with members of the clan, but I'd also gone through a period of years when Ethel Kennedy hadn't spoken to me because of a *Nightline* interview with Sirhan Sirhan. Geraldo, nonetheless, plunged on, and soon I was seeing my name in print preceded by the phrase: "the embattled president of ABC News."

Then I got lucky. Geraldo's assistant/girlfriend—take your pick—was nabbed using an ABC messenger to pick up an ounce of marijuana.

Gee.

Bright and early, I gave Geraldo a buzz.

"I want you to quit," I said.

"Bullshit," he said. "I have a contract."

"Sorry about that," I said, "but the only contract I've been able to find here isn't signed. Isn't that just the darnedest thing?"

I let Geraldo word the press release. Geraldo denied then and has consistently denied since that he had anything to do with the marijuana. It talked about the "honorable work" he'd put in—true enough—and ABC's "sincere regret" that he'd decided to "pursue other opportunities." And it closed with the traditional, "We wish him well in his endeavors."

20/20's ratings, which I worried would plummet, instead spiked, and *World News Tonight* was now scoring highest in the demographics advertisers coveted most. Best of all, the nonsense of recent months had gone relatively unnoticed, largely because the media critics and pundits were having a field day with what was going on at the competition.

At CBS, much earlier in the year, Jesse Helms's public campaign to rid the nation of Dan Rather had collapsed, only to be replaced by Ted Turner dangling $5.3 billion in junk bonds and cash to buy the company. CBS had fought him off by going $1 billion into debt to buy up its own stock, but that put the company in what Wall Street calls "play." A presumed "white knight" appeared in the person of the aforementioned Larry Tisch, billionaire proprietor of Loews, a hotel, cigarette, insurance, and watchmaking conglomerate, who soon owned a controlling interest in CBS and, on November tenth, got himself elected "acting" CEO. Ed Joyce, whom Van Gordon Sauter had put in as CBS News president while he pursued larger ambitions, was gone by then, having incurred the displeasure of Dan Rather. Meanwhile, 125 employees of CBS News found themselves casualties of the worst advertising downturn since 1971, the year tobacco commercials were banned from the airwaves. Don Hewitt, sometimes allied with Rather, sometimes not, proposed a rescue by buying CBS News, which was not for sale. Soon enough, Sauter was back at the helm and, so it was said, planning even larger layoffs.

NBC, where my college classmate Larry Grossman was the fourth news division president in six years, had just come under new ownership as well. Its parent company, RCA, went to General Electric for $6.28 billion, and Jack Welch, chairman of GE, was known as "Neutron Jack," so-called because, once GE took a company over, he allegedly left the buildings standing but the people inside had disappeared.

All ABC did in the crisis was sell off its small collection of Pollocks and de Koonings—one day, when I walked into the executive dining room where they'd hung, they were simply gone, casualties of change, replaced now by some inoffensive works—and cut 615 jobs, which hurt like hell. One person learned he was out of work in the middle of celebrating his forty-sixth anniversary at the network. The layoffs were presented as the decision of ABC management, because Cap Cities technically didn't own us yet, but whether they happened because Cap Cities wanted them or because ABC management thought Cap Cities wanted them was moot.

Then the other shoe dropped—the one I'd been worried about.

I knew that David Stern, commissioner of the NBA, had been talking with Jim Spence about bringing pro basketball back to us after a number of unhappy years at CBS. I hadn't been thrilled by the idea initially, given the history of how we'd lost the NBA before, but then I discovered that, despite getting clobbered by "Roone's Revenge," (the lineup of programs I'd slotted against CBS's weekend telecasts), CBS had been clearing $15 million a year in profits. Maybe we'd had enough revenge? Furthermore, ABC Sports could use a new winner, and the price—$160 million for 160 games, including play-offs and championships, spread over four years—made the numbers awfully attractive. If any deal was a sure thing, this was it.

Fred Pierce concurred, and just before Christmas took the package to Tom Murphy and Dan Burke, expecting instant approval. He called that afternoon.

"Ixnay on the NBA," he said.

"*What!*" I exclaimed. "Didn't they believe the numbers?"

"Numbers aren't the problem. Murphy says he quote 'wants to send a message.' He thinks we 'won't be taken for granted anymore' when we start coming in second on bids."

"Oh, come on! What about Dan?"

I knew Dan Burke was an avid sports fan.

"Sorry, Roone. That's their decision."

I couldn't help wondering: If a premier event like the NBA could be turned down for "message sending," why not the Kentucky Derby next? And the World Series, the U.S. Open, then the Olympics? Didn't they know it was crazy to give away events to the competition? Didn't they realize that we'd spent years striving for a position of dominance and how valuable that was to the entire company?

No, apparently not. Apparently Murphy and Burke didn't get it.

As far as I was concerned, it was high time I got out of Sports.

There was something a lot worse going on for Fred, as I found out shortly, than losing the basketball contract. As I've mentioned, he'd been in line to succeed Leonard, and the Capital Cities people had apparently agreed. But now, although Tom Murphy apologized to him for changing his mind, they wanted him back in his old job, just running the network.

I could understand it both ways. From Cap Cities' point of view, the network was where the trouble lay, and specifically the Entertainment division. But Fred had certainly paid his dues.

"What are you going to do?" I asked.

Fred let out a bitter chortle. "Well, first thing, I'm going to get on a plane and head for Aspen for a couple of weeks. I told them they'd have their answer when I get back."

"I'm sorry to hear this, Fred," I said.

"Oh, don't worry about me. I've got four years on a contract they'd have to buy out. Worry about yourself, Roone. This isn't the old candy store anymore. Don't take anything for granted. And I mean *anything*."

Paranoia time. But neither was I given to paranoia nor did I think it justified, as least as far as I was concerned. The times I'd spent with Tom Murphy, he'd been all back pats and affability. In addition to being a genuinely nice man, I found him incredibly smart, and I liked him personally and thought it was mutual. When I worried out loud about looking for a successor to run Sports—something that had been plaguing me for some time—he advised me not to rush it. Relax, he'd said. When the time came, I'd pick the guy. He was bubbly about News, too. Loved it, he said; in fact, it was one of the few things he watched. "We just don't interfere in any way with our editorial people," he'd assured me. "You can't get good editorial people when you do that."

To a reporter's question at a press conference, he'd said I was "one of the assets we bought when we bought ABC." Okay, so to Tom I was "an asset." No one had ever called me that before, but at Cap Cities maybe it was a very good thing to be.

The formal handover took place on January 3, 1986. Six days later, we were summoned to the fortieth-floor conference room to hear that Fred Pierce was becoming a Cap Cities/ABC "consultant."

The new president of the network was John Sias, a former ad salesman who'd been running the Cap Cities publishing division. Tom Murphy introduced him as being responsible for 48 percent of the company's profits and 63 percent of its revenues.

"Interesting choice to head Programming," I whispered to David Burke.

Sias told us "the party's over"—hardly a wonderful way of introducing himself, although it may have played well with his bosses—and he made a few remarks about ABC's "product." Then we adjourned. In the margin of that meeting, Tom Murphy and I had a chat about the future. Tom said he thought the time had come for me to concentrate on news. Fine, I said, and I'd really put my mind to choosing a successor.

But that, it seemed, might already have happened.

The next day, I had a meeting with John Sias.

Did I have a candidate to propose for Sports? he wanted to know.

In the aftermath of this meeting, I would kick myself for not having given Jeff Ruhe the job when it was mine to give. Jeff had been my senior assistant, I'd promoted him to vice president after his performance as coordinating producer for the L.A. Games, and I knew he had a terrific future in the business. But Jeff was only thirty-two, and Dan Burke, who'd recognized him as a comer in the organization, had arranged for him take a "sabbatical" from ABC at the Harvard Business School. Besides, I didn't feel I could overlook Jim Spence totally. Although I believed Jim had his shortcomings, he'd certainly earned his spurs and, I thought, at least deserved consideration. Fred Pierce and Leonard, however, had been negative about him.

Now, in the meeting, I put forth Jim Spence's name again.

Sias shook his head. Jim Spence, he said, wouldn't be considered for the job.

"But what about Larry Pollack?" Sias said.

"Larry Pollack?"

Larry Pollack, it will be remembered, ran our Philadelphia station. He was the one who'd given me grief over *Nightline* in the beginning, and later over *This Week,* which, because it interfered with his scheduled Sunday-morning movie, I'd had to give him a second feed at an hour's difference from the rest of the world. (To this day, as a result, *This Week* is seen at different times in different cities.) A powerful figure, in other words, in the ABC firmament, but president of ABC Sports?

I told Sias I didn't think so.

He paused. I got one of those uneasy feelings that there'd been conversations on the subject in which I'd played no part. And the feeling became a certainty with Sias's next candidate.

"What about Dennis Swanson?" he said.

Dennis Swanson, for the last ten months, had been head of ABC's O & Os, and before that, general manager of stations in Chicago—where he had put Oprah on the air at a time when stardom was still in her future—

and Los Angeles. He'd caused us problems once before, during the L.A. Olympics, when Dennis was general manager of our Los Angeles affiliate. Peter Ueberroth had changed his mind about an arrangement we'd made in which he would furnish appropriate feeds to the athletes' facilities. In other words, the French athletes would see the French broadcast, the Japanese the Japanese, and so on. Instead, they all got Dennis's KABC feed, thereby saving the L.A. Olympic Committee a few bucks, but exposing them to the constant booster "Let's go, USA" rooting section of KABC staffers at station breaks and an embarrassingly jingoistic, pro-America atmosphere. The athletes from 139 nations thought—mistakenly—that this was what their fellow citizens were being subjected to back home. They raised an unholy stink, Dennis wouldn't change things, and the network was declared the villain of the piece.

Still, I thought of him as a good administrator—such was his reputation—if something of a martinet, which was logical enough for he was also a former captain in the marine corps. The combination, I gathered, made him just Cap Cities' can-do type.

I temporized with Sias.

"We'll be glad to consider Dennis," I told him. "We'll put him into the mix."

"Well, I'd really like to move this thing along," Sias said. "Unless you can come up with someone better quickly, we're going to go with Swanson."

And so it turned out. Whatever misgivings I might have had about Dennis, I myself hadn't been able to come up with an acceptable candidate, and I was happy to get rid of the day-to-day burden of Sports. In the new arrangement, I would be group president, ABC News and Sports, and Dennis Swanson would report to me, but I was going to spend most of my time at News. With one exception. As Dan Burke told me, he'd promised our major advertisers that I would personally produce the Calgary Olympics.

I had then the painful task of breaking the news to Jim Spence. I decided to wait until after *Wide World of Sports* that Saturday, knowing he'd be watching at home. But I couldn't put it off any longer because I was flying to Phoenix for the Capital Cities financial-meeting-cum-reunion, the major event on their annual calendar, and I didn't want Jim to hear about it elsewhere.

It was a very short conversation.

"Capital Cities," I said, "has decided they want Dennis Swanson to head Sports. They want you to stay on under Swanson."

"I appreciate your calling me, Roone," he replied.

That was that, but I could tell he felt I'd betrayed him. Two days later, while we were all in Phoenix, he cleaned out his desk.

Phoenix. Another world.

As soon as we arrived at the Arizona Biltmore, the famous Frank Lloyd Wright hotel where big companies loved to hold their meetings, we were given a "Hi, my name is" badge and half of a $10 bill. The game was to find the holder of the other half. (It was unclear what you were supposed to do when you did. Maybe flip to see who got the ten?) I put mine in my pocket, and went into the meeting room, where baskets of little gifts were laid out. I took a jar of relish.

"How many of you have a jar of relish?" Dan Burke asked from the stage when we'd settled in. By then, I'd given my jar to Dave Burke and his hand went up.

"Look inside," Dan Burke instructed.

David unscrewed the cap. A gold Kruggerrand gleamed up at us.

That set the tone. It was totally foreign to us, a kind of Cracker Jacks and detailed year-end financial review rolled into one, punctuated by serious exhortations and admonitions about the business.

Almost immediately, after Dan's welcoming remarks, he introduced ABC as the newest member of the Cap Cities firmament and, as the room darkened, a screen came up showing Peter Jennings on the *World News Tonight* set.

"ABC has ever attracted executives of talent and uncommon modesty," Peter intoned.

Quick cut to shot of Roone Arledge.

"I can certainly agree with that," said Mr. Arledge.

I have no idea where they'd found that or when I'd said it, but there were hoots of laughter all around.

Later on, a guy I didn't know named Aaron Daniels, who ran Cap Cities' radio stations and was a very funny fellow indeed, came onstage, dressed in Middle Eastern garb, a lookalike to Johnny Carson's "The Great Karnak" quizmaster. He called himself "Aaronak." He was accompanied by Phil Beuth, a Cap Cities executive who played "Aaronak's" Ed McMahon.

"The answer," Beuth called out, "is the Khmer Rouge, the PLO, and the KGB. Now what is the question, Almighty Aaronak?"

Silence.

Then the Almighty One's response: "The question is: Name three organizations that have better health plans than Capital Cities."

And again:

"The answer is: St. Thomas Aquinas, Abraham Lincoln, and Roone Arledge. Now what is the question?"

Pause. Then: "Who are three people who never answer your phone calls?"

Raucous laughter and catcalling. Well, the guy *was* funny, and I thought to myself in the general mirth that if you can't beat 'em, join 'em. At one point, Tom Murphy had all the ABC people stand up and applaud all the local station people, because the local station people were the ones making all the money. And in the traditional review, which lasted a full day, when Dan Burke went through the financial results of all the divisions, those that were ahead of the average in making profits and cutting costs were shown in green, those behind in red.

ABC had a lot of red.

"Shock therapy," Dan called it from the podium.

Another culture, a new order. It all ended in a dress-up banquet where I was seated at the same table of honor with Tom Murphy and Warren Buffett. Clearly the Cap Cities people were trying to make us feel at home, but meanwhile—as befit owners—they were calling the shots.

Back in New York, traces of the new order were everywhere to be seen. Multiple mail deliveries each day had been cut to one. A memo had come saying that all limousine rentals required written authorization. The executive dining room had been put on notice. Urine tests had been put on every new employee's agenda as a way of weeding out druggies. And I was meeting with Dennis Swanson, whose proudest possession was the University of Illinois football helmet in his new office.

We were civil to each other, even though we both knew he was John Sias's choice, not mine, and, among other things, I suggested I put a dinner together for him with the guys who ran ABC Sports.

"That won't be necessary," he said. "I'm calling everyone at Sports over to a special meeting. Wednesday morning."

I think he said "0900 sharp," but I confess I'm not 100 percent sure. I wasn't in attendance at his meeting either, but a number of those who were took notes.

Dennis started off with his CV. "I didn't go to an Ivy League school. I went to a land-grant college in Illinois because my family didn't have the money to send me to an Ivy League school. I had to get into the marines to go through graduate school. I worked my way up."

The truth was, we'd all worked our ways up, I first and foremost. I'd started at $66 a week at NBC, and that was my second job. The same was true even of those of us who'd attended Ivy League schools, which included not just me but Chet Forte and Dick Ebersol among others.

"I've worked in Stations," Dennis said. "A lot of you don't know much about Stations because you think you're so hot for having worked for a big sports network. But we do a little thing in Stations that maybe you're not familiar with either—we make money."

He next made a jab about salaries. "I'm only the president of this organization. I'm not paid what Chet Forte is paid." And another about superstructure—"We've got so damn many vice presidents around here that you don't know when you are going to bump into somebody in the hall who's vice president of something. We've got a vice president of production; we've got a vice president of production *affairs*. We've got a vice president for administration. Jesus, even Jeff Ruhe's a vice president." And, just in case anyone had been missing the point—"If Roone were Jimmy Carter's adviser, the U.S. would surely have gotten all its hostages out of Iran, because Roone would have had enough helicopters."

This last, in fact, was taken as a compliment, in that we would have done whatever it took to get the job done, but Dennis apparently saw it otherwise. Then he laid down a few precepts.

"I'm old-fashioned in a lot of things. I think people should come to work on time. I think they should work hard while they are here. I think they should answer the phone before it rings three times."

Ties were to be worn.... There was to be no screaming in control rooms.... "God made Saturday to get haircuts"... the "arrogance" of the old ABC Sports would not be tolerated. There was nothing to be arrogant about, because there was nothing special about the quality of ABC Sports productions.

"Everyone does not have a vote here," Dennis finished. "This place is going to be run like a dictatorship. And I am the dictator."

Needless to say, people came out of the meeting like victims of shell-shock. We'd built a great and highly profitable organization, but the marines were now in the process of dismantling it. "Razing it," someone quoted, "in order to save it." A few months later, in a sign of the times, Joe Namath and O. J. Simpson were unceremoniously dumped from *Monday Night Football*—"Those people are really *rude*," Broadway Joe said—and Al Michaels and Frank were told there'd be only the two of them in the booth. Frank was shunted into an analyst's role after sixteen years. There was a big howl from Namath when Dennis stopped paying off Namath's contract, after *Newsday* quoted Joe as saying that the games had gotten dull, but the matter was quickly settled. Chet Forte departed, after telling the *Detroit Free Press,* "It's just not been a fun year," and Chuck Howard, who'd been removed as head of production, also left. Dennis demanded to know if Chuck was talking to me. He replied, "None of your goddamn business."

Monday Night Football has since never recovered. Sadly I watched the proceedings, but from the sidelines because ABC Sports was Swanson's shop now, and Dan Burke, who was something of a sports freak and loved hanging out with the jocks, was now conducting the negotiating with Pete Rozelle.

"We aren't in business to subsidize professional football," Dennis said. Nevertheless, in the next NFL contract, the price per game went up $500,000.

Some message, I thought, thinking back to the NBA fiasco of the preceding fall.

Finally, I went to Dan and told him I'd like to drop the "Sports" part of my title. Why, he wanted to know. Because it didn't mean anything anymore, and I found myself disagreeing with too much of what was going on.

No objection from Dan.

At News, I thought that salvation lay in avoidance, and, whenever possible, I ducked encounters with the top brass. Inevitably, though, I'd be cornered, and the "suggestions" would pour forth. Tom said I ought to get pointers from the news director at the station in Raleigh/Durham, North Carolina, which, like all Cap Cities outlets, was being run on the

Eyewitness happy-talk formula of murders and car crashes. Like all Cap Cities stations, it was number one in its market.

"Get to know this guy," Tom said. "He could be a big help to you. He really knows how to do news."

Dan, meanwhile, had specific program ideas. *60 Minutes* was making a fortune for CBS; why didn't we do our own version at the same hour? Except our correspondents would be young unknowns, so we wouldn't be stuck with Mike- and Morley-level salaries.

His ardor cooled when I told him that *60 Minutes* didn't make a pfennig the first seven years. Well, but if prime-time News programs could be produced for $400,000—half the cost of an Entertainment hour—why didn't we do more of them?

I gave him his wish with *Our World*, a weekly walk down stock footage lane to sepia-tinted years gone by. Av Westin produced, Linda Ellerbee and Ray Gandolf, whom I'd hired away from CBS, hosted; the critics swooned; and, given half a chance, the program might have built a following. But John Sias took care of that personally. He put *Our World* opposite *Cosby,* the most popular show in television history, then told the affiliates it was "filler." "I feel like a kamikaze pilot taking off on a mission," I told the press. *Our World* was struck broadside: last place in all the prime-time polls.

Sias, himself, remained on the case. Why did News need so many correspondents when so few were on the air every night? How come *World News Tonight* devoted two minutes to Honduras? Did anyone care about Honduras? Why were there three-hour election specials in prime time, and gavel-to-gavel coverage of the national political conventions? Polls said Americans were turned off by politics. How did CNN manage to produce twenty-four hours of news for a third the ABC News budget? Was there really a need for a network evening news?

Not that Sias was grim all the time. He could be a lot of fun to be with. He'd brought to the job a reputation as a great practical joker, and on Lincoln's birthday, he appeared in the newsroom dressed up like Honest Abe. Other times, he patrolled the hallways with a squirt gun, searching for targets, and sounded a boat horn to call meetings to order. He put whoopee cushions on office chairs. He liked to hide the briefcases of visitors. And one April morning at eight-thirty A.M., he clambered on top of a newsroom desk and bellowed. "Where's Roone?"

Probably I was seeing to the additional $25 million Dan Burke wanted whacked from the News budget. Another seventy-five jobs were cut. Bureaus in Warsaw, Chicago, and London were shrunk. A dozen correspondent slots were eliminated. Programs made do with freelancers. Productions were farmed out to nonunion shops.

"It's a beginning," Sias said.

Watching the goings-on at the competition offered some respite. At CBS, the *Evening News with Dan Rather* fell to last place for the first time in four years, the *CBS Morning News* was canceled altogether, and in a fine example of what goes around comes around, Van Gordon Sauter was out on the street a few months later, fired twenty-four hours after Larry Tisch dropped the "acting" from his CEO title.

About the time Sauter exited Black Rock, I was on my way into the office tower next door for a News division budget review. Dave Burke, Dick Wald, and finance vice president Irwin Weiner were along, and fat files full of figures were tucked under our arms. We looked like the Four Horsemen from Touche Ross.

I didn't understand the need to spend the next three days sitting across a conference table from Dan Burke, Sias, and a covey of network finance execs, but Dan had stiffly told me that this was the Cap Cities way. At the same time, I wasn't expecting trouble. ABC News made a profit, after all, $37 million in 1986, a year when not even *60 Minutes* could drag CBS News into the black, and NBC News was on track to lose $64 million—*excluding* overhead from its numbers while we always included it in ours. Not least, we'd been good soldiers in cutting costs.

Dan Burke, however, didn't see anything to cheer about.

"Wipe that smile off your face," he barked at Dick Wald when Sias demanded to know exactly how many newspapers the Dallas bureau subscribed to. 'This is the most serious business you will do this year."

Perhaps it was.

How many phone lines were in the newsroom? What was "a fixer" and why was one employed in Beirut? (A fixer, an indispensable figure in countries like Lebanon, was someone who fixed things—from getting you through customs to dealing with local politicians and terrorists.) Why was Sam Donaldson being paid more than the vice president for Administration? Couldn't Peter Jennings get by with one assistant rather than two? Why did ABC News have so many video machines? Did we really need a new graphics generator?

We had answers for some questions, shrugs for others, such as the last time the L.A. bureau had been painted. When we provided our expense figures, Sias yelled, "Cut them in half!"

It lasted three days, but we took it. I agreed with a lot of what they pointed out, and, as I kept reminding David and Dick and Irwin and the others, what counted was News, not the frills that were being winnowed away. Our job was to keep our core intact, and if some countries like Haiti could no longer be covered, if the midterm elections of 1986 were not reported in prime time, if *World News Tonight* was moved to six-thirty so that WABC in New York could air *Jeopardy* at seven, things were no better across the street. I continued to believe that, if we just weathered the storm, like monks in the Dark Ages, we'd come out okay. Meanwhile, our core programs—*World News Tonight, 20/20, Nightline, This Week*—all continued to flourish, as did our specials. While Sports floundered and Entertainment went in the toilet, News proudly held its own.

Until the kind of thing I'd worried about came to pass.

To an extent, it was an old battle. In all my years at ABC, there'd been tension between News and Entertainment, and while I'd gotten on famously with some of the Entertainment people as individuals, people like Marty Starger, Barry Diller, Michael Eisner, and Tony Thomopoulos, a quasicultural difference prevailed between the divisions. They were West Coast, we were East. They monopolized prime time with mostly forgettable shows, some of which cost the company millions of dollars in write-offs, while we, who made money, had to beg, borrow, and steal to get airtime. And so on.

But there was a difference this time.

On May fifteenth, 1987, I took Dave Burke with me to the thirty-eighth-floor conference room at 1330, Avenue of the Americas, for Entertainment's show-and-tell on the upcoming season. Tom Murphy was there, Dan Burke, Sias, and some forty others from Sales, Research, and the Stations group. Brandon Stoddard, who'd succeeded Thomopolous as president of Entertainment, was master of ceremonies. The worst I expected was an afternoon of bad pilots, but something else turned out to be on the agenda.

Brandon Stoddard, who stood maybe five-six in lifts, had been around the network forever, and what he lacked in physical stature, he more than made up for in smarts and cunning. In his previous job, he'd brought in the three most-watched miniseries in history (*Roots, The Thorn Birds,* and *The Winds of War*); overseen the release of big-grossing theatrical features (*Silkwood, Prizzi's Honor, The Flamingo Kid*); and been behind made-for-TV movie successes (*The Day After*).

But he'd been a flop in his new job, turning out a string of sitcom bombs and investing a total of $164 million in two miniseries—*Amerika* and *War and Remembrance*—that looked like turkeys-in-the-oven. So far, though, it hadn't hurt his standing. Tom, who admitted that his Entertainment knowledge was limited to liking Clint Eastwood, was mesmerized; and the affiliates—whom Brandon continually asked for "one more year of patience"—were also in his thrall. Up till now, I had gotten along with Brandon, too. He ran his domain, I ran mine, and the two of us were ships passing.

In the conference room, Brandon was pacing back and forth in front of a large, magnetized board marked with schedules of the three networks, each show represented by a movable plaque. Brandon was casually flipping one of the plaques in his hand. It was marked "*Dolly.*"

Dolly was Dolly Parton, and according to Brandon, her new variety show would be the network's salvation. From what I'd heard of the deal, it had better be. New shows usually got thirteen-week runs to prove themselves; Stoddard had given *Dolly* a forty-four-week commitment—two full seasons—at $1 million per week.

I watched as with a loud *thwack* Brandon slapped *Dolly* onto the nine P.M., Sunday slot—the most watched hour of the most watched night of the week. Brandon twiddled the *Movie of the Week* plaque that had been there, as if trying to decide the best place to put it. He reached for the plaque at Thursday, ten P.M., and moved it two positions, to eight o'clock, across from the plaque in the NBC column marked *Cosby*—the highest-rated half hour in the history of television. *Our World,* Sias's so-called filler that had faced Cosby, was taken off the board entirely. As Stoddard slipped *Movie of the Week* into the nine o'clock Thursday slot, I could feel every eye in the room on me.

The plaque opposite *Cosby* was now *20/20.*

I stared at the board, momentarily too stunned to say anything. Didn't they realize? It had taken *years* to build *20/20* into prominence, but once we'd made it, it had been as solid as the rock of Gibraltar!

Now, with a flick of the wrist, my most popular, profitable show, hosted by my biggest star, had just been given a death sentence.

"In the interests of truth in advertising," I heard Stoddard's deputy, Ted Harbart, say, "you should know that some of these movies don't run exactly two hours. We can't cut into the local 11:00 news, so 20/20 will accordion. If *Movie of the Week* goes 2:07, 20/20 ends at 8:53."

"Stop right there!" I shouted. "Are you crazy?"

Dave Burke jumped in, almost like a manager getting between his player and the umpire. "Why don't you run *Dolly* Thursday at eight?"

"Are *you* crazy?" Stoddard said. "*You* tell Dolly she's opposite *Cosby*!"

"*You* tell Barbara!" I shot back.

I'd shoved back my chair, ready to leave the room, and now I poked David to do likewise.

"If 20/20 goes to eight P.M.," I said, "we won't produce the show!"

Tom Murphy himself chased us out into the hall, pleading with us to calm down.

"I know you're upset," he said. "I'm upset, too. Brandon's so damn imperious. But I'll fix this. Trust me, guys, I will."

Tom and I went at it, arguing back and forth all that day. How could they even have imagined putting us up against *Cosby*? And the accordion idea, did he really think that was in the realm of possibility? Tom took it upon himself to try to negotiate "a compromise" with Dan Burke and Stoddard. What compromise? There was none that I could see. *Our World* was gone, 20/20 was going. We'd walked right into the middle of a well-planned setup!

Finally, late in the day, I told Tom that if there had to be a resolution, we could possibly live with Friday at ten P.M., but that I was damned unhappy about it. The next morning, I got in unusually early.

Tom delivered the news just after nine. Brandon, he said, was "very unhappy," but he'd forced a solution "in the best interests of everyone, including the company."

20/20 would air Fridays at ten P.M.

By this time, though, I'd decided against it.

"Opposite *Falcon Crest* on one of the two least-watched nights of the week?" I put it to him. "Tell me, Tom, how is that in the 'best interests' of the American Broadcasting Company?"

We went around and around for almost two hours, but there was no budging him. Friday at ten, take it or leave it.

Reluctantly, I took it.

"You want Dan and me to come over to explain it to your people?" Tom asked.

Typical Tom. I thought it was very decent of him, and I told him so. But I warned that they'd want to vent.

"I've already had a day of Stoddard venting," Tom said, "I can handle some more. How about two o'clock?"

"Two o'clock's fine," I said.

We met in the fourth-floor News conference room, where, once upon a time, Leonard used to eat his goose-liver sandwiches. David, Dick Wald, and Irwin Weiner, among others, were with me. If I took a backseat in the argument, it was because I'd already argued, and failed, and because I wanted "my people" to get their chance.

And vent they did.

I expected it from David Burke. Nothing gets an Irishman's Irish up, I would say, as two Irishmen.

"I know you think we're arrogant at News," David said, "We *are* arrogant, but there are reasons for it. For one thing, we make money. For another, we're the only ones around here who feel the weight of public responsibility. That little twit on the West Coast has no right to push us around. The network is in the shithouse because of him."

Tom denied that Stoddard was a twit but, ever the diplomat, he said he understood why we were hurt. It had been hard for him, too.

"This," he said, "is the toughest decision I've ever had to make."

But Irwin? When it came to negotiating with the outside world, Irwin Weiner had a take-no-prisoners mentality, and many a time he and I had played the bad cop, good cop routine with excellent results. But inside the company, particularly vis-à-vis our bosses, he'd never been one to speak out.

"Why are you constantly busting our nuts?" Irwin wanted to know. "Why are we the ones always sucking hind tit? Don't you realize what Roone Arledge has done for this company? Don't you realize that there wouldn't *be* an ABC without him? So why do you do nothing but jerk him around? I don't understand that, Tom, I really don't. I don't understand why you listen to people who always fail."

No one said anything for a long, long moment.

I thought that Irwin, bless him, had just slit his throat.

Not so.

But the meeting broke up soon after without our getting anywhere, and so, the next morning, I sent a memo to all hands, which read, in part:

> As you may know, the management of ABC News feels very strongly about this matter. We argued strongly in opposing the change for over three days. In the end we did not succeed primarily because of the enormous pressure placed on the decision-makers by the extraordinarily poor performance of ABC's prime-time programming, and the resultant economic loss facing the network. *20/20,* regardless of its strength, its importance, and its great success, simply could not prevail against those seeking a way out of an historic entertainment failure.

It sounded hot, and it was meant to. I was tired of playing the good sport.

We got past it—most of us, that is—but in time it took its toll. On David Burke, for one. He and I agreed on many things, among them that Tom Murphy and Dan Burke didn't care much for our kind of News, and we shared the fear that they would continue to cut as long as they could get away with it, regardless of the impact on content. Tom, in particular, had made his position plain. He was in business to make money, he'd said in our first conversation after the takeover. He didn't pay attention to awards, or even to ratings, except as they translated into profits. "What I care about is shareholder value and that's what I see as my role," he said. "I like being a broadcaster and it's a great profession. But my real bottom line is the bottom line."

Where I parted with David was on questions of tactics. He had an inbred pugnacity toward Murphy and Burke. He was Horatio at the Bridge holding off the Visigoths, the keeper of the flame, the fighter for the boys in the trenches, the brawler not only ready but eager to get his nose bloodied for a good cause.

David's fixation was on how terrible things were; my focus was on how much worse they might have been. Say what you would about Tom and Dan, they weren't Tisch and General Electric. They looked after the people cut loose, bent over backward to place them, ensured that their settlement packages were twice what they would have been elsewhere. ABC was Sunnybrook Farm compared to CBS.

There were also facts that couldn't be ignored. Ten cable channels were making more money than ABC; profits for the networks were half of what they'd been four years before.

David liked to tease about our different styles. Over the last year, however, he'd done so with less humor, and I could feel his restlessness. He'd been with me nearly a decade—longer than he'd worked for Ted Kennedy, Hugh Carey, Howard Dreyfus, Luther Hodges, or Willard Wirtz. He wanted, at last, to be boss.

The offer came in July 1988. Howard Stringer was being promoted to head up the CBS Broadcast Group, and Larry Tisch wanted David to be president of his News division.

"I hope it happens for you," I said, the night he was to meet Tisch for final inspection. "But for us, I genuinely hope it doesn't."

This was the understatement of the millennium. David was much more to me than the person I could call at two o'clock in the morning to plot with, more than the friend who would tell me when I was full of shit and in just those words. He was like my alter ego. And I didn't know what I was going to do without him.

But I was going to have to learn. David wowed Tisch, as I knew he would. The only remaining hitch was keeping the deal quiet until Tisch got the approval of his board. I realized I had a duty to tell Tom Murphy. He and Tisch, I knew, had made a no-raiding pact on CBS and ABC personnel, and there was a risk he'd howl once he heard.

This was a Friday, and Tom, I knew, was flying to L.A. on a business trip. If I left a message at his hotel that I needed to talk to him, then made sure I wasn't around when he called back, it'd be midday Monday at the earliest before he could get hold of me, and I still would have done my duty—to David as well as to ABC.

Rope-a-dope, in other words.

When he called back, Tom was terrific. "David deserves this," he said. "I'm not going to do anything to hurt him. But I guess it means that all bets are off."

The new president of CBS News was introduced to the press July 13, 1988.

We got past that, too. In fact, we got past a lot of things. The truth was that Tom and Dan had taken over ABC just when the industry in general had entered a period of ever higher costs, flat revenues, and increased competition. While they knew instinctively how to deal with the first of these, nothing in their backgrounds had taught them how to navigate a crazy business like network television through difficult times. Consequently, they made some disastrous mistakes in their hires and found themselves, to their own surprise, caught up in internecine squabbles like the one over *Dolly* and *20/20*.

But on a personal level, Tom Murphy couldn't have been more respectful and nicer to me.

"He's afraid of you," a mutual friend explained.

"Afraid of what? That I'll go to the competition?"

"Well that, sure. But that's not the reason."

"Then what?"

"He knows you know things he doesn't," Tom's friend said. "He doesn't understand how you do the things you do. He says you have some magic he can't get at. He calls you 'a sorcerer.' "

I leaned back, laughing and shaking my head.

"A *sorcerer*?"

"That's right."

Well, okay, a sorcerer. It was better than being an "asset," at least. Come to think of it, much, much better.

Landing Diane

Network news stars, like diamonds, have many facets. They are great journalists, the kind who will walk through walls to get a story. They are smart. They are good on their feet. They inspire trust. They possess that indefinable something that makes them leap off the screen. There are very, very few who combine all those qualities.

Barbara Walters is one of them. Diane Sawyer is another.

I wanted both.

In fact, I'd been aware of Diane since shortly after taking over the News division in 1978. I was trying to beef up our correspondent corps then, and Ben Bradlee had suggested Bob Zelnick, a lawyer and former chief of National Public Radio's Washington bureau, who'd worked with David Frost putting together David's famous interviews with Richard Nixon the year before. The four-part syndicated series was Nixon's first public grilling since the resignation, and his "I gave them a sword" ruminations about Watergate were a sensation—as was the $1 million Nixon was paid to make them. Bob was everything Ben had advertised, and I was happy to hire him. As we were discussing his new duties as a Capitol Hill correspondent, he mentioned a recently departed Nixon aide who'd also make a great addition. The daughter of a Republican Kentucky judge, and a former Miss Teen USA, she'd worked in the White House press office and had accompanied Nixon into exile at San Clemente to assist in the writing of his memoirs. According to Bob, she was now looking for a job in television, where her only experience was a pre–White House stint as a Louisville "weathergirl." Her name, he said, was Diane Sawyer.

It turned out that Bill Sheehan had already seen Diane's audition tape and had decided against her, apparently because of Washington bureau worries about her service with Nixon, not exactly glittering résumé material in those days. Although I looked at it now and was blown away by her poise and her intelligence, as the new boy on the block, and having only recently learned to stop referring to correspondents as "announcers," I decided not to pursue her. Bill Small of CBS News did and, despite some opposition from Rather (who had his problems with Nixon), hired Diane as a Washington reporter.

For her first year on the job, the only time Diane made air was when the camera caught an inadvertent glimpse of her ear; her role was to gather information for correspondents. During the Three Mile Island nuclear accident, however, Diane was thrown into the on-air breach. The steadiness of her reporting led to other assignments, and, in 1980, CBS posted her to the State Department, a crown jewel in any network news operation. Charlie Kuralt loved her work on the Iran hostage crisis, and in 1981 twisted the right arms to have her appointed his cohost on *CBS Morning News*. CBS had always failed in the morning, but Diane and Kuralt were great together. By the summer of the following year, the program nudged past *Today* and into second place in the ratings, and Diane had become a television star. Two years later, on the tenth anniversary of Nixon's resignation, Diane scored again with an interview of her former boss, the third after Frost's and Barbara's. Like Barbara, she was polite and respectful, but also relentless trying to get Nixon to explain why he'd done the things he'd done, and the session removed any doubt I might have had about Diane's readiness to break china for a good cause. A few months later, about the time Cap Cities was swallowing us, Don Hewitt named her *60 Minutes'* first-ever female correspondent and dispatched her, with seemingly perverse delight, to the world's hellholes. But nothing stopped her. She was dogged and tough, fearless and beautiful—even wearing an Iranian chador.

As the expiration date of her contract came into still distant view, my acquisitive juices began to simmer.

Diane's agent was none other than Richie Leibner, our sparring partner in the Dan Rather negotiations. Richie was letting it be known that Diane would leave CBS only for a coanchor slot, and Peter had already made it clear that he was not interested in sharing. As he put it to journalist Ken Auletta, "I didn't take this job and go through all the crap I did for three years in order to divide up twenty-two minutes." Peter didn't specify what travail I'd subjected him to, but I presumed it was not collecting the salary I was about to nearly double. In any case, I was getting used to his pique, and probably could have handled him. Tom and Dan, I could not; they cut dead any notion of going after Diane.

For one thing, there was Tom's nonaggression pact with CBS. I'd run into Larry Tisch, who'd said the same thing: that the networks had to get along and not raid each other's talent. Besides, wasn't Barbara our female star? Why did we need another?

Why, I countered, were we limited to only one? Besides, they were different. Barbara was a peerless interviewer, but Diane, as she was amply proving on *60 Minutes*, was a peerless investigative journalist. Stars were what brought ABC News its growing clout, I said, and stars like Diane came on the market almost never. If we grabbed her from a network whose news division was synonymous with prestige, we'd become *the* game in town. Knowing Dan's fondness for jocks, I even resorted to a sports analogy: Would the Yankees, the most talent-laden franchise in history, *reject* the opportunity to acquire a Sandy Koufax or a Willie Mays?

I all but stood on my head trying to get them to unbend.

Their intransigence wasn't just penny-pinching. Tom and Dan regarded talent as—their word—"fungible" (meaning "interchangeable"). As proof, they loved to relate the story of Larry Kane, their Philadelphia station news anchor, who so completely dominated his time period that competitors were but a blip. One day, a New York station offered Kane bundles to defect. Off to the Big Apple he went. What had entranced Philadelphia, however, somehow got lost on the Metroliner, and the out-of-work prodigal was soon looking to return. Cap Cities wouldn't take him back: The Philly station's newscast, it turned out, hadn't lost a viewer in the interim. The moral, as Tom laid out to me, was simple: "If they can get you ratings, fine. But the minute they can't, to hell with them."

Rope-a-dope. Someday, somehow, I believed, things were going to change. In the news business as in life, after all, nothing lasts forever, including policies at ABC and contracts at CBS. Meanwhile, I was going after Diane. So, confiding only in intimates and carefully covering my tracks, I embarked on a clandestine courtship.

We'd meet for lunch or dinner every few weeks, usually at Nanni's. Our initial get-togethers were getting-to-know-yous, since our only previous contacts had been at industry functions in ballrooms with a thousand people. She chatted about life at San Clemente, where staff jeans were banned and Nixon showed up for work every day in his Oval Office blues; I chatted about the army, big-game hunting, and sports—testosterone topics she relished. We were feeling each other out, getting a sense of what we liked and disliked, filling in portraits of who we were. On occasion, her questions left me tongue-tied, as when she asked, "What do you dream about at night?"

As we got to know each other better, Diane now and again invited me to the apartment she shared with Richard Holbrooke, the investment banker and sometime diplomat whom she'd met when he was an assistant secretary of state in the Carter administration. To my surprise, it was rather sparsely furnished. She simply wasn't into possessions, things, and although she dressed beautifully, she wasn't that interested in clothes either.

And all the time, we talked shop. Little by little, she made it clear that, as much as she loved Don Hewitt and her own contributions to *60 Minutes,* and as proud as she felt to be a part of it, she'd never quite made it into the club—Mike, Morley, Ed, and Andy. She liked them all as individuals, but there was a kind of old-boy camaraderie she'd never been permitted to share. At the same time, it would be hard as hell for her to give it up.

All this I could believe and understand. If, furthermore, there was one thing I'd learned from negotiating with Dan, Tom, Barbara, Peter, Ted, and Howard, it was that network stars, however rosy their present, were always focused on their future. "Whom do I want to share it with?" "Who will guide my career?" "Who can I trust?" Questions like that were uppermost to a person like Diane. She needed a soul mate, not so much a protector as someone she could count on to always be there for her.

Although in one sense going after Diane was far easier than a Dan Rather or a Tom Brokaw had been—ABC News was no longer a smoke-and-mirrors operation but had become numero uno in the network firmament, the place people wanted to work—Diane didn't know us. That was both a plus and a minus. To her, we were another corporation, and to join us would require a leap of faith on her part. It became clear to me, therefore, that I had to become more than a friend who sat across the dinner table listening to her hopes and dreams. I had to be ABC to her. If she believed I was her future, she'd be our newest star.

Such, at any rate, was my calculation. For it to work, a number of things had to fall into place, and, in the fall of 1988, after I'd been quietly wooing Diane for more than a year and a half, they began to. The first was David Burke's leaving us to become president of CBS News, an event that ended the raiding ban Tom and Larry Tisch had agreed to. The elevation of David's predecessor, Howard Stringer, to the presidency of the CBS Broadcast Group was marked, ironically, by a celebratory soirée at Don Hewitt's home. "Hey," Don said, inviting me, "why don't you bring Diane Sawyer? She doesn't have a date, and it'll give you a chance to get to know her."

"Great idea," I answered shamelessly, and so I did.

The second planet to align was ABC's getting clobbered every Thursday by *E.R.,* NBC's number-one-rated show. Having sent a series of contenders into battle, with uniformly bloody results, the Entertainment division threw up its hands. This gave me the opening I'd been waiting for. And I had a plan.

In the past, I'd often started with a concept, then had set out, as it were, to fill the empty house with people. But in this instance, I had the star—Diane—whom I believed needed to be paired with a man, not just because the couple combination seemed to work best in television newsmagazines but because I wanted Diane to be able to pursue investigative reportage outside the studio from time to time while her partner held the fort. Without going into all the mental permutations and combinations that brought me there, I'd come up with the man too, and knowing him, his strengths and his weaknesses, helped me define and refine the concept. I took it then to Tom and Dan. We'd do a newsmagazine, I told them, but not just any newsmagazine—not a clone of *20/20* or *60 Minutes* and certainly nothing resembling the late, lamented *Our World,* which John Sias had destroyed, coming out of the box, by calling it filler. We would go live and we would have a studio audience. We would be of the moment, tracking breaking news and using reporters all over the world, and in the absence of hot news stories, we would specialize in hard-hitting investigations. But most of all, we would have cohosts whose pairing would send heads snapping: Diane Sawyer and Sam Donaldson.

It would be called *Prime Time Live.*

Tom's and Dan's heads snapped, all right, and not entirely happily. Dan was no fan of Sam, and though Dan's own observance of the separation of church and state wasn't the best (he wanted to phone our polling results from our own control room election night to operatives of his good chum George Bush, but I wouldn't let him), he continued to rail about a supposedly objective correspondent spouting liberal opinions on *This Week.* But I knew something else about Sam. As good as he was as a Washington journalist and a panelist on *This Week,* he was dynamite in front of a live audience. His whole personality came alive, and in a totally different way from what viewers were used to.

I could tell that Tom wasn't pleased by the prospect of snatching Diane. Still, my proposal had one appeal they couldn't dispute: producing newsmagazines was relatively cheap. Before proceeding, though, I insisted they commit to keeping the new show on the air for at least two years. Whatever chance *Our World* had had was doomed by yanking it so soon. Ambitious new entries required time to find their footing and build a following. There was *60 Minutes,* of course, but the long gestation of our own *Good Morning America* demonstrated it, too. Besides, I knew I couldn't get Diane to leave the most successful news program in television history for something that might disappear in thirteen weeks.

Tom and Dan agreed, but not before Dan had grilled me about Diane. When had I first talked to her? Was there any risk we could be accused of tampering? What made me believe she'd join us?

I answered factually. I'd first talked to her years before, always with the idea of wanting her to come to ABC. I wasn't trying to induce her to break her contract (which might have constituted tampering). I didn't know that she would join us, but I sure as hell wanted to try.

I called Diane the next day and said I wanted to get together. I had something important to discuss. She asked me to come over to Mike Nichols's town house. This I did, and when I showed up, Nichols was in the living room with Steve Martin and Robin Williams. The three of them at the time were preparing a revival of *Waiting for Godot.* I made my hellos, and Diane waved me into the kitchen, where she was making tuna fish sandwiches. We sat down. I told her ABC had agreed to make a commitment to the program I was about to describe to her, and that if she left

CBS, she wouldn't be bridge jumping. Far from it. Then I laid out what I had in mind in detail.

She got it, got it all. She was excited about every element in the concept, especially the idea that she could combine hosting and reportage. Her coupling with Sam, whom she knew and liked from her Washington days, startled her at first, but the more she thought about it, the more the Beauty and the Beast casting appealed to her. "Emily Dickinson meets the Terminator," she took to calling it. She didn't say she'd play Emily, but I left feeling better than ever about my chances.

Over the next few weeks, Diane and I met often, talking about the show and working at ABC. She wanted to know who was who, whom she would be working with, and so on—all encouraging signs. The rare times the subject of CBS came up, I trod cautiously, avoiding any criticism that would arouse her intense loyalties. My only slip was a crack about CBS using her as a podium reporter that summer at the national political conventions. "That antenna sprouting from your head," I said, waving my hands up. "Come to ABC and I'll never make you look like a rabbit again."

Diane laughed, but she didn't say she would.

I needed a decision from her, though, and soon, in order to ready the show. One night over dinner, I finally pressed for an answer. Diane said, "Look, right now, I'm not going to tell you yes or no, I'm not going to wink or make a deal under the table. To begin with, if word got out that I was talking about leaving, it would hurt *60 Minutes* and all the people I work with. The press would be all over us. Second thing is, I don't want to be in a position of having to lie if a reporter asks me, 'Are you going to ABC?' I want to be able to say, 'I have not made any arrangements or plans,' and be honest about it. Until my contract expires, you are just going to have to trust me."

I decided I would. By then, we were close enough that I knew she wouldn't string me along. If she didn't want to join ABC, she would have said so. But she hadn't. So, even though I was taking a huge gamble, I assumed everything would work out. Tom, Dan, and the few other senior execs aware of what was going on thought I was crazy. "Where's Roone?" they snickered. "Oh, he's tying up Diane Sawyer."

The next six weeks we talked far less than before. The times we did speak, the conversation was the fleeting, temperature-taking variety. We both knew what was at stake; there seemed no reason to hash it over. Finally, in mid-January 1989, with only days left on her contract, Diane called.

"I'm yours," she said.

I suppose I should have felt giddy, ecstatic, triumphant—anything but what I did feel, which was almost matter-of-fact. I'd trusted she'd come, and here she was.

Before we rang off, Diane said she had only one stipulation about her ABC contract. "I don't want more money than I'm making at CBS. I don't want people to say, 'Oh, she's just going for the money.' I want them to know that I'm leaving for a better opportunity."

That's when it became real for me.

Knowing Dan, I wasn't expecting paeans of praise when I gave him the news. But I didn't expect him to be highly put out, which he was, when I begged off attending the upcoming affiliates' meeting in Phoenix in order to handle contractual negotiations with Richie Leibner and the counteroffensive I knew was in store for us from CBS.

The meetings, in the Cap Cities vision of things, were sacred. Besides:

"No way in hell that dame's coming to ABC anyway," Dan scoffed. "She's just diddling you to jack up her price at CBS."

Truth was, I was a little edgy myself. Though I didn't for an instant believe Diane was using me as a pawn, I was asking her to leave the only serious corporate home she'd ever known. I was also well aware that she'd acquired some very powerful and very persuasive admirers. Bill Paley, CBS's founder, was said to fairly swoon in her presence, while Larry Tisch publicly called her "my golden girl." Any minute, CBS would begin its counterattack.

Directing it, I had no doubt, would be Dave Burke. While we were still partners in crime, I'd waxed eloquent endlessly about Diane's virtues and how important I regarded her for our future. I'd left nothing out, including what a blow I thought it would be for CBS to lose her. David, the best scalp collector in the business, had no need to guess my game plan; I'd already laid it in his lap.

Thus far, however, I hadn't picked up any intelligence that Dave was moving on the Sawyer front. I knew he was preoccupied with trying to bring Dan Rather to heel, in particular Rather's habit of airing soiled CBS underwear, and his effective control of correspondent assignments.

Because David had told me so on a number of occasions, I also knew he found beautiful women intimidating. May Diane be looking even more gorgeous than usual, I kept on thinking, and may Rather be a larger than usual pain in the ass for David.

I sat down to deal with Richie Leibner and Diane herself. Richie immediately played the anchor card. Just as quickly, I told them there was no way Diane was going to anchor or coanchor *World News Tonight*, which was not only Peter's and number one in the ratings, but a job Diane and I had never discussed during our many get-togethers. The on-the-spot finality of my turndown seemed to impress them both, and the rest of the contract details went swiftly.

The next piece of the puzzle was Sam, who was in career limbo thanks to a recent decision on his part to leave the White House beat that defined him. He was bored, he'd told me, he needed a new challenge beyond *This Week* and a change in venue from the White House. Well, I had both for him, and it was in part because he was being underused that had set me on his trail for *Prime Time Live*. Sam being Sam, I assumed he'd find something to kick up a fuss about when I presented the proposal—his compulsion for causing televised trouble was a prime reason I was casting him, but with the brilliance of the spotlight I was offering, I thought that the squeaking and squawking would be minor, and we'd get down to a normal negotiation: Sam would try to get all the money he could, and at a certain point, I'd say "no more," and he'd say "okay."

Was I ever wrong.

Without divulging what I wanted to talk about, I asked Sam to come up from Washington for a meeting. He arrived with booming cheerfulness, and his mood held as I sketched his big step up. Diane he thought great. Same with going live, the studio audience, the whole approach. The sole worry he expressed was Diane's making him second banana. I assured him he wouldn't be, and suggested he take Diane to dinner. He'd know how easy she'd be to work with after an evening together. We organized it on the spot. Though I didn't say so to Sam, it was Diane I was worried about locking in, not him, and I was counting on his charm to help.

Before he left, I told Sam that the only promises I'd made to Diane were that she could open the show by saying "Hello," and that her name would be first in the introductions. She'd hadn't asked for either, I said; I'd offered.

Peter Jennings called. He'd picked up rumblings of Diane's coming aboard, and wanted to know what it would mean for him. "Nothing," I said. "Anchoring or coanchoring is not part of this deal." Peter seemed satisfied. Assuaging Barbara, I knew, would be a lot tougher. Though we'd been through it all together, she appeared to enjoy keeping me on edge at regular intervals by hinting that there were other offers out there. I was certain there were, just as I was that Tom and Dan were totally in her thrall.

I was at my softest soap when I reached her at home that evening. After extended pleasantries, I said, "There's a fairly good possibility that the Diane Sawyer thing may happen, maybe even this weekend. I'm calling so you won't be taken by surprise if it does, number one, and number two, to assure you that, if it happens, it won't affect you in any way."

"That's terrific," Barbara said. "I'd be delighted to have Diane here. I think she's awfully good."

It wasn't, I could tell from her tone, quite the clarion endorsement I'd hoped for, but I hung up relieved. Half an hour later, though, my phone rang. It was Barbara. Apparently, she'd been talking things over with her husband, Merv Adelson, who ran the highly successful TV production company Lorimar, and I could feel the telephone receiver icing up in my hand as she went on.

"Now that I've thought it over, I'm totally opposed to her," she said, disdaining even to mention "her" name. "It *has* to affect me. How is someone of my stature supposed to divide up things with *her?* With all the things I do for ABC, bringing in an obvious competitor like her is going to make it very tough . . ."

She didn't finish the sentence, but I thought the missing words were: "for me to continue working for you." I told her she was foremost in my heart and would continue so everlastingly. I told her not to worry. I told her I wasn't going to let her get hurt. I told her I would personally look after her interests. If not totally convinced, at least she wasn't issuing direct "or elses."

She finally did take my word for it—well, sort of, as I shall explain— but I knew I had a lot of refereeing ahead of me.

The next morning, Irwin Weiner, my point man on contract negotiations, reported that, overnight, Sam's agent, Bob Barnett, had called him at home. The dinner with Diane had gone swimmingly, Barnett had said, but Sam had come away believing I hadn't been fully truthful. " 'Sam is hurt,' " Irwin quoted Barnett as saying. " 'What else has Roone promised Diane?' " Whatever Sam believed it was, Barnett stated that Sam wanted absolute parity with Diane at all levels, including salary and saying hello. Not getting both, Barnett said, could be a deal breaker.

"You must be exaggerating," I told Irwin. "What rational adult—even Sam—would walk away from such an opportunity over a 'hello'? This has to be about money; what do you think?"

Maybe I was willing to give Sam almost as much as Diane, but not quite. Diane was a proven superstar. Sam at the time had no news-magazine history, whereas Diane was a star on the most successful news-magazine there'd ever been. Yes, Sam was super on *This Week*—so long as Brinkley was on hand to moderate the mud wrestling—and arguably the best White House correspondent there ever was, but how or whether these talents would translate into *Prime Time Live* remained an open question.

Well, Barnett, I was confident, would back down, once reality sank in.

Except Barnett wasn't the problem.

Meanwhile, later in the day, the ever helpful Leibner called to say that Dave Burke was at last on the case and had "cautioned" him about letting Diane go to ABC. Richie wasn't sure whether David was posturing or threatening. I thought it likely a bit of both, but either way, David could be extremely persuasive once he focused.

The following Monday, Diane was scheduled to meet with Hewitt and Burke in the morning, lunch with Paley in his private dining room at noon, and dine with Tisch in the evening. My biggest fear, knowing Diane, was Paley. The others she could handle—for one thing, she was as smart as they were, and she would read their arguments, rightly, as those of businessmen out to protect a bottom line—but I could hear the old founder holding forth on the hallowed traditions of CBS and Diane's obligation to carry them on. He'd pull out all the stops: guilt, money, loyalty, Ed Murrow and the boys braving the London blitz.

"Roone, I'm sorry, I just can't."

I could hear that, too.

These depressing ruminations were interrupted by the appearance of Irwin, Barnett in tow. Irwin, always pale, looked positively ashen, Sam's agent resolute, as if about to step into the ring. Sam, Barnett informed me, was awaiting developments in the office of Dorrance Smith, the producer of

This Week. Full, across-the-board parity with Diane, "hello" equivalence at the top of the list—that was what his client had to have. Unconditional surrender, in other words. In addition, Barnett hinted that, even now, Sam was being pursued by an unnamed, deep-pocketed network.

David? I wondered.

I held the fort the rest of the afternoon and early evening. The only movement was Barnett scurrying back and forth to Sam, always bearing the same answer, always bringing back the same response. Sam wasn't budging on "hello," and neither was I. Diane was jumping off a cliff in the belief that I kept promises; I wasn't going to start breaking them now.

On the slender chance that some nourishment might do us good, at nine-thirty, I suggested adjournment to Nanni's. We hadn't yet opened the menus when Sam started in.

"What did you offer Diane?"

"Exactly what I told you I did," I answered for the umpteenth time. "She gets first billing and she says the hello."

"I should say the hello," Sam said.

"Nope, I made a promise."

"Why should I believe that you don't have an understanding I don't know about?"

"Because I told you I don't."

"But how do I *know*?"

On and on like that, round after increasingly exasperating round. He'd serve, I'd volley back, permanently stuck at love–love. I couldn't puncture Sam's skepticism. If Mother Teresa told him the time, he'd look at his watch. During one of Sam and Barnett's frequent men's room caucus breaks, Irwin and I figured the worst-case scenario: CBS keeps Diane, lures away Sam, and they cohost our program for the enemy.

That wasn't even allowing for what NBC might be up to.

An hour slipped by. Then another. And another. And another. It was now one-thirty, the restaurant was deserted, and the waiters were standing around waiting for us to go. They must have thought we were crazy. I did. Then, as I was signing the check, I threw out what had to be a winner.

"Who's the star of *20/20*?" I asked Sam.

"Barbara Walters, of course."

"Check again," I said. "Hugh Downs says hello and his name comes first."

Game, set, and match to Mr. Arledge, I thought.

Wrong again.

"I should still say hello."

On that note, I went home and to bed. My service had a message from Leibner: Diane had resisted all entreaties. Even the Founder had failed.

The next morning the ever early-to-rise Sias called from the Cap Cities meeting in Phoenix. Diane's plan to jump ship had surfaced, and the affiliates, he reported, were in a tizzy of excitement. So was Sias himself, who was burbling about the brilliance of the Sawyer coup—exactly the opposite of what he'd been saying twenty-four hours before. As he waxed eloquent—well, eloquent for Sias—I groaned internally at what he didn't know. How the hell was I going to deliver what everybody thought I'd already delivered?

I decided I'd better say something to Sias before our "coup" turned into a disaster. I mentioned that Sam had created a problem, and that there was a chance David Burke was pitching him for CBS, even as we spoke.

"If I were David," I mused to Sias, "that's exactly what I'd do. I'd go after Sam, put him on *Face the Nation* or something, and make it seem like an even trade. That'd take out a lot of the sting of losing Diane. Of course, it wouldn't be an even trade, but after CBS got through playing it that way, it would look like musical chairs."

Sias called back a little later. Obviously, he'd been talking to others at the meeting.

"*We can't lose Sam!*" he shouted. For the second time that morning, I couldn't believe what I was hearing. Suddenly Sias was acting as if Sam were the embodiment of all that was wonderful about ABC News.

Things got worse from there.

Hardly had I hung up from talking to Sias than word came that David was, indeed, going after Sam, the plan being to give him a news-magazine to replace *W. 57th St.* That news was followed shortly by a message from Leibner saying that Diane had heard of Burke's gambit and that if Sam wasn't going to do our program, *neither would she!* Suddenly I saw the work of years dissolving in front of me—all because of the paranoia of one insecure man!

And the meeting in Phoenix was already celebrating.

There were days when I *hated* the effing business, *hated* dealing with the effing prima donnas of both sexes! More than anything, I wanted my hands around Donaldson's neck!

Instead, I made one last attempt to bring him around. I got him at his hotel, where he was packing to go back to Washington, and told him the trip was off; I wanted one more conversation, in my office. I didn't feign coldness for negotiating's sake; I was terminally fed up.

Sam came in, accompanied by Barnett, still fulminating about what I must have promised Diane and was denying him. I told him to sit down. To sit down and listen.

"Look," I said, "I don't think we can make a deal. I think we are going to lose Diane and lose this program. I care because I care about ABC News, and for us to lose this would break my heart. But I also think that you are blowing a huge opportunity. You're convinced I have a secret understanding with Diane. That's absolutely insane. I've told you I don't. I've given you my word, but you don't believe me. Bottom line, you're saying I'm a liar, and leaving aside everything else, I find that offensive as hell."

For possibly the first time ever, Sam didn't have a comeback.

"There comes a point in any negotiation when you have to trust somebody," I went on. "Either you trust me or you don't. Ask yourself: 'Has this man been good to me or bad to me? Has he ever lied to me? Has he ever mistreated me?' You want to walk out this door right now? That's your right. If you do, I'll call Diane and that'll be that. The end. So stop this 'How do I know?' crap and make up your mind."

There are moments you wish you had a camera to preserve. The look of consternation on Sam's face was one of them.

"Well," he said, "as long as you put it on a personal basis."

I wanted to take a victory lap, but this was no time to celebrate.

Message from Leibner. CBS was now threatening to sue both him and Diane. Either we had to indemnify them against damages or the deal was off.

Conversations with lawyers. Before we agreed to indemnify Diane, the lawyers insisted on reviewing her CBS contract so we'd know what we were getting into.

Leibner, at first, didn't want to give us the contract. Finally he did—it had become a condition of the deal. The lawyers took a look and said, "Fine": CBS had no case.

The next day, February 1, Irwin went to Leibner's office for the contract signing. Before pen could be put to paper, Jay Kriegel, Tisch's top deputy at CBS, called, instructing Leibner to have Diane leave immediately for Dave Burke's office.

Irwin reported the news by phone. It was all I could do to keep from going over to Leibner's office and closing the deal myself, but it would take too long for me to get there.

"Pass me Richie," I said. Then, to the agent, "Absolutely not. There'll be no more meetings. Whatever's going on, I want it resolved right now."

Irwin called me back on an outside phone.

"I think Leibner's stalling," he said. "I'm worried that he's still negotiating with CBS."

I told Irwin to hang tough.

The minutes dragged by. I tried, not altogether successfully, to avoid thinking the worst. At Leibner's, meanwhile, Irwin's fears were turning out to be misplaced. It was Richie who was hanging tough, telling Kriegel to say whatever he had to say to Diane on the phone. It took only moments: Kriegel told her CBS would give her anything she wanted if she would stay—the sun, the moon, the planets, and a galaxy or two thrown in.

But Diane Sawyer was—and is—a trouper. She said no to Kriegel, and she signed.

I was watching the clock when the phone rang. I picked up and heard Irwin saying, "The eagle has landed."

In the House of ABC News, prosperity reigned, the omens were good (sanctified by Nielsen), and there was peace—oh, for a month or so.

Early in March, I went to a memorial service for Lee Stevens, the long-time president of the William Morris Agency. On March 21, I had lunch at San Domenico with Lou Weiss, *capo di tutti capi* of the agency now that Stevens was gone but someone, I knew, who craved retirement.

"Barbara says she knows nothing of Lee's dealings with you," he said.

"What dealings?" I asked, not knowing what he was talking about.

"Well, Barbara's been working without a signed contract. You know that, don't you?"

What I did know was that the negotiations with Stevens had been protracted, with corrections on top of corrections, and it turned out that the signing hadn't happened before Lee died. On the other hand, Barbara was being paid for a year and a half under this new agreement.

None of this, by the way, was particularly new. Deals worth millions are made orally all the time in television, or on handshakes, and the paperwork limps along afterward on its way through the legal departments.

But there already was a deal!

"She knows nothing of what Lee was up to," he said. "Look, Roone, all I want is to be able to tell Barbara I think we can work it out."

"Work what out?"

"Look, she doesn't want to go anywhere else. That wouldn't make any sense, for any of us."

And what did Barbara want?

Lewis suggested the numbers, in fact, weren't that far out of line. What was, was that Barbara wanted only a two-year deal. Plus she wouldn't give us the right of first refusal at the contract's expiration, that is, the right to match anyone else's offer. In other words, at the end of two years, she'd be totally free—either to negotiate with the competition or use same to strike a deal with ABC.

Irwin thought Merv Adelson was behind it all, and maybe he was, but it made no difference. I asked Irwin and Dick Wald to work it out, with Weiss and Art Fuhrer on the William Morris side, knowing—as Barbara certainly knew—that in the end, she and I would have to work it out between us.

It took about a month. Quicker than usual, I thought. By that time, Barbara had appealed to John Sias, who had told her, correctly, that it was News's call, not his. The subject of her old shows, the Barbara Walters specials that we'd coproduced over the years with her company, inevitably came up—she wouldn't accept any deal unless we gave them back to her. (The next time, I knew, she'd insist we buy them back from her once again.) Irwin, at least once, told Lou Weiss to go fuck himself, when, as I recall, Lou threatened to take Barbara to CBS and Irwin told him he couldn't under the existing contract, and Lou said worst case, he'd take her in two years.

And Lou Weiss reported that Barbara was very upset. "The girl feels abused and wronged," Lou Weiss said.

"They don't appreciate me," this last, allegedly, from Barbara, too.

That, as always, was my sign that we were close. Also that it was time to step in.

We met in late April, like diva and impresario, and made our deal over dinner.

Was that the end of it?

Of course not.

A day or two later, Lou Weiss called Irwin, saying Barbara wanted the deal retroactive to March first. Irwin refused, telling Weiss to call me if he wanted to change the deal. Instead I got a letter, asking us to reconsider our position in, as I recall, the "best interests of both sides."

Finally, I said that if we could get a contract signed by May fifth, I'd make it retroactive to April first.

On May fifth, we signed.

What did I say?

That there were days when I hated this effing business? And its prima donnas?

Not true. I loved it. Still do. Loved them, too, particularly Barbara. Just that there were days, now and then, when I loved them a little bit less.

Moscow Town Meeting

Mission to Moscow

Building and competing in network news required continual investment—investment not only in star talent but in production values too, all
those off-camera people who generated the content and gave us the visual
excitement of what we put on the air—producers, directors, editors, cameramen, researchers, and so on. There was no question that the conservative bent of Cap Cities, their milk-the-cow-and-feed-her-as-cheaply-as-
possible philosophy, constituted a drag on our operations. What made the
situation the more ironic—and putting aside the question of whether the
network, like the industry as a whole, had to go through a period of
retrenchment and consolidation in order to survive (much less thrive)—ABC
News's projected numbers for the year 1990 were pretty darned impressive.

They called for total revenues of just under half a billion dollars, generated by a staff of 1,312 people. (This, in passing, was five people fewer
than we'd employed five years before.) The heaviest of the heavy hitters
was *World News Tonight*, which brought in just under $140 million (for five
half hours of airtime a week), followed by *20/20* at just under $80 million,
Nightline at about $60 million, the new *Prime Time Live* at $40 million, and
on down. (*Good Morning America* wasn't yet part of News at the time; its
revenues belonged to Entertainment.) As the newest member of our major
programs, *Prime Time Live* in its second year still had the highest ratio of
expenses to revenues, but it was also our fastest-growing venture and well
on its way to solid annual success.

The expenses side of the ledger had two components. About half, for each individual program, were direct costs. The other half were allocations from general expenses, which included the bureaus (domestic and foreign), Broadcasting Operations and Engineering, News Coverage, and all the myriad Administrative costs from inside and outside the division. But the sum and total of all our expenses was projected at just under $400 million. This gave us approximately a 20 percent return on revenues—maybe not all that Cap Cities believed could be squeezed from the business but proof that News *was* good business and far less volatile and more predictable than the roller-coaster ride of Entertainment.

The same could—or should have been—said of Sports. We'd been dominant and highly profitable in the seventies, but I could only watch now as the golden enterprise we'd built staggered and finally crumbled. To a degree, this was no one's fault. From the high-water mark of the L.A. Olympics in 1984, television sports advertising had never fully recovered. Competition among the networks for the star franchises—pro football, grand-slam events in golf and tennis, the World Series, and so on—had sent licensing costs skyrocketing. And cable, not yet a serious factor with the major events, was nonetheless nibbling at the edges. ESPN, for instance, was airing programs that were competitive with *Wide World of Sports,* and for the first time, there was some draining, however slight, of the advertising dollars.

But Dennis Swanson had been having a tough time of it. In February 1987, he'd renewed *Monday Night Football* at a per-game price $500,000 higher than our previous agreement (CBS and NBC, meanwhile, signed contracts that *lowered* their pro-football costs an average of 7 percent), and the cash cow we'd created became a perennial loser. NCAA football ratings were off 30 percent; the World Series down 16 percent; and ABC's stripped-down broadcast of Super Bowl XXII turned in the worst Nielsen share in the history of the event.

A number of Dennis's best producers and directors had defected, and our sports coverage had more than its share of errors and bloopers, like our telecast of the first New York City Marathon to be won by a black man, Ibrahim Hussein of Kenya, which failed to show the victor crossing the finish line. (Dennis blamed the cameraman, the president of the cameraman's union blamed Dennis's director, and the Reverend Al Sharpton accused them all of racism.) To top it all off, Dan Burke suspended Dennis for a time for screaming obscenities at a subaltern during a Cap Cities budget meeting.

Under the circumstances, I tried hard not to have to produce the Calgary Winter Games, which was shaping up to be ABC's first money-losing Olympics and where I knew I'd have the company brass looking over my shoulder. Turning a profit on $400 million in rights and production costs would be an unlikely trick, but any loss, I'd figured, would be more than covered by the additional $19 million in profit that Calgary would generate for the O & Os, and the $30 million' worth of promotion for the Entertainment schedule, which was in the midst of its fourth straight last-place season. However, I'd made these calculations prior to Dan Burke's deciding to allow several major advertisers to back out of their contracts, among them Coca-Cola, whose business I'd help secure by accompanying Dan on his sales pitch. I'd also failed to account sufficiently for the overflow of VIPS, advertisers and the like, who, because of the proximity of Calgary to the United States, showed up in meganumbers and whose costs—from transportation and lodging to wining and dining and outfitting in cowboy boots and Stetsons—were dumped into our Olympics budget. Finally, even though Calgary set viewership records, Sales had so oversold the prospective size of the audience that rebates to advertisers would reach the tens of millions. Added up, the total loss with which I was about to become associated amounted to $65 million—a little over half, it should be noted, of what Entertainment blew on *War and Remembrance*.

All this failed to fill me with enthusiasm about the prospect of spending twenty-one days in an Alberta control booth. I had lots else to do this presidential election year, and I didn't know most of the crew I'd be working with, nor did they me. But I'd agreed, and once we were up and running, my enthusiasm for the Games revived. This was my tenth Olympics production.

The Games themselves were, well, Canadian: well mannered, well mounted, a tad boring. Nothing terribly untoward occurred except for the weather's being hotter than Miami (I showed split-screen thermometers to prove it), which melted the ice on the bobsled run, turned skiing into slushing, and necessitated continual negotiations with the International Olympic Committee as we tried to juggle events for prime time. I decided precisely which events we rescheduled where, but at the end of each working day when, exhausted, I stumbled back to my trailer office, it was to find it standing-room-only with kibitzers and well-wishers—ABC brass, advertisers, and the like—who wanted to find out what was happening the next day. Meanwhile, the tricky and highly diplomatic task of dealing with the IOC and other interested parties I left to a polished and resourceful emissary who'd begun his career working as Jim Spence's assistant. In fact, he'd made an important contribution to ABC Sports for many years, and Tom and Dan, who'd come to Calgary to look over my shoulder, were so impressed by his abilities and personality that a year later they sent him to Hollywood to replace Brandon Stoddard and euthanize *Dolly*. It was the first of many major executive posts in the company for Bob Iger.

The Calgary Games, in spite of everything, dominated prime time for three weeks, enabling ABC to eke out its first win in the February ratings "sweeps" since . . . well, since the Sarajevo Games. Larry Tisch, whose network was pushed down to third in the process, took notice, and three months later purchased the rights to the 1992 Winter Games at Albertville, France, for $243 million—$68 million more than the best offer of runner-up NBC. ABC, home to ten of the last thirteen Olympics, submitted no bid. NBC and CBS split the next six Games, and then, in 1995, NBC Sports president Dick Ebersol—the onetime Yale sophomore who'd been my research assistant way back at the Mexico City Games—fittingly took over the mantle. Working with me, Dick had come to believe passionately in the Olympics, and now he championed their cause at NBC. He concluded a $3.55-billion deal with the IOC for all television rights through 2008, made it big at Atlanta, suffered through Seoul and Sydney, but overall has brought a wonderful asset to his company.

ABC was no longer the "Network of the Olympics."

So be it.

On to Moscow!

But first some background.

It was an amazing story—the story of the century—totally unforeseen by those of us in the West who'd lived most or all of our lives in the shadow of the Cold War, and it happened with such astonishing suddenness.

I'm talking about the collapse of the Soviet Empire. Who could have dreamed it?

I first went to Moscow in 1961 for *Wide World of Sports,* for the U.S.-

USSR track meet, and I'd been back some fifteen or twenty times since. I remembered vividly—even fearfully—what it had been like, how hard it had been to get visas, the sinister entry at the airport, how Intourist had kept our passports locked up in their office at the National Hotel where we'd stayed and didn't give them back till the last day. I still remember with a shudder one such visit when, on the last morning, I happened to break a cheap hotel glass while shaving in my room. A little later, when I was in the street outside with my luggage, a babushka-wrapped behemoth—I believe she was the floor supervisor—grabbed me, literally strong-armed me back inside the hotel, and refused to let me leave until I had paid for the glass!

The city was so cold, so dark, and so ominous in those days. And the people so afraid to talk. I remember the silent throngs waiting to walk past Lenin and Stalin's tomb in the Kremlin (Stalin would later be "removed" to the Kremlin's "heroes' cemetery") and similar lines outside the GUM store, with its empty shelves. I remember passing the infamous Lubyanka, the KGB headquarters and prison in Dzherzhinsky Square, which invariably made me think of Arthur Koestler's *Darkness at Noon*. I always tried to give it as wide a berth as possible—out of superstition, perhaps, but how did you know you mightn't be seized and arrested—"You say you have no passport, American spy?"—and never heard from again?

It was a time when whom-did-you-know was a key question. One of the most interesting and useful of the people to know was a Russian Jew, Gabe Reiner, small in stature but mighty in chutzpah, who ran a New York–based travel agency called Cosmos. In Moscow during the years when Nikita Khrushchev was first secretary of the Communist party, Gabe went to a July the Fourth bash at the U.S. embassy and there ran into none other than the first secretary himself. It was a very liquid and convivial day—as all fêtes are in Russia—and before it was over, Gabe and Nikita were dancing with their arms around each other. Amazing! But that was how Cosmos Travel got to be the official travel agency in America for the USSR, and almost anything you needed having to do with getting in and out of the country, as I found out, had to be negotiated with Gabe.

All this may sound strange, even melodramatic in ways, but even after the coming to power of the arch-reformer Mikhail Gorbachev, in the mid-eighties, and the new policies of *glasnost* and *perestroika*, the Soviet Union remained the enemy, "the evil empire," home of the gulag, and even though it represented a huge ongoing story for ABC News, one we had to cover, one we were desperate to cover, I always heaved a huge exhale of relief whenever we took off from Moscow Airport on the return flight to the West.

1989.

It has been called "The Year of Miracles." In the course of one year, the Berlin Wall came tumbling down, the old Warsaw Pact nations of Eastern Europe freed themselves in a largely bloodless revolution, and the first free elections were held inside the Soviet Union. To one who had grown up with the dread of nuclear war, who had experienced the confrontations over Korea, Cuba, Vietnam, the entire Middle East, and points north, west, east, and south, these were unbelievable, totally unforeseeable developments. But we seized the opportunity. In 1989, capitalizing on the spirit of *glasnost,* Diane Sawyer and Sam Donaldson did a magical *Prime Time Live* called "Behind the Kremlin Walls," a sort of Moscow version of Jacqueline Kennedy's memorable tour of the White House in the early sixties. Our cameras took viewers on a private tour of the Kremlin, including Lenin's bedroom (actually, his whole apartment) and the tsar's private apartments, all of which had been kept miraculously untouched. Tom Murphy eavesdropped on the show, and I think this, more than anything, convinced him that News had magic. In fact, we had already been pursuing a Moscow connection most vigorously. Beginning in 1987, we had launched a groundbreaking series called *Capital to Capital,* produced by the ever fertile Rick Kaplan, which brought U.S. congressmen and members of the Supreme Soviet into live dialogue and debate via satellite. This in itself was a first for American television, but there was another first to it at least as exciting: via Gosteleradio, the Soviet national television network, the series was also broadcast—*live!*—throughout the Soviet Union. To Russians who had lived through over half a century of media censorship, this was an incredible event, filled, as the open discussions were, with topics like political corruption in Russia, religion, crime, and so forth. While we preempted *Nightline* with the ninety-minute programs, they were broadcast in the early morning hours in Russia—to, we were told, huge audiences.

Fulfilling *Nightline*'s old motto—"Bringing people together who are worlds apart"—we'd done three *Capital to Capitals* in 1987, then one each year in 1988, 1989, and 1990. As good as they were, though, I kept looking

Roone

for something bigger, something that could use the relationships we'd already established with the Russians but which would attract the appetites of a truly mass American audience. Of course, we knew Gorbachev and he knew us from numerous interviews we'd conducted during his visits to America as well as in Moscow. Boris Yeltsin, who'd come to prominence as chief of the Moscow Communist Party, was, in marked contrast to the urbane and friendly Mikhail, a big bear of a man, blunt spoken, hard drinking, something of a bully but a hero to the Russian man-in-the-street. The contrast between the two seemed tailor-made for great television. But how to get them to appear together on the screen when they were clearly on a collision course for political power?

It came to us like the proverbial lightbulb—bring them both together, yes, but if a face-to-face with each other was unthinkable, why not with the American people? Why not a "town meeting" format? This old broadcasting chestnut—back in the days of radio there'd been a highly successful weekly program, *Town Meeting of the Air*—had been revived in the presidential campaigns of the eighties, bringing the political candidates together with questioners from a live audience of voters, and we'd often used the same concept on *Nightline,* encompassing questioners from a variety of sites across the country. In the satellite age, bringing these two Russian "candidates" into contact with Americans was a technical piece of cake, and having them answer questions from overseas, i.e., from Americans, would allow them to appear together, at least on the surface, in a nonadversarial posture.

The key to the situation was Gosteleradio, and in particular its chairman, Yegor Yakovlev. If anyone did, Comrade Yakovlev had the clout to make it happen at the Moscow end, and Rick Kaplan and Peter Jennings had come to know him and his people well through the *Capital to Capital* series. We sounded out Yakovlev informally. He loved the idea, which I then pitched in a formal letter of invitation, and the next thing we knew, a whole group of us were packing to leave for the Kremlin, with a late August airing in heady prospect.

But as so often happened in those charged days of rapid and unpredictable change, events intervened once again.

On July twenty-ninth, 1991, Peter Jennings and I were in Moscow, where Peter was doing a two-hour interview with Mikhail Gorbachev in the Kremlin gardens.

On August sixth, Gorbachev left Moscow with his family for their annual vacation in the Crimea.

On August eighteenth—it was the weekend, and I was in Sagaponack, on the east end of Long Island—I got a call from the News desk in New York, relaying a bulletin just in from Moscow. Mikhail Gorbachev, it had been announced, had fallen ill and was taking a medical leave. Pending Gorbachev's "recovery," a "State Committee on the State of Emergency," led by Vice President Yanaev but numbering such notables as Minister of Defense Yazov and the KGB chief, Vladimir Kryuchkov, among its members, was assuming power.

"That's so much bullshit!" I exclaimed into the phone. "We just saw him less than a month ago and he was in the best of health. This is a coup, a goddamn coup! I'm coming in."

I outran an incoming hurricane into the city—"Bob" was its name—by which time the story had begun to break. As it turned out, Gorbachev was being held under house arrest at the presidential compound at Foros, by the Black Sea, and, under the pretext that Gorbachev was too ill to rule the country, a group of conspirators, most of them from Gorbachev's own inner circle, had seized power. There had been rumors of a coup before. The hard-line Communists, their power progressively weakened, were about to be totally disenfranchised by the signing of a treaty, scheduled for August twentieth, under which the old USSR would be dissolved and replaced by a loose federation of its member republics. But now they'd done it, and the fate not only of a fledgling new regime but of the whole Russian people hung in the balance.

The most amazing part of the coup, though—and maybe it was as telling a sign as there was of the rot inside the old Communist leadership—was how poorly prepared the conspirators were! The first task in overthrowing any regime is securing the support of the military, but this the conspirators had simply failed to do. There was one highly dramatic moment of equilibrium in which Yeltsin, the emerging hero of the new democracy, was besieged in the Russian White House, home to the Soviet Parliament, surrounded by growing crowds of loyal Moscow citizens who built barricades against the tanks and armored cars of the Red Army. Those images electrified television viewers around the world, the more so because of those of Yeltsin himself astride a tank. The key army units refused to support the coup. Shortly thereafter, the conspirators were arrested, and Gorbachev came home from the Crimea, to be greeted by his savior, Boris Yeltsin.

ABC News had an enormous stroke of luck. We just happened to have one of our stars already in Moscow on another assignment and she managed, on August twentieth, to get an interview with Yeltsin inside the Russian White House. Picture it: a ravishing Western blond journalist making her way, with total sangfroid, through the cordons of military and civilian protectors to interview the hero.

None other than our own Diane Sawyer!

Even after the coup collapsed and Gorbachev was back in Moscow, I assumed our town meeting would be a casualty.

But not so. Not at all!

The Russians, we learned, wanted it to go on—for reasons that would become clear only when we got there.

So it was that on Saturday, August thirty-first, a group of us flew to Moscow, including me, Joanna Bistany, and Judith Kipper of the Council of Foreign Relations, who had wonderful connections in Moscow and served as a consultant to ABC News. We were met on the spot by Ned Warwick, our London bureau chief, Jim Laurie, former Moscow chief who'd moved to London, and Steven Coppen, a Brit who'd taken over our Moscow bureau chief post at the beginning of the year. And also by the marvelous Irina Rachkovskaya, a dark-haired five-foot, eight-inch Russian who worked for the ABC bureau and was as well-placed as anyone in the city. Her husband was a former dancer, now an executive, at the Bolshoi Ballet, and her son was in the Bolshoi, too. She herself was friendly with Yeltsin's daughter and with Raisa Gorbachev. We couldn't have had a better interpreter and fixer.

We checked into the Penta Hotel, Lufthansa-owned, next to the Moscow Olympics venues, and got ready to meet the next day with Yakovlev and his people (which we did). The program was supposed to air the night of September second. That morning, I was interviewed on *Good Morning America,* and I could feel excitement throughout the whole organization for what we were about to do.

But it wasn't to be. At a meeting later than day, the chain-smoking Yakovlev informed us that the program would have to be postponed. Not canceled (in hindsight, I believe it would have been too great an embarrassment to the Russians to cancel it), but the principals, Gorbachev and

Yeltsin, and the people around them, weren't ready to go on the air. We only had glimmerings of it, but we found ourselves on the margins of a so-far peaceful revolution. The political infighting that was going on nearby in the drafting of the new constitution was apparently fierce, and Gorbachev and Yeltsin, those twin heros as seen from America, were locked in a struggle that, if its outcome had already been determined and if the facade was one of politesse, was nevertheless bitter and protracted.

Meanwhile, Yakovlev stalled, and we had meetings, and we saw the "new," post-Communist Moscow, the stores with goods in them (still for the few), and the expensive German cars (also for the few), and the women more stylishly and colorfully dressed and wearing, so Joanna noticed, rather less makeup than in the Communist days. We had dinner with Senator Sam Nunn one night, who was in Moscow for behind-the-scenes talks on the control of nuclear arms, and lunch, the next day, with Vitaly Ignatenko, the editor in chief of *Tass*. But the most striking phenomenon of the new Russia was that, everywhere we went, people were talking— talking infinitely more freely than in the old days.

One extraordinary example of this was the off-the-record session Judith Kipper and I had with Yevgeni Primakov, who was a close friend of Judy's and whom we met, one evening, in his office in a largely deserted Kremlin. Primakov was a highly resourceful politician, a former journalist and academic who had been a member of Gorbachev's inner circle but who would emerge later as Yeltsin's foreign minister and, eventually, prime minister. Of course one of the great topics for all Russians, that week, was the coup and the idiocy of the plotters, only one of whom, the minister of internal affairs, Boris Pugo, had had the decency to commit suicide on August twenty-second, just before his arrest. But Primakov regaled us with tales of another of the "gang of eight" who'd been inhaling vodka in the Kremlin and, weeping, full of contrition and self-abasement, had begged Primakov to help save him. It was another sign of the new Russia, as Primakov pointed out, that not one of the gang of eight had been tortured and summarily executed.

But the greatest shock of all—given the Moscow I had come to know and fear across the decades of the Cold War—were the extraordinary hours that we spent with Vadim Bakatin. Bakatin was one of the "progressives" in Moscow politics. In fact, he had been fired as Gorbachev's minister of the interior in 1990, as a sop to conservatives who supported

Gorby, for being too soft on the Baltic states. Now he was, of all things, head of the KGB, and thanks to Primakov and Judy, he agreed to receive us—in the KGB headquarters.

I couldn't believe it. Just going there—to that legendary building—was an event that inspired awe and just a touch of dread. But since I'd last skirted Dzerzhinsky Square, it had undergone an astonishing, if impromptu, renovation. After the coup failed, on August twenty-second, the crowd that had amassed around the Russian White House had gone looking for some token or symbol to express their victory and the final downfall and humiliation of the old regime. Some 10,000 to 15,000 of them had marched to Dzerzhinsky Square where they tried to pull down the huge statue there of Felix Dzerzhinsky, founder of the Cheka, the forerunner of the KGB, while some thousand KGB employees cowered inside their headquarters. It took the victorious throng till the night, but finally, with the help of a building crane, they lifted "Iron Felix" off his pedestal and towed him away through the streets of Moscow.

Vadim Bakatin turned out to be an urbane, loquacious, and amazingly frank politician, another former academic who wanted to talk about everything too, including American mystery novels and James Bond! (He was a fan and something of an expert.) He'd promised us twenty minutes and gave us over two hours, in his office inside KGB headquarters. One of the hot topics at the time, for journalists and historians generally, was whether the KGB was going to open its vast archives. Bakatin said they couldn't, not fully in any case, and the reason he gave constituted an incredible postmortem indictment, in its way, of the whole Soviet system.

The problem the KGB had with total *glasnost*, Bakatin said in accented but impeccable English, was that, for decades and generations, Russians had been spying on each other, reporting on each other—brothers on sisters, wives on husbands—and that the opening of the files would paralyze society and lead to new cycles of revenge-seeking (much like what had already happened when the regime toppled in East Germany and the Stasi files were seized by angry mobs). But the more immediate problem the KGB faced was money, money to pay personnel to manage the vast network of information gathering that had been in place. What good were taping and wiretapping if there was no one to listen? Amazingly, Bakatin said there was even a movement on in the emerging regime to dismantle the KGB entirely. He himself expected to be there for no more than a transition period.

As mind-boggling as this was—remember what the KGB and its pre-decessors (the Cheka, the GPU, the NKVD) had stood for for over seven decades—and as revealing that the old Communist society had been seized by the neck and shaken hard, there was at least one thing in Russian life that hadn't changed.

The waiting.

Days gave way to nights, nights to days, and we continued to meet every day with our Gosteleradio partners. And nothing happened. Meanwhile, it was costing ABC a fortune—the open satellite time booked and rebooked, the town-meeting sites kept at the ready in America (night after night), the staff on hand in Moscow and New York (plus the local-station venues), the promos upon promos—and meanwhile, we had begun to say to each other, well, we can't wait here forever, can we? Even though Yakovlev—a nervous wreck by now—kept telling us it was going to happen.

It was Yeltsin, we began to hear. He, or his people, were the obstacle. He kept backing out.

And then—we were literally packing to go home—Yakovlev delivered! So Russian!

Thursday night, September fifth, New York time; eleven-thirty P.M. Friday morning, September sixth, in Moscow.

The great hall—St. George's Hall—in the Kremlin. A fantastic venue with arched, inlaid white ceilings, a series of gigantic and ornate chande-liers, an ambience that recalled at the very least the elegance of the Hall of Mirrors at Versailles. A long red carpet stretching down to two armchairs that sit in a sort of rotunda in front of a giant television screen. These chairs are for the two presidents—Gorbachev, of the newly formed Coun-cil of the Republics (the umbrella group that will include the presidents of each of the former Soviet Socialist Republics that made up the USSR), and Yeltsin, of the all-powerful Russian Republic. And there is a third chair nearby for Vladimir Posner, of Moscow television, who will serve as moderator for the Russian telecast just as Peter Jennings is, likewise, wait-ing to do in New York.

Everybody is there, awaiting the two principals.

No matter. Amazingly, at long last, *A National Town Meeting*, an ABC News special, was on the air—live in Moscow and live not only in New York but in San Francisco, Los Angeles, Houston, Chicago, Detroit, Miami, Atlanta, Philadelphia, and Brooklyn, New York, where audiences were gathered and questioners primed. Peter opened in New York narrating a brief overview of the history of the Soviet Union from the revolution on down, then broke to Morton Dean, who reported on the current crisis. Then the across-the-world dialogue was supposed to begin.

Only one problem.

Still no Gorbachev! No Yeltsin!

It fell to Peter and an unsuspecting Jim Laurie to wing it. Peter was onstage in New York, while Laurie stood, a little nervously, near the two empty chairs, conversing with Peter before millions of viewers, while the rest of us, TV people from Russia and America and Russian plainsclothes security, milled around anxiously in the background.

Their unrehearsed dialogue, I'm proud to say, was first-rate, and highly informative. Two smart pros who knew their stuff. What had been going on in Moscow, they pointed out, was without precedent—akin, say, to a constitutional convention in America in which the delegates (many of whom would be congressmen) were obliged to vote themselves out of existence. The eventual compromise, in Russia, took the form of the members of the now defunct legislature being allowed to continue to collect their salaries, and their perks, for the next several years as an inducement to giving up their power, but the result of all their deliberations, as Peter and Jim made clear, was that Mikhail Gorbachev was left as president of the state council, which included the heads of all the old republics, now independent, while the presidency of Russia, and true power, was firmly in Yeltsin's large hands.

At last!

Here they came walking together down the red carpet, trailed by their entourages and by the omnipresent Yakovlev. The two men wore dark suits with white shirts and red ties, but they were as different as two fellow countrymen can be. Both had been through makeup, both now sat in the two armchairs while lapel mikes were adjusted and I came forward to them, in my own dark suit and white shirt and patterned navy tie, to explain in some detail, through their interpreters, how the format of the show worked and what they could expect.

And now, *A National Town Meeting* aired live—from New York to Vladisvostok!

The questioners came from all across America. They took turns at the

microphones in their various venues, their faces huge on the large screen
before us, and here came the questions, on a kaleidoscope of topics. A
Cuban exile in Miami wanted to know what Russia's intentions now were
toward Castro's Cuba. An Eastern Orthodox clergyman asked what the
two presidents' religious beliefs were (Gorbachev was a self-proclaimed
atheist, Yeltsin someone who went to church for "moral cleansing,"
adding, as an afterthought, "You never know!"—much to the general
mirth and his own broad guffaw). A woman in San Francisco then asked
President Gorbachev how Raisa was doing! (So American. He answered,
with a smile, that she was very well indeed.) There was a touching
moment when a self-styled defector from Atlanta, a young man named
Myshkin, with a faintly Dostoyevskian air, asked what was going to happen to the KGB, because he wanted to visit Russia. Both presidents held
forth on the subject of change at the KGB, but it was Yeltsin who said,
"Please come back, Citizen Myshkin. Don't be afraid."

There were questions on agriculture, on business, on nuclear disar-
mament and the security of nuclear weapons, on the role of women in the
USSR, on anti-semitism (no more, both candidates agreed), on technology, and even—in the voice of "an actor" from Los Angeles, one Ben Stein
(the same Ben Stein who later became a star on the Comedy Channel)—on
the future of Communism. Since Communism had been such a dismal
failure in Russia, what did they expect of it in the future? (Yeltsin said it
was too bad it had been tried in such a vast society as Russia, and specu-
lated that the experiment might have been more interesting in a smaller
country. Gorbachev pointed to all the countries of Europe and elsewhere
who were led by Socialists, in Social Democratic regimes.) But the greatest
single interest in the program lay not so much in their specific answers
but in what their answering styles, and their mannerisms, their expressions, their body language, said about the power struggle they'd waged. It
was very clear, just observing them, which one had won.

Peter Jennings brought the subject up, how Yeltsin had saved Gorbachev from the conspirators and Gorbachev was now signing over power
to him, and what, Peter wanted to know, did they feel about each other?
Both responded in kind—about the new spirit of cooperation that prevailed in Russia—and it became clear that the chance to express this, to
show their solidarity in answering the big questions, and to convince their

Russian public, as well as the American one, that they really were working together to forge the future was why they had agreed to the town meeting in the first place.

Despite, though, their polite and easy deference to each other—"You should answer that question before me," "No, please, you should"—the two men couldn't have been more different. Gorbachev's fine features and sensitive dark eyes, under the strange archipelago of the birthmark on his balding pate, expressed a kind of nervous, quick, even cheerful intelligence, and he had a tendency to sit forward in his chair, his hands active, as though he had to try to make a last-ditch impression. Yeltsin, by contrast, filled his chair with his big body, his large square dour peasant's face mostly impassive although it broke now and then into the familiar beefy grin. He seemed relaxed, totally at ease, and seen close up, his head filled the television screen. His answers, for the most part, were shorter, more direct. Gorbachev seemed incapable of giving a short, direct response. Instead, even his sentences—at least as translated by his interpreter—came across as lengthy and hedged, clauses modifying clauses, because he was either trying to refine his thoughts as he went or was avoiding making direct statements. Gorbachev, nevertheless, came across much more the polished Western-style reformer-politician-diplomat. Yet Yeltsin was the one who stood for democracy-in-action and it was he who seemed to capture the mood of the moment in the dramatically changing Russia of the 1990s.

From the point of view of television, it was a great and absorbing event—exactly what television should have been doing more of, and in America, occupying the normal *Nightline* slot and running much beyond, it averaged 40 percent more than the standard audience. Much to the dismay of Yegor Yakovlev, though, we ran over the allotted hours, past one-thirty A.M. New York time, and that made the head of Gosteleradio a nervous wreck. He kept saying he'd promised—given his solemn word—to the two presidents that they would be finished at the agreed-upon hour. In some atavistic, gulag archipelago way, he seemed terrified that an awful punishment awaited him if he didn't keep his word. I, for my part, refused to stop these dramatic proceedings for anything, and for theirs, the two speakers seemed ready to talk all day long.

Finally, it was Joanna Bistany, herself a devout smoker, who figured out what was wrong with poor Yegor.

"He's dying for a cigarette," she whispered to me, "can't you tell?"

There was no smoking in St. George's Hall.

At that, she whisked Yakovlev into the adjacent corridor where, presumably, the two of them puffed away to their hearts' content. And when they came back, it was to hear the wrap-up, Peter thanking the two presidents for their time and their illuminating frankness, Gorbachev, true to form, apologizing for their having delayed the program at the start.

I just said, "what television should have been doing more of." If anything, however, this *A National Town Meeting* was the last of its kind, at least at ABC News. Just a decade later, I'm not sure it would even occur to a news executive to initiate this kind of program, to absorb the costs and live with the uncertainty. Getting two major foreign leaders to sit down in the midst of revolutionary times and talk to the American people about their differences, the future of their country? You've got to be kidding! The operative word, perhaps, is "initiate." The idea of "initiating" a program of such size and substance goes against the spirit of twenty-first century TV. The cost-conscious, highly structured, corporate-managed news divisions of today *cover* events as they happen, as best they can—and, at their best, they still do this brilliantly—but otherwise, in terms of the political leadership of the United States and the rest of the world, too much of the time they take handouts, bringing microphones and cameras to set pieces orchestrated by the political powers themselves.

To me, our Gorbachev-Yeltsin "summit" of September 1991—created and pursued and developed by us—was the high point in the history of ABC News. It also marked the true end of the Cold War.

And life went on—for all those who participated in the town meeting. A couple of years later, Joanna Bistany and I, in Moscow on another mission, went to visit Mikhail Gorbachev. He had long since been removed from power, having resigned at the very end of 1991, and Boris Yeltsin and his entourage now ruled supreme. Gorbachev was devoting himself to the Green Cross, an organization he had started that dealt with environmental issues, and he was making a living, I gathered, giving speeches on the subject to audiences all over the world.

Joanna, Irina Rachkovskaya, and I drove some twenty minutes out from the center of Moscow to a rather anonymous office complex. We went without cameras or mikes—it was nothing more or less than a courtesy call—and when we were ushered into Gorbachev's own office, even though he greeted us with his habitual courtesy, he seemed subdued, as though he didn't know at first who we were or what we were doing there. But then, taking a closer look, he seemed to recognize my face.

"Ah, so it's you!" he said, or some such, as he shook my hand warmly. And then, suddenly, he was the old Gorby, glad to see us, delighted that Western journalists who had known him when he was the great leader of the USSR were still interested in him, and he became his old animated, proselytizing self. At a glance, he looked about the same, somehow perhaps a little smaller physically than he had been before, and as we chatted about the old days through an interpreter about the world leaders he'd known—Margaret Thatcher and Ronald Reagan among them—it became clear that he missed power.

He still seemed to have an entourage of bright young men in the offices of the Green Cross, just as he had in those headier days when, as first secretary of the Party, he had tried to lead the Communist regime into radical self-reform. But I got the feeling too, as I had with other political leaders in retirement (whether forced or chosen) that somehow the times had gone past him. So there he was, with memories of old arguments, old debates, old positions taken that were no longer altogether relevant to the world as it had evolved since.

Let's go back, though, to September 1991. It was a month of high drama for me, swinging from the great high of *A National Town Meeting* to the unsuspected nadir that awaited us. For no sooner had I returned to New York from Moscow than I discovered that Dan Burke had new plans in store for me and ABC News.

Weiswasser

Why Not Quit?

Dan Burke called, saying he'd like to come over. It was nearly five o'clock, the usual close of the workday for him, and I sensed that something important had to be up, something he wanted to pop on me when the hour wouldn't allow debate. I asked if it could hold till the next morning, Friday, September twenty-seventh. Yes, it could. I also said I'd come to his office. We were in adjoining buildings, but mine, the newer one, having been built in the corner-cutting Cap Cities style, had paper-thin walls, and whatever Dan had to say, I didn't want it to be overheard.

I wondered what was up his sleeve. The most likely possibility, I thought, was the announcement of a new network president. John Sias, I knew, was getting ready to cash in his Cap Cities stock options, and one leading candidate was Steve Weiswasser, a Harvard-educated lawyer out of Lloyd Cutler's Washington firm. Steve had advised Tom and Dan during the merger and come aboard with them as general counsel. As such, he attended board of directors' meetings. More recently, having replaced himself with David Westin, another ex-Cutler attorney, he had been learning the corporate ropes as Sias's deputy.

Like many corporate men as they approached the magical retirement age of sixty-five, Tom and Dan were preoccupied with questions of succession and orderly transitions. Tom, himself, was on the brink of retiring and ambivalent about it, but Dan, as he never tired of announcing, couldn't wait. Although I didn't know all the details of it, I knew that they had very sensibly earmarked a certain number of younger executives and, in effect, moved them around the company for on-the-job training that would prepare them, eventually, for the upper reaches of management. One of them would turn out to be Bob Iger, my onetime colleague in

Sports. The aforementioned David Westin would be another, Steve Weiswasser a third. What I didn't know at the time was that Tom and Dan had interviewed five men (Iger, ironically, wasn't one of them), asking each in the process if he aspired to become chief executive of ABC, Inc. Sias had been one of the five, but had turned them down. And Weiswasser had been another, and had said yes.

He had all the Cap Cities requisites. He rose early, fought a chronic overweight problem via maniacal jogging, and possessed the toughness one might expect from the son of a Midwestern county prosecutor. He also didn't lack ambition or brains. The only apparent blot on his résumé, and a source of great notoriety in Cap Cities' dining rooms, were table manners that would have done Henry VIII proud. He seemed to surround a meal. He didn't so much eat it as inhale it, slurping noisily away, and he thought nothing of reaching out and expropriating leftovers on other people's plates.

The next morning, Dan was all sweetness, congratulating me on the Moscow program, which the critics were still showering with rose petals. "Bold idea, beautifully done," he said. We chatted about it. I related a few anecdotes from our travels, and if there was any criticism in his mind over what it had cost, he kept it to himself.

But I knew that wasn't why I was there, and finally, Dan came to the point.

By way of background, I should point out that, before I left for Moscow, I'd asked Irwin Weiner to draw up a worst-case scenario of what we were looking at in the way of salary increases in the forthcoming fiscal year. We had a lot of contracts coming due at once, Peter's leading the list, and now that ABC News was number one, our competitors found our people at all levels highly desirable. They were primed to raid us, just as we'd once raided them, and I wanted us primed to avoid the bidding-war trap that lay in store for us. The worst case, Irwin had calculated before my trip, but after protracted negotiations, would be close to 15 percent. In order to get to the 4 percent increase in expenses that we knew would be our target, we would have to implement the $25 million in savings from other sources that we'd been mulling over.

It turned out, though, as I now learned to my consternation, that while I'd been away, John Sias had asked Irwin to give him a News division budget forecast. And Irwin had given him the only one he had on paper, that is, the worst-case one that gave Peter & Co. the sun, the moon, and the stars thrown in.

Before I could even get a word of explanation in, Dan started to rant at the forecast.

"Horrendous," he said, adding, "obscene" and "intolerable," followed by, "I've got to tell you, Roone, this is absolutely unacceptable."

"Of course, it's unacceptable," I said. "Those weren't the real numbers."

But there was worse.

Apparently, Dan himself had called Irwin on the carpet and Irwin, he said, had told him I'd frustrated his every effort to keep costs in line!

"Maybe I was a little rough with him," Dan said, "and the guy was really upset."

It was probably difficult for Irwin—or for that matter, me—to explain anything to Dan Burke. He didn't want to hear about savings or worst cases or be reminded that at a time when the News divisions of NBC and CBS were losing money, and ABC's Entertainment division was hemorrhaging cash, News was bringing in annual profits in the $100-million range.

"I think the time has come for us to give you a helping hand," Dan said. "The people around you just aren't good enough. I want you to take Steve Weiswasser on as executive vice president of the News division. Let him take control of your budget and your major expenditures."

"Whom does he report to?" I asked.

"Well, to you, of course," Dan said. "You're still the boss. We're just trying to help you out, for God's sake. Steve will take the financial burden off your shoulders if you'll let him. That's not stuff you care about anyway."

I knew that Dan came into ABC convinced I had the financial mark of Cain on me. I knew too, nothing had transpired since, including two rounds of bureau closings and staff trimmings during the last fifteen months, that had changed his opinion. Profits? They could always be more, according to Dan, who still relished telling the Roone and the three limos story from the L.A. Olympics. Tom, at least, I could reason with; in a crunch, he was a brake on Dan. But Tom was on his way out the door, and I just wasn't Dan's kind of guy. I didn't schmooze, I didn't keep nine-to-five hours, I didn't do many of the things Cap Cities executives were supposed to do, I'd been living a bachelor life, which Dan somehow assumed meant I was swinging on the chandeliers, nights, with all kinds of showgirls. Whereas all I wanted—perhaps naively—was to be judged on my work!

Dan, I'd noticed, had a document on his desk, with sections highlighted in pink. Proof of Arledge's first law? (He who brings the paper to the meeting controls it?) Now he handed it across to me.

"This outlines Steve's duties," he said.

I scanned the pages. The precise legalese told me Weiswasser was their author. As I read through the highlighted sections spelling out the division of powers, I remembered how Leonard Goldenson handled an old executive favorite who'd outlived his usefulness: gave him a big title, terrific salary, and absolutely nothing to do except wander the halls. Well, I'd be damned if I was going to let that happen to me.

"You'll see that Steve has no editorial role," Dan said, as if sensing what I was thinking. "It's still your shop, Roone. All the editorial content, the programs, that's all you. He's money only."

"It's an impossible separation, Dan," I said. "You must know that. What happens if I want to invent a new program? Design a new set for *World News Tonight*? Hire a new anchor? Am I supposed to go to my own executive VP for *approval?*"

Clearly we had different ways of looking at an organization. But Dan only shrugged.

"Talk about it with him," he said.

"If I agree to this," I said, "and I'm saying *if,* I'm going to have to make him part of every decision. He'll have to work together with me and everybody else. Otherwise it'll make no sense."

Dan nodded. He stood up then and, at the door, shook my hand, saying, "Just talk to him about it. You've got a decision to make."

I nodded back.

Sure, I thought, but you've already made it, haven't you?

Naive as I was, it didn't even occur to me that I'd just let the fox into the henhouse.

There were two things I thought about Weiswasser.

One was that, from the contacts we'd had, he seemed an okay guy.

Besides being smart, he had a sense of humor and, presumably from his Washington years, a worldliness well beyond the Cap Cities executive norm. He certainly was a refreshing change from his general-counsel predecessor, who was very conservative when deciding which investigative pieces shouldn't air. Steve, by contrast, was always figuring how they could. Our sole run-in had come during the Gulf War, when, as Sias's assistant, he'd wanted me to agree that News would preempt time "only with the approval of the network president, or, in his absence, his designee"—meaning, clearly, Steve.

"Why do you want to come down in the middle of a huge crisis like this, when everyone is working twenty hours a day, and pick a fight over some silly control issue?" I said. "You know it's going to upset us. And it's so goddamn *needless.* Don't you realize we're the only one of the networks *not* systematically tacking an extra half hour onto the evening news? We only do it when events actually require it. The same goes for specials. Nobody is abusing anything."

Weiswasser had blanched that time. "I don't consider it picking a fight. This is an organization, and ABC News is not any different from Entertainment or anybody else."

"Fine," I said. "A month from now, maybe we should sit down and have lunch and talk about how maybe we didn't inform you enough, because all of a sudden something broke and we had to make decisions at the last minute. But right now we're in the middle of a war. And I'm not gonna agree to this"—I was tempted to say "bullshit"—"this thing."

Our dealings since, however, had always been cordial, including a dinner a few months before Dan's announcement. "Let me give you a tip," Steve had said, at one point during the meal. "They're getting antsy at the network about spending. You might want to get in a finance guy as number two."

I thanked him for the tip.

It was obvious now that I should have paid Steve's warning more heed. Nonetheless, I wasn't panicked. Leonard's financial people had bitched about spending, too, when I was at Sports. Rather than fight the problem, I took a leaf from my high school wrestling days, and embraced it, jujitsu style, appointing a notorious network hatchet man, Stan Frankel, as vice president of finance. "Look at anything you want," I told him, "any event, salary, expense account, whatever you like. You see something excessive or wrong, change it. And if someone gives you a problem, come to me; I'll back you up." After thirty days, he gave us a clean bill of health. I'd employed the identical tactic on several other occasions during the intervening years, successfully every time. I saw no reason why it wouldn't work again with Steve.

"I don't want you doing just the financial stuff," I told him over dinner at Nanni's. "I want you fully involved in everything, starting with coming to the editorial meetings. If you're not around, and I make a decision, I'll tell you; and if I'm not around, and you make it, just tell me."

As I went on, describing the rudiments of how we operated, Steve's head bobbed sympathetically. News being news, I said, there was no predicting expensive, must-cover events. Our reporting on the Gulf War, for instance, had eaten $20 million from profits. But our competitors had taken similar hits, and for spending the equivalent of a couple of failed pilots at Entertainment, we'd trounced them in the ratings. He seemed even more impressed when I revealed the existence of the savings program that would make up for that shortfall, and more.

"If this is going to work," I finished, "we have to be partners. I want us to be like Murphy and Burke."

"God," Steve said, bursting into a smile, "you don't know what a relief it is to hear that. I didn't want this job. Dan's been forcing it on me for months. Last night, I could barely sleep, worrying about how you'd accept me."

"Steve," I said, covering my surprise at the news of Dan's plotting, "if I'd known you were the person I'd be working with, I'd have been for this a long time ago."

Outside Nanni's, Steve put his arm around me. "We're going to be a great team," he said.

The next morning, a call was waiting from Dan, who'd clearly been briefed by Steve on dinner. "I can't tell you how thrilled I am," he said. "This is going to be wonderful. You'll be happy to have strength in there. It'll be like getting a tooth removed. Hurts for a little while, then you'll feel so good, you'll wonder why you didn't do it sooner."

I had Sherrie Rollins and Patti Matson from ABC press relations draw up a release, announcing Steve's appointment and duties. I told them to include the clause that Steve would be reporting to me.

Weiswasser didn't like that at all. "I'm not a jerk about these things," he said, when we met with Sherrie and Patti.

I was startled by his vehemence, the more so in front of publicity people, but to fight over a press release seemed a silly way to start a relationship.

"Never mind," I said. "Take the line out."

I'd already told the people closest to me about what was happening, but now others had picked up the rumblings. We had an editorial meeting that morning in which Tony Cordesman, our national security expert during the Gulf War, was briefing us on the ins and outs of nuclear war, lecturing about "throw weights," "megadeaths," and the like, and the moment he departed, I held forth.

"I guess you've all heard about Steve Weiswasser," I said. "It's true: He's coming on as executive vice president, and he'll have authority over our spending. He won't be making any editorial calls, but I'm going to have him sit in on our meetings so he'll know why we need what we need. Don't look so somber. I think, all things considered, it's a very good thing for us. He'll take a big load off. The bad news is that I'm still in charge, and that with Steve handling the money, you'll have me breathing down your necks even more."

There were no smiles, though, and no questions. Silence. Finally, it was Diane who spoke for the community.

"I guess we'll just have to love him to death," she piped up.

One person who decided not to love Steve to death, unfortunately, was Irwin Weiner. The next morning, he told me he was quitting, and how sorry he was for having gotten me in trouble.

I knew he meant it—he'd never threatened to quit before—and I tried like hell to talk him out of it.

"We've been through the wars together," I said. "Besides, you didn't cause me any trouble."

"Oh, no? Who gave Sias that report? If I hadn't done that, none of this would have happened."

"Not true," I countered. "It turns out that Burke's been planning on dropping Weiswasser in here for a long time. You know what these guys think of News. Dan just used your report as his rationale."

He shook his head adamantly.

"Their putting Weiswasser in here is a vote of no confidence in me," he said. "That's all there is to it. I couldn't stay. I could never report to him."

I'm not sure if I laid on Irwin the line I'd been using on myself, and still was, i.e. that Weiswasser's stay with us would turn out to be purely temporary because he was headed for bigger things in the corporate firmament. In Irwin's case, I fully believed, their putting Weiswasser in News had nothing to do with Irwin. But the combination—that he'd let me down and that the corporation had no confidence in him—was too much for me to overcome.

Off he went, my colleague of so many years, of Sports and News and a thousand and one negotiations. In many of these, we'd played bad cop good cop, but through it all, he'd earned the respect and friendship of people in the company, and his departure only added to the prevailing gloom.

Weiswasser, meanwhile, was busy symbol building. Move one was to transfer Dick Wald from the office next to mine. Move two, which came three days after Steve's appointment, was to say he'd like to cut a door in our shared wall, so he would have free, and scrutiny free, access.

"You want a door," I said, "you got a door."

Move three was the firing of a receptionist and the remodeling of the space she no longer occupied. None of this concerned me particularly. The receptionist came from a corporate pool and didn't really belong to our team.

But move four, that same week, did bother me in a symbolic sort of way, and I wasn't the only one. ABC News was hosting a dinner and reception in Washington on the anniversary of *This Week*, with David and Susan Brinkley to be fêted and a full complement of Washington VIPs and power brokers as guests. Tom Murphy, David and Susan, and I were to greet the reception line. Somehow Weiswasser found out about this arrangement and started to raise a fuss. It was vital that he be included. I decided to ignore him—a mistake, to be sure, but also a long-term plus, for the next thing I knew he'd taken the issue to . . . Tom Murphy!

Tom, needless to say, didn't have the foggiest notion why he was being involved—after all, it was an ABC News event—or why on earth Weiswasser was bringing such a petty problem to the chief executive officer, so he sent Weiswasser back to me.

And I—"accommodationist" to the end—said okay, that he could join the reception line.

I'm well aware that the incident was as interesting for what it said about me as about Steve Weiswasser. I honestly believed that Steve's need to be seen doing everything I did was "his problem," and most of it I wrote off as harmless. There were other moments, as when the promotion department staged an ensemble picture taking of our so-called Magnificent Seven—or the Mag Seven as they came to be known: Barbara Walters, Peter Jennings, Diane Sawyer, Ted Koppel, Hugh Downs, David Brinkley, and Sam Donaldson. Promotion wanted me to be photographed with them in a separate shot. Feeling awkward, I desisted until the last minute, but then I did it, and there's an amusing shot of the Mag-Seven-Plus-One, in which Diane and Peter have their arms around my shoulders.

When I left the session and rode to the fifth floor, Steve was standing there, waiting for the elevator, smoothing his lapels. "Just called to a meeting," he said hastily when the door opened, slipping past me and into the car. "They want me right away."

The "meeting," I later learned, was one of his calling. For, sure enough, there is another shot, somewhere in the archives, of the Mag-Seven-Plus-Weiswasser.

He had by then embarked on a campaign of talent wooing. During the week, there'd be dinners with Barbara, Diane, and New York–based correspondents, easy to arrange for Steve, who was bunking alone in a hotel due to his wife's refusal to move to New York from Washington. On weekend visits home, the pattern would repeat, except the dinners would be with Ted, David, Sam, and the senior members of the Washington bureau. That his invitations were readily accepted was no surprise. Charming and well informed, he also clearly possessed some kind of mandate from on high, the dimensions of which remained a mystery. Despite my tries at assuring everyone, the questions persisted: Was I being forced out? Grooming a successor? All that people in News knew for certain was that someone named Stephen A. Weiswasser suddenly loomed large in their lives.

At the same time, he treated me with something bordering on awe. He was with me one day when a producer came in with plans I'd asked him to draw up for an "overnight"—or wee-hours-of-the-morning—news show. We wanted one partly to beat off the competition from cable, but it also was a good place to experiment and to try out new talent. (Aaron Brown, for instance, came out of our "overnight" show incubator.) Looking over what the producer had come up with, which amounted to Ken-

and-Barbie, local-news version, I said, "No, no, no, that's not it at all. Visualize it with me. Imagine Associated Press headquarters after midnight. The place is almost deserted, plastic coffee cups litter the desks. There are only a few people on duty, and they've got their ties pulled down and their shirtsleeves rolled up. It's loose, it's gritty. But they know from their own experience that they've got these incredible tentacles out there, all over the world. At any minute, all hell could break loose somewhere, and the alarm bells will start going off and they'll be glued to their monitors. That's the feel I want."

After the producer left, Weiswasser, who'd been listening open-mouthed, said, "That guy spent weeks on the wrong concept, and you turned it around in five minutes. You just invented a whole program. And he went charging out of here like he'd thought it up himself. Now I understand what people say about you."

The real trouble started with our $25-million savings plan. Irwin had given it to Steve before he left, and Steve was impressed all right—sufficiently to take it to the Capital Cities brass. When I called him on it, he said, "So what? It's a good thing I did. You'd never have done it anyway. That's what I'm here for, and it's only the beginning." With that, he segued into a series of changes. Among the first to leave was Sandy Vanocur, who'd been used primarily as the host of a marginal Sunday-morning business program we were now scrapping.

A few weeks later, we were at it again, this time over a new news-magazine the network had asked me to mount, to fill an expected hole in the prime-time schedule. *Day One* was to feature softer content than the investigations and breaking-news pieces that were *20/20* and *Prime Time Live* staples. Creating such programming, without descending into "Freak of the Week" sensationalism, required meticulous planning, and a host who projected exactly the right tone was equally crucial. The talent who best fit the bill, I decided, was Connie Chung, who, having been misused, first by NBC, then by CBS, both of which had put her in dreadfully produced newsmagazines of their own, was now on extended leave from CBS, having jumped the second sinking ship to have a baby with her husband, syndicated talk-show host Maury Povich. She would be a reclamation project for us, but I thought the effort could pay dividends.

At least I thought so until I ran into the double buzz saw of Weiswasser and Burke.

Steve was appalled by the prospect of employees "sitting around for months doing nothing," as he termed planning and banking stories. Dan, of course, agreed. They wanted *Day One* on the air that spring, fall at the latest. They weren't looking for production perfection, Steve said, simply for me to run "a properly organized division." Then Dan put so many restrictions on our hiring Connie Chung—not only would she have to be totally free from CBS but she would practically have to beg us for a job— that I dropped the idea of using her at all, either for *Day One* or for *Turning Point,* a Sunday-night show we were beginning to get together that would focus on decisive historical and personal events. "The way you do shows in this environment is not to go find somebody else's talent," Weiswasser opined to author-journalist Marc Gunther, parroting Dan Burke. "Maybe, in hindsight, if we had passed on Diane Sawyer, *Prime Time Live* wouldn't be where it is. Maybe it would. But we haven't ever tried to do it the other way."

This last, needless to say, conveniently ignored Peter Jennings, Ted Koppel, Sam Donaldson, and Charlie Gibson, among others, who'd been homegrown at ABC News.

Weiswasser now turned his attention to *Nightline*—specifically to the $1 million that could be picked up by shuttering the show's facilities in New York and shipping its producer to Washington. I was well aware of the savings, as I'd been the one who'd calculated them. But in bringing the figures to Dan prior to Steve's arrival, I'd said that it was a foolish economy. Ted, with the addition of each new Nielsen point, became harder to keep on the lively, provocative track that had brought *Nightline* to popular and critical success. In his heart of hearts, I think he'd have loved to have worked for PBS (provided he could continue to be paid like a network anchor), and if both the producer and Ted were in Washington, removed from my ability to ride herd at least on the producer, I feared *Nightline* could become "PBS line."

Originally Dan had seen my logic and agreed. By this time, though, I'd hired Tom Bettag to produce *Nightline,* and Bettag himself wanted to move to Washington. In the end, knowing it was a mistake but unable to prove it before the fact, I capitulated. With Tom Murphy retired, Dan in as CEO, and Weiswasser as his agent, the whole of *Nightline* was moved to Washington.

(Interestingly, what I feared was exactly what happened in time—the erosion of *Nightline*'s nightly preeminence—and led eventually to the igno-minious embarrassment of the Letterman fiasco, when ABC tried to woo David Letterman, unsuccessfully, as a replacement for one of the great news programs of all time.)

Cost cutting now became a regular drumbeat. "Part of your job is to think of ways to run your shows that cost less than the way you did it yes-terday," Weiswasser lectured the staff, seconded by a Harvard MBA armed with printouts of savings projections. "The guy who succeeds is the low-cost provider." We were operating with fewer correspondents, fewer crews, fewer bureaus, fewer bodies everywhere, from the library to the control rooms. The stories we were reporting were less ambitious. Our aim was lowering and our reach was shrinking, and I began to understand that the rope-a-dope tactic I'd adopted was failing.

You remember "rope-a-dope," don't you? It was what Ali did in Zaire—the so-called Rumble in the Jungle—sliding into and along the ropes and covering up until George Foreman wore himself out. It was the same tactic I'd used in landing Diane, keeping my pursuit of her going until such time as Dan and Tom no longer stood in the way, and I'd figured with Weiswasser I would simply duck and let the storm blow itself out.

Meanwhile, early in 1992, I learned I had prostate cancer.

I was told that it is not necessarily fatal, and I could have an operation whose aftereffects almost made me wish it were: incontinence, impotence, and no guarantees.

The moment—obviously—had arrived for other opinions. I asked Dr. Tim Johnson, our medical editor, for a recommendation, and he told me of a surgeon at Johns Hopkins, Dr. Pat Walsh, who'd invented an opera-tion that spared the nerves surrounding the prostate, allowing continued function of that which I feared was over. Tim said Walsh was usually fully booked, with a clientele that included kings and sultans, but he'd see if he could squeeze in a beleaguered network news president. Dr. Walsh could, and after consultation and examination, we set surgery for April twenty-second.

The day before I checked into the hospital, I gathered the staff to tell them why I'd be away for a while. By that time, of course, I'd already long since alerted Tom and Dan, and Barbara, Diana, Ted, Peter (who, to my amazement, had tears welling out of his eyes as I told him), and the inner circle, too. And Weiswasser as well, who'd be minding the store in my absence. "I'll come to the hospital right after the operation," he said. "I'll bring your briefcase and a lot of papers, so you'll be up to date on everything. It's important that you be seen working."

This was the good Weiswasser in action. But at the same time he was taking actions I would not have taken.

I've read of the things that go through people's minds when they think they're facing the beyond. What went through mine wasn't in any of the books. As I lay on the operating table, waiting for the anesthesia, I was thinking of a time in Africa. It was a perfect, high-skied day, as days can be only in Africa, and a professional hunter and I, half a mile from our four-wheel, were stalking half a dozen or so Cape buffalo, the most dangerous big game on earth, the only animal that, wounded, will come back, stalk you, and kill you. We were following a narrow path the herd itself had pounded through the grass. Then we heard them coming, and, all of a sudden, we could see them—an awesome sight. "Stand perfectly still," the hunter said, grabbing my arm. "If they don't veer away first, wait till the lead animal is right in front of you. Then put your gun on his nose, and shoot. Otherwise, he'll kill you."

I stood frozen, as the great beasts thundered closer. They kept coming, the noise of their hooves deafening, until the lead animal was no farther away than the length of my office. I could see his eyes, huge and blood streaked; his mouth, bathed in white foam; his nostrils, wide, runny, and slick. I braced the gun stock hard against my shoulder. As darkness closed over, he did veer off, and I was remembering the shake of the wind as death rushed by.

I awoke hearing Pat Walsh say, "It's over."

He had come to see me in my room while I was still in the hospital. He wasn't sure they'd gotten it all. In any case, there could be no guarantee it would, or wouldn't, come back. From our discussion, I deduced that there was a 75 percent chance it *would*—probably in seven or eight years.

Joanna Bistany was one of my sources, during my convalescence, of what was going on at the office. One week after the surgery, Los Angeles erupted in riots, following the acquittal of the cops who'd beaten Rodney King. As vast swaths of the city began to burn, Ted called Joanna from Washington to say that he wanted to take *Nightline* to L.A., and to alert Weiswasser. "You sure that's safe, Ted?" Joanna said. "It's dangerous as hell out there." "I'm going," Ted said. Joanna told Ted to call when he got to the airport and she'd put Weiswasser on the line. But Steve, who'd yet to dispatch additional news teams to the scene for budget reasons, wasn't buying. Too expensive, he told Joanna; he'd explain to Ted.

Moments later, Koppel rang, and while Joanna listened in, Weiswasser said, "Gee, Ted, do you really want to go? You do? You're that insistent? In that case, okay. I was just worried about your safety."

I felt lousy still, but well enough to have an editorial meeting at the apartment. Steve objected. He wanted to do it by speakerphone from the conference room at work. We compromised once, and I had a caterer bring in sandwiches and salads for the whole gang, Steve included.

The rest of the time, Steve served as my principal funnel to the office. One morning, I remember, when I called in, he said he was too busy to talk but that he'd drop by after lunch.

At four o'clock in the afternoon, I called again. "What happened? You said you were coming by."

"You're a liar," he snapped at me. "I said no such thing."

"What?"

"That's what I said. You're a liar."

I was so taken aback, it took a few beats for the words to come out.

"You know," I said finally, in as controlled a voice as I could muster, "my father grew up in a different era and in a different part of the country. But he always said to me that there are certain things that you just don't tolerate, and being called a liar is one of them. That happens, he said, you are duty bound to fight. You know another thing, Steve? That happened once with my roommate in college. He called me a liar over some trivial thing, and I did just like my father taught me."

The silence on the other end of the line was prolonged.

"I didn't mean to upset you," he finally said.

Things were better for a day or so. Then reports began coming in. One of them was that Weiswasser had summoned Joanna to his office and offered her a promotion. All she had to do was cease reporting to me and begin reporting to him. Joanna had turned him down. Eighteen U.S. servicemen had been killed in a firefight with warlords in Somalia, bodies had been dragged through the streets of Mogadishu. Weiswasser had refused to rush in coverage. "Who cares if we get there late?" he'd said. "We save $100,000 right there."

Then came the capper: They'd made a move on Sam.

The story that came back to me was that, within the framework of all the salary negotiations that had to take place that year, Weiswasser had informed Sam that the company had decided to cut his pay at the expiration of his current contract, to the tune of $500,000. The rationale given was that costs were being slashed all over the network, and fairness dictated that the burden not fall exclusively on the little people. Anchors must sacrifice as well. Sam had apparently taken understandable umbrage, and rejecting the appeal to his liberal instincts, as well as Weiswasser's protestation, "I'm just doing my job," had stalked off. Proclaiming himself "insulted," he was now said to be negotiating with other employers.

Sam could be a trial at times (viz. his behavior during the Diane negotiations), but his was a unique talent, and losing him—particularly when *Prime Time Live* had become a hit—would be a major blow. I knew too, that cost cutting was only part of the salary slice. If there was one thing Weiswasser shined at, it was being attuned to the prejudices of superiors. Dan disapproved of Sam, always had. Steve wouldn't have required a further cue.

As ironic as it was that Sam had to be saved, on the morning of May twenty-ninth I swapped my pajamas for business blues. It was time for a showdown.

I was tired when I got there, and pale faced, and Weiswasser was already in Dan's office. He didn't seem delighted to see me, and I didn't pretend I was glad to see him. It took two hours to lay out the arguments and rebut Weiswasser's rebuttals. I emphasized the storm we'd whip up by driving Sam out, especially if Sam portrayed himself as a martyr for telling it straight, as Sam no doubt would. "Sam's been at ABC for twenty-five years," I said. "Can you imagine how it's going to look? This guy is synonymous with ABC News. How are we going to recruit talent? Even cheap talent? Who's going to want to come here if we reward a quarter century of work and loyalty by cutting a paycheck?"

But the brunt of my argument was as follows: "Why do you want to put two of our best shows at risk? If you take Sam out of the mix in *This Week* and try to find someone else to joust with George Will, there's no telling what might happen. Sam may not be the star of the show, but he's certainly a catalyst. And *Prime Time Live* has worked far better that anyone believed it would. It's a hit, and Sam is a big part of that. You've been at this long enough to realize how hard it is to create a winner from scratch.

We've done it. But now, you're putting two better-than-solid franchises at risk, and I think that's a terrible mistake."

Dan lifted his hand in surrender. He sketched a compromise: We'd reinstate the cut, continue Sam for a year at his current pay, and, if his ratings held up, he'd get an increase his next contract. Steve looked deflated, but didn't protest; his master had spoken.

"Fine," I said, "but aren't you forgetting Sam's pride? Steve has wounded it, and Sam's not the sort who'll easily forgive. I'm not sure I can hold the fort with him, but at the least we need to give him a tangible token of our amends."

"What sort of 'token' do you have in mind?" Weiswasser said, looking to recoup.

"I want a check for $500,000 paid to the order of Sam Donaldson," I replied.

"You want to give him half a million dollars so he'll *feel* good?" Weiswasser's eyeballs were on the carpet.

"I'm not 'giving' Sam anything," I said. "This is what you cut from his salary. We're giving it to him as an advance against next year."

Dan looked from one to the other of us.

"Get him the check, Steve," he said.

I called Sam immediately afterward, and asked him to come up from Washington.

"This has been an unholy mess," I said, "but I think I've straightened it out. Anyway, we need to catch up."

We met at Nanni's, and though Sam was bursting to let loose and vent, I stayed him. "Listen to me, Sam. I know what's been going on. Some people made a terrible mistake. It happens. But you know how crucial I think you are, to *Prime Time*, to *This Week*, to ABC News."

I pulled the envelope with the check in it out of my pocket and handed it to him.

"What's this?" Sam said.

"Read it," I said.

Sam opened it, and stared at the numbers.

"What does this mean?" he asked.

"It's your salary cut, reinstated. Why should you have to wait for it?"

He looked at me, beetle browed. Then the corners of his mouth creased into a smile.

"I love you, Roone," he said.

Saving Sam, though, proved only a respite in the Weiswasser struggles. Once I returned to work full-time, he dropped any pretense that we were partners. "Oh, didn't I tell you about that meeting?" he'd smirk, after I'd belatedly learned of the latest trim he'd enforced. "Gosh, it must have slipped my mind."

The staff no longer had to speculate about Weiswasser's intentions either; he was advertising them. "Poor Roone," he allegedly told one of the executive producers. "Life will be so much better here when he's gone." And, although I didn't learn this till later, Phil Beuth, who had recently been put in charge of *Good Morning America,* had met with his staff to unveil plans to "improve coordination" between the News division and the program, which had recently been bested by *Today*'s addition of Katie Couric, after 155 straight weeks of being number one. Charlie Gibson had asked Beuth whether the idea had my backing. To which Beuth had replied: "What you don't understand, Charlie, is that Roone Arledge is not in charge of ABC News. Steve Weiswasser is."

Weiswasser, for his part, let me know that he was regularly meeting not only with Burke but with members of the board, including the heftiest of the big gorillas, Warren Buffett.

"You didn't bargain on the fact that I had my own power base, did you?" he said to me one day.

"I assumed you did," I said. "After all, you were the lawyer for the company."

"Well, I'll tell you something you didn't know," Weiswasser said. "I have a constituency of two: Dan Burke and Tom Murphy. They're the only ones I care about."

His sureness of himself was total, and so was the inevitability of his rise (with me serving as a stepping-stone). Having apparently tamed the supposedly untamable Arledge, nothing seemed to faze him.

"Good for Bob," he said, after the appointment of Bob Iger, my former colleague at Sports, as network president. When I looked at him questioningly, assuming he'd be shattered by Iger's taking over a post predicted for him, Weiswasser said, "I never wanted that job anyway. I want to be chairman."

In hindsight, I can only question my sanity. Why did I take all this stuff? Things were unlikely to get better. Dan, I knew, was marking off the days to his sixty-fifth birthday, less than a year away, and talking more and more of the delights of retirement. (He would end up running a minor league baseball franchise he bought in Maine, the Portland Sea Dogs.) If Steve replaced him, the final gutting of News wouldn't be long in coming. NBC and CBS were already talking about selling off their News divisions, why not ABC? I couldn't prevent it; with Steve as CEO, I'd be out, no doubt about that. It seemed that all I was accomplishing by sticking around was delaying the inevitable.

Furthermore, two of the genuine heavyweights in the business had been trying to get me to leave ABC. One was Jack Welch, head of GE, the parent company of NBC. The truth—and I told him the truth—was that every part of NBC was worse off now than when GE had taken it over. Entertainment was last, *Today* had been overtaken by *Good Morning America,* and even late night was not as strong. As for News? Well, it was bad and getting worse.

Welch wanted me to take over NBC News and, in essence, duplicate what I'd done at ABC. He put a lot of money on the line, more than I was making, although not a long-term deal. The day after one of our meetings, champagne arrived at my office with a note reading, "This is only the beginning of what it can be like."

The other was Rupert Murdoch. While I had—and have—a great deal of admiration for him as a businessman, I was less admiring of the content of his multiform media empire than of the business acumen that built it. Murdoch wanted me to take over the Fox Network, the so-called fourth network, and we had several meetings on the subject. Again, the money was impressive, but the job concerned me. Whatever I ran, whatever my work was, I plunged in wholeheartedly, 24/7 as we say today. But somehow, I couldn't imagine myself spending my weekends viewing Fox's teen-oriented pilots and negotiating deals with Hollywood agents.

But there was another side to it, too. Call me Pollyanna, but ABC News was my baby. I'd sweated blood building the place, and it had taken years, and I was proud of it. I'd made promises and commitments to all sorts of people I'd induced to come build it with me. Diane Sawyer may have been foremost among them, but she was far, far from the only one. Diane would never have come to ABC if it hadn't been for me and my presence. While I felt no particular loyalty to the corporation that was Capital Cities/ABC, I did, intensely, to the people in News, and furthermore, I wasn't going to let what we'd built be dismembered, limb by limb, like ABC Sports. Not without a fight anyway. Not as long as there was a chance in hell of saving it. If there was, I was going to take it and come swinging off the rope-a-dope ropes.

In the winter of 1992 to 1993, I made a pact with Weiswasser. I would let us implement a reorganization scheme that we'd been talking about for a long time if, once the pieces were all in place, he would agree to leave News. The scheme reorganized News into tidy, B-school boxes. There would be a chief for the newsmagazines, a chief for hard news, a chief for administration, and so on, each supported by separate bureaucratic structures and reporting to the executive vice president. One of its effects would clearly be to marginalize the influence and direct control of the president. He—that is, I—would be chief of chiefs, but I couldn't help but think of Mikhail Gorbachev in 1991, presiding over a council of independent republics.

Still, if it was my way of getting rid of Weiswasser, who, I thought, was headed for the upper reaches of the company, I could live with it, the more so since the candidates for the assignments were all people I'd hired in the first place. Bob Murphy, slotted as vice president for hard news, was a no-brainer. He had a news portfolio that gave him the necessary background, and he was well liked. Paul Friedman, currently the executive producer of *World News Tonight,* was similarly a logical choice as Weiswasser's replacement. Paul had his allies in News, Peter Jennings being one, but he also had his enemies, and he might have lacked some of the man-for-all-seasons characteristics that I thought the job required. But I could work with him.

Then we came to the sticking point. I wanted Joanna Bistany to take charge of the newsmagazines, a job I thought was tailor-made for her talents.

Weiswasser didn't.

"She's just a nurturer," he said. "That's not what we need."

"Steve," I said, "a least half the job in question is nurturing people. Don't you understand that by now? If you're going to get Barbara and Diane to work together, or Peter and Ted, it takes a lot of handling. That's what nurturing is. Do you really think that's a luxury?"

"You don't need someone to hold people's hands when you give them this much money," Weiswasser replied. "They ought to just go do their job."

The truth was that Joanna was the one Barbara would call at two A.M. to say there was a shot at getting O.J.'s lawyer. Joanna was the one who smoothed, deflected, explained, *managed* the entire 1,100-person ABC News operation, better than I ever could. David Burke, my old cohort, had said before he left that I should prepare Joanna for his job. Funny thing, in many ways that's who she had become.

But that wasn't the point. I did everything I could to turn Weiswasser around peacefully. If he didn't believe Joanna knew the magazines backward and forward, I said, he should talk to the executive producers, to the talent, to the stagehands. I had Diane and Barbara call him, and Ted and Peter behind them, all describing her importance and how indispensable she was for our functioning.

But that wasn't the point either.

If we couldn't agree on Joanna, my next choice was Phyllis McGrady. Phyllis had been a crackerjack producer for us for years, and she too was highly regarded throughout the organization. But Phyllis, when I sounded her out, turned the job down. She wanted to be a producer, not a manager.

Weiswasser's candidate for newsmagazine vice president was Alan Wurtzel, then head of ABC News Research. Alan's personal qualities were sterling, but his Nielsen crunching to the exclusion of all else made him, I thought, exactly the wrong man for the job. Newsmagazines had never been overnight successes. They had to be built over time, with patience and hard work. And, yes, they had to be "nurtured."

I vetoed Wurtzel's appointment. Suddenly, there was no compromising. The issue was Weiswasser and me, with Joanna Bistany as an unwitting football.

Now he wanted Joanna out entirely. She'd be gone with the next layoffs. There was no place for her in the reorganization.

But there was no way I was going to let it happen.

"I'll tell you what, Steve," I said. "You want Alan Wurtzel?"

"Yes, I do. He's the man for the job."

"Well, you can have him. But Joanna stays with me, as my number two. There's no way under the sun you're going to get rid of her."

I could almost see the smoke rising from his ears.

"Take her," he said tersely.

The reorganization of ABC News was announced in February 1993, but though I'd kept my end of the bargain, Weiswasser now showed no sign of leaving. Relations had deteriorated to the point where we were barely speaking, and I almost never attended his morning management meetings. When I did come in, it was usually to find him huddled with Paul Friedman. I'd slam the door and announce, "Hey, you've done enough plotting. Time for our editorial meeting."

Meanwhile, I was doing some plotting of my own. News of the tension in the division had now spread throughout ABC and beyond, and I was contemplating a frontal assault on Dan Burke, winner take all. Dan, however, was so close to retirement that he was capable of saying, You two guys work it out together, I'm out of here, and I hated to think of the infighting that would result and the dire effects it would have on News.

There remained the alternative of leaving. I hadn't yet closed the doors that had opened to me elsewhere. But in some funny way, I'd gone past that possibility.

Then, late one afternoon while I was in my office, I had a visit from an unexpected ally. Leonard Goldenson showed up, founder and builder of ABC, my old boss and someone I was extremely fond of. He was also still on the ABC board of directors, and he was having dinner with Dan Burke that same evening. We chatted for a while—I couldn't begin to say about what—but then, in a very understated Leonard way, he said, "You know, you don't look happy to me, Roone. What's wrong? Is there anything you want me to say to Dan?"

I don't know to this day if this was a purely chance encounter, a courtesy call on Leonard's part, or whether he'd been asked to ask. But the time had come.

"Yes there is, as a matter of fact," I replied. "I'd like you to tell him that if he doesn't get Steve Weiswasser out of here by next week, I'm not coming in to work."

It's odd, sometimes, how the smallest of stimuli—the butterfly stirring its wings in New Guinea, so they say, can bring about twisters in Oklahoma. I've no idea of everything that took place in between, but lo and behold, Weiswasser was transferred by the weekend.

I can tell you that I went to see Tom Murphy.

At the time, I was still considering the proposals I've mentioned from outside the company. I hadn't said yes, but I hadn't given a definitive no either. The truth was that I didn't want to leave, for the reasons stated, but I felt that a great deal of damage had been done to News—unnecessarily—and if I was to stay, I wanted some reassurances.

I told Tom that was why I wanted to talk to him.

"If I'm to stick around myself, now, I never want to go through another thing like this. I want your word that Steve Weiswasser will no longer play any role, of any kind, that will affect my life at ABC News."

"He will not," Tom said. "He might still have a job with this company, but nothing that could affect you in any way."

Tom Murphy was a man of his word. Shortly thereafter, Weiswasser was transferred to Americast, a cable operation that not even he was able to whip into a minor league power base. He stayed there less than a year. After that, he returned to his old Washington law practice. As far as I was concerned, he disappeared off my radar screen and into the Stygian mists and shadows.

Sorry about that, Steve.

But you know something? Maybe at the end of the day it was your table manners?

Changing the Guard

I had a lot going for me. Even as I struggled through the Weiswasser turmoil, there came an extraordinary piece of luck. I was off on vacation, playing golf in Ireland before attending the Ryder Cup matches in England, when I had a call from Pierre Salinger inviting me to a dinner party he was hosting in London. Most of the guests would be French, he said, but there was one woman in particular he wanted me to meet. I went, and there I met a charming and beautiful Frenchwoman, Gigi Shaw, who had just a touch of Jeanne Moreau in her looks and persona (some say Catherine Deneuve) and a disarming twinkle in her eye. One thing led to another, as they say, and thence to marriage, and Gigi and I have lived most happily ever after.

I'd recovered my health too—a reprieve, at least, from cancer—and I had the pride and pleasure of watching my four children, now grown up, making their way in the world. And despite all the inner strife at ABC News, not even Weiswasser had managed to dent our position: *World News Tonight* was closing out a fifth consecutive year at the top; *20/20* was as solid as a rock; *Nightline* was beating Leno most nights and Letterman almost every night; *Prime Time Live* had become a hit; and *This Week with David Brinkley* still dominated Sunday mornings. We also had two new programs making their debuts in prime time: *Day One,* hosted by Forrest Sawyer, and *Turning Point,* alternating Barbara, Forrest, and Diane.

Dan Burke's retirement, in February 1994, and Tom Murphy's return as CEO, touched off a chain reaction in the corporate hierarchy that led to Bob Iger becoming Murphy's designated heir at Cap Cities, and David Westin, who'd followed Weiswasser into the corporate counsel's office, becoming president of ABC. I liked both Bob and David and knew I could work with them.

What, then, was wrong? Why the sense of foreboding? Was I the only one to feel it?

Like it or not, Weiswasser—or Weiswasser's ghost—continued to haunt ABC News, and the damage he had wrought could never altogether be undone. The worst of it was his role in politicizing the organization. It's almost inevitable that a network news division, with its high quotient of creative, motivated, and talented people, will tend to form fiefs and cliques and rivalries, complete with backbiting and infighting. After all, how can people who thrive on studying power and its uses in the political arena be unaware of it in their own? The ABC News that I'd inherited back in the seventies had had its share of this. There was Harry versus Barbara, to name one, and the Washington bureau with its us-versus-them, man-the-barricades attitudes. But I had worked long and hard to depoliticize us, to make room for prima donnas of both sexes, to encourage big shots to work with little shots and to make room for people on the way up, to stretch everyone's abilities without squashing anyone. To a very large extent, I thought I'd succeeded. During the period of new ownership—of GE and Larry Tisch—people marveled at how we managed to stay out of the gossip and rumor mills. There was speculation about Diane versus Barbara, but much the greater tension, very largely unpublicized, was that between Ted and Peter. (With one exception—our invasion of Panama—Peter didn't want to substitute on *Nightline,* and even the one time he did, he refused to be introduced as "substituting for Ted Koppel." Ted, on the contrary, did fill in on *WNT* when Peter was on vacation, but he wouldn't participate in any of the preparation—the rewriting, the correcting, and so on—that went into the program.) At the least, though, I'd cultivated a mutual respect among our power centers—*World News Tonight, 20/20, This Week, Prime Time Live, Nightline,* and so on, and over the years we'd been able to attract and bring in talented new people simply because ABC News was where they wanted to work.

But the quasi-collegial atmosphere we'd achieved had been eroded in less than two years of Weiswasser's involvement. He had obliged people to choose sides. You were either with him or against him, and God help you if you were with me. Paul Friedman, as executive vice president, had also managed to alienate some of the staff. A competent producer, Paul was well liked by the *World News Tonight* people, Peter Jennings first and foremost—their relationship went back to their London days, before Peter became anchor.

Newsmagazines, to Friedman, were unworthy tabloids, whereas *Nightline* was nothing but a competitor of *World News Tonight*. In manner as well as words, he was impatient with others. He had a habit, for instance, of leafing through mail at editorial meetings, suggesting how little he thought of what was being said or who was saying it. If someone complimented a piece or a producer in Paul's presence, he would invariably be heard to comment: "You should have seen what I had to do to get that piece of crap on the air."

Finally, there was his relationship with me.

A holdover from the Weiswasser days?

Maybe so.

One day I had a phone call from Ted Koppel.

"I just had a very interesting visitor from New York," Ted reported.

"Oh?" I replied.

"Yes, Paul Friedman."

"I was wondering where he was," I said.

"It was a brief encounter," Ted said. "He came into my office, closed the door, and announced, 'I'm your new boss. From now on, you report to me, not Roone.' "

"So what did you say?"

"I said I work for Roone Arledge and unless I hear otherwise from him, I will continue reporting to him.

But there was another key factor contributing to the trouble, and that was me.

Okay, so the last thing I'd wanted had been for News to split into factions and, consequently, I'd stood aside and let Weiswasser have his way all too often. But a lot of people had interpreted this as my seeming powerlessness, a sign that I was on my way out. They'd put together rumors about my leaving with what they perceived of my acquiescence to Weiswasser and, now, Paul Friedman, and came, logically (and with a little help from both these gentlemen), to a very wrong conclusion.

If, in one sense, rope-a-dope had worked—Weiswasser had punched himself into oblivion—in another, it had produced the opposite result from what I'd intended. And the fact that Weiswasser was gone didn't diminish the feeling that there was a power vacuum inside the division.

I'm tempted to call it the Giuliani syndrome. Rudy Giuliani and I couldn't have been more different—I lack the prosecutorial temperament, with its single-minded tyrannical edge, and I never used my position as a license to bully people—but the enormous change that came over the mayor after his prostate surgery, the softening, the humanizing of the man when he saw his own mortality staring back at him in the mirror, resembled what happened to me. I may never have expected to live forever, but I'd never expected *not* to live forever either. I'd simply been too busy to worry about such things.

Now I too had been grazed by mortality, and it affected me in strange, sometimes contradictory ways. On the one hand, I was as devoted as ever to ABC News. On the other, I was tired of the bureaucratic wars, and I wasn't averse to the idea of some new challenge, a different activity, a life, I'm tempted to say, after ABC. I was well aware that, as the nineties swung into full gear, we'd entered a period of enormous transition insofar as the preparation, delivery, and consumption of information and entertainment were concerned. (At the beginning of the decade, remember, virtually none of us so much as knew what the Internet was; by the end of it, most of us were on-line.) In news, CNN, which had come into its own as a serious twenty-four-hour-a-day deliverer, would have cable competition of its own, and while the three networks' evening news programs would still command over 50 percent of the viewing audience, the networks, in general, felt the pressure of high tech, of cable and satellite, then of the Internet, with HDTV (high-definition television) and broadband somewhere in the future. Some of the corporate managers in communications, information, and entertainment, afraid to be left behind, allowed themselves to be sold into making mammoth investments in the "new" media—and in some cases had equally mammoth write-offs. Some were indeed left behind, and struggled to catch up. All felt the hot pressure of competition, and the threat of eroding market share and profits. Many sought partnerships, alliances, and mergers, with varying outcomes—the ultimate example of which would be Time-Warner and America Online, the former one of the great American media franchises, the latter a company no one had ever heard of before the 1990s.

ABC, needless to say, was hardly exempt from these waves of change, or from the pressure to change. Even though our top executives came out of the "old" media, they were a new, and younger, breed. I'm thinking of Bob Iger, who effectively ran the company as Tom Murphy's heir apparent, and David Westin, who'd taken over as general counsel after Weiswasser (David had been first in his class at Michigan law and he'd done a Supreme Court clerkship with Lewis F. Powell), and now served under Iger as president of the network.

Both were well aware of the "new world," and both were fully capable of making mistakes as they sought to navigate their way through it. One of their lesser ones had to do with me.

One day, David Westin called to make a dinner date, and when he called again to tell me Bob Iger would be joining us, I knew it wouldn't be just a social occasion. In fact, David and I had had inconclusive discussions before about when we might activate the clause in my contract that gave ABC the right to make me chairman of News and appoint a new president, someone who would run the day-to-day operations of the division. The topic of my eventual successor had first surfaced after the Capital Cities takeover. Even though we got along well personally, I just wasn't Dan Burke and Tom Murphy's kind of guy. Maybe I was "the sorcerer" in their eyes, but suppose "the sorcerer" got it into his head to leave his post and take his magic with him to one of their competitors? Or what if he was hit by the proverbial truck? Who, in that case, would run News?

Whence, Weiswasser.

Now Bob Iger and David Westin had inherited the worry, and, mindful of Weiswasser, they wanted to make sure I had a number two I could live with, and they could, too.

So, at dinner that night, the subject came up again. They were in no rush to make the change, they said, but they wanted my successor lined up and in place. Even before I could mention Paul Friedman—after all, he was my executive vice president—it was clear that he would not get the appointment.

What had brought them to that conclusion I couldn't say, but I happened to agree.

"What do you think of Tom Bettag?" David said. "Ted Koppel loves him and everyone else seems to. And he sure does know the business."

That he did. It was why I'd hired him as executive producer for *Nightline* after he left the *CBS Evening News,* and why I'd accepted, however reluctantly, moving the production end of the program to Washington.

I thought about it for a minute. I'd always tried to put producers in key roles—they understood news inside out, it seemed to me—and Tom was solid, a first-rate producer. I liked him, too. Finally, I felt strangely relieved by the choice.

"I think he'd be terrific at it," I said. "Have you talked to him about it?"

"Not yet," Bob said. "He's awfully wedded to working with Ted, and we think only an appeal from you could get him. We were hoping you'd agree to ask him."

"I'd be happy to," I said.

We did Nanni's a week or so later, and after focusing on *Nightline,* swapping reactions and new program ideas as we usually did, I asked him if he'd ever thought about moving into management.

Not really, he said.

Well, I went on, I thought the time came for all of us who were producers—the good ones, anyway—to at least consider it. It was a natural career progression.

He seemed strangely noncommittal.

"What I'm really doing, Tom," I said with a smile, "is offering you the presidency of ABC News."

To my surprise, he didn't react. Had he possibly not heard? I talked on for a few seconds, filling up the silence, but it was an awkward moment.

Finally, I said, "Did you hear what I said, Tom?"

"Yes," he replied.

"Well? Aren't you at least surprised?"

"No."

I didn't get it.

"Why is that?" I asked him.

"Because Bob and David have already offered me the job," he said. "I told them I wasn't interested. And I'm still not."

I couldn't believe it! There was no point in my expressing my embarrassment to Tom. Instead, I questioned him about when this had happened. They'd been in Washington the week before, he said. And why had

he told them he wasn't interested? In the first place, because he loved
what he was doing and loved living in Washington. But in the second, as
he'd told them, he'd never do anything that would hurt me or that could
be seen as trying to push me out.

End of discussion.

I was royally pissed off. Not that Bob and David didn't have the right
to sound him out on their own, but why in Hades hadn't they told me
about it? Instead, they'd make me look like a prime jerk.

The next day, in Iger's office, I called them on it. They were all embarrassment and apologies, although less, I thought, than what was war-
ranted by the situation they'd put me in. The last thing they'd wanted was
to offend me, they said, and that's exactly what they'd done. As far as they
were concerned, everything that happened had to be in accordance with
my wishes. Yes, they wanted me to have a number two, but it had to be
someone I'd be comfortable with. What Tom Bettag had actually told
them about the job was that never in a million years would he do anything I didn't want, or that might sabotage me. They'd realized then that
the only way of getting Tom was if I asked him. Etc., etc., etc.

Okay. But why hadn't they told me they'd already talked to Tom?

Well, they should have, yes, but they'd realized it was a mistake for
them to have talked to Tom without having talked to me about it first,
and they'd thought maybe they could get away with having done so.
Dumb, and embarrassing, and they were sorry for it.

We got past it, and if I'd harbored any feelings of expendability, Bob,
who was soon to take over from Tom Murphy as CEO, dispelled them.

One of our projects that had been shunted for years from front
burner to back burner, and forward again, was a twenty-four-hour cable
news channel. Back in 1982, our cable people had set up a partnership
with Westinghouse in a venture called Satellite News Channels, which
was to be to television what WINS's "You give us twenty-two minutes,
we'll give you the world" was to radio. On paper, it was an intriguing
idea. ABC had an increasingly successful News division, with bureaus
and outposts strung around the world, and Westinghouse was in the
process of adding TelePrompTer to its already substantial cable holdings. CNN, on the other hand, was available on only 25 of the country's
115 cable systems. We intended to lower that number to none by paying operators 50 cents a household per month to carry SNC. Ted Turner,

who'd already dropped $77 million on CNN, wouldn't be able to compete for very long.

That, in any case, was the logic behind the move, but our business plan had never met Ted Turner. I've never forgotten one exchange we had, standing at adjacent urinals during a state dinner at the White House, back when CNN was just beginning. "I'm going to kill you network guys," Ted had said. "I'm going to hire college kids and you're going to pay grown-ups, and I'm going to kill you." Now, at hideous cost ($1.00 per household, just to be carried), he launched a new channel, CNN2, which would become *Headline News,* and he was up and running six months before SNC's June 1982 debut.

Then it only came down to which one of us would blink first. Sixteen months and $85 million in losses later, we and Westinghouse did. Satellite News Channel was sold to Turner for $25 million. After the deal was signed, the gutsy entrepreneur admitted that he was glad we hadn't hung in for two more months. If we had, he said, he'd have been bankrupt.

CNN, by the mid-nineties, was in 67 million homes in America, had worldwide distribution on top of that, and had merged into Time-Warner. I'd been working for a long time trying to bring together pieces of an international network of our own. I'd succeeded in wresting the prestigious BBC away from their agreement with NBC, one that went back to the Sarnoff glory days. They used some of our material now, and we used some of theirs. The alliance offered us access to their vast distribution in Europe and all corners of what had once been the British Empire in Africa and Asia and had the potential to save both partners money while increasing their coverage. We had a similar relationship with the Japanese network NHK, as powerful in Asia as the BBC was in Europe. We also owned 80 percent of World Television News, a London news-gathering agency that had bureaus in a number of overseas locales where ABC News didn't and served as a powerful wire service for the airwaves.

With all this worldwide potential, though, we still couldn't compete with CNN's global distribution. That, and the fact that NBC owned a spare cable channel and ABC didn't and had been gearing up a twenty-four-hour news operation for more than eighteen months, led me to believe that we and CNN had mutual interests to discuss.

Bob Iger seconded the motion.

"Let's get together," I said to Ted Turner over the phone. *"Quietly."*

I laid out my plan in his office a few days later. ABC and CNN, I pointed out, would soon be facing a common enemy: NBC's forthcoming cable news channel. "Their pockets are as deep as Time-Warner's, maybe deeper," I said. "And as highly as you may think of your stars, when it comes to Tom Brokaw, et al, who do you think is going to win? The same goes for ABC. You can't match us on the talent side. What you've got is distribution. You're all over the world, twenty-four hours a day. What we've got is the top-of-the-line news organization—Peter and Diane and Barbara and Ted and you name 'em. Put us together in a joint venture and NBC cable will be stillborn."

I could see Ted sparking to the idea. When it came to the "vision thing," to quote the first President Bush, Ted Turner had it in abundance. But there were obstacles, and the more meetings we had with Ted and Tom Johnson, CNN's president, and other of his colleagues, the more they surfaced. The truth was that Ted was still interested in buying a network of his own. Old dreams are the hardest to die, and before he sold out to Time-Warner, he'd made a strong run at CBS. In addition, they'd have wanted ESPN, which was ours, to be part of such a venture, joining their own regional sports programming, and that we weren't about to do. In the end, the obstacles won out over the vision and the initiative was lost.

Meanwhile, though, Bob wanted us to go forward on our own. It was now or never, he thought, if we wanted to keep from being swamped by the competition. As to how we were going to squeeze our way onto cable systems, he wasn't worried. We had a certain amount of muscle to begin with. Furthermore, Time-Warner, the largest cable operator in the country as well as the owners of CNN, would be too afraid of the FCC, the antitrust division of the Justice Department, and other government regulators not to give us space on their systems.

"And the plan?" I asked.

"I'm leaving that to you and Herb," Bob said.

Herb Granath, as mentioned, had been our resident cable guru for years. He was a real pro and someone I liked a great deal. We started to put together the pieces on a crash basis—the organization, the people, the formats, the business plan (including the inevitable losses we foresaw in the start-up years). Because of the latter, I had my private doubts that we would ever go all the way, and I worried that we were too late. But then something else intervened that put all such concerns into a totally new perspective.

Amazing.

I'm talking about Disney.

Although the news—that Disney was acquiring ABC—hit the world like a bombshell, there was great logic to it on both sides. Dan Burke and Tom Murphy had both retired and this was their chance (and the chance for their fellow shareholders) to cash in. From Disney's point of view, in a world in which entertainment and communications were globalizing and it was fast becoming apparent that fewer and fewer huge companies would control more and more of the content, production, and distribution outlets, it was a chance to capture a missing piece of the pie and at the same time solve an old problem. For years, Disney had had to worry about network distribution for its programs, making licensing deals without having the total control the company always wanted. Now it had both—distribution and control—at the price of $19 billion, the highest figure ever for a non-oil-industry acquisition. The result, at least for the moment, was the world's largest media and entertainment company.

In fact, I knew little about our acquirers except for our new boss himself, Michael Eisner, the CEO of Disney, who knew television inside out. We'd first met during the seventies, when I was at Sports and Michael, who'd started off as an NBC page and had become a key player at ABC Entertainment, was helping to bring in hit shows like *Happy Days, Welcome Back, Kotter,* and *Starsky and Hutch.* I'd known him to be unconventional, creative, and also sports happy.

At the takeover press conference, August third, Michael described me as "a visionary," which was highly gratifying, and ABC News as "profitable brand names," which, if somewhat less felicitous as language, nonetheless expressed part of what we'd achieved. The important thing was that he said he was pleased with ABC News and its management, and would not be touching either.

Cap Cities, however, wasn't gone yet. It would be months before the sale cleared regulatory-agency hurdles and Disney officially took over, and Tom Murphy, in the meantime, would let nothing get in the way. Including a $10-billion libel suit that had been brought against ABC News by the Philip Morris Tobacco Company.

It had come about because of a 1994 *Day One* investigation into the tobacco industry's alleged practice of adding nicotine to cigarettes artificially for the express purpose of increasing addiction. Producer Walt Bogdanich, who'd won a Pulitzer for medical reporting at the *Wall Street Journal*, and correspondent John Martin had put together a painstakingly documented report, singling out Philip Morris—the historic bully boy among the tobacco companies—for particular attention. I reviewed their evidence and found it overwhelming, as did others in the company, including our attorneys. But as Tom Yellin, *Day One*'s executive producer, warned me, we might well be headed into a war with Philip Morris, one in which the combat would be hand to hand.

"If we've done our job carefully," I told my people, "and we have, that's all that matters."

That was true of the *Day One* segment, but it didn't take into account the promo for the show. It's always the promo that gets you into trouble, I thought to myself when I first saw it on the air. Promos are made at another department, and this one included a highly damaging phrase, not found in the main script, that had somehow gotten past everyone who was supposed to review it. In any case, on February 28, 1994, the first installment had aired, and twenty-six days later, Philip Morris filed federal suit in Richmond, Virginia. "The essential allegations made by ABC on those broadcasts was that cigarettes are *'artificially spiked'* with nicotine during the manufacturing process 'in order to keep people smoking,' the Philip Morris statement said. "These allegations are not true, and ABC knows they are not true."

There was the damning phrase: *"artificially spiked."*

How far we might have gone in defending the suit I can't say, only that in many meetings with our outside lawyers, we were told that we were in fine shape to defend it. I never knew for sure either whether Disney insisted that Capital Cities get rid of the potential liability before the deal went through or Tom feared they might do just that. I did know, though, that he'd been a Texaco board member—he often referred to it—when a Pennzoil lawsuit, accusing Texaco of tampering in its acquisition of Getty Oil, had won a multibillion-dollar award from a Texas jury and had come within a whisker of bankrupting Texaco. In any case, one afternoon when I was out of the office, he called me suddenly into a meeting.

When told I wasn't there, he said it didn't matter, he'd take Paul Friedman in my place. When Friedman got to Tom's office, our corporate counsel, Allen Braverman, was already there.

Philip Morris and Braverman, it appeared, had crafted a deal: Philip Morris would drop the lawsuit in exchange for an on-air apology by ABC for the "spiking" charge. Just before hands were raised, Tom said to Paul, "You don't get a vote."

I often wondered if he would have said the same thing to me, as opposed to my second in command. Probably. But I was outraged when I got back and found a distraught Paul in my office. Tom didn't want to hear my protests, not a word, and it fell to Diane, who'd had nothing to do with the tobacco story but happened to be subanchoring that night, to read the apology on *World News Tonight*. We took a heavy publicity hit. Walt Bogdanich, the producer, quit—most understandably—and Philip Morris took out full-page ads across the country, trumpeting its victory.

God damn. I still believed we were right. I'd have bet the farm on it. And in fact, some months later, in sworn testimony before Congress, the chief executive officers of Philip Morris and the five other major tobacco companies, retracting statements they'd made under oath, admitted to having artificially added nicotine to cigarettes. They also admitted to knowing that their products were addictive and potentially deadly.

The rest is history—the judgments against the tobacco companies, the multibillion-dollar deals they've had to make to extricate themselves from wrongdoing, and so on—but our *Day One* was the rock that started the landslide.

In all fairness to Tom Murphy, I can't say for a fact what would have happened to the Disney takeover if he hadn't agreed to the deal with Philip Morris, but nothing else stood in the way of the merger, including the Justice Department's antitrust experts, and the Capital Cities era formally ended. Then, in early December 1995, Bob Iger, who'd recently added "Disney chief operating officer" to his titles, called to tell me that Strategic Planning at Disney corporate headquarters in Burbank, California, had approved going forward on the twenty-four-hour news channel.

Could Rupert Murdoch's announcement the day before—that Fox would mount "a really objective news channel" to compete with CNN—have been incidental to Strategic Planning's decision?

Bob laughed over the phone.

"Look," he said, "we've still got a lot of numbers to run, but we're cleared to hold a press conference."

"When are you thinking of having it?" I asked.

"The day after tomorrow," he answered.

I assumed that Iger would be doing most of the talking. Wrong. On the way in to make the announcement, he said he'd only be introducing me. Then it was mine, all mine.

I winged it, mostly. I didn't disclose what the channel would be called or who would head it or how much it would cost—not out of coyness but simply because I didn't know the answers. The one specific I did toss out—that we'd launch in early 1997—was a pure guess.

"During the Gulf War . . . the Clarence Thomas hearings . . . the O.J. hearings . . ." I proclaimed, "even though there was a twenty-four-hour service available when these stories broke, more people still turned to ABC for coverage." Many of these breaking stories hit, by chance, on Thursdays, by far our weakest evenings compared to NBC and CBS, but we still came out tops when it came to switching channels for special news reports. "We want to make sure that continues, and we think it will, only more so, once we're up and running twenty-four hours a day."

In a way, I had support from an unexpected source. Geraldine Laybourne, the legendary impresaria of Nickelodeon, had since become head of Disney cable programming, and while the go-ahead for us had come from higher up in the corporate food chain, she still would have to bless the event. We liked each other a lot, with mutual respect, and her first words to me on the cable venture were distinctly less than encouraging.

"Doesn't anyone in this company realize that this is a nonstarter?" she grumbled privately. "Nobody wants another news channel. It's never going to happen."

But making it happen was Gerry's job, and she had a plan. Our channel wouldn't go after Ted Turner's fogies who watched CNN; we'd take direct aim at the eighteen- to forty-nine-year-olds, the key objects of advertiser lust.

"I don't want to be a damper," I said, "but these people don't watch news. They're interested in sex and sports and cars and starting a family and sending the kids to school. News they get interested in later."

Gerry gave me a "What do you know?" look, and said she'd prove her point with research.

Focus groups were assembled. Scientifically selected eighteen to forty-nines were paid to watch hours of television. Questions were posed, responses examined. And out of this precisely tracked, maybe scientific survey, a startling finding emerged: Eighteen- to forty-nine-year-olds, according to Gerry's investigation, yearned not for less news, but for *more.* They just didn't like network news shows.

I didn't believe a word of it, but Disney and Gerry, as far as ABC News was concerned, were holding the cards. I went into action. I lured Jeff Gralnick back from NBC and set him up with a ten-person staff. By 1997, if not sooner, we'd be ready to take on the world.

In January 1996, though, NBC joined forces with Bill Gates and Microsoft, a most powerful alliance. MSNBC, as their new cable channel was to be called, would have no problem bearing the estimated $100-million loss on the road to profitability.

Five months later, Bob Iger told me that Disney was pulling the plug. I'd heard, by that time, that the Disney planning and finance people, who'd been opposed to a cable news channel from the beginning, were continually devising new ways to inflate the projected loss that we might incur. It was now being put at a hypothetical $400 million.

Still, I was surprised. Michael himself had been supportive.

"What happened?" I asked Bob.

"I had a talk with Michael," he said. "He put one question to me: 'If this were your company and your own money, would you invest it in this venture?' "

"I told him I guessed I probably wouldn't," Bob went on.

To which Michael had apparently replied, "I didn't think so. Neither would I."

Done. Predictably, a series of talent raids followed—someone had to man all the cable news channels—and we lost Brit Hume to Fox, John Hockenberry to MSNBC, and later, Jeff Greenfield and Forrest Sawyer to CNN. Still later, a terrific blow, Rick Kaplan went off to become president of CNN.

Meanwhile, I had other new concerns. In an ill-considered moment, just before Disney formally took over, I had agreed that ABC News would become the savior of *Good Morning America,* which was getting a thrashing from Katie Couric and the *Today* show. A reluctant savior, I should add. The idea was nothing new. Iger and Westin and I had had numerous conversations about it, and at one point I'd tried to withdraw, only for Iger to say they had no other solution. The negatives on their side were that News might make the program too "serious" and "hard news." On my side, I didn't like the habit the producers had of turning ABC News correspondents into gossip and recipe reporters. But we could hardly do worse than Entertainment, I figured, and in the spirit of helping a beleaguered program, we went for it.

It took time. In fact, it wasn't until Joan Lunden left the show and we could revive a visibly burned-out Charlie Gibson with the piquancy and talent of Diane Sawyer, who took to the challenge despite my misgivings about what this might do to her other work, that we could challenge *Today* again for morning supremacy.

In the meantime, there were two other passings that, though of a very different kind, yet marked for me the end of a great era.

The first of these was the death, on April twenty-fourth, 1995, of Howard Cosell, at seventy-seven, of a heart embolism after years of cancer. His wife, Emmy's, passing in 1990 seemed to have marked a turning point for him. I'd seen relatively little of him since. This wasn't my doing, to say the least. It was Howard's. Embittered by his perceptions of the past, overwhelmed by the loss of Emmy, and enfeebled by disease, he'd become a recluse and even his closest friends were turned away from his door.

Shortly before Howard's death, Frank Gifford, on a ruse, had succeeded in paying him a visit. He told me about it, with huge sadness, reporting how he'd found Howard rocking back and forth in his chair, watching cartoons on television, a gnarled and shriveled figure. "Where have you gone?" Howard was singing to Emmy, his long-lost wife. "Where have you gone, now that I need you?"

Some of us go out nobly, some horribly, but either way, it is never any fun. He'd been due to get a lifetime achievement Emmy, and at the request of his daughters, I accepted it on his behalf. I said, among other things, "He became a giant simply by telling the truth in an industry that wasn't used to hearing it"—and that, to me, was his legacy.

My other loss was David Brinkley, not to death but to time and age. The affiliates had been clamoring for me to take him off the air, even though *This Week*, number one on Sunday morning its fifteenth straight year, hadn't declined—it had become more popular than ever since the addition of Cokie Roberts. But David was seventy-six, and beginning to make mistakes. He'd blow a cue or forget a name or reread part of a script. Nothing earthshaking, but enough to alarm the affiliates.

For my part, I was determined not to repeat CBS's tawdry treatment of Walter Cronkite, and for more than a year, I used one question to keep the hounds at bay: "Who would be better?"

But David's fumbles were increasing, and he and I agreed that he should cut back to a commentator role. I'd always thought that Ted Koppel would be the logical successor, but Ted refused to work on Sundays, and so we made Sam and Cokie cohosts. David and I had also concluded that *Election Night '96* should be his tenth and final turn presiding over democracy's quadrennial drama. When I announced the news in mid-October, the front page of the *Washington Post* headlined: "Brinkley Decides to End an Era." And that was the truth.

I pulled out all the stops to mark the occasion, and the ratings for the evening blew the doors off CBS and NBC. But, with Bill Clinton's victory over Bob Dole called at nine o'clock, it was a very long evening, made all the longer by Clinton's delaying until nearly midnight to deliver a twenty-seven-minute victory speech. By the time it was over, David had been on the set for seven hours without a break.

"That's the worst thing I've ever heard," he said, when the camera came back, post-speech. "We all look forward with great pleasure to four years of wonderful, inspiring speeches, full of wit, poetry, music, love, and affection—plus more goddamn nonsense."

Cokie laughed, but Sam gently admonished, "You can't say that on the air, Mr. Brinkley."

"Well, I'm not on the air," David snapped.

Peter Jennings repeated that he was, and when David twice ignored the warning, tried to head off additional damage by asking David to deliver "the last word" on the evening.

"Okay, fine," David said. "I'm not going to say much. Among the things I admire, almost near the top, is creativity, and everyone in this group has it. It shows in your speech, what you do, what you write, what you say. And it's one reason why this group is so terrific. Bill Clinton has none of it. He has not a creative bone in his body. Therefore, he's a bore, and will always be a bore."

I was furious that we hadn't gone to commercial the first moment that David was in trouble. But, in the end, no major harm was done. Calls to ABC divided evenly between outrage and congratulation; the *San Francisco Chronicle* opined that the ratings of *World News Tonight* would "shoot up like Roman candles" by letting Brinkley loose every night; and David opened his final appearance as host of *This Week* by apologizing to his previously scheduled guest, none other than President Bill Clinton.

"The vice president," the president opined with a smile, referring to Al Gore, "was very happy when you said *I* was boring."

And life went on.

"Orderly succession" was back on the agenda, part of the Disney culture too, and I had no objection. Bob Iger told me we had a new candidate to become president of ABC News, serving under my chairmanship. Much to my surprise, it was David Westin. I knew he'd become restless, ever since Bob had taken Sports and Entertainment from his supervision and had the two division presidents report to him. But *News?* It didn't make sense: He was the president of the network, which made him my boss in a formal sense. If he became president of News, I'd be his! But if that was what David wished, he'd be a good choice; potentially, a great one.

I talked to him about it, and to Bob, and eventually to Michael. By the time we got around to the announcement—that the "succession" would take place in June 1998, which would be my twentieth anniversary at ABC News, until which time David would report to me in the hierarchy of things—it was the un-surprise event of the media year.

"I am not retiring," I told a group of reporters looking for gossip. "I am not stepping down, I am not being kicked upstairs, and I am not changing my duties," I said. "And ABC News is not in trouble."

To which Michael added a troubling, if true, addendum: "I wish the rest of our company was in as good shape," he said.

Chapter 23

Roone Arledge, Sage

On July 1, 1998, as agreed—that is, twenty years to the day after I'd taken over—I handed the day-to-day keys to the kingdom of ABC News to David Westin. In a way, it was a good thing. Times had changed. We had entered, as Bob Iger put it, "a period of lowered expectations," one in which our task would be to maintain what we'd built rather than to innovate, and though I continued to come to the office every day and David continued to consult with me on all major decisions, I was happy enough to have become "Roone Arledge, Sage," rather than someone who would be fighting the same old corporate battles.

Which didn't mean I didn't fight some!

A major case was the combining of all the evening newsmagazines, particularly _Prime Time Live_, into _20/20_. Or, in the language of marketing, "extending the brand." The truly spectacular success Michael Eisner and his colleagues had enjoyed in turning a sleepy (some would have said moribund) company like the old Disney into an entertainment powerhouse was based to a very large extent on the brilliant marketing and exploitation of a relatively small number of brand-name products. To this day, the Disney theme parks, the merchandising, the publishing, all continue to exploit the "stars" on which the company was built, like Mickey Mouse and Donald Duck, and others, like Winnie the Pooh, which were acquired through licensing. It could even be argued that the wonderful, and greatly profitable, animated films of the 1990s—_The Little Mermaid,_

Beauty and the Beast, and so on—were, conceptually and visually, spin-offs of the great old Disney successes like *Snow White* and *Fantasia.*

Another factor that pushed my colleagues to "extend" the brand of our newsmagazines was the failure of the Entertainment division to compete successfully across the time slots of prime time, which in turn brought into play the old temptation to plug up the holes with newsmagazine "filler." This is exactly what NBC had done with *Dateline,* taking a once-a-week newsmagazine of no particular distinction and making it virtually a nightly one, still of no particular distinction, but which nonetheless helped the network work its way through the competitive schedule at relatively low cost. Of course, the difference between *Dateline* and *20/20* was that *20/20* was a long-established success. But the *Dateline* situation also impressed a crucially important personage at ABC News. Diane Sawyer had been complaining constantly that our newsmagazines competed with one another, that she, on behalf of *Prime Time Live,* had to go head to head over and over again with Barbara Walters and *20/20* every time there was a choice "get" for an interview. She saw the *Dateline* model, applied to *20/20*—that is, expanding the *20/20* umbrella with different stars every night—as her way out, and she started lobbying for it as only Diane can lobby.

I thought she was wrong about both *Prime Time Live* and *20/20.* Both programs had identities of their own. *Prime Time Live* was intimately associated with Diane, and now she was running the risk not only of losing that identity but of stretching herself too thin. But Diane didn't see it that way. Furthermore, NBC had been trying, at different times, to lure Diane and Barbara to *Dateline,* promising each, so it was said, that all their reporters, even Katie Couric, would do pieces for the program. (To me, this sounded suspiciously like a negotiating ploy, the kind of blandishment one might use to attract a star and have to wriggle out of later on. But rare indeed is the TV star who is not vulnerable to blandishments!)

My opposition to the idea, though, went beyond Diane. In over four decades of producing television, my strategy had always been to invent a program, develop it, improve it, nurture it, build it, and then—if and when it became an established hit—*protect* it against any and all temptations to exploit it beyond its own limitations. It was the stand I took, early in my career, against the pressure not only of the network but a major sponsor to take *Wide World of Sports* to prime time one summer, with an eye, if it worked, to continuing in the fall. The head of Sports sales at the time actually said he wanted to get rid of the "mystique" of *Wide World of Sports* so that he could package it with other programming and so tie media buys together. Get rid of the "mystique"? Its "mystique" was precisely what made *Wide World* thrive! At the same time, I knew in my bones that the program couldn't compete in the prime-time hours. Maybe it could have survived the summer, but to go up in the new season against the high-concept dramas and sitcoms the general public has always favored on weekday nights? *Wide World* would have been dead in the water if we'd abused it in this way, and we would have lost the Saturday-afternoon franchise. The *franchise,* mind you. I managed to protect it that time, and *Wide World* ran on and on, for forty years, and it's still running in the new millennium, if under changed circumstances.

The operative word is "franchise." *20/20* had the franchise on Friday nights at ten P.M. One solid hour out of the twenty-one that constitute prime time. Next to *60 Minutes,* it was the most important repeating franchise on television. It was like owning a piece of land. Once we owned it, and as long as we nurtured it, no one could take it away from us. But my colleagues somehow failed to realize this, or how hard it was to establish a franchise, or how valuable it was once you had it.

My advice was unavailing. *Prime Time Live* became the second *20/20*. A third would follow in 1999, and an edgier fourth, *20/20 Downtown,* a year later. By then, the prime-time entertainment schedule had fallen into last place among the networks and had lost nearly a quarter of the coveted eighteen- to forty-nine-year-old audience. So *20/20* and its various clones became filler for ABC. It became impossible to keep track of who was on which version or which night, Charlie or Diane or Barbara or someone else. Eventually an effort was made to resuscitate *Prime Time Live,* but in the process, the "mystique" was lost, and so was the franchise.

The moral of the story ought not to have escaped our remaining competitor in the newsmagazine business, CBS, but somehow it did. After treating *60 Minutes* with special care from the beginning, protecting it through thick and thin, the powers that be at the network couldn't resist the temptation to launch *60 Minutes II.* They did so over Don Hewitt's dead body, but so powerful was the original franchise that, for several years, the original Sundays-at-seven program suffered no noticeable damage and Don was chalked off as an old curmudgeon who'd failed to keep up with the times.

But guess what?

Lately, the original *60 Minutes* has indeed slipped. Not in its own time slot on Sunday evenings, but it has dropped out of the weekly top ten. And—second guess—who are the powers that be at CBS now blaming for that slippage?

You've got it. None other than Don Hewitt who, at eighty, has been unceremoniously asked to step down!

Sic transit gloria mundi, or so I seem to remember from Latin II.

While my own focus, as resident Sage, was ABC News, our troubles were only part of an industry-wide trend. This didn't make our reductions in personnel any easier to bear, or the pruning of the assets that went with them. One regrettable casualty was the aforementioned Worldwide Television News (WTN), the London-based news-film agency of which we owned an 80 percent majority interest, and which I'd once looked on as a key element in our worldwide network-in-the-making. In fact, WTN had been a major aid in keeping ABC's news-gathering costs in line, and by selling footage to other outlets, it had also generated a small profit for the network. But "Strategic Planning" in California, I was told, wanted no part of it. For one thing, Disney didn't like partnering with anyone. For another, Strategic Planning judged the margins "too low." As a result, WTN was unloaded to the Associated Press for $48 million. (Interestingly, not only did the deal make the AP fully competitive with Reuters, which was its goal, but the new owners recouped their investment in three years, and as far as I know continue to turn a tidy profit on WTN, in addition to enlarging their services.)

While it is true enough that, in the seesaw of competition, all networks and their divisions go through hot and cold periods, the ABC News franchises we had worked so hard to build to dominance over a twenty-year period began to yield to the competition. And once that process began, it accelerated with surprising speed.

Nightline, at eleven-thirty P.M., by the end of 1998 was third in the ratings. As I'd feared, the program had become an independent duchy since production had moved to Washington. Ted Koppel was on hand several weeks less out of the year with each new employment contract, and we failed to groom a substitute of sufficient stature during his lengthening vacations, among other things in a contract negotiation letting Forrest Sawyer go. With control of the program gone from New York, Ted and

Tom Bettag's choice of subjects had drifted from the topical and the gripping toward the never-never land of the timeless and the esoteric.

At the same time, *World News Tonight* was passed by Tom Brokaw and NBC and was left to fight it out with the *CBS Evening News* for *second* place. Actually, the three networks were very close to each other in audience share and all evening news programs continued to be successful, but the era of ABC's dominance was over. According to Peter Jennings, *World News Tonight* was a victim of the end of the Cold War and the accompanying plunge in appetite for foreign news, which was his forte. I had my doubts. The Cold War, after all, had already been over for several years. Nor were Messrs. Rather and Brokaw any better qualified to deal with the domestic scene than Peter. Part of the problem may have been that Peter himself thought second place was an okay place to be. On the other hand, ever since his electric performance on September 11, 2001, *World News Tonight* has been back jockeying for first place with NBC.

This Week—without David Brinkley—was being beaten by Tim Russert and *Meet the Press*, which had been transformed and reformatted into a virtual facsimile of *This Week*, down to the colors of the graphics. The problem was simple: As good as Sam and Cokie were, they weren't David. There was only one Brinkley and he, taking his retirement, had ridden off into the sunset. To make matters worse, NBC's and CBS's Sunday-morning lead-ins continue to be much stronger than ours. It remains to be seen whether ABC's refurbishing of *This Week*, now hosted by George Stephanopoulos, can make its mark against both *Meet the Press* and a *Face the Nation* that now also copies our *This Week* format.

A bright spot for ABC News, as we closed at the end of the millennium, was *Good Morning America.* Charlie Gibson, who at one point was rumored to be ready to go off to A&E to host *Biography*, had been talked out of leaving and Diane had moved from temporary cohost to permanent one. Once we abandoned the magical age-range target of eighteen to forty-nine (all efforts to bend the program toward that audience having failed), the combination clicked well enough for *GMA* to be a solid number two to *Today,* and so did the mix of soft and hard news that has always characterized morning television. We also had our share of out-and-out successes. Like it or not, one of our all-time ratings busters came on March 14, 1999, when some 70 million Americans tuned in to *20/20* to watch Barbara Walters interview Monica Lewinsky. And given the opportunity, despite all the layoffs and the budget cuts and the corporate tin-kerings, ABC News can still rise to the occasion and outperform every-body. Our millennium special, anchored by Peter Jennings, followed the celebrations of the countdown in venues all around the globe, ending in New York City at the magical midnight hour, and it was as moving as it was exhilarating for millions of viewers. And our awesome performance on September 11, 2001, not only made me so very proud to be connected to Peter and a great team of news professionals but brought our whole ABC News organization back to the top.

By the turn of the century, a quick-buck mentality had permeated almost the entire American business community. It was a product, in part, of the new-economy, dot-com way of looking at success, in which profits were somewhere beyond the horizon; even revenues took a backseat to "hits" on a Web site and the all-important measurement—the only one that counted in many instances—was the price of a company's shares on the stock exchanges. Not that the price of a company's shares was a new concern. Tom Murphy had said that he didn't care about awards, stars, ratings, or anything else that didn't have a positive effect on our stock price, which remained his number one interest. But in the late 1990s, the big, estab-lished corporations got caught up in the fever, too. It may be that the shocking business scandals of the early twenty-first century occurred largely in new, high-tech companies in telecommunications, energy, and biotechnology, and that a collusion between their executives, their account-ing firms, their Wall Street promoters, and the politicians in Washington to whom they contributed vast sums of money made it possible, but the fever and the greed that characterized them spread into every corner of our soci-ety. Managers and boards of directors in all kinds of companies felt the pressure for instant success, as blessed by compliant auditors and endorsed by Wall Street, and their compensation in the form of stock options matched or outstripped the staggering earnings of pop stars and sports heroes. It became essential for the established companies—particularly in volatile star-driven fields like entertainment and communications—to gen-erate profits *now,* not to build for ten years hence or even next year, and in my judgment, every company in my field suffered from that pressure.

It was not a world in which I felt particularly comfortable. It was one that exploited much and created little, where buying and selling far outstripped content, and where the older concepts I'd grown up with—of building, of loyalty, of integrity—had less room. It was a world, furthermore, where companies themselves were bought and sold like commodities. Over a fifteen-year period, two great communications independents, Time and Warner, became Time-Warner became AOL-Time-Warner, and Turner Broadcasting disappeared somehow into the maw. MCA-Universal became part of Matsushita became part of Seagram's became part of Vivendi and will become part of who knows what? CBS went from Paley to Tisch (Loews) and on to Redstone (Viacom), who had already swallowed Paramount and Blockbuster Video. Bertelsmann, the German publishing giant, bought every American publishing company in sight, and record companies, too. Disney swallowed ABC whole. And so on and so on and so on.

The era of the founders vanished into history.

Needless to say, I miss it. For while I know and personally like and admire many of the people involved in the emerging corporate world of communications and entertainment, I cannot say—nor do I think anyone can fairly claim—that any of the individual companies acquired during these past fifteen years is better off, stronger, healthier, than it was before.

As for me, I might well have moved on from ABC and found some new experience to challenge me, for the role of Venerable Sage was a little too sedentary for my taste. But it was not to be. Instead, the millennium greeted me with the news that my cancer had spread to my bones.

I'd been told after the prostate operation that the odds were high of a reappearance within five years, but since I'd now gone three beyond that—eight years in all—I'd thought I was home free. Now the oncologists went to work, with radiation, shots, and medication. I'd thought that, after a certain period of treatment, I'd be able to resume a more or less normal life, but the steroids hit me hard. On my worst days, and there were many of them, I was unable to walk, unable to turn over at night in bed. Nevertheless, I was finally on my way back, or so I thought, and beginning to go about my business, when I ended up suddenly in the operating room, urgently needing a triple bypass and a valve replacement.

The bad news was that it would be a cold day in hell before I could play golf again. The remarkable news was that I was still alive. Along the way, in a kind of enforced busman's holiday, I watched a great, great deal of television—including all the cable news shows, the sports, and a personal favorite, the Food Channel—because when I have the time, I love to cook, as I have ever since my dad taught me as a boy.

And I learned a lot, watching TV. Some of it was obvious enough, but some of it was startling.

As far as news was concerned, the pendulum had begun to swing away from the networks. When you added in MSNBC, CNBC, the two CNN channels, even Fox, and BBC World News, plus the old *Lehrer* hour on PBS, there was a breadth in coverage, from the point of view of the consumer, that outstripped anything we'd offered before. On the other hand, there was an excruciating sameness to it, all too evident to a convalescing channel surfer, and, on the cable news channels, an obsessive competition for the hot sex-and-murder story of the moment, the more so when it involved little girls who'd been abused or kidnapped or killed or— best of all—all three.

Probably this trend can be traced back to before the O. J. Simpson case in 1994, but from then on, by way of Monica Lewinsky to Gary Condit and Chandra Levy and the Beltway sniper, the cable channels have homed in on the freak-of-the-week type of story like vultures circling in the sky, pushing local news channels out of the way when they find the hot one and fighting to the death to steal victims and victims' families away from *Larry King Live*. The most disturbing aspect to me has been the degree to which this tabloid approach has influenced network coverage, particularly on the "softer" morning shows. When it came to war zones and global hot spots, however—from Kosovo to Afghanistan—the cable channels could, and often did, do a fine job, although it sometimes seemed that Christiane Amanpour was everywhere at once, a kind of one-woman network. (Unless, unbeknownst to the public, she'd been cloned?) And while there were fewer American journalists regularly stationed overseas, the pick-up people who took their places, many of them British and from British news services, were in many cases excellent, and it was not hard to imagine careers in the making.

The competition on cable was just as vigorous as it had once been among the networks—viz. the panic that set in at CNN when Fox went ahead of it in the ratings—and the "star system" prevailed in cable too, from Bill O'Reilly to Lou Dobbs to the up-and-coming Brian Williams and Paula Zahn, whom CNN captured from Fox for its morning news. What was particularly gratifying to me was the realization that ABC

News, over the past decade or two, had been a kind of school for reporters and producers. Everywhere I turned, I found alumni and alumnae from our ranks. Among the reporters and anchors, in addition to O'Reilly and Zahn, were David Ensor, Sheila MacVicar, Willow Bay, Jeff Greenfield, and Brit Hume, while the less well-known but equally important producer ranks included David Tabacoff, executive producer of *The O'Reilly Factor,* Neil Shapiro, executive producer of *Dateline* and now president of NBC News, Kathryn Kross, now a CNN vice president, and even, straddling the fence between reportage and producing, a one-time associate producer at ABC, now the MSNBC anchor, Ashleigh Banfield.

The same went for sports. Our alums were all over the place, led by Dick Ebersol, who'd literally transformed NBC Sports. But the same pressure for instant success that permeated the communications industry in general has also done its work on sports. More and more, as I switched channels, I was reminded of what the new owners of Madison Square Garden, the Dolans of Cablevision, proclaimed when they took over not just the arena but the Knicks and the Rangers, too. "We're going to put good product on the floor."

"Product." The great contests that enthralled us for years and occupied my working life for so long are now reduced to "product." What's more, I discovered, it is too often true! What, for instance, has become of baseball's once-hallowed All-Star game, which, in 2002, by the commissioner's fiat, was declared over—in a tie—after eleven innings? The contempt for the public implicit in that decision reflected not only the smugness and arrogance of Major League Baseball as it is run today, but the sad decline of what was once one of the great competitive events of the sports year. Not long ago, I happened to watch (on ABC) a made-for-television pairs golf match between Jack Nicklaus and Tiger Woods, and Lee Trevino and Sergio Garcia. At the end of the match, the real estate developer who'd put up the money for it was interviewed and what did he talk about? Not what we'd just witnessed, or the glories of golf in general, but how briskly he was selling real estate lots thanks to the event!

This isn't to say I'm over my addiction to televised sports. It's in the blood. It's where I "made my bones" professionally, and I still find it absolutely astonishing that I was once actually paid to run ABC Sports! I'm still fascinated by golf on TV and think it admirably well produced, even if it lacks the great announcing personalities of yesteryear. Wimbledon is wonderful, and I still root just as ardently for the Yankees. One of the dividends for the devout fan in the proliferation of cable sports channels are the pregame and postgame specials, many of them excellent, that one finds on MSG and the newer Yes channel, as well as ESPN, that are tied into the games themselves and may well be telecast on network TV. In other words, for the devout sports fan, even if the integrity, the dignity—I'm tempted to say the grandeur—that used to characterize the televising of great sporting events has worn thin, there is simply more to watch today than ever.

And so with news.

At the summit—even after all the reports of their demise—remain the three networks' evening news and their star anchors, Jennings, Rather, and Brokaw. They are now the true "venerable sages" of our culture, the faces and voices we turn to for information, intelligence, and reassurance, just as people a generation earlier turned to the "irreplaceables" of that era, Walter Cronkite and Huntley-Brinkley, and those before them tuned their radio dials to Murrow, Kaltenborn, Heatter, and Raymond Graham Swing. Jennings, Rather, and Brokaw, to my mind, remain at the pinnacle of broadcast news, and I happen to think they're terrific at what they do. Indeed, the high point of Peter's career, I believe, didn't come until the World Trade Towers tragedies of September 11, 2001, when, as I've already mentioned, he took control of our whole network for a full day of brilliant impromptu reportage.

As hard as it is for me to imagine broadcast news without this trio, I know the day is coming, and in the case of NBC, the succession has already been announced. The next generation of anchors will determine the face and flavor of television news for years to come, and in a strange way, they will be as important to our society as the choice of new justices for the Supreme Court. Unless, that is, we are ready to write off the network news divisions as fading dinosaurs from the late twentieth century?

Some are. I, for one, am not. Whether we will continue to function as we do now is hard to say. Now that cable has come of age and commands a still small but growing segment of the market, we networks find ourselves at a severe structural disadvantage, for cable channels have two sources of revenue—advertising and fees paid by cable operators—whereas the networks, which pay to have their programs aired, have only advertising. There are also new technologies on the way—HDTV, broadband, wireless, et al.—but what effect they will have on the delivery of broadcast news is beyond my crystal ball. Don Hewitt, wearing his pundit's hat, has recommended that the networks, in order to save money, cease expensive competition and run a single unified newscast every evening!

I think this an absolutely monstrous idea. Eliminating competition, eliminating, that is, the investigative impulse, the fighting for stories, the striving to be first and best would leave us instead with the blandest and most homogenized, corporate-approved programming imaginable. Who would watch it? (How much poorer our society would be, for instance, if the *New York Times* were the only newspaper we could read!) If and when change does come, I believe it will be through a series of arrangements of the kind I tried to create with my global schemes at ABC (which my colleagues have resuscitated in renewed conversations with CNN), and which NBC is now able to achieve in a different way, spinning out many of its news-generating costs over two cable channels as well as the network. ABC, in fact, has been doing the same thing in sports for some time, combining the network and the ESPN channels in acquiring major sports licenses.

As for the industry in general, I'm not ready to say that television once enjoyed a lamented Golden Age—whether one puts it in the fifties or sixties or seventies—and that it is now long gone, although I can't help but be reminded of an old quip of Elton Rule's. "Some day," he once told an affiliates' board-of-governors meeting, "you're going to look back on where we are today. So enjoy it now, because these *are* the good old days."

Be that as it may, if I personally miss the era of the founders, it is as a septuagenarian who undoubtedly misses the vitality of his own youth. There was programming I once thought fabulous that we have never seen since—live TV drama, for instance, as it was produced in the 1950s—but today's audience never experienced it and has other icons to cheer about. I may mourn the great television comedians of yesteryear—the Gleasons, the Skeltons, the Berles—but today's viewers have *Seinfeld* and *Cheers* to miss, as they will one day miss David Letterman and Jay Leno. And on the negative side of the equation, may I remind us all that forty years ago, in the 1960s, TV was already being called "a vast wasteland" by none other than Newt Minow, then chairman of the FCC. What impresses me most on television today is the talent. The industry continues to attract the best of the new generations, people who are smart, talented, ambitious, and innovative. The opportunities, in fact, are far, far greater for aspiring reporters, writers, cameramen, directors, and producers than they were when I came into the business in the 1950s, and if you watch television, as I did, with a knowledge of what goes on behind the scenes in the control room, the studio, the mobile unit, you begin to realize how the industry has grown up in my half century. However the chips of ownership may change hands in the future, and whatever new technologies may come to the fore, the industry to which I've given my professional all will continue to grow and, meanwhile, shows no sign of ceding its great appeal to masses of viewers to any other medium.

It has changed, that is all I can say.

And may it continue to change.

Gradually, but with setbacks, my health improved. It was a slow process—a lot slower than I'd have liked—but in painful stages, I graduated from bed to wheelchair to walker to crutches, and ultimately to a cane. Not up to playing St. Andrews, I told well-wishers, but edging closer to the first tee.

It would turn bad again in time—that's been the way of it—but meanwhile, another invitation arrived. I'd turned so many down, but this one I couldn't, no way. A reunion had been organized for all those who'd been the members of ABC Sports at the time of the Munich Olympics, that incredible moment in history in which we'd participated that might even be called the dawn of modern terrorism. Organized down to the last detail by Geoff Mason, Carol Lehti, and Paula O'Connell, among others, it was set for July 16, 2001, at Tavern on the Green, the place where four decades before I'd sat with Ed Scherick over beers, trying to come up with a title for my new show, to be dubbed *ABC's Wide World of Sports.*

By the time the day came, I was still uncertain about whether I was going to go or not. For one thing, it still took some doing for me to get myself dressed and on my feet. The steroids I'd been taking, plus the shots, caused me pain. Already exhausted from that effort, I thought of just phoning in my good wishes. But Roger Goodman, director of so many of our great sports and news telecasts, came to escort me and make sure I didn't back out, and Orlando, my faithful driver who's been with me for years, was waiting for me downstairs. Gigi encouraged me to give it a try.

And so I did.

Lest I seem to overdramatize, this was literally my first time leaving the apartment for such an event in over a year. I was still on crutches. I waited till the last moment to see if I was up to it, then, when we got close to Tavern on the Green, I had Orlando drop me off around in the back of the famous restaurant. I simply didn't want to be seen until I was ready. Even as I started up the path from the car, though, I was perspiring in the summer-evening sun and in pain from the crutches digging into my underarms. I felt bloated and weak. The path rose slightly upward, and at one point I caught myself just as I was about to fall down. I stopped, hesitant again, but through the glass walls of the main room that gives out onto Central Park, I spotted Jim Spence, whom I'd been out of touch with ever since the call I'd made that Saturday, telling him of Swanson's appointment in his place; and Jim McKay, who, at eighty-one, had just signed a deal with NBC to cover the Olympics through 2008; and Jim's son, Sean, who'd been six years old sitting in the control room at Munich, and was now president of CBS Sports.

Damn.

I pulled myself erect. Head up, shoulders back, hands manipulating the crutches. I went up the rest of the way. They couldn't see me in the shadows, but through the windows I saw Frank Gifford and Dick Ebersol and Donna De Varona; Dick Button, Julie Barnathan, and Herb Granath; Bob Beattie, Kurt Fuchs, Barry Frank, and Andy Sidaris; Geoff Mason, Doug Wilson, Jacques Lesgardes, Marvin Bader, and John Wilcox, and what looked to be two or three hundred more people.

I thought fleetingly of those who weren't there—of Howard Cosell and Chet Forte and Chuck Howard. But nearly all the rest who'd worn the yellow blazer of ABC, all those years before, were present and accounted for.

And I was, too.

All of a sudden, all the things I wanted to tell them flooded my mind. In the entire history of network television, I wanted to say, there'd never been a division, not even CBS News at its zenith, that had so dominated its field as ABC Sports. We'd had the best events, the best announcers, the best producers and directors, the best programming by a light year or ten. We'd pioneered all the techniques that were now commonplace throughout our industry.

And how goddamn proud I was of all of us.

I was inside by then, making my way through the corridors, until, just as I turned the last corner, I glimpsed the evening sun streaming through the wall of windows and the masses of green foliage outside. I stopped one more time to suck in my gut and hold myself as erect as possible, then paced the last few steps.

The sound when they saw me was like walking into a stadium. They were all on their feet, applauding. And I saw Peter Jennings, brushing at his eyes with one hand and holding a mike in the other. And I heard him say, a big smile now on his face, "Ladies and gentleman, the Boss is back."

Index